Whispering in the Wind

by

Carmen Bostic St. Clair

and

John Grinder

J & C Enterprises

Scotts Valley, California 95066

ISBN 0-9717223-0-7

Cover design by the Type Factory (Santa Cruz)

DEDICATION

We dedicate this book to our parents:

Charles and Renee Altomare,

Eileen Grinder and

Jack Grinder

What strange and mysterious ways our parents influenced each of us to have brought us to a place where the thinking and expression contained in this book became possible!

Thank you,

We love you

Carmen Bostic St. Clair   *John Grinder*

Acknowledgements

We would like to acknowledge the special contribution of our friends:

Tom Malloy

Chris Mitchell

Frank Tall

whose intelligent reading and comments on a draft of *Whispering* significantly improved this work.

Table of Contents

Authors' Guide for the Reader/Preface to Whispering in the Wind

It is with great excitement and pleasure that we offer this book to the Neuro-Linguistic Programming (NLP) community. Its publication seems to us to be most timely. The legal controversies surrounding Neuro-Linguistic Programming have been recently settled in such a way that there are at present no further obstacles to an intelligent and appropriate professional development of this field that holds such great promise (see appendix A for documents detailing the legal settlements that have cleared the way for this development).

NLP has been carried on the wind to all corners of the earth in the short time it has existed. The initial work by its co-creators, John Grinder and Richard Bandler, was done in the mid – 70's in California. The patterning coded by them in their initial modeling of geniuses has been translated into many languages, adapted to a large number of cultures and integrated into countless domains of application. It has touched profoundly the lives of hundreds of thousands of people, making positive contributions to the quality of their lives.

Our motivations for writing this book are multiple. First, we were moved by a concern about the emphasis and direction that NLP has recently taken. In particular, we refer to the lack of modeling – the very activity that defines the core of this discipline NLP. Our thought was that if we could identify cleanly the primary strands of influence, both intellectual and personal, that shaped the context in which NLP was formed, it would give some depth to the enterprise. Further, there is nowhere available any published descriptions of the processes by which the initial modeling that created the field of NLP occurred. Similarly, the contexts in which these processes occurred have never been revealed. It hardly seems appropriate (and it is certainly not effective) to exhort people to do something without offering some guidance on how to accomplish it.

We begin by identifying the epistemology underlying the entire enterprise of NLP. We subsequently present the principle threads, both personal and intellectual, that were woven together to create this fabric of many colors.

We then select and describe a series of key incidents in the modeling activities that created NLP. Our intention for so doing is that by presenting such narratives, we could point to specific strategies (both literally and metaphorically) that have proven effective in the modeling of excellence. In particular, we develop extended descriptive narratives that define what philosophers of science refer to as contexts of discovery. Our intention, then in this enterprise, is to encourage others to think and act with clarity in responding to the tremendous opportunities that the technology called NLP offers to intrepid explorers. Such enlightened self-interest will hopefully drive the further development of the field as a natural consequence.

Without an appreciation of its foundation, historically and epistemologically, there is a tendency for a new discipline such as NLP to drift on the wind. We present a number of tether points, strong enough to resist inappropriate drift but with enough slack to allow flexibility and some grace in its movement.

Finally, we offer extended commentary on the practice of NLP and how we as a community might refine and extend such practice. These include specific proposals about how to improve the actual application of the patterning created through modeling processes. We conclude with a set of recommendations about how we might organize ourselves as a legitimate research community, and a commentary on its possible application to wider social contexts.

The discipline of Neuro-Linguistic Programming had a reasonably spectacular infancy and has, more or less, survived a tumultuous adolescence. We propose that it is now time to establish it as a professional discipline taking its rightful place along side other approaches to the study of human functioning. NLP has and will continue to contribute significantly to the study of human behavior and in particular, to that extreme form of human behavior we refer to as excellence. The field is far more important than the two men who founded it: it now has a life of its own. In part, what follows is an attempt to make transparent certain aspects of its creation and development if for no other justification than to allow it to move beyond the personalities of its co-creators.

Whispering is not a typical NLP book - in particular, those seeking another how-to presentation of NLP patterning of excellence should look elsewhere. The book assumes a certain level of familiarity with NLP patterning and concerns itself with larger and more profound issues – ones that, in our opinion, will determine whether NLP reinvigorates itself and continues to develop or simply is swept away on the wind.

Nor will we use this book to offer a report of the patterning in large organizations – corporations, institutes and governments - that has been the focus and principal activity of Quantum Leap and its principals, Carmen Bostic St. Clair and John Grinder during the last decade. Our intention here is quite different.

The book is organized into 3 sections, each with multiple internal chapters as follows:

The Lull Before the Storm

1. Preface

2. Prologue: offers some simple opening remarks about the current context in which we find NLP and some typical contemporary perceptions of it.

Part I: A Freshening Wind

Chapter 1: Epistemology – an explicit presentation of the epistemology underlying NLP. The reader is warned that this section requires close attention. While it is possible to appreciate many portions of the succeeding material without an explicit understanding of the epistemology presented in this section, we consider it crucial to any serious student of the technology. We argue for a sharp distinction between the set of neurological transforms that process the incoming data stream from the world up to the point where we as humans first gain access to it (primary experience) and the set of transforms subsequent to that point, focusing on the linguistic mapping and their effects (secondary experience). Korzybski's famous map/territory distinction is challenged and refined. Some of the implications for NLP are explored.

Chapter 2: Terminology: a number of key terms in NLP and in particular for this book are defined with commentary.

Chapter 3: Intellectual Antecedents of NLP: here we identify and characterize the most influential sources of the strategies, methodologies and patterning that deeply influenced the co-creators, John Grinder and Richard Bandler, and the processes that they used during the creation of NLP.

Chapter 4: Personal Antecedents: a representation from the point of view of one of the two co-creators of NLP of the personal characteristics that played an important role in the discovery processes that created the field of NLP. The reader is reassured that the accidents of one person's tortuous personal history represents only one (and a quite unlikely one) way of achieving the skills necessary to engage in the modeling of excellence.

Part II: The Eye of the Storm

Chapter 1: Contexts of Discovery: a series of historical narratives with commentary in which the reader is invited to consider how specifically the initial modeling of genius and the associated activities that created the field of NLP occurred. Special attention is paid to the contexts and processes of discovery.

Chapter 2: The Breakthrough Pattern: we make explicit the features of NLP that distinguish it from other systems of change. We then offer a historical narrative, describing the emergence of the breakthrough pattern that casts a revealing light on certain unfortunate choices made by Bandler and Grinder in their enthusiastic initial coding of the patterns of excellence in the NLP's classic code. After an analysis of the breakthrough pattern, we offer a critical analysis of the classic code illuminated by the differences revealed in the breakthrough pattern.

Chapter 3: The New Code: we establish the historical context in which the New Code emerged. This is followed by a presentation of design strategy behind its creation and a teasing out of some of the implications. The new code change format is presented with a specific new code game. The topic of multiple perceptual positions with special emphasis on that privileged set of perceptual positions – Triple Description - is offered.

Part III: A Steady Sea Breeze

Chapter 1: Some Key Issues in NLP modeling

  a. Coding issues: the presentation of a number of issues associated with coding, including the tension between elegance in Modeling and pedagogical requirements.

  b. Ordering Functions: a study in the ordering relationships common found in NLP patterning. Distinctions are drawn between linear and hierarchical orderings and a number of different relationships by which such orderings are created are examined.

  c. Logical Levels and Logical Types: a brief excursion in

the historical development of the notion of logical type. This is followed by an analysis and a proposed reform of usage, given the distinctions uncovered and explicated

Chapter 2: Some Key Issues in NLP [application] and NLP [training]

   a. Sorting functions: the beginning of an explicit strategy for knowing, given a specific presenting problem, how to select the appropriate pattern for an effective intervention.

   b. Chunking and Logical Levels: the development of a careful argument beginning with ordinary chunking exercises and resulting in the precise sorting of two of the most common ordering relationships in hierarchies: logical level (generated by logical inclusion) and part/whole hierarchies. Several applications are described.

   c. Form and Substance: Process and Content: a preliminary effort to make explicit one of the key differentiators in NLP activities, both modeling and application.

Chapter 3: Recommendations: an invitation to consider a series of specific recommendations to the NLP community of how specifically the quality of work in NLP can be improved and what specific steps we as a community might take to ensure that NLP takes its rightful place in making useful and insightful contributions to an appreciation of how we as humans function, with, of course, special focus on performances of excellence. This discussion is followed by a commentary on how the patterning of NLP might be applied in wider social contexts.

One final suggestion on the use of this book – one of the co-authors, Grinder, worked as a professional linguist prior to participating along with Bandler in the creation of NLP. In the tradition of linguist research, there is a tendency to put in the footnotes some of the most interesting observations, albeit ones that have yet to be adequately explicated. While footnotes in a book are typically considered something of a requirement and incidental to the material – we have chosen to follow the tradition of linguistics. Our footnotes offer commentary and description that are quite rich and we urge the reader to consider them carefully. The reader will note that we have decided to handle the gender bias inherent in natural language by more or less randomly alternating masculine and feminine pronouns in their generic use.

Carmen Bostic St. Clair   John Grinder

Alamo and Bonny Doon, California, December 2001

The Lull Before the Storm

It was yet another crystal clear day – the wind moved over and around us, fresh and cool having last touched land in Siberia. The swells marched from the northwest to the land, one by one. They came in concert, perfectly spaced although larger than usual, and at the last moment drew up and threw themselves forward, crashing upon the beaches of the central coast of California. The movement of the air was strong enough to support the raptors that glided effortlessly above the terrain features that collected and pushed it up beneath them. All the creatures of the central coast of California busily went about their common routines under the gaze of an apparently benevolent sun.

PROLOGUE

The adventure known as Neuro-Linguistic Programming (NLP) began over a quarter of a century ago in the Santa Cruz Mountains. These mountains rise up from the restless blue Pacific in ancient sea bench after sea bench along the central California coast, remnants of former sea levels that existed in deep time. From within this damp environment that nurtures such an array of life forms as the towering redwood trees, banana slugs and delicate Douglas irises, two rather peculiar young men, John Grinder and Richard Bandler, emerged like the early morning sea mist that curls its way up and over the ocean cliffs to create a set of patterns that launched a ship of many different practices into the sea of personal and professional change work and then sailed on into the uncharted oceans beyond.

These initial patterns were in significant part extracted through a complex process of modeling the behavior of a number of famous psychotherapists. As you read the chapters entitled *Personal Antecedents of NLP* (chapter 4, Part I) and *Contexts of Discovery* (chapter 1, Part II), you will discover much about these two adventurous men, so eager to learn and test their abilities. They were largely ignorant of the existing orthodoxy that defined the field of psychotherapy – a field that had few explicit ideas on how to play in the game of change. Grinder and Bandler had little conscious appreciation that they were launching a discipline that would extend well beyond the confines of the field in which they had begun their adventure.

At the time Grinder and Bandler began this adventure, there was a veritable Tower of Babel - a proliferation of schools of therapeutic work (Gestalt, Transaction Analysis, EST, Rogerian, Rational Emotive, Kinesics, Behavior Modification, Self Actualization…). While differentiating themselves from traditional psychoanalytic practice was a common theme in these various schools, they each presented themselves wrapped in terminology more or less unique to their practice. This rendered them nearly mutually incomprehensible to practitioners of all the other schools. Amusingly, while clearly attempting to challenge the dominance of the traditional psychoanalytically oriented approaches to change work, each of these new contenders (with the exception of behaviorist-inspired therapies) unconsciously accepted many of the presuppositions of analytic practice:

1. that the roots of initial experiences (typically, early childhood) had to be uncovered as an integral part of the change process – what we will refer to as an archeological approach.

2. that the material (reference experiences) to be re-worked had to be brought into the light of consciousness before deep change could occur. The primacy of consciousness

was thereby enshrined in these more recent schools of psychotherapy, awarding it the same privileged position that it occupied in traditional psychoanalytic practice.

3. that the processes of change had to be managed by a professionally trained practitioner who operated on the client or patient in order to create the changes that would liberate the client/patient from the psychological obstacles that presently blocked their continuing development and growth. The general position that the professional agent of change occupied was quite analogous to a surgeon operating on a patient, a mechanic fixing a vehicle or a software engineer correcting a bug in a program. In none of these cases was there any significant attention given to making the patient, the car owner, the owner of the flawed program or the client/patient autonomous and capable of making changes in the event of future difficulties.

Largely ignorant of these presuppositions and without much interest in what they perceived to be a poorly organized and incoherent set of competing and questionably effective patterns of change work, Grinder and Bandler set forth on their adventure.

In spite of these inauspicious beginnings, the meta-discipline that Grinder and Bandler created has spread like wildfire throughout the world. This widespread dissemination can be accounted for by a simple observation – the patterning they modeled and coded works. It works across cultures, generations, genders, age groups and fields of application.

There are now hundreds of thousands of the people in the world whose lives have been profoundly and positively impacted by the application of this patterning called NLP. If they were to say what NLP is, the range of their responses would be breathtaking:

For Ralph S., NLP is what saved his marriage and the integrity of his family. It gave him the tools to learn to adapt his communication to fit with the requirements of the unconscious preferences of his wife. Both Ralph and his wife now find great pleasure in one another's company as they work side by side to provide the context for their growing children.

For Susan D., NLP is the key that unlocked her potential as a independent woman by allowing her to challenge and ecologically change the no doubt well intentioned injunctions about what is proper, correct and acceptable with which she was inculcated as a young girl in a very traditional family. She now moves through the world with grace and self-assurance with an array of choices that she now realizes is available to her.

For the B. brothers, Jorge and Oscar, NLP provided them with the patterns they needed to convert a failing family business into an expanding profitable enterprise in which they and their employees take great pride. They incubated several new businesses put together by former employees.

For Arthur J., the congruent application of the patterning of NLP literally gave him a new lease of life. He was diagnosed with a type of cancer generally considered to be untreatable. Arthur is "in remission" without symptoms and has been for some 11 years. He looks forward to a long and fruitful life.

Marian W. is a professional athlete – she was always very good at her sport but exhibited a clutch problem. She would perform beautifully until the finals - then she would choke. She now finishes in front, and does so on her own terms.

Edward S. was unhappy in his job – sales. He knew the products; he had the desire to succeed but lacked the patterns necessary to convert the knowledge and desire into effective operational behavior. Having integrated certain of the patterns of NLP, he is now faced with the delicious problem of selecting his assignments and accounts as top dog in sales.

Linda and John V. had a dream of having a child of their own. After some ten years of marriage and a host of applied fertility techniques, they were discouraged. A deep application of NLP patterning succeeded in removing the unconscious obstacles to conception. They are presently more than bit crazy about their lovely daughter of two years and Linda is expecting their second child, a son, in several months.

George U. was always a dedicated teacher – his passion is mathematics and he carries a burning desire to pass his enthusiasm on to young people, to open the magic portal of formal thinking for the next generation. He was frustrated by his inability to instruct and inspire his students. How is it that some of the students "get it" and others just never do? He now calibrates with care, gleefully adjusts his presentation for the precise unconscious learning strategy requirements of his students, and while he is not yet at 100% success in his work, he is living his dream.

Cynthia D. had an idea she wanted to take to Silicon Valley. She knew intuitively that what she had developed was close to a "killer app". Her low self-esteem prevented her from making the necessary connections to recruit and organize the team she needed to transform her work into a dynamic high tech firm. With the aid of specific personal change patterning, she is now preparing for a very lucrative IPO.

Jim O. is a family therapist. He says that he has always known that the deepest satisfaction for him would be to serve as the context for families to find their way through the almost inevitable crises of family life, using the challenges as an occasion to advance as a family and as individuals within that family system. With a thorough grounding in the change patterning of NLP, he delights in his sessions with families and marvels at the precision and speed with which he can guide his clients to new choices that allow them to realize their yearnings.

Kathy P. is a physician – weary of her limited success in exhorting her patients to follow the regimens that would lead to a recovery of health, she now employs patterning from NLP to tap into the motivational structures of her patients with nearly 100% compliance. She feels deeply confirmed in her work.

Lynda R. is the COO in a production company. She has a lightening fast thinking and action style. This style has opened some doors for her and slammed others in her face. With her intelligence, she recognized easily enough that she was succeeding almost completely by an enormous personal expenditure of her own efforts. Trained in the patterning of NLP, she has learned what it means to be a leader – the ability to create a context in which other players are enthusiastic and own the projects that drive the success of the company. She has become an expert at the formation and deployment of self-directed and highly successful teams.

Jorge B. is part owner and CEO of a re-manufacturing, sales and service company in Mexico. He acquired a deep appreciation of the NLP patterning and brought his company through the deepest recession and monetary crisis in the recent history of Mexico into a stronger position than it had prior to the crisis. He accomplished this in significant part through his disciplined and creative application of NLP patterning.

Luc B. had all the qualifications for his position as CEO of a bulk manufacturing company in Belgium – he was being held hostage by a member of his staff whose unique contribution and tacit knowledge made the difference between a high rate of rejection of bulk product and a low one. With the patterning of NLP, he discovered a way of shifting the perceived context for this critical employee in such a way that that employee became thoroughly committed to and highly effective in making his contribution as a member of Luc's team.

Suzette T. heads up a research and development group for a pharmaceutical company. Well qualified herself and excellent at managing people, she was nevertheless dissatisfied with the quality and quantity of new projects generated by her staff. She learned and incorporated a number of NLP new code games into the activities of her group resulting in an explosion of projects that she is confident will carry the company into a new and highly profitable future phase in the business.

...

Clearly for each of these people, NLP and its applications means something quite different. This is to be appreciated and respected – they have had the direct experience of the positive impact of changes in their lives. This is a book about what lies behind all these diverse experiences and how specifically the enterprise might continue to make such extraordinary contributions to our quality of life.

We congratulate these people and the NLP trained agents of change who assisted them as well as the thousands upon thousands of others who have successfully applied NLP to achieve their professional and personal dreams. The differences they have made are an important measure of the effectiveness of our work and are highly confirming to us personally.

However, we will argue in this book that these stories represent surface consequences of something much deeper. Further we will put forward a concern that unless the distinctions that we propose (or some equivalent set) are appreciated, accepted and operationalized, the wildfire adventure called NLP (in its core activity, modeling) may smolder and burn out for lack of oxygen. NLP would then have a quite limited life span on the planet, while the patterns of application as its ashes may be spread on the wind, as minute indistinguishable particles.

As a species, we distinguish ourselves from other inhabitants of the planet in a number of ways. One of the deepest of these differences is the compulsive way in which we order the world around us. We name, we categorize, we classify, we stack hierarchies, we argue over meaning, we dispute the claims of others when they differ from our own... These activities occur in the natural course of everyday life for all of us.

There are also those of us who devote ourselves to the study and elaboration of these activities at the professional level as well - scientists, philosophers, makers of public policy, owners and leaders of businesses, educators, physicians...

We are a contentious species. We excel at finding differences that we then will spend extraordinary amounts of resources, time and effort to resolve. From time to time we even fall into a madness in which we do violence to ourselves, to one another and to innocent bystanders (the other species on the planet) over such differences.

Other species display no mark of this activity, at least as far as we have up to now been able to tell. They seem to act as if what they perceive is identical with what is and as if any differences in their perceptions are simply differences, not stimuli for dispute in whatever form.

These other species will never develop explicit formal systems such as logic or algebra or C+ – those sanitized, explicated segments of another and more ubiquitous code called natural language - again, a system as far as we can determine unique to our species. Our companion species will never rejoice nor worry, neither will they fret nor obsess nor feel guilt... These are all activities that require the comparison of what they are doing with what they might be doing. Neither will they dance nor sing. Nor will they paint, play music or sculpt...and most telling of all they will never dare to dream!

Thus we are adrift on the planet with this set of odd and powerful gifts – albeit one with most dangerous consequences. In our history on the planet, we have had the luxury of making stupendous mistakes and still find a way through. With a burgeoning population, the awesome power of technology, our predilection for shaping our own environment as we choose and without any well developed ability to foresee the consequences of our actions, it is not clear we still have this luxury. If the other inhabitants of the planet had a voice, they would surely ask that we pause and consider where we are going and the consequences of the paths we have chosen.

We propose that NLP has significant contributions to make to these issues. In what ensues we attempt to make explicit what some of these contributions are. Such potential contributions can occur only if NLP can survive its adolescence and find its way to take its rightful place alongside other strategies for exploring the realm of human possibility.

Part I

A Freshening Wind

The first indicators of the approaching storm were available to anyone with the sensibilities to detect them. For most, however, these harbingers were non-existent. With their heads bowed and their attention fixed on the tasks immediately before them, the signals of the approaching storm literally passed them on the freshening sea wind.

Then there were those, more alert to the movement of the world around them, or by some strange accident of the moment were touched by these messengers of things to come, who paused and looking about them, read the future. Breathing deeply, they dropped their implements and moved with dispatch to a vantage point from which they could appreciate what was arriving on the wind. The surf was now pushing hard upon the coast and the wind began to insist on moving all before it.

Chapter 1: Epistemology

A marsh hawk swoops swift and graceful over the damp meadow and then with a shrill cry falls like a broken dream precipitously to the earth... only to rise again triumphant in the hunt, its prey grasped firmly in its talons.

For that suspended moment we witness without words, filled with rich textured sensory knowledge, confirmed in our identification with living things. We are for this brief passage of time close to our non-human companion species. Our eyes focus with precision, capturing and savoring the grace, speed and precision of the falcon, our ears tune themselves to the sounds of the desperate movements of the prey's futile attempt at escape and the last wisps of the morning sea fog giving way before the rising sun cools our face and hands even as we silently and smoothly shift position to follow the unfolding drama before us. We are alive; we are present. We witness without emotion, without judgment...

> *" Did you notice the way he turned on his wing to fall upon the rabbit?"*

asks our companion... and the moment vanishes along with the coastal fog and we are again human, for better or for worse.

Whether we respond to the question or simply nod, the web is rent; the identification passes on the wind. The query throws open the gates to a gust of images, sounds and feelings triggered by the words, generated without effort, indeed, without choice. The images of the specific way in which the harrier completes the drama are now replayed, not for appreciation but for comparison and analysis.

Did he pivot on his right wing or his left?

You remember seeing clearly the flash of the white band across his tail during the pivot and now examining your images, you realize that he actually turned on his right wing before falling upon his mark. The word *rabbit* drags a long sequence of sounds, images and feelings ranging from an incredible launch by a jackrabbit you once saw out in the high chaparral through the warm furry sensations of the first time you, as a child held a small rabbit.

But wherever the words take you, they most assuredly take you out of the moment: the marsh hawk and the rabbit, the morning's mists and the rising sun, and all the experiences of those suspended moments are lost in a maelstrom of associations that rush through your awareness dimly,

9

converting this unique experience into another entry in the associated files within your neurology. Through language, the specific has transformed itself into the general.

Later that day, you will hesitate, only partially aware of the difficulty, as you relate the story to a friend and attempt to remember whether the last squeal you remember hearing occurred before the hawk dropped out of sight or immediately afterwards, whether the wind rose from your left or right, whether this marsh hawk was larger or smaller than the one you saw last week or whether the rabbit was fully grown... Sensory impressions sink into memory as you reconstruct that moment.

But did that moment actually happen? Did the mist cool your face or did a complex heat and moisture driven interchange occur between skin and air that reduced the temperature of your face and hand? Did you see the marsh hawk out there in the meadow or in the area known as V-1 on your occipital lobe?

Why, of course, that moment happened...as surely as the sun rises. There is, of course, the problem of finding an educated person who will agree that the sun did actually rise as opposed to the earth having turned on its axis to reveal the sun precisely where it always was with respect to the earth.

Neurology and language – those two great sets of transforms that both separate us from, and connect us to, the world around us. Thus do neurology and language make fools of us all, each and every one of us!

A brief excursion into epistemology

> *If there were no difference between appearance and reality, then there would be no need for science.*
>
> **Karl Marx**

We propose that NLP, both in its core activity, modeling, and its applications can be usefully understood to be a higher order operational epistemology. By this statement, we mean several things: first that the operations defined both by modeling and by the application of many of the coded patterns of excellence that result from this modeling are operations that are designed to challenge the very processes by which we form portions of our mental maps that we normally accept without question. These challenges are designed to force a critical revision of significant portions of our mental maps, calling for a fresh perspective about the relationship between the conclusion we typically draw from our experiences and the evidence that we use to justify such generalizations. In effect, such challenges, sensitize us to the mapping operations ranging from our receptors to the higher level codes by which we consciously attempt to make intelligent decisions about ourselves, one another and the world about us. This is the sense of the term *operational* in our proposed characterization of NLP.

By higher order in this characterization, we more specifically intend to point out to the reader that the patterns that are the focus of NLP are not the patterns of the physical world; those patterns of the physical world are the domain of physics and associated disciplines. The patterns that are the focus of NLP are the representations that have already been subjected to neurological transforms prior to our first experience of them – what in this book we will call First Access (FA). To appreciate what we are proposing requires a brief excursion into the world of epistemology. We will state our position without attempting to motivate it in any great depth. The interested reader may wish to examine the full argument we make in *RedTail Math: the epistemology of everyday life* (working title), Grinder and Bostic, 2002.

The epistemological positioning of the field of NLP can be stated quite simply. Under normal circumstances what we as individuals refer to as our experience of the world is actually a set of events that have already been significantly transformed with respect to the world. We name these sets of events First Access (FA).

To aid the readers in orienting themselves, we anticipate the distinction that is the major focus of the epistemological section. We propose that it is essential to distinguish between neurological transforms (all the mappings that occur between stimulus/receptor contact and the point at which we gain first access to experience) and all the transforms that occur subsequently – referred to here as linguistic transforms. We will focus initially on the neurological transforms. The opening metaphor of the hawk is, of course, an integration of these two great classes of transforms, as is our typical everyday experience. The experience of the rabbit will not change as a function of the reports offered by the observers.

In the above paragraph, we use the term *mapping*; this concept is nearly ubiquitous in our thinking and in the presentation we offer here. To ensure that we as the authors and you as the reader are well aligned, we offer the following informal representation:

> Mapping: is a means of associating members of one collection with members of some other collection. The domain of a mapping is the elements in the initial collection while the co domain (sometimes, called the range) of the mapping is the collection of elements in the second set with which the elements of the initial collection are associated. The term *function* is sometimes used synonymously with mapping. The identification of what specific rule of association there

11

is between the two collections is the definition of the mapping involved – the specific way in which the elements of the two collections are associated.

As a concrete example, consider a collection of sports fans and the collection of seats in a sports stadium. There is an assignment algorithm (opaque as it may be to us as sports fans) by which the management of the stadium sells tickets to those fans interested in attending some particular game. When you purchase your ticket, printed on the ticket is a level number, section number, a row number and a seat number. Thus, we have a mapping or an assignment of fans to seats such that each fan is assigned to one and only one seat. Further if the ticket I have purchased has the number that occurs on the seat immediately to the right of the seat that has the number that is on your ticket, then I will sit to your right during the game. Thus a difference in the numbers on the tickets and on the corresponding seats (relations covered by the phrases *to the right of, to the left of, above, below, higher in number, succeeded by this letter*) is preserved by the actual positioning of the sports fans that happen to have purchased those specific tickets.

Note that certain relationships among the tickets (and their corresponding seats) are preserved under the mapping – such as the examples above, *to the right of...* Other relationships are not preserved. For example, all the tickets (and their corresponding seats) weigh the same, but not all the fans who hold those tickets or who sit in those seats do.

There is a frequently occurring (privileged) mapping we mention here, as we will appeal to it a number of times in the ensuing discussion. An isomorphic mapping is one in which each member of the initial collection is associated with one and only one member of the second collection such that the relationships among the members of the first collection reoccur among their counterparts in the second collection. In the example above, the relationships of the numbers on the tickets (corresponding to the physical location of the seats in the stadium) are preserved by the physical location of the fans when actually seated. For example, the higher the numeral on the fan's ticket, the further to the right/left he or she will be sitting in the stadium. Thus, the mapping is said to be isomorphic with respect the numerical/physical variables involved. The fact that all the tickets weigh the same but the fans do not is understood in this universe of discourse to mean that the mapping is not isomorphic with respect to this property.

Data Streaming to First Access (FA)

The events presented to us at First Access (FA) are the product of a set of neurological transforms beginning at the point where our receptors and the external world of actual stimuli collide and terminate at their respective cortical projections. Linking the receptors and the cortex are a series of neurological structures whose functions we will call neurological transforms.

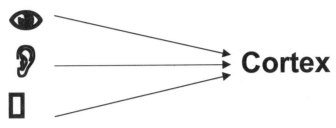

For example, photons (units of electromagnetic energy) of wavelengths between 400 and 700 nanometers strike receptors in the retina of the eye. All wave lengths above and below this range pass as a whisper on the wind, wholly undetected and undetectable directly by us. Those photons within the specified narrow range are detected by our receptors, general or specialized, and are transformed into electric impulses that begin their extended journey along the optic nerve. These impulses will pass through a number of larger complex structures (e.g., distinct nerves, the lateral geniculate bodies, the hypothalamus...) and the ensuing portions of the neurological network leading to the occipital lobes. At each stage of this complex process, the news of difference from the world is subject to mappings by the neurological processes such as summation, lateral inhibition... among others that in effect remove, change and/or add to the data stream that serves as initial input to the receptors.

The optic nerve is a jungle of hundreds of thousands of cells, arranged in complex connections and combinations that transform the input data in ways that are not yet understood. The structural arrangement of these neurons as well as the biochemical conditions found at each of the linked connections (the synaptic junctions) determine whether this data stream will pass and in what specific form.

Who knows what data is actually present before my eyes? Whatever the nature of that input stream, that data is registered on my retina which in turn passes it along to that astonishingly complex bundle of nerve fiber - my optic nerve - and finally, arrives at the occipital lobe. At the occipital lobe, the data which is a stream of electric impulses from the two dimensional surface of the retina, must be mapped (by some set of rules that shame the exquisite techniques of western artists even since the Renaissance) onto the occipital cortex transforming itself into a three dimensional representation of the original data in front of me and then and only then, do I see.

Parallel sequences of transforms can be described for each of the other sensory channels. The product of each of these sequences of transforms in each sensory channel yields our primary experience. This is the first point we have access – thus, First Access – to any of the sensory systems - visual, auditory, kinesthetic... to what is around us.

Each of these transformative sequences in each of the sensory channels occurs prior to consciousness, before we have access, before we have the ability to experience it. Each of the sensory channels has their specific projections onto the cortex. At the point where the impulses carried in parallel by the different sensory modalities are projected onto their various cortical areas, a (at best) poorly understood complex synthetic operation (no doubt involving the synesthesia or cross modality mapping) occurs, resulting in a seamless illusion of integrated experience and we have First Access.

We "see" an image of something we take to be in front of us; we "hear" sounds originating from directly unknowable real world events; we "feel" differences in temperatures, textures, moistness...all of which are the complex products of the original stimuli as they interact with the various neurological transforms in the chain of events that occur in our visual, auditory and kinesthetic systems.

Then, and only then do we have First Access (FA) [1]

All of this occurs typically without any ability on our part to influence it and certainly without any possibility of knowing directly in real time what is occurring. While we reassure readers well trained in NLP models of Ericksonian hypnotic patterning that we are aware that with great discipline it is possible to learn to influence even some of those events prior to FA, the typical situation is that we are entirely unaware of these events.

The image we see of what we take to be in front of us is actually behind us on our occipital lobes. We "know" that that occipital lobe image corresponds to some event in front of us through learning and especially the multiple descriptions of our experience of the world that we create through a comparison of the products of the neurological transforms that define the individual sensory modalities - in particular touch and audition. The sound we hear emanating from behind us is an event that is actually occurring on our temporal lobe - but we have learned as in the case of vision through coordination with the other modalities and in particular by arrival time differentials as refined as 1/250,000 of a second between the two ears where in the space around us the source of the sound is located. Again similar descriptions are available for the other sensory channels.

Critically for our analysis, FA occurs pre-verbally, prior to the imposition of language that by its very nature carries with it its own quite unique transforms.

The various sensory channels we have are tiny windows onto the flux of the real world we take to be out there. Simply stated, there are no conditions under which we have direct access to the world. What we can get to is First Access. But what are these events at FA and in particular, the crucial epistemological question is,

> *What is the relationship between the events in the world and the representation of those events at FA?*

Limitations to the Data streaming to FA

There are two marked limitations that we encounter when we attempt to answer the question stated immediately above: first, the vast majority of the events that are occurring around us in the gale of electromagnetic movement are simply NEVER detected by us as they fall outside the narrow bands of access that we call our sensory channels; secondly, those sharply reduced sets of events that do fall within our sensory limitations are processed by a set of neurological transforms whose specific operations are as yet not well defined – we simply do NOT know how the processing mechanisms influence the data stream that they manage:

First Limitation on FA

The first of these limitations guarantees that the vast majority of events occurring around us are eliminated as possible sources of experience simply by the limitations inherent in our connection with the world about us - our sensory channels.

Take a substance as common in technologically developed societies as stainless steel. What is the characteristic advantage of stainless steel as a material for, say, common applications such as utensils, engines of certain classes, jail bars, bank vaults and sinks? The answer that anyone familiar with the substance would offer is simply that stainless steel does not rust.

In a recent piece in the *Scientific American* (August, 2001, page 96), the following description is offered,

> *This form of steel* (stainless steel – authors' clarification) *remains stainless or does not rust, because of the interaction between its*

alloying elements and the environment. Stainless steel contains iron, chromium, manganese, silicon, carbon and in many cases, significant amounts of nickel and molybdenum. These elements react with oxygen from water and air to produce a very thin, stable film that consists of such corrosion products as metal oxides and hydroxides. Chromium plays a dominant role in reacting with oxygen to form this film. In fact, all stainless steel by definition contains at least 10 percent chromium.

This stable film prevents additional corrosion by acting as a barrier that limits the access of oxygen and water to the underlying metal surface. Because the film forms so readily and tightly, even just a few atomic layers of the material reduce the rate of corrosion to very low levels. The film is much thinner than the wavelength of visible light, and so is difficult to see without the aid of modern instruments. Thus, although the steel is in fact corroded at the atomic level, it appears stainless to the unaided eye.

> *Endpoints, Why doesn't stainless steel rust?*
> Written by Michael L. Free, Nancy Avery (editor).

The critical point is contained in the phrases,

The film is much thinner than the wavelength of visible light,

and

Thus, although the steel is in fact corroded at the atomic level, it appears stainless to the unaided eye.

In other words, the film of rust has a dimensionality below the threshold of light visible to us as humans (below 400 nanometers) and thus is undetected and undetectable by our visual system. With the usual disregard (or ignorance of) the actual state of events, we accept the situation as it appears (or in this case, fails to appear) as reality and award this material the title *stainless*, instead of awarding ourselves the description *clueless*. The point is even clearer in Spanish – *acero inoxidable* - literally, unoxidizable steel.

But one need not search for exotic examples; we live in the midst of such events:

You are likely sitting in a comfortable chair holding this book in your hands as you read these words. You are sensing a vast number of things; most of them occur without your being aware of them; some force their way into your consciousness. We invite you to back out of your present perceptual position for a moment and look at this reader seated comfortably in a chair, holding a book. What is the larger context in which you observe him or her holding the book?

This reader whom you are observing is awash in a sea of electromagnetic energy - the entire electromagnetic spectrum is in active play in, around and through her, her chair and her book. The reader has very limited access to this vast spectrum of events. Her eyes are capable of detecting wavelengths between 400 nanometers and 700 nanometers. Her ears register the arrival the sound waves, alternating compressions and attenuation of sound waves generated between 20 cycles per second and 20,000 cps. The tactile sensitivity of her skin responds to differences in position, temperature, moisture… within extremely limited ranges. The rest of what is happening - indeed, the vast majority of those events that occur in the electromagnetic spectrum that defines the actual world - occur without any awareness, in fact, without the possibility of unaided awareness (that is, without instrumentation) by her. In the time that it took her to read the last paragraph, a large number of sub atomic particles have literally passed through her body.

The channels of access – her sensory apparatus - to this booming buzzing riot of movement, energy and flux are as small knotholes in a fence through which she attempts to peer as if to catch a fleeting glimpse of the great game being played out there.

Even if we confine our attention momentarily to these tiny apertures through which we receive news of events occurring in the vast electromagnetic spectrum, there are serious epistemological questions regarding this sharply reduced flow of information.

Second Limitation on FA

By the second of these limitations, we are pointing to the fact that the FA representations (those portions of the electromagnetic spectrum that do fall within our limited ability to detect events) can be demonstrated to be different in important ways from what we can convincingly argue is the actual world – the chaotic winds that swirl about us. These differences are most apparent under conditions known as illusions and most importantly under an operation of comparison with the results of a special set of what we will call epistemologically privileged operations - specifically, those associated with instrumentation and measurement [2]. A warning – when using the phrase *epistemologically privileged operations* we are not proposing that such operations (instrumentation and measurement) are revealing the "true" nature of the world outside of ourselves but rather that they have a number of characteristics that sharply distinguish them from naturalistic observation as done by us as humans:

1. consider a simple black box representation both for humans making observations and for some simple instrument – a spring scale (as in the following example). Both accept as input certain elements from the world – in the case of the human, the stimuli striking the various receptors within the boundary conditions of what our receptors will respond to and in the case of the spring scale, the gravitational forces acting on the mass of the object placed on the weighing platform. The critical difference is that in the case of the spring scale, we know with precision what the set of transforms are between this input (object placed on the weighing platform) and the output – the number indicated on the scale for the units of weight detected under the operation of weighing. We engineered the spring scale; we calibrated it to some independent standard; we constructed it – we have explicit knowledge of its mechanical transforms. In the case of the human being, it is precisely the lack of explicit knowledge regarding the nature and contribution of the neurological transforms that intervene between input and output (our experience of the world) that presently constitutes the barrier to having any deep confidence in the representations – our mental maps - that we call the world

2. the spring scale has a highly restricted and unambiguous output vocabulary in which its reports are offered – the number system. However complex in the case of some particular instrument the transforms that are engineered into the structure of that instrument may be, the result is reported as one of a highly constrained set of robust symbols. These are numbers that indicate the quantity of some one-dimensional aspect of the object under scrutiny. In the case of the spring scale, the number of grams, ounces… are the result of the measurement operation. Note that this single clear report of the quantity of the dimension of the object being measured is robust enough to pass without significant degradation through the transforms of the human nervous system.

    When humans offer reports of their experience of the inputs they have received, they do so in natural languages with all their richness, vagueness and ambiguity. Further, for us to understand what is being proposed in such a report, we must activate complex sets of meaning making processes. These sets of processes are as yet only minimally understood.

3. the sensing instrument is not subject to the same logical type of

internal shifts that we as humans are. We note that the actual performance of a spring scale will vary as a function of humidity, the presence of rust on the spring, the direction and force of wind present at the point of the weighing operation… These variations are, however, well understood and can be factored into the final result in well-defined ways to achieve arbitrary precision. The state shifts of humans, while profoundly influencing the reports they offer about various experiences in the world that they sense, are not well understood. In addition, there are no well-defined formulae for factoring in their contribution and thereby correcting for an accurate report.

While there are other important distinctions to be made between these two classes of events (human sensing/reporting and instrumentation /measurement operations), these will suffice to justify the distinction. Note that we are proposing therefore, not that the instruments and measurements associated with them are disclosing the "real" nature of the world about us, but that they are distinct from direct human sensing in certain explicit ways and therefore offer a second description of those portions of the world they are applied to. This, by the way, suggests with some urgency that future epistemologists will want to turn a critical eye to the design of instruments as an essential part of developing a sound epistemology.

Using one of the special epistemological operations, standardized measurement - using the simple spring scale we have just discussed - to weigh a series of objects. We ask a naïve subject to lift the objects, two at a time, and decide in each case whether the two objects weigh the same or different. If the person decides "different", he will indicate which of the two is heavier. If at the end of this process, we compare the results obtained by using a human being as the sensing instrument with the results of our special epistemological operation - weighing on a standardized scale - we will discover a pattern.

The pattern is what psychophysicists well over a century ago call the just noticeable difference (jnd). If the difference in weight between the two objects lifted is more that a certain percentage of the weight of the heavier of the two boxes, the difference will be detected. If the difference in weight between the two objects is less than some specified percentage of the weight of the heavier of the two objects, no difference will be detected and the human will classify the two objects as having the same weight. Thus comparing the results of the two measurement operations: one the weighing operation utilizing the spring loaded scale and the other one utilizing the ability of a human to detect difference - we discover that the human will consistently judge as equal in weight events that can be demonstrated by the scale to be different. This experiment demonstrates that separate events in the world, distinguishable by instrumentation and measurement, are experienced by the human as the same.

This simple experiment can be repeated in each one of the sensory channels: in the auditory channel, the volume or pitch of sounds, taken two at a time; in the visual channel, the brightness of lights taken two at a time. There is (for most of the range of the phenomena) a constant ratio of difference arrived at through the epistemological act of weighing the boxes with a standard scale that predicts which pairs of boxes will be classified as same and which as different. [3]

Thus, even in the simplest of judgments in each and every sensory modality, we find a difference between what we can demonstrate through measurement with instruments exists in the world and our experience of it – the FA representations. While it is not difficult to demonstrate that there are such differences, the precise nature of all but the simplest of such differences between FA and the world itself is at present largely unmapped. We are therefore, at this moment, unable to explicate what precise relationships obtain between the elements in our experience (FA) and the actual world.

Few of our readers will have had the experience (or any desire) of lifting a series of objects, two at a time, to verify the conclusion offered. Turning to more common examples of illusion that occur about us on an everyday basis, we offer the following examples.

> *You are sitting in a car at a stoplight. There is a large bus to the left of you in the left - hand turn lane. You fall into the typical driver's trance, musing over whatever as you wait for the red light to turn green. You suddenly feel as if your car is moving backwards and quickly push hard on the brake. What has occurred, of course, is that the bus has begun to move forward making its left turn. In your peripheral vision, you unconsciously detected the forward motion of the bus and interpreted it through these same sets of neurological transforms into a see–feel sensation (synesthesia) of your moving backwards. The movement of the bus was actual; your experience of sensations of moving backwards was the consequence of the neurological transforms under discussion here. Those colleagues in Paris, Vienna or any other world class city with a well developed metro system of transport will find the same illusion occurring when two trains are initially at rest side by side and the one you are NOT in, begins moving.*

The difficulty, of course, is simply that the neurological, physiological, anatomical and biochemical structures that are responsible for moving the news of difference from our sensory receptors to FA are not simply a passive conduit through which the incoming data stream passes. They are, in fact, a set of neurological operations defined over this incoming data stream that transforms it in ways as yet unspecified. Until the fundamental research on how precisely the processing of the incoming data stream between sensory receptor and FA transforms this data stream, we are limited to making statements about the structure of the transformed data stream but not the source of the data stream, the world itself. [4]

While the great majority of what occurs passes without the reader's knowledge, even many of the things that do fall within that sharply reduced range covered by her sensory apparatus can occur too quickly or too slowly for her to sense or at scales too large or too small for her to detect.

Returning momentarily to the image from above of the reader seated comfortably holding an apparently stable book in her hands. If our local physicist arrived on the scene, he would assure her that the apparently stable book she cradles in her hands, the chair that comfortably holds her, the floor on which her chair rests are all illusions: in fact, in the case of each one of those objects if she could freeze them into immobility at this instant, she would discover that they are vastly more space than substance. The solidity of each of the objects is a consequence, an artifact, of the tremendous speeds at which their individual components move and the inherent limitations of the reader's sensory apparatus.

To further illustrate this point, we ask you to remember the first time you ever approached a revolving door. How old were you in that moment? Maybe you stood in awe in front of the revolving door and just watched for a moment as individuals moved into the space between the dividers and walked out the other side. Maybe you took someone's hand. You and the person with you, each of you, calibrated the movement of the door and unconsciously knew, and basically trusted, that this revolving door was designed by humans for humans for the scale of events manageable by our sensory apparatus. On this day the door was moving at a speed well within your ability to discriminate. You were able, therefore, to judge when it was appropriate to step into the space between two of the dividers of the revolving door and subsequently exit out of the space between the two dividers in order to safely leave the space it defined.

Now suppose you are standing before a revolving door at this moment and that the revolutions of the door are accelerated to speeds more rapid than you have ever previously experienced and certainly more rapid than your reflex times. This door could now constitute a danger. You would be unable to judge when it was safe to enter after a divider had passed and you could not move quickly enough once within the space to exit without being struck by the divider behind you.

If it were possible to speed up that same door to the velocities typical of electrons at the atomic level, we would have converted the revolving door into an impenetrable barrier. This "door" now represents no danger to us as the tremendous speed at which it is traveling now creates the experience of solidity for our sensory apparatus - it is now simply a rounded section of the wall in which it is set. We may lean against it, push on it, bounce a ball off of it… with no more fear of injury than you experience when you settle yourself into the chair you are now sitting in. What we as individuals consider the world to be is a set of complex dynamic relationships between what is actually out there (unknown) and our sensory and neurological processing abilities as we sense a small and selective portion of those events that are occurring.

Glance through a window; hopefully you can see a tree that is planted within your view. Is it growing? You can see that lush green new growth appears in the spring, but can you watch the tree growing? To answer these questions, we can call in our local naturalist who can produce measurements that demonstrate that the tree outside our house is growing constantly, but again our senses betray us. We simply cannot detect those activities except through instrumentation that reveals a scale of differences beyond our normal sensory abilities to discriminate. Isn't it amazing how much your child or grandchild or niece or nephew grows when you have been away for even a few days?

As you face east at sunrise, watching the apparently rising sun, can you sense that you are moving "forward and down" with respect to the sun; that you have simply been carried by the rotation of the earth to a new perceptual position from which the sun looks "higher" in the sky?

Select any specific nerve cell in the complex nerve bundle mediating vision at any point between the optic chiasm and the occipital lobe. What are the conditions for the firing of this nerve cell? Does this nerve cell require inputs from a single preceding nerve cell or some combination of nerve cells? Is this particular nerve cell wired like a logical AND gate - that is, does it require the near simultaneously firing of all of the impinging nerve cells - or is it wired like the OR gate of formal logic - requiring only some portion of those preceding nerve cells to fire for it to respond? If only a portion of the preceding nerve cells is required, which preceding nerve cells specifically and under which conditions?

These questions appear to be questions that define some of the most important research issues in neurology. Our point is *that these questions simultaneously define some of the most crucial issues in the field of epistemology.*

Thus, at present, it is impossible to say with any precision or completeness what portions of the world end up represented in our maps, or conversely, what elements in the world are patently not mapped onto our representations (this is partially known for the simplest cases at present), or what elements in our maps are uniquely the contribution of the processing mechanisms.

The conclusion is clear enough - that FA is already a set of transformed representations: products of transforms defined over the incoming data stream. These transforms are not some simple isomorphic mapping of what there is all around us. We know that the vast majority of what is out there never enters our sphere of representation, never makes it into our sensory channels and therefore onto our representations, our mental maps, as the structure of our sensory receptors is simply not capable of detecting and reporting their presence. Further the sharply reduced set of events that happen to fall within our sensory capabilities is in turn only partially reported since variables such as the speed of presentation and scale will further reduce what can be detected and reported.

Finally, and most interestingly, the reports of events that escape this initial filtering are inputs to a sequence of complex neurological operations whose structure is yet to be elucidated - operations that transform these reports in ways as yet unspecified. These transforms remove once and for all the possibility of a simple correspondence between what is out there and what we experience.

Second Set of Transforms: linguistically mediated experience

In our examples we have thus far focused on examples of the neurological transforms: operations that occur prior to any awareness, beyond our ability to influence [5], prior to FA and well before any linguistic mapping.

We are now at the point in our description of the processing of the incoming data stream where we apply a second set of transforms; the transforms of natural language and its derivative forms - formal systems such as logic, algebra, geometry, automata theory… We hasten to clarify: we are NOT proposing that the set of formal systems mentioned are in any current sense dependent on language – we are well aware that mathematicians, physicists and logicians as well as architects are perfectly capable of and, indeed, do spend significant portions of their professional life thinking visually in effective and creative ways without the use of natural language. Similarly, dancers and athletes think exquisitely with their bodies without the aid of language forms – indeed, liberated from such "aid" for the critical portions of their professional life known as performance. Composers and musicians find deep satisfaction in their professional activities working auditorily without language. What we are proposing here (see *RedTail Math: the epistemology of everyday life (working title)*, Grinder and Bostic, 2002) for a fuller presentation) is that natural language was historically the first subsystem within the human neurology to develop what we now refer to as finite recursive rule systems.

Further developing this point, there are a number of common experiences in which people react to situations in the world of great importance without language playing any part:

> *You are driving at relatively high speed on a freeway and suddenly two cars immediately in front of you collide. You take a series of extremely quick actions that allow you to avoid hitting either of them and finding a way through without entanglement. During those fractions of seconds, you are making excellent decisions and implementing them without any verbal experience, using what we refer to in NLP as see-feel and hear-feel (synesthesia) circuitry. None of this involves either reflexive consciousness or language.*

> *You are asleep – it is 5:00 AM, before sunrise. Suddenly, you feel your bed put into violent motion. You hear deep creaking and groaning of the structure of your home. You leap from your bed and find yourself racing to the snatch your baby from her crib and exit the house. It is much later, once safely outside that you discover, for example, your feet are bleeding from running over broken glass to rescue your child and flee from the tottering house. Oops, you are without an adequate night garment - another California earthquake.*

> *You are in the kitchen, preparing one of your favorite meals. You are aware of classical music playing softly in the background, the chatter of the neighbors visiting over the back fence, the children playing on the swing set... The air is sweet with the aroma of the freesias in the vase in the center of the table. The last rays of a magnificent sunset capture your attention as our life-giving orb slips quietly beneath the far edge of the placid Pacific. During none of this did even a whisper of language enter into the experience. This is indeed of great importance as it defines in part the quality of your life.*

Implications for the traditional Map/Territory Distinction

We know that the processes that deliver the data about the world are a set of operations that act on that data transforming it in ways that we are not fully explicit about. We know that there are significant differences between the world and our representations of the world. However, we are as yet not in a position in most cases to make any precise statements about what those differences are. Thus the world as we know it is not the territory, it is the product of a set of neurological transforms. One of the most commonly referenced clichés of NLP is the distinction attributed to Korzybski who proposed that we create mental maps that come to represent the territory (the actual world in which we live) and act upon those maps as if they were the things they themselves represent. This is captured by the mantra:

The map is not the territory.

We are proposing that Korzybski was far too conservative when he said that the map is not the territory. Indeed, we propose that his territory isn't even the territory. [6]

The Criterion of Utility

We are faced now with the question of how specifically these natural language transforms further shape our already transformed representations of what is around us. This second mapping, the function called language, is *in principle* freed of all constraints except utility, a criterion near and dear to any NLP modeler's heart. By utility, we are referring to the fact that as in the creation of all models, the fundamental evaluation metric is the simple question,

Does it work?

In other words, does the way that we use language to carve up the transformed world as presented to us at FA lead to a relatively effective ability to manipulate the perceived world to achieve our objectives?   Does this utilitarian way of linguistically segmenting the perceived world at FA - the product of the set of neurological transforms - serve us well? Note that we are applying these imposed categories NOT to the world but to a set of transforms of the world (FA).

We believe it important to emphasize that there is no commitment to truth (whatever that might mean) in this linguistic mapping exercise; no necessary correspondence between the way we divide up our perceived experience (FA) and the actual structure of the world; no isomorphic mapping (1 to 1 association with relationships among the initial elements and their counterparts preserved) between the world and the first point at which we gain access to it – FA. Further there is no isomorphic mapping between the representations called FA and the linguistic coding of them. Clearly as in the case of any NLP model, the universal modeling activity that language represents does not alter the structure of what it names. That structure presumably remains constant however certain we may think about what we have created through the languaging process.

However, the same criterion applies to the creations of language as for NLP models, too much of a discrepancy between our attempt to impose structure through language and the actual structure and behavior of the things and processes so named results in an inability to effectively manipulate the perceived world. Under such circumstances, driven by feedback, we reorganize our model – our assignment of linguistic categories to the world as perceived. In this sense, our natural languages and the structures they impose on our primary experience (FA) are statements about a long evolutionary process of trial and error in carving up the perceived world with language. As such, these mappings between FA and the linguistic categories of our languages represent the accumulated wisdom of our ancestors and a summary statement of what they have historically found useful in their manipulations of the perceived world through language.

> *The suggestion is that the function of the brain and nervous system and sense organs is in the main eliminative and not productive... The function of the brain and nervous system is to protect us from being overwhelmed and confused by this mass of largely useless and irrelevant knowledge, by shutting out most of what we should otherwise perceive or remember at any moment, and leaving only that very small and special selection which is likely to be practically useful...To make biological survival possible, Mind at Large has to be funneled through the reducing valve of the brain and nervous system. What comes out the other end is a measly trickle of the kind of consciousness which will help us to stay alive on the surface of this particular planet. To formulate and express the contents of this reduced awareness, man has invented and endlessly elaborated those symbol-systems and implicit philosophies that we call languages. Every individual is at once the beneficiary and the victim of the linguistic traditions into which he has been born – the beneficiary inasmuch as language gives access to the accumulated record of other people's experience, the victim in so far as it confirms him in the belief that reduced awareness is the only awareness and as it bedevils his sense of reality, so that he is all too apt to take his concepts for data, his words for actual things.*

> Aldous Huxley, *The Doors of Perception*, New York, Harper and Row, 1954, pages 22 - 23

Thus, we organize these linguistic transforms in ways that are in principle relatively free of whatever structure is presented at FA – itself some poorly understood representation of whatever structure there may be in the world plus whatever contributions the structure of the processing mechanisms themselves induce.

We incessantly order and re-order the products of the neurological transforms at FA with language structures, operating by a logic wholly independent of whatever actual structures (if any) the original events in the real world may have originally expressed.

The Naming Function

If some object in front of us has as part of its structure physical properties that will absorb all the wavelengths in the limited spectrum of visible light that correspond to what we can see except green, then with breathtaking epistemological disregard for the technical aspects of what is occurring in that small portion of the electromagnetic spectrum to which we have access, we ascribe to that something the color name *green* – note not because the object itself is green but because it absorbs all the colors of the visible spectrum *except green*. This example is simply to point out that the assignment of some arbitrary sound sequence to some portion of FA is entirely conventional, both in the sound that is assigned and in how we make the assignment. [7]

Common everyday examples of this arbitrary naming activity are frequently found in the naming of objects by young children and especially within families where there is no standard non-technical way of referring to common everyday objects. For example, with the introduction of the remote control for operating televisions, CD players... at a distance, there has been a proliferation of terms referring to that object – *clicker, remote, control, switcher, changer...*

Language has enabled us to create advanced post-FA mental maps, mental representations, which ascribe characteristics to objects, people, processes.... which are pure artifacts of our requirements as human beings. Consider the questions that follow:

> *What is the difference between a weed and a flower, a freedom fighter and a terrorist, noise and music?* [8]

We are inviting you to recognize that language is an additional layer of distortion in perception. It is another source of illusion – an apparently uniquely human transform layered on top of the neurological transforms we have been discussing.

As mentioned above, we have proposed that Korzybski was too conservative. We find it useful in the extreme to refine Korzybski's analysis known as the map/territory distinction. More specifically, it is essential to distinguish between two classes of mappings produced by two fundamentally different logical types of transforms: the first, the neurological transforms prior to First Access (FA) and second, the linguistic transforms, subsequent to FA. The transforms operating from receptor to FA are the first set of transforms (neurological transforms – we will sometimes refer to this set of mappings as f^1) that induce a mapping onto a set of representations whose product is called the FA. As we have stated previously, FA is the set of images, sounds, feelings… that constitute what we call our first experience of the world. The second sets of transforms (linguistic transforms – sometimes referred to as f^2) map what we call our experience of the world (FA) onto language structures. [9]

The Distinction between Neurological and Linguistic Transforms

The fundamental refinement that we are proposing is the distinction between the set of neurological transforms (receptor to first point of access (FA) to the sights, sounds, feeling…) and the set of transforms called language (and its formal derivatives). This difference is motivated by a number of considerations, among them and perhaps most compellingly, the difference between the internal relationships that dominate each of these sets of transforms.

> *I see on the one side the totality of sense-experiences, and on the other, the totality of the concepts and propositions. The relations between the concepts and propositions among themselves and each other are of a logical nature, the business of logical thinking is strictly limited to the achievement of the connections between concepts and propositions among each other according to firmly laid down rules, which are the concern of logic. The concepts and propositions get "meaning" viz., "content" only through their connection with sense-experiences. The connection of the latter with the former is purely intuitive, not itself of a logical nature. The degree of certainty which this connection, viz., intuitive combination, can be undertaken and nothing else, differentiates empty fantasy from scientific "truth". The system of concepts is a creation of man together with the rules of syntax, which constitute the structure of the conceptual system.*

Albert Einstein, *Autobiographical Notes*, p. 13

We offer the following examples to motivate the distinction in the logics (the internal relationships) within the two sets of transforms – neurological and linguistic transforms and therefore between the two sets of transforms:

Ask a child to sort out a pile of toys. The child will group the toys into piles based on some perceived similarity: size, color, use… The child will NOT sort by manufacturer or price. This first set of criteria the child uses for sorting we will call natural partitions. Natural partitions are naturally perceived classification categories or grouping based upon characteristics that are the consequences of the interactions between the objects and the structure of the perceptual (receptor) and subsequent processing (neurology) systems that are uniquely human. Natural classifications are *confined to distinctions available in FA*. Through her actions, the child is implicitly communicating that she is creating a grouping on the basis of selecting some one dimension of the objects involved (color, size, shape...) and ignoring all other differences. The selected dimension or part represents the whole – evoking a classic iconic relationship.

Be careful here; we are NOT saying that this first set of partitions or groupings is a sorting by aspects of the objects themselves. We don't have access to the objects themselves, only to the results of the complex perceptual and processing operations to which these objects are subjected and thus transformed by our nervous system - more specifically, the f^1 transforms from receptor to FA.

Sorting by price or manufacturer is an example of an artificial partition: that is, the partitioning in these latter cases has absolutely no basis in the perceptual experience of the child; rather they represent categories that are the unique creations of our species - categories developed and imposed upon those objects independent of any inherent perceived features of those objects as presented in FA. Artificial partitions are consequences of the linguistic transforms operating on FA. [10]

Take as an example, a detached arm of a plastic super hero in the original heap of toys. How will the child classify this object? The most likely decision will be to place the detached arm with intact plastic figures of super heroes. Here is an interesting contrast between the two classes of logic. The logic present in the product of the neurological transforms tends to be iconic - part/whole relationships. Thus the detached arm is perceived to be *part of* the class of plastic super heroes.

Most of us use language without consciously being aware of the structures and processes we are employing. The example of the child sorting the toys demonstrates the difference between the logics of the neurological transforms and those of the linguistic transforms. We are asking you to note that language further transforms representations of what we perceive and that these resultant perceptions result in a different logical type of mental maps – mental representations. Those of you experienced in NLP applications will recognize the importance of mental representations in respect to change work.

At this point we will delve into the structure of the internal logic of language and how it acts to transform our mental maps. In the process we will explore the logic of ordering relationships [11] (sets). Please note that we are using the term *set* in a colloquial sense not in its formal sense as used in mathematics) and their role in classification.

The internal logic of the natural language system (and many of its derivatives) is usefully and well modeled by the logic of sets. A logician would likely classify the detached arm into a quite different set than the child, putting it into a stack called *parts of toys* along with a loose wheel from a tractor. In what Korzybski called the territory - the neurologically transformed representations to which we first have access - there are no artificial sets such as the set of parts of toys. FA has no such groupings. The linguistically based transforms that operate on primary experience to produce our linguistically mediated maps excel at such groupings. Consider the following sets:

> a. the set of all toys purchased before the child was 3 years old

> b. the set of the child's favorite toys

> c. the set of toys placed in the green toy box at the end of a play period

> d. the set of toys purchased and given to the child by her maternal grandparents

The sets explicated in a-d are further examples of artificial sets generated by the logical structure of language - none of which have any necessary correspondences to the resultant perceptible distinctions available in FA.

Being somewhat more precise, then, natural partitions are those partitions defined over all and only those differences available in the product of the neurological transforms - FA. Natural sets consequently are those sets generated by natural partitions. Artificial partitions and the resultant artificial sets are formed by set membership rules defined on criteria NOT necessarily available in the products of the neurological transforms. Such resultant artificial sets use linguistic or linguistically derived criteria as their set membership rules.

One of the principal language-based transforms by which artificial partitioning is accomplished (and artificial sets are generated) is what linguists call relative clause formation. Take the noun, *boat*, as in the sentence:

> I am looking for a boat!

The noun *boat* is itself a partition defined over the set of outputs of the neurological transforms (FA) and the partition induced by the noun, *boat*, is the name of a potentially very large set. Suppose that the reader were interested in understanding what the speaker of the sentence meant, what she was referring to by the noun - *boat*. [12]

Applying one of the most fundamental verbal tools of NLP we could ask a specification of the speaker with such questions as,

Which boat specifically?   *A boat that is sea worthy*

Which sea worthy boat specifically?   *A sea worthy boat that is capable of a voyage from California to Tahiti*

....

In diagrammatic form, we have an ordering,

A boat

A boat that is sea worthy

A boat that is sea worthy and that is capable of going from California to Tahiti

....

This dialogue could continue until a unique referent - a specific boat - is identified. The formation of each relative clause has two consequences: the set under scrutiny (e.g. boat) is further partitioned, creating a more restricted set - that is, one that has fewer members in it. Please note that this observation holds if and only if the sets in questions are finite.

At the same time, the new sets and all sets that result from further partitions inherit the set membership rules for the original partition, *boat*. Whatever the set membership criteria are for the set *boat*, they will be preserved under any partition of that set by relative clause formation.

Logical Levels as Structure in the Linguistic Transforms

We shall call all hierarchical orderings that respect these two formal criteria hierarchies ordered by logical inclusion, or more simply, logical levels. The two criteria, then, for logical inclusion are:

1. constriction - reduced coverage under each successive partition induced by relative clause formation

2. inheritability - the preservation of the set membership criteria under partition by relative clause formation

As stated above, the events presented to us at First Access (FA) are the product of a set of neurological transforms beginning at the point where our receptors and the external world of actual stimuli collide and terminate at their respective cortical projections. Linking the receptors and the cortex are a series of neurological structures whose functions we will call neurological transforms.

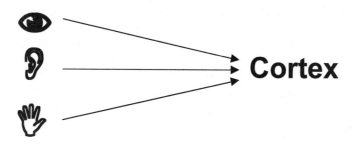

The hierarchy generated by the decomposition of the original set *boat* into its component parts is certainly a legitimate ordering relationship - indeed, one that finds resonance in the products of the neurological transforms in the same way that the detached arm is a part of a plastic super hero toy, an iconic relationship.

Now apply the formal criteria that define a hierarchy of logical levels. Note that the new hierarchy fails to qualify as a hierarchy of logical levels on both criteria. The formal criterion of constriction fails by the simple observation that there are more bolts in the world than there are boats (equivalently, more threads than bolts). The inheritability criterion misses as well as the set membership rules that define the set of boats simply is not present in the definition of the set of bolts. One of the set membership criteria for the category *boats*, for example, would be that they float; bolts are typically made of substances heavier than water and patently do not float. Clearly, then, ordering relationships called hierarchies generated by part/whole relationships are of a different logical type than hierarchies generated by logical inclusion. [13]

The distinction between natural and artificial partitions (and their resultant sets) constitutes a clear example of one of the differences between the internal logic governing the neurological transforms and the internal logic dominating the linguistic transforms. We further note that the hierarchies generated by natural language processes (e.g. relative clause formation) result in logical levels - the ordering principle for hierarchies defined by natural language is logical inclusion - a well-defined formal ordering. While there are tantalizing hints present in the current research as to what might constitute a natural part in the domain of FA (see Hoffman's comments on pages 102 – 105 in his excellent work *Visual Intelligence*), to the best of our knowledge thus far no corresponding formal characterization of the part/whole ordering relationships or hierarchies natural to the product of the neurological transforms at FA is available.

We briefly mention two additional examples of differences that distinguish neurological and linguistic transforms and invite the interested reader to review the more extended arguments presented in *RedTail Math: the epistemology of everyday life* (working title), Grinder and Bostic, 2002.

One interesting classification within language is that there are content words (normally all the nouns and verbs of the language, and their derivatives) and function words (the prepositions, articles, connectives, negation...). It is relatively clear that the nouns *dog, cat, plane*... and the verbs, *strike, touch, see*... refer to objects and actions respectively that correspond to specific portions of our perceived experience. To what then do the function words *to, at, on, over, under, the, a, not* refer? The usual answer is that they do not refer but rather are linguistic operators that indicate what the internal relationships among the content words are. The succeeding pair of sentences differs only by the contrasting pair of function words *under* and *on*:

> *The plate is on Jessica's table*

> *The plate is under Jessica's table*

The usual analysis is that the function words *on* and *under* specify the spatial relationship between the nouns *plate* and *table*. This seems intuitively satisfying. Now consider the sentence,

> *The pit bull is not attacking the German Shepard.*

As speakers of English, it requires little effort to summon up an image, set of sounds and feelings that correspond to the sentence presented. However, consider the situation from the point of view of the dogs involved. Here we quote Gregory Bateson's excellent analysis of the situation.

> *In iconic communication, there is no tense, no simple negation, no modal marker.*

> *The absence of simple negation is of special interest because it often forces <u>organisms into saying the opposite of what they mean in order to get across the proposition that they want the opposite of what they say.</u>*

Two dogs approach each other and need to exchange the message,
"We are not going to fight. But the only way in which fight can be
mentioned in iconic communication is by the showing of fangs.

Gregory Bateson, *Style, Grace and Information* in *Primitive Art*
in *Steps to an Ecology of Mind)* pages 140-141

The two non-linguistic entities (the pit bull and the German Shepard) have a problem – how to communicate the absence or negation of an action in a communication system that does not contain negation as it is found in human linguistic systems. The point is that at FA – the only domain in which the two animals operate – there is no negation.

The reader familiar with NLP application work with the unconscious will be aware of the issue in other contexts. In the analysis of effective communication, a speaker using negation will mention precisely the thing/action that he does not want and then negate what his words have stimulated in the listener by the use of one or the other forms of negation. This leads in the naïve use of language to the typical schizophrenagenic class of communication by parents, for example, with their children such as,

Don't play with fire!

The sentence elicits through the natural meaning-making processes at the unconscious level in the child, images, sounds and feeling of the action *playing with fire* (that is, the child sees the image of a fire, feels its heat, and hears its crackling and then feels the movement within himself to play with it). Unfortunately for the child concerned, the adult then proposes its negation, that is, delivers the injunction NOT to carry out the actions stimulated within the child by the adult's sentence. This is, in effect, a sequence that stimulates representations of precisely what the parent does NOT want and having stimulated those representations, offers an injunction against what has been so proposed. From the perceptual position of the child, the adult has proposed representations and then indicated that those representations are NOT permitted. The child is caught between carrying out the actions named and the injunction NOT to carry them out.

A more intelligent, effective and congruent strategy, of course, is for the adult who wishes to signal the child that the ongoing (or future) behavior is unacceptable (*playing with fire*) to name another activity (one appropriate for the context, the child and the intention the adult has and mutually exclusive of the activity from which the adult wants the child to desist) such as,

Gather up all the matches, bring them over here to the table and let's build a house with them! [14]

While mental maps occur at both of the levels that we have distinguished (FA and subsequent to the linguistic mappings that follow) we have presented this example to explicate one of the essential differences between the set of neurological mappings that occur between receptors and FA and the set of linguistic mappings that occur between FA and the mental maps to which we are accustomed, subsequent to the linguistic mappings. Primary experience (and its associated mappings onto FA) does not have a representation for negation and thus sharply distinguishes itself from what we find in the linguistic mappings common in our everyday experience.

As a final example of these fundamental differences, consider the contrast between the following two "syllogisms":

Syllogism A (a conscious mind pattern from classic deductive logic)

> *All women are mortal*
>
> *Nicole is a woman*
>
> *Nicole is mortal*

Syllogism B (an unconscious mind pattern from a logic not yet explicated)

> *Birds fly*
>
> *Words fly*
>
> *Birds are words*

The first syllogism is typical of conscious mind linguistic/logical patterning while the second is found variously in dreams, poetry, schizophrenic rantings and a keynote presentation by the current authors at the 2nd World Conference of Psychotherapy in Vienna in July 1999. Syllogism A is one of the set of deductively valid forms for verbal conscious mind reasoning, first coded explicitly in our traditions by the Greeks. Syllogism B, then, we propose, is a member of a set of patterns of the associative logic of the typically unconscious, non-linguistically mediated world of FA.

Freud, of course, used the term primary experience to refer to the product of the neurological transforms – what we are calling FA. Secondary

35

experience refers to experience already operated on by linguistic transforms.

We have offered several examples of the difference in logical types between the neurological transforms and those induced by language. While there are other quite fascinating differences between the logics governing the products of the two great sets of transforms (neurological and linguistic), those that we have explicated here are sufficient to motivate the distinction between the two classes of transforms.

Our larger point is, of course, independent of the naming of the distinctions involved. There are three sets of events (and, of course, the mappings within and among them) to be appreciated:

WORLD

First Access

Linguistically mediated descriptions of the FA

Further, other activities – additional analysis, formal, mathematical, the use of instrumentation and measurement... can easily be added into this ordering at various levels.

Some Implications of the Epistemological Argument

> *It is wrong to think that the task of physics is to find out how nature is. Physics concerns what we can say about Nature.*
>
> Niels Bohr quoted in *The Ascent of Science*, Brian Silver, page 36

Bohr takes a surprisingly conservative position with respect to the field (physics) to which he made such powerful contributions. We propose, in contrast, that physics does have as its objective the coding of patterning in the world external to us. Such activity has historically begun with qualitative observations of the relations within FA. As the relationships become better understood, there is a movement to quantitative representations of the patterning. The next phase is typically to develop standardized measurements and to design experiments to verify the explicit and then the implicit consequences of the explanatory vehicle onto which the patterning is mapped – these are called theories. Instruments are constructed to allow measurement of aspects of the theories that lie outside of FA – beyond our ability to detect, sense and measure directly (that is, without instrumentation). When findings in this last phase begin to accumulate that are inconsistent with observations within FA, the physicist posits entities that are outside of the domain of FA – hypothetical elements that serves both to allow the patterning detected to be described and then explained in such a way as to fit into the extended theory.

For example, as of the first draft writing of this book, the CERN facility (the principal research center in western Europe for fundamental research in particles physics located in Switzerland) is close to announcing that they have detected the last of the elements posited by the standard theory – the Higgs Boson element. This particle was proposed originally purely to fill a gap required to make the standard theory complete and consistent. Thus, there is great excitement that the scientists at CERN have identified events that they believe likely to be the first physical evidence for the actual existence of this theoretically required element.

Clearly, there are absolutely no events in FA that correspond to this element although if verified, it will take its place alongside other particles in the standard theory that the physicists hope will explain all physical events parsimoniously.

It is important to appreciate that the differences between appearances and reality are precisely the domain of physics in its current form. It is equally important to note that when physicists move from observation to description and then explanation, their work is subject to the same linguistic transforms that other disciplines are subject to. This occurs as the essential activities of description and explanation necessarily involve the neurological and linguistic (as well as the derivative forms of the linguistic code such as mathematics, logic…) transforms we are normally subject to. Thus the neurological and linguistic transforms apply with full force in these aspects of their work.

For us, the two most compelling aspects of the work of disciplines such as physics are:

1. there is an ongoing commitment to an instrumentation strategy that maps from the portions of the electromagnetic spectrum that are outside of the domain of FA back into FA where observation and patterning become possible.

2. Instrumentation is also deployed to gain access to the very large and the very small, the very fast and the very slow – that is, to aspects of the world that in some cases fall within our tiny

apertures of perception in FA but because of variables such as those mentioned – size, speed… - the sensory apparatus that we have as the legacy of our species are incapable of mapping them into FA.

The practical applied successes of these rarified theories of physics serve to remind us that while we will never have direct sensory access to the real world, it is possible to detect and codify patterns that apparently operate in that domain to great practical advantage.

The twin-intertwined strategies of instrumentation and measurement give physics and associated fields of science a special epistemological status *in those portions of their activities that are confined to these strategies*. They are, at present, the only candidates for activities that approach touching directly on the real world (whatever strange domain that may be). This follows from the fact that the instruments are not subject to the same set of neurological transforms that define the processes that yield the events in FA.

Next consider the implication of the epistemology that we have proposed for the field of neurology. We characterize them as one step more removed in their professional focus from the actual world. By this we intend to point to the fact that the vast bulk of their work does not touch directly on the world. In fact, their domain is two-fold:

1. first, the sets of mappings between the real world explored by the physicist and FA. Their task from our perspective is the identification of the structure and function of the neurological transforms. Their ultimate contribution will be to allow us to appreciate the systematic patterning that yields the direct experience we have named FA.

2. secondly, the relationships that obtain among the transformed elements of FA. FA will be found to have patterning which while partially independent of the world of the physicists still carries its own inexorable logic - the internal logic imposed by the organization of the human neurology.

We turn our attention to the linguists, the logicians, the mathematicians… in light of our epistemology. Their task includes two domains as well:

1. first, the mapping between FA and the mental maps the vast majority of people in the world believe to be reality. Indeed, it is their reality. This position is well expressed by the linguist Derek Bickerton,

Conflicts of representation are painful for a variety of reasons. On a very practical level, it is painful to have a model of reality that conflicts with those of the people around you. But why should this conflict worry people, if a model is only a model, a best guess at reality that each of us makes? Because nobody thinks of it in that way. If the model is the only reality you can know, then that model is reality, and if there is only one reality, then the possessor of a different model must be wrong.

Derek Bickerton, *Language and Species*, 1990, page 249

The answer to Bickerton's provocative question is precisely the points we have made above with respect to the special epistemological operations of instrumentation and measurement by physicists. In this special context, it ultimately does matter greatly.

2. secondly, the patterning of the internal logic of natural language and its derivatives – the formal systems we have developed and constantly impose on FA (for example, the syntax of natural language..

Coordinated with this sequence of professions are different sets of activities. Disciplines such as physics, chemistry, physiology... represent a systematic exploration of the set of mappings between the world and a special set of mental maps known as theories. This activity typically occurs in several phases or levels of activity, although these distinctions are not in general sharply made or deeply appreciated. As mentioned above, typically such activity begins with observations among the elements in the set defined by the product of the neurological transforms - FA. As the observations become more refined, instrumentation and measurement plays an ever-increasing role in aiding researchers in their work. The instrumental and measurement operations offer such scientists a second description of the world. These operations (instrumentation and measurement) have a special epistemological status as we mentioned above as they have a number of characteristics that distinguish them from all classes of direct (within FA) observations. We mention two here:

1. these operations are not directly subject to the normal set of neurological transforms that define the human neurology. [15]

2. these operations are performed externally and their results are typically mapped onto a single unambiguous object – a number or set of numbers robust enough to pass our neurological transforms without significant degradation.

In pursuit of these mappings, comparisons utilizing those special epistemological operations known as instrumentation and measurement between the world and our normal experience - FA - occur. The ultimate goal of this work is a working model of the relationships among the elements not within FA but within the world itself.

As the scientist attempts to describe the differences obtained by a comparison between normal observations of FA and these special epistemological operations, his activity is subject to the second set of transforms. More specifically, the linguistic transforms and their derivatives – linguistics, mathematics, logic... This portion of scientific activity is clearly within the set of higher order epistemological operations – more removed from the patterning in the real world.

The set of neurological transforms between activity at the level of receptors and FA is the domain of the neurologist, the anatomist, the physiologist... and may be said to be epistemological activity once step further away from real world patterning. Once again, as the neurologist moves to explain her findings, either to herself or colleagues, her behavior is subject to a set of even higher level epistemological activity – namely; the linguistic transforms (and its derivatives).

Sitting on top of all these professional activities are disciplines such as linguistics, logic, mathematics... which have as their focus the set of mappings between FA and the product of the linguistic mediated maps as well as mapping within the domain of linguistic activity and its derivatives. These operations do not comment on the world itself, only on the mapping between FA and our descriptions of the world and on the mapping within its own domain.

Implications for Neuro-Linguistic Programming

NLP as a discipline is a higher level operational epistemology; its domain being the mappings within FA, between FA and the linguistically transformed representations, as well as the patterning within the set of linguistic and higher order transforms. For example, the set of transforms in natural language called syntax is one of the most important sets of f^2 mappings shaping the final product – our linguistically mediated mental maps. What is clear in the extreme is that representations are the domain over which NLP patterning is defined. Note that this positioning of NLP and its operations as a set of higher order epistemological operations has as its corollary that NLP operates solely and exclusively on representations (mental maps) *and at no point does it touch upon any questions of the nature of the real world.* The domain of NLP is representations, pure and simple. The mappings that are within its domain are those that connect FA to various descriptions of FA and its internal relationships.

This, then, is the epistemological positioning of NLP. At both levels, at the level of FA and at the level of the linguistic transforms, we are operating with representations – mental maps – never the world itself. It is apparent that the domain of Neuro-Linguistic Programming (NLP), then, is representations and the application of NLP patterning is expressly the manipulation of such representations. As Bandler and Grinder stated in the book that founded the field of NLP,

> *Human beings live in the real world. We do not, however, operate directly or immediately on that world, but rather we operate with a map or series of maps that we use to guide our behavior. These maps or representational systems, necessarily differ from the territory that they model.... When people come to us in therapy expressing pain and dissatisfaction, the limitations they experience are typically in their <u>representation</u> of the world not in the world itself.*

> Bandler and Grinder, *The Structure of Magic*, vol. I, page 179

A cursory examination of the consequences of the epistemology developed for the practice of NLP will reveal among others the following;

> 1. In modeling, the core activity of NLP – the mapping of tacit to explicit knowledge – it is relevant to note that all modeling has a certain arbitrariness to it. Given any complex human behavior, and especially any set of dynamic interactions between humans, there is a large number of ways of carving up such interactions so as to create a model. This arbitrary quality of modeling is constrained by several variables that reduce its arbitrariness, although these constraints do not approach making it deterministic.

> A concrete example will serve. Take a common and relatively simple mechanical system such as a flashlight. Now consider the following two models or descriptions of the same flashlight:

>> Model A – Flashlight. Congratulations, you have just purchased a superb EverLite flashlight. The operation of your EverLite is simplicity itself: all you have to do is push the silver strip on the side toward the glass end of the device. Presto! You now have lite even under conditions of absolute darkness. Remember to put the two batteries into the device before attempting to activate the on/off strip.

Model B: Flashlight. This mechanism consists of a single circuit connecting a power source (2 or more "C" batteries arranged serially) with an incandescent bulb located at the extreme end of the mechanism. A simple sliding lever when advanced toward the end holding the bulb will complete the circuit and activate the bulb, creating a source of illumination.

Clearly both of these models/descriptions are useful albeit for fundamentally different purposes. This points to the importance of purpose or intention in the activities collected under the title *modeling* and the closely associated issue of the vocabulary onto which the modeling of excellence is to be mapped. [16]

This mini exercise in descriptive coding makes apparent the value of making explicit the intention of the modeler during the modeling. Of even more importance is the requirement to test the model through its actual presentation to learners and the resultant feedback by which the modeler observes the performance of the learners and learns where modifications in the coding of the model will facilitate learning and thereby improve the model.

2. As stated above, we wish to focus on the fact that NLP in no aspect of its work impinges on the real world. The domain of application of NLP, both in its core activity of modeling as well as in its multiple applications, for example in change work whether personal and therapeutic or professional in large and powerful organizations (corporation, Institutes and even countries) is representations and *nothing more*.

We point out an example of the liberating consequences of this epistemology in a concrete area of application. A professional change agent is faced at many points in his or her career with clients who have suffered horrendous experiences of inhumane actions. Put yourself in the perceptual position of such an agent of change: across from you is a person who has suffered multiple acts of personal aggression, a traumatized refugee from Bosnia, Northern Ireland, Afghanistan, Rwanda or a suburb of Los Angeles. The person in front of you is seeking to escape the tyranny of this horrific personal history. As a consequence of these traumas, she is unable to mobilize her resources and clear the effects of what she has suffered to move into a productive, even creative, phase of life and personal development.

Now if the professional fails to recognize that he is in the business of manipulating representations – the domain over which the application patterning of NLP (or any system of change) is defined, the task is literally impossible, undoable. How can he assist the client in changing the brute historical experiences of assault, rape, abuse... - all events that actually occurred and did so in a past beyond present reach.

The answer, of course, is disarmingly simple: it is the observation that none of the horrific experiences that occurred in the past are occurring now. What is occurring is that the client sustains within herself the representations (the images, feelings, sounds, odors and tastes) of those experiences and any attempt to move into productive appropriate behavior triggers, reactivates (through the relatively well-explored phenomenon of what we call in NLP anchoring) those representations from the past in the present.

Understood in this way, the agent of change is empowered to create a context in which the client can free herself of these no longer appropriate responses quickly and cleanly. No one (we would hope) is capable of accepting and tolerating such abusive behavior but we are capable, once we recognize that the representation is not the thing itself, of systematically and ethically manipulating those representations so that the client frees herself of these obstacles and moves forward in her life to creative and satisfying new experiences without the burden of her personal history. This, indeed, is liberating, creating choice both for the client and the agent of change.

The Distinction between Science and other legitimate human activities

The *nothing more* comment above is absolutely unsurprising given the epistemology presented and has significantly wider application. While identifying as unique and deserving of special treatment the fascinating special epistemological operations of measurement and instrumentation, all sciences have as their domain *only representation*. Further, consider even these specialized areas of endeavor such as physics. Once the robust numbers emerge from the instrumentation employed to capture and quantify the phenomena under scrutiny, the resultant activity is conducted or interpreted in language and its formal derivatives – mathematics... This makes the activity fully subject to the transforms that induce further uncertainty as the contribution of the transforms themselves are unknown.

This recognition has immediate and concrete consequences, among which is the final (we hope) burial of a particularly viciously flawed nominalization called *truth*. To some, such a death is unsettling. To others, quite liberating.

We hasten to add that this epistemology is likely to be understood by so-called relativist/constructionists centers of thought differently than we here intend – with a resultant inappropriate blurring of important distinctions. In Parts II and III of this book, we develop and propose specific practices that, if congruently implemented, would allow NLP [modeling] with its special focus on the extreme of human behavior (genius) to take its rightful place alongside other systematic and scientifically based approaches to the study of human behavior. We identify and explicate certain characteristics that distinguish scientifically based disciplines from those not proceeding under this set of constraints. Among those human activities not sharing such constraints, one finds numerous activities of great importance in the history of our species, such as religion,

> In an email message from the American Association for the Advancement of Science, I learned that the aim of this conference is to have a constructive dialogue between science and religion, I am all in favor of a dialogue between science and religion, but not a constructive dialogue. One of the great achievements of science has been if not to make it impossible for intelligent people to be religious, then at least to make possible for them not to be religious. We should not retreat from this accomplishment.
>
> Steven Weinberg, *A Designer Universe*
> The New York Review of Books, Vol. XLVI,
> No. 16, page 46

There are relativists/constructionists who will seize upon portions of our epistemological presentation to argue that given the inescapable conclusion that all knowledge, by definition, must pass through those two great sets of transforms that define the human condition; the neurological (up to FA) and the linguistic (thereafter) in order to achieve the status of knowledge. Thus there is no essential difference, they may argue, between scientific knowledge and religious "knowledge". The ongoing parallel monologues issuing from the creationists and researchers in the field of evolutionary biology with regard to school curricula in the US educational system come to mind.

We reject this conclusion. There is no intent on our part to blur this important distinction. We simply point out that in the resolution of strongly held but fundamentally different opinions, whether dignified by the term *theory* or not, there are some essential process distinctions. We develop one here to drive home the point and as a way of supporting the importance of maintaining and strengthening the difference.

In all scientific activity, by definition, the practitioners accept as an appropriate and natural part of being a member of such a community, the discipline of public presentation. Not only are they committed to reporting their conclusions but of the most extreme importance, their procedures.

This allows other researchers to verify (or not) the conclusions through something approaching the replication of the original observations/experiments. Any differences then are resolved not through appeals to authority, whether written or oral, living or dead, nor through arguments from consequence now personal intuitions, but rather by provoking the world through systematic observation, experimentation and the reporting of results of such provocations in publicly available standard formats.

It is difficult to identify where, if anywhere, differences of opinion (often referred to as beliefs) that occur in the realm of religious activity are subjected to the discipline of public presentation of results and procedures. Nor is there any commitment through systematic observation and experimentation to resolve such differences. It is hard to even imagine what evidence, if any, would have the effect of changing the opinion of a so-called pro-life, anti-abortion advocate, or for that matter, that of a so-called pro-choice, pro-abortion supporter. The procedural requirements of scientifically based activities, the discipline of public presentation of the results, the procedures of investigation, the evidentiary requirements by which hypotheses are formulated and tested, all represent the distinctions that deserve recognition by all intelligent and well-intentioned participants in these debates.

We are, of course, proposing the final internment of a certain nominalization – *truth*.

Footnotes for the Chapter 1, Part I

1. The informed NLP reader will recognize this point (FA) as what we have designated historically in NLP as the 4-tuple – a decidedly user unfriendly label unless you happen to be trained in Automata Theory.

2. Indeed, an illusion is defined as a difference between our sensory perception of some aspect of the world and what we can demonstrate through epistemologically privileged activities such as instrumentation and measurement is actually there.

3. This is a version of the classical experiment of the jnd. Gustav Fechner, a physicist from Leipzig, formulated what we are discussing in the text - the constant ratio of differences between weights determined by the special epistemological operations - weighing with a standard instrument, a spring-actuated scale - and by human sensing. The intensity of sensation is proportional to the logarithm of the stimulus. He called this Weber's Law after an earlier researcher who had explored the matter in detail but had not formalized the ratio. Fechner's formulation of Weber's Law occurred some 150 years ago as of the writing of this book.

4. The exception is the set of instrumentational and measurement operations. These have a special epistemological status, as they are not subject to the same set of neurological transforms as all direct observation and experience. Bostic and Grinder develop this point more adequately in their work: *The Epistemology of Everyday Life* (working title), Grinder and Bostic, 2002.

5. We are aware that with discipline, training and/or the use of hypnotic patterning it is possible to influence portions of ones physiology at levels well before FA. Development of this topic is well beyond the scope of this book.

6. There is an ambiguity in Korzybski's writing as to whether the territory he referred to is what we call here FA or the actual world itself. The more general point – the distinction between the neurological transforms and linguistic transforms - we are making is independent of which way you read Korzybski.

7. The sole exceptions are onomatopoetic terms such as *splash* where the sound sequence is (at least) a partial mapping (auditorily) of the event it names. In other words, *splash* sounds like the event it names.

8. Native Japanese speakers, for example, apparently process western music in the same way they process mechanical repetitive noise. See Tsunoda *The Japanese Brain* for an astonishing description of this as well as other such differences in cerebral organization between native Japanese speakers (and Polynesian speakers) and non-Japanese, non-Polynesian speakers.

9. We are aware that what we are calling the linguistic transforms must ultimately have a neurological representation as well. The distinction is pedagogical - we motivate the distinction in the ensuing text.

10. We argue that the distinctions induced by language are *artificial* as in the phrases *artificial partition* or *artificial set.* We intend these terms to be descriptive not evaluative. We invite the reader to read the more detailed arguments presented in *RedTail Math - the epistemology of everyday life* (working title), Grinder and Bostic, 2002 where the argument is made that it is, indeed, precisely the ability to create *artificial* sets through *artificial* partitions that in significant part accounts for our creativity as a species.

11. We offer a full discussion of ordering relationships as they occur in NLP [applications] in chapter 1, Part III of the book under *Ordering Relationships.*

12. We are not proposing that the referent and the meaning of a noun are the same thing, only that one useful strategy for appreciating what someone is talking about is the ability to identify what the referent, if any, of various portions of their statement is.

13. In subsequent comments (see chapter 1, Part III, under *Logical Levels* and *Logical Types*), we will there more formally define logical types in order to be more precise about the distinction between them. Indeed, we will propose a linguistic reform of the historical use of these two key terms.

We are also aware that we are proposing non-standard terminology. More specifically, we apologize to any logicians and mathematicians reading our book for the discrepancy between standard usage in their disciplines and what we are proposing here. We have argued for a distinction between part/whole or iconic orderings and what we are calling logical levels (generated by what we are referring to as the ordering relationship of logical inclusion). While the arguments for the distinction between the two types of hierarchical orderings are sound and their mapping onto the distinction we propose between FA and post FA structures intact, the assignment of terms is clearly non-standard.

There are two difficulties we are attempting to manage: for well over two decades, the term *logical levels* has been used in a very loose way within NLP in general although my (JG) particular usage has been consistent. Thus I have trained a significant number of practitioners who have accepted this terminology. It is therefore most unfortunate that while I have been consistent in my usage, I have simultaneously been at complete variance with the standard terminology in logic. Thus through my ignorance of the standard usage in logic, I have inadvertently applied the term *logical levels*, a term that the logicians used to designate the part/whole ordering relationship to a different ordering relationship, logical inclusion and simply refer part/whole relationships as part/whole or iconic. This makes our usage here at variance with the standard usage in the fields of set theory, formal logic...

14. Clearly, the adult will have to instruct the child in what is and is not appropriate play with matches and other fire-producing implements at some point, addressing the issue head on. Presumably, this will occur when both the adult and the child are in a context and in states that permit such instruction, presumably through the explication/ demonstration of the consequences of the actions the adult wants the child to NOT engage in - the playing with fire. What is clearly schizophrenagenic is to stimulate in the child internal representations of precisely what the adult does NOT want the child to do and then place an injunction on the stimulated representations.

15. It follows from our remarks here that great value will accrue to this entire endeavor through the development of an epistemology of instrumentation. One of the research questions would then be,

> *What mappings or transforms are built into the design of instruments?*

Clearly until these epistemological studies are developed, the special epistemological status of such operations remain unexplicated.

Further, there is a body of literature (*the Experimenter Effect* – investigated by, for example, Robert Rosenthal) that scientists are unconsciously influenced in the act of observation itself by presuppositions and the hypotheses they carry into their work. This would seem to make more urgent the investigation of the design of instruments.

16. We again invite the reader to peruse the more developed and

extended presentation of these themes in *RedTail Math: the epistemology of everyday life* (working title), Grinder and Bostic, 2002

Chapter 2: Terminology

Neuro-Linguistic Programming NLP

(NLP) is a modeling technology whose specific subject matter is the set of differences that make the difference between the performance of geniuses and that of average performers in the same field or activity. In this sense, the objective of modeling studies in NLP is to explicate in a transferable and learnable code these sets of differences. [1] The core activity, then, is the mapping of tacit knowledge onto an explicit model. This meta-discipline was created by John Grinder and Richard Bandler in the early 70's.

Modeling, Application or Design

In actual usage over the last several decades, the term *NLP* has come to refer to the general set of activities that includes not only modeling, but applications of the product of the core activity of modeling – the patterns of excellence coded from the sets of differences discovered - as well as the teaching and training of these patterns. In part, the drift in the meaning is a measure of the ineffectiveness of the co-creators to make clear and precise what NLP is.

The required distinction is the same as the distinction between physics and engineering, or medical research and clinical practice, or chemistry and pharmacology. Physics, for example, is the study of the patterns that govern the physical phenomena about us. Such studies over centuries have resulted in the coding of certain patterns, principles, laws of nature... An engineer designing a bridge will draw upon this body of tested and verified patterning (especially the computational formulae) to carry out his work. He is said to be applying the principles of physics in order to work how specifically the bridge should be constructed. Physics – the study of the fundamental patterns of physical phenomena – can be applied in multiple instances from bridge building to the design of extraterrestrial vehicles. Such examples are applications of physics, pure and simple.

Comparably, the modeling of geniuses done by Grinder and Bandler created the field of NLP, resulting in a series of models of excellence. These models coded patterns that govern the patterns of interactions among people in certain contexts (change work, hypnosis...). A business consultant addressing a challenge within a client company will draw upon the patterns. She will be said to be applying this body of tested and verified patterns in order to determine how specifically to resolve the challenge.

NLP – the study of the fundamental patterns of excellence in human performance – can be applied (in the context of business practice, for example) to management practice, strategic planning, personnel, recruitment, new product design... Such examples are applications of NLP, pure and simple.

The meta model can, for example, be usefully understood to be an application of the modeling of linguistic patterning inspired by Transformational Grammar.

It is important to note that in the coding of a large number of patterns in the initial modeling done by Grinder and Bandler is a set of variables. These variables (for example, state), inherent in each of the coded models, constitute an initial vocabulary out of which the patterning of excellence is composed. Such variables may function as the design variables for creating and testing additional patterns. While these may be largely variations on the patterning initially discovered and coded by Bandler and Grinder, it is possible to use them to develop genuinely new patterning and models. The new code (covered in Part II under *The New Code*) is an excellent example of pure design, a pure manipulation of these variables. Thus, we identify the distinction between modeling and design.

Indeed, from our limited point of view, there is little activity in the general field known as NLP [modeling] that strictly speaking should be so labeled. In fact, part of the motivation for writing this book is our concern that unless the distinction we are presently proposing is recognized and more importantly, the activity of modeling becomes in fact a significant activity of what is loosely called NLP, the technology of modeling that produced such powerful patterning will simply fade away. It is, for example, almost impossible to attend a high quality management seminar in the USA or Western Europe without encountering any number of NLP coded patterns of excellence such as representational systems or much of the verbal patterning. Thus, unless renewed activity in modeling and the coding of new patterning of excellence becomes the touchstone for NLP, then it is quite likely that the patterns of excellence initially modeled and coded will simply be incorporated in the various applications areas. Once such an integration is completed, there will be no justification for anything called NLP.

Thus we are faced in this book with a difficult linguistic issue – how shall we refer to NLP and its various activities. If we adopt the common usage of the term *NLP*, the critical point concerning modeling is lost. If we insist on the distinction between NLP [modeling] and NLP [application], we are swimming upstream in the river of usage.

So, may we swim strongly!

For purposes of the exposition here then, we will use NLP as a generic label referring to the entire range of activities from modeling through applications to training. In any usage in this book, where in our opinion it makes an important difference, we will specify whether we are referring to core NLP – that is, as presented above, NLP ^{modeling} - or to some application of NLP – therefore, NLP ^{application}. At times we will further distinguish application from training with the use of NLP ^{training}. In some cases, the intended distinction is clear from context (the surrounding text specifies the intention of the writers adequately) and we will avoid the artificial device we have selected for a written presentation by leaving the specification out of the presentation. Our hope is that the distinction will be clear and cogent enough to activate interest on the part of some of the readers and inspire them to commit to becoming proficient and active in the modeling of excellence – that is,

$$NLP\ ^{modeling}.$$

Pattern

The key unit of analysis in NLP modeling is the pattern, the natural work product of a modeling process. A pattern itself is a redundancy or, borrowing from Gregory Bateson's work,

> *any aggregate of events or objects (e.g. a sequence of phonemes, a painting, or a frog or a culture) shall be said to contain a "redundancy" or a "pattern" if the aggregate can be divided in any way by a "slash mark" such that an observer perceiving only what is on one side of the slash mark can guess with better than random success, what is on the other side of the slash mark.... Or, again from the point of view of a cybernetic observer, the information available on one side of the slash will restrain) i.e. reduce the probability of) wrong guessing.*

> Gregory Bateson, *Steps to an Ecology of Mind,* page 131

The work product of a NLP modeling project then is always (minimally) a pattern.

As a common example, observe birds moving from perching behavior to flight. Their sequence always includes a point in their behavior where they push down on the surface upon which they are perched prior to achieving flight. Thus, if we were to write out a description of the bird's activities beginning while the bird is perched and terminating when the bird is airborne, we would be able to place a slash mark between the portion of the description when the bird pushes down on its perch and its achieving flight.

The typical form an application pattern takes in NLP is a sequence (partially or totally ordered) of statements (for the most part injunctive as opposed to declarative) containing variables that identify what is to be manipulated and instructions indicating which operations to perform on those variables. In the context of application, the term *format* is often used synonymously with *pattern*.

A deeper analysis of the actual application patterns reveals that such application patterns are actually a series of attention points that indicate where and how to fix either the client's attention, the agent of change's attention or both.

This discussion leads us to a very specific research proposal. We urge that all patterns proposed in NLP ^{modeling} and presented in the field either in the literature or through oral presentation, satisfy the following three minimal requirements (or their equivalents) – specifically:

Presentation of Patterning

1. <u>Description of the pattern</u>: a sensory-grounded description of the elements in the pattern and their critical ordering (that is, the sequence in which those elements are to be applied – historically, in NLP, this has taken the form of steps in a format which define what the practitioner is to do first, second…).

2. <u>Consequences of the use of the pattern</u>: a sensory-grounded description of what consequences the practitioner can anticipate through a congruent application of the pattern.

3. <u>Selection criteria</u>: the identification of the conditions or contexts in which the selection and application of this pattern is appropriate (as known at the time by the modeler) – for example in the field of change work, making the distinction between the pattern's appropriateness for 1st and 2nd order changes [2]. This description should include any contraindications (conditions under which the pattern is expressly NOT to be selected and applied).

Our intention in proposing the above format, Presentation of Patterning, is to create a standard format whereby modelers can report their findings (patterning) in a manner that allows easy evaluation of their work, the ability to build on it with further patterning and a clear procedure for its application. Our inclusion of selection criteria is expressly designed to develop, refine and promote this less well-developed portion of reporting of patterning in NLP [modeling].

Model

More typically than a single pattern, the work product of a NLP modeling project is a collection of patterns – that is, a model. Models are to be sharply differentiated from two other associated notions, replicas and theories.

A model is simply that, a model – a description of some portion of the source's behavior, a mapping from a complex set of interactions onto a reduced set of elements. Thus the resulting description is always a reduced representation of the complex behaviors offered by the source. This is the distinction between a replica and a model. A model does NOT represent any attempt at achieving an isomorphic mapping between the source's performance and the description purporting to describe it. Indeed, the value of a pattern/model is to offer the interested party a simplified description of the complex behavior(s) the source himself or herself displays. This reduction is essential if the pattern/model is to meet the requirements of being learnable and transferable in a relatively efficient manner.

The reader is alerted to the distinction between a reduced representation and reductionism. Reductionism is a movement (found in many disciplines) to reduce the patterning under scrutiny to a fixed set of elements, typically at what is considered a more fundamental or elementary level of description. For example, any attempt to map the patterning of biological phenomena onto a purely chemical and physical vocabulary is an example of reductionism. Indeed, it is only replicas that may be said to not undergo a mapping onto a reduced representation.

A reduced representation does not necessarily imply a fixed set of elements or some fixed vocabulary. It simply recognizes that the mapping done by a modeler in NLP during the coding phase (when accomplished successfully) is a mapping from the complex performance of the man, woman or group under study (the source of the patterning of excellence) onto a model that simply ignores those aspects of the performance of the source not required for the learner to reproduce the excellent behaviors of the original source in the context in which the modeling occurs. This is fundamentally a sorting of essential from accidental aspects of the person or group serving as a source of the patterning, and is, in the obvious sense, a reduced representation.

The collections of patterns or models that result from the modeling of excellence contrast not only with replicas but critically also with theories.

Theories are, for example, subject to a number of criteria for their evaluation including internal consistency, explicitness, elegance (minimal description – Occam's Razor) and fit with "reality" or as it is sometimes expressed, "truth"... Models are simpler creatures; the sole criterion (at least thus far accepted) for their evaluation is,

> *Does this pattern/model work – that is, is it learnable and upon learning it, does the learner display behavior similar in results and quality to the source from which it was extracted?*

Collections of patterns associated by some common principle(s) will be called a model – we can identify two such classes of models:

1. common source principle - a set of patterns all of which were modeled from the same source. For example, the patterns discovered and coded by Bandler and Grinder from their observation, assimilation and testing of the specific strategies employed by Dr. Erickson and named the Milton model.

2. common function principle – a set of patterns all of which are designed to serve the same function. For example, the hypnotic patterns that have in common the purpose of communicating directly with the unconscious of the person to whom they are directed without the conscious participation of that person. These include not only the patterning modeled by Grinder and Bandler in their extended study of Dr. Erickson, but patterns designed using the variables discovered in that modeling as well as other sources of hypnotic patterning.

The term *model* in NLP is used in a systematically ambiguous manner; it can refer either, as suggested above, to collection of patterns (e.g. the Milton model) or to the source of inspiration for the patterning (in the case of the Milton Model, Dr. Milton H. Erickson himself).

Models (in the sense of a collection of patterns associated by some principle(s)) may be pure or hybrid; by pure model, we intend that all the patterns in the collection have a common source (e.g. the Milton model) while by the term *hybrid*, we intend reference to a collection of patterns whose source is not unitary – that is, that has more than one source of patterning. An example of a hybrid model is the Meta model (whose sources include Perls, Satir and the field of transformational syntax).

Collecting all of these comments, we have the core activity of NLP – NLP modeling – that results in the creation of a set of patterns or a model. The vast majority of the actual activity at present in what is loosely referred to as the field of NLP is application and training – more specifically, application and training of the sets of patterns (or equivalently, models) that are the work product of modeling projects to specific areas of endeavor (change work, for example, either remedial or for the purposes of optimization of performance, business practice, sports, medicine, art...)

Historical Models: Classic and New Code

Historically, the work products of modeling are variously referred to as patterns, formats, and strategies. In this book, we distinguish between the classic code of NLP and the new code of NLP. These terms are to be understood as follows:

1. Classic code: the set of patterns coded by Grinder and Bandler during the collaboration (1973 through 1979) that created the field of NLP [modeling] through their initial modeling of geniuses (e.g. Perls, Satir, Erickson...). It is important to note that the patterns typical of this period of collaboration are a mixture of two types of patterning:

a. Patterns modeled directly from the sources as mentioned above.

b. Patterns designed by Grinder and Bandler by manipulating the essential variables they had uncovered and partially coded as the result of the modeling of the original geniuses who served as the inspiration for the studies in excellence in the field of change work.

Note that this second source for patterning is not modeling in the sense defined here but design – more specifically, the manipulation of the variables discovered in the initial modeling studies and their use as essential design variables in the creation of new patterning.

2. New Code: the initial set of patterns designed (1984 – 1986) by Grinder and Delozier during their collaboration and its more recent extensions and refinements.

Grinder has continued since 1986 to extend, refine and design additional patterning consistent with the characteristics of the new code. Since 1989, he has been collaborating with Carmen Bostic St. Clair in this work. Bostic St. Clair and Grinder have also focused their efforts during this interim on the modeling and design of patterning of excellence in the context of large organizations (companies, institutes and in some cases governments).

Thus, the classic and new codes are examples of models.

First Access (FA)

First Access is defined as the first point where we gain access to the information about the world. Present best research neurologically indicates that this occurs for the visual system, for example, at the point (V-1) on the occipital lobes where the two-dimensional stream of impulses reconstitute themselves, producing the three-dimensional image (see Hoffmann's work *Visual Intelligence* for a brilliant presentation of the processes involved) that we are accustomed to seeing – and which most people call reality or the territory. Specific cortical projections for the other input channels identify where FA for that modality occurs. This is equivalent to what we understand Freud to be referring to as primary experience. These are linguistically unmediated mental maps. We have argued that the internal relationships (or logic) within FA are systematically distinct from the internal relationships (or logic) of linguistically mediated mental maps. In previous work in NLP, especially by Grinder and Bandler (in, for example, *Patterns of the Hypnotic Patterning of Milton H. Erickson, M. D.* or *Neuro-Linguistic Patterning*, or *Turtles All the Way Down*, this privileged level of representation was referred to as the 4-tuple.

f^1 and f^2

These designations refer to the sets of mappings that occur before FA (the f^1 mappings or transforms) and after FA (the f^2 mappings or transforms). Thus the f^1 mappings occur between receptor and FA while the f^2 transforms refer to the mappings between FA and the form that our final linguistically mediated representations take – our linguistically mediated mental maps.

Commentary

We elaborate on several of the points made in the presentations of the above definitions:

1. the subject matter of NLP [modeling] is high performers and their functioning – the study of excellence. More specifically, the focus of research in NLP is the identification and codification of the differences that make a difference between the performance of a genius and an average performer in some field of valued human activity.

2. the core method of NLP is modeling and invariably uses contrast as one of its systematic tools (contrasting, for example, at the highest level, the performance behaviors of the genius who serves as the model with the performance behaviors of an average performer). The behaviors of the model (source) that are also found in the

performance of the average performer are not described – only those that distinguish the model from the average performer.

3. the term *genius* (similarly, the terms *excellence* and *high performers*) is, of course, an evaluative term not a descriptive one, and further one that has at present no satisfactory independent criteria. Historically, and continuing to the present, given the lack of definition of the term, the actual practice has been to accept as valid the sampled opinions of other professionals in the same discipline in identifying who is and is not a genius in any particular discipline as well as the personal assessment of the modeler involved. There is much room for work on this point, especially since it is often the case that professionals will ignore renegades (e.g. the AMA's historical response to Dr. Erickson) or even denigrate their work.

4. The criterion for the evaluation of a model or patterns is simple enough;

> *if an intelligent human being learns to implement the descriptions of patterning which result from the modeling of a genius in pursuit of a similar set of objectives in the same professional context as the original performer, does that learner achieve a similar quality of results in roughly the same time frame as the original performer did?*

If the answer is affirmative, then the pattern/model is judged to be successful. If not, the pattern/model is judged unsuccessful. Absolutely no commitment is made to fit with "reality" or the "truth". Indeed, the co-authors systematically and provocatively warn participants in the adventure called NLP that the patterns being presented are "lies" [3] – systematic misrepresentations of what is actually occurring. Such participants are further advised that the important issue is whether a congruent application of these "lies" yield performances that approximate the elegance and effectiveness of the original genius. In other words, are the "lies" useful?

Given the epistemology develop in Chapter 1, Part I of this book regarding the possibility of knowing whether a description matches the "truth", NLP could hardly take another position in this matter.

5. It is possible to punctuate patterning in multiple ways. Take any one of the patterns from the meta model, say, the challenge to modal operators of possibility,

client: *I can't express my feelings in front of my spouse*

NLP agent of change: *What would happen if you did?*

Using Bateson's definition of pattern, we have a client and an NLP trained agent of change in a loop. We could place the slash mark immediately after the initial statement by the client containing the modal operator of possibility (*can't*) as the challenge that the agent of change will offer is fully predicable given the syntax of the client's statement. Equally valid would be the placement of the slash mark after the challenge by the agent of change. What occurs on the other side of this slash mark – the next set of responses by the client - is (at least partially) redundant or predictable? Change is underway.

In the first case where the slash mark occurs immediately after the client's statement – the specific set of challenges available to the agent of change is determined by the algorithms presented in, for example, the meta model – that is, we are able to predict with better than chance probability what the verbal responses of the agent of change will be. If we position the slash mark after the challenge by the agent of change, we could say with confidence that what occurs subsequent to that challenge is an exploration of consequences that extend and enrich the mental map of the client leading then to increased choice in his or her experience.

6. NLP is a meta discipline in the sense that all disciplines (including recursively, NLP itself) are subject to NLP modeling activities – that is to say, that the geniuses in the disciplines of physics, chemistry, psychology, architecture, religious practice, business activity, sports… are all potential sources of these sets of differences which distinguish top performers from average performers – in other words, such geniuses are potentially sources for NLP modeling projects.

7. The question of the vocabulary for coding the results of modeling projects is a non-trivial one and will be dealt with in chapter 1, Part III under *The Coding of Pattern.*

Footnotes for Chapter 2, Part I

1. During our research on the written material published on NLP over the last 15 or so years, we were surprised to learn that even such an eminent practitioner of applied NLP as Robert has defined NLP in a published interview as the study of the *thinking* patterns of geniuses. Perhaps this is simply an artifact of his particular focus on his *modeling* of people who are dead (Disney, Jesus Christ, Einstein...) through their writings and biographies.

2. This distinction, essential in NLP application, is more fully presented in chapter 2, Part III of this book under *Sorting Functions*. Few of these points (for example, the distinction between first and second order change) were explicit to myself and Bandler at the point that we created the initial patterns for the classic code that established NLP. The above distinction is offered only with the benefit of years of work in applying the patterns – that is, in hindsight.

3. the term "lies" as well as "truth" and "reality" appear in quotation marks to remind the reader of the epistemological position developed in Part 1, chapter 1 of this book. In brief, it is not at present possible to make any general comparison between a description of something and the actual thing itself as both are corrupted by the structure of the human nervous system and language (f^1 and f^2) in ways not yet understood. The sole *partial* exception to this statement as noted in the epistemology section above is instrumentation and measurement strategies. The exception is partial in the sense that the instrument designed, built and deployed by humans does not contain the same set of transforms as the human nervous system and thereby offers a second description independent of those transforms.

Chapter 3: The Intellectual Antecedents of NLP

General Background for the Western Scientific Paradigm

We begin this section on intellectual antecedents with a provocative statement from a recent book that contextualizes our largest historical frame as we work our way toward more and more specific influences on the development of NLP.

Steven Shapin in his monologue *The Scientific Revolution* (1996) lays out with broad brush strokes the historical development of certain ways of thinking, certain modes of perception and understanding that have characterized the more or less systematic attempt by our species to investigate and arrive at some useful representation of the world in which we live.

In his reconstruction, Shapin has identified certain styles of thinking (implicit epistemologies) about the world and the way it works, starting with the classic Greek paradigms usually attributed to Socrates and Aristotle and has traced their wanderings through various developments in the Middle Ages through the events of the 17th century - a point in time that many commentators about the development of science have claimed as the origin of the modern scientific method. Shapin is careful to eschew such broad claims, instead stating with a charmingly deliberate provocation in the first sentence of the introduction to his book,

> *There was no such thing as the Scientific Revolution and this is a book about it.*

> Steven Shapin, *The Scientific Revolution*, page 1

Our intention in presenting the intellectual antecedents of NLP is to engage the reader in thinking about how epistemologies change or evolve. The historical development of science is a model of the evolution of man's thinking and perceptions - a model of how mental maps can and do change.

> *Have you ever thought about awakening in a time when there were few explanations about the physical world surrounding you? Imagine that you are a youngster of five years living on a farm near a river, the furthermost farm at the end of a long dusty dirt track – your closest neighbor is a six-day horseback ride away.*

On this particular day, everyone is busy with chores – you have just finished yours. It is one of those hot sticky summer days; you are hot, sweaty and thirsty. You know the land well, and especially a partially shady area with a pool of cool water. You walk to the clear pool of water with a light sandy bottom. You satisfy your thirst.

As you rest cooling off in the shade of the trees, you idly drop a stone into the clear pool. You watch it tumble lazily, and, as it rests on the bottom, you notice that the stone appears larger than when you held it in your hand. You toss in another stone. This time your attention is on the water's surface, you notice concentric circles radiating from the point where the stone entered.

You sit there and think about what you have just experienced. You see the reflection of the trees and the sun in the pool. Those images blur at almost the same instant that you feel a slight breeze ruffling your hair. You hear the rustling of the leaves in the trees above you. Your eyes still focused on the pool perceive a slight dimming of the brightness of the reflection of the trees and the sun. Curious, you turn and look up to see a cloud partially obscuring the sun. From experience, you deduce that it might begin to rain, so you start walking towards home.

As you walk, you smell a strong odor and you hear the raspy caws and then see ravens circling above. You walk toward the smell and the birds. You see a partially eaten carcass of a young fawn. The entrails are exposed. There are flies.

What questions are in your mind? What explanations do you hallucinate? What theories do you project? What do you think you have just learned about the world in which you live? What are your conclusions about that part of the natural world that you have just experienced? What proofs do you seek – if any? Are there patterns in what you have observed? How do you generalize the patterns? The answers to these questions would be dependent upon the processes by which you place your attention, your personal experiential history, your ability to think in a systemic manner, your mental maps of your world, your ability to make generalizations, and your curiosity – to even notice, anyway.

The human being is a curious beast and that curiosity in a systemic form about the world of nature within which she lives has given us the discipline of science, as we know it today.

Science is our way of trying not to fool ourselves!

Richard Feynman

In any discussion of a legacy of thinking, regardless of the classificatory domain of that thinking, it is important to be cognizant of the contextual paradigms that existed at the time of that particular thinking. If you lived at the time of Homer, as the youngster in front of the clear pool of water, how would you answer the questions above? Would you say that, *the gods are sad, and therefore it will rain?* Or that *the gods were hungry, and therefore the fawn was sacrificed to satisfy that hunger?* Or during the time of Aristotle - *the rock fell to the place it was meant to be.* What mental map (representation) would you formulate to understand what you had experienced from the natural world around you?

The point we are making is that the answers to these questions are highly context dependent. The presuppositions of the culture and the society in which you live, the historical time, your personal experiential history, your own mental maps of the world and the conditions under which you were asked the questions and on, and on...

How much of the residue of the thinking of our predecessors still finds expression in our thinking today? By way of answering this point, we offer you the following example. Let us look at some of the pre-Socratic ideas about the nature of their world. The notion of animism which is a loosely woven thread through out the fabric of Greek thought presupposes a world in which it is inherent within the nature of objects to behave as they do – a world in which desires, purposes, intentions - are not limited to animate or even human agents; but which are characteristic of all objects distinguished in the product of the f^1 filters – call it the epistemology of animism. Post- Freudian thinking would identify this process as a projection: the imposing of human attributes onto the inanimate world. There is little doubt that this unique way of perceiving the world is still alive and operating in a number of contexts even today as the following letter to the editor of *Science News* demonstrates:

> *"It should surprise nobody that animism is popular among sophisticated adults in any culture, including our own... A firefighter facing a blazing building, prairie, forest or oil refinery has neither the time nor the means to develop a three-dimensional finite model to predict the fire's future evolution. It is much more efficient to model the fire as a hungry animal that can be stopped by depriving it of fuel to "eat" and air to "breathe".*

Animism is the first resort of anyone trying to deal with a situation that is too complex or has too many unknowns to be modeled in a more "rational" way. When the chips are down, sophisticated adults use the best mental approach available, and really don't care whether theologians, psychologists or philosophers approve of it or not. "

Charlie Masi
Golden Valley, Arizona
Letter to the Editor
Science News, Vol. 156, No. 6,
August 7, 1999

Charles Masi's remarks are perfectly congruent with the spirit of the core activity of NLP ^{modeling}. He is proposing that this animistic epistemology is of utility in specific contexts where we are required to make responses to overwhelmingly complex phenomena under time pressure conditions where the decision we make may make the difference between disaster and success, even life and death.

Nevertheless for all the variations of that time, the most well known epistemology of the Greeks was the Aristotelian version. Such a worldview contrasted sharply with post-Cartesian epistemologies. So does the weighty historical pendulum of philosophy swing.

The most prevalent worldview of the same generality as that we assigned to the Greeks in the world of medieval Europe is the machine metaphor. Under this new world view, not only are inanimate objects stripped of all the mental characteristics that the Greeks has assigned to them, but large portions of the animate world are reduced to simple mechanisms without any trace of such mental activity. Animals are automata whose inner workings are best captured by the image of a complex clocklike mechanism. There was a great fascination with the construction of animal-like machines – an icon that seemed to capture the spirit of the time.

Descartes is a useful symbol of this age, one that continues into our present experience. Descartes was a philosopher/mathematician living in an age dominated by religious interests and influence. He clearly wanted to differentiate humans in particular from machines. He happened upon a solution of immense harm when applied to everyday life. He proposed that we are of two parts: mind and body. The body was a mechanical system, much like an automaton, while the mind was, well, something else. It seems that this dichotomy has significantly defined the terms of discourse of philosophy ever since. Once we have been cloven asunder, there is, in particular, the problem of connecting the two "distinct" parts of ourselves.

Descartes drew a line that split the entity, the human being, into two parts and thereby created the problem of finding specific ways in which these two now distinct parts could influence one another. This question has exercised philosophers greatly ever since as well as promoting high rates of employment among physicians who are called upon to clean up some of the consequences of Descartes' original sin – his cleaving of the human into mind and body.

20th Century Contributions

We warn the reader that whenever a review of historical efforts is undertaken, whether it is a present researcher seeking positive support from a predecessor or a negative criticism from some historical era, there is always the tendency to evaluate that distant work in terms of the current perceptions and present practices, all, of course, with the benefit of hindsight. Such intellectual raiding parties from the present into the past are nearly always self serving, whether consciously or not.

In the present modern era, much of the ongoing dialogue is intelligible only if the reader appreciates that the discourse is occurring in a context of reaction to the highly influential epistemological form known as logical positivism. [1]

The logical positivists solved many of the traditional philosophical issues by neatly sidestepping them; they simply restricted the domain of scientific activity to exclude asking certain questions. The positivists defined the domain of science as the description, analysis and explanation of a restricted set of data – that is, the only data acceptable for scientific discourse are what could be observed (in some schools, only that which could be measured). While such strictures may appear to us from our historical vantage point to be extreme, an appreciation of the intellectual context in which this philosophy of science arose makes it far more understandable albeit if seriously over-extended. One great issue of that era was how one could characterize the difference between living and non-living systems. Distant rumbles and echoes of religious influences still reverberated in the distance and the logical positivists were determined to remove such influences from the realms of science, once and forever.

On the one side, the vitalists insisted that there was a force, a principle that informed living systems which was not reducible to some physical principles. The positivists, whatever their personal beliefs might have been, drew a line separating the domain and activity of science from other endeavors. This line of separation was articulated such that only the tangible, sensory-verifiable and measurable portions of our world of experience were within the domain – all else belonged outside of science, in whatever realm.

The echo and reflection in psychology of logical positivism was called behaviorism (with its most well known figures being the founder Watson and subsequently Skinner) while the counterpart in linguistics was based on the work of Leonard Bloomfield and his associates. The influence of this paradigm showed up in a number of ways in linguistics. For example, in the Bloomfield paradigm, syntacticians were encouraged to record the utterances of native speakers of the language in which they were working. The set of utterances thus captured formed what was called the corpus or body of data to be described, analyzed and explained. This all seems straightforward enough, and was accepted nearly universally by working linguists as standard doctrine during this era.

Chomsky's Contribution to Neuro-Linguistic Programming

The single most pervasive influence in NLP is the paradigm that was current in linguistics at the time of the creation of NLP. This paradigm – called Transformational Grammar (TG) - was one of the most brilliant contributions to the study of human behavior offered in the 20th century. While no paradigm arises without precedent, without precursors, without important intellectual influences from other people and disciplines (indeed, the point of this portion of the book), TG was very much created through the efforts of a single man, Noam Chomsky.

While linguistics has evolved since the founding of NLP, it is important to point out to the reader that the description of TG offered in the succeeding passage is one that uses the TG of the early to mid-70s as the base for description. Since our purpose is to offer some *historical* insight into the intellectual antecedents of NLP, this choice is entirely appropriate and well-motivated. Where significant differences have evolved that impact the issues we are presenting, they will be identified.

The field of TG has, of course, continued to advance and there have been a number of significant developments. Indeed, there are those who would argue (as Grinder did in 1972 in the preface to *On Deletion Phenomena in English*) that Chomsky's model of TG of the 60's and 70's was so well-defined and rigorous that it guaranteed its own demise. Equivalently, and more sympathetically stated, it led naturally through its very success to its elaboration and finally its replacement.

In the intervening years since TG was used as the reference point for many of NLP's initial procedures, some of TG's key presuppositions and methodologies have been challenged and even in specific cases overthrown. However, even though some of Chomsky's original operating assumptions for the field of linguistics have been challenged, the paradigm current at the point historically that the field of NLP was created acted as a catalyst, was generalized and proved useful in the extreme for one of the co-creators (JG) and was key in successfully launching the field of NLP.

The brilliant burst of syntactic studies inspired by Chomsky's paradigm shift burned so brightly that it extinguished itself several decades ago. All this was quite natural in a field as dynamic as linguistic studies with its many able practitioners.

Some readers will find the new field called Cognitive Grammar (see R. Langacker's two volume work 1987 and 1992, *Foundations of Cognitive Grammar*, for a comprehensive statement of the differences) a natural paradigmatic successor to the TG of the era in which NLP was created. The domination of the sentence as the primary unit of analysis, the research strategy that proposed that syntax could be usefully separated from semantics and patterning thereby greatly facilitated, the strict boundaries by which linguistics isolated itself from psychology and neurology as well as other allied disciplines, the deployment of hypothetical entities such as Deep Structure and the use of logical forms as the base for the transformational component of the grammar present in the flowering of syntax in the 60's and 70's have been successfully replaced or are presently under siege (depending on whose work you read). [2] Still, many of the foundation stones continue to have applicability to NLP as well as other disciplines.

It has fascinated us enormously in our own review in preparation for the writing of this section to focus on the question of whether the essential elements from the TG of that era (over a quarter of a century ago) pressed into service in the creation of NLP still serve. We offer the descriptions below for the reader's consideration and decision.

Methodological Contributions of Transformational Linguistics to NLP: The Competency/Performance Distinction

Chomsky was a student of Zellig Harris, one of the leading American linguists at the close of the Bloomfield period of dominance in linguistics at the University of Pennsylvania, and was himself (Harris) deeply influenced by Bloomfield and his particular interpretation of logical positivism in the theory and practice of linguistic research.

Chomsky challenged Bloomfield's model, in part by proposing a crucial distinction. An analogy may serve here. There is a piece of music called Beethoven's Fifth Symphony, presumably composed by Ludwig van Beethoven and first performed in 1808. Now any competent classical musician (and many skilled amateurs) can consistently distinguish between Beethoven's Fifth played by, say, the Berlin Philharmonic and the London Philharmonic. Clearly then these two musical events are distinguishable, creating different experiences for the listener. Yet both orchestras purport to be playing Beethoven's fifth. The question then is,

> Which of the performances, the Berlin or the London Philharmonic, represents the "real" Beethoven Fifth?

But, many students of classical music will protest that the question is decidedly odd. If enough interest is present and enough time is allowed to work it all out, they will arrive at a statement something like:

> Well, each of the orchestras is offering its interpretation of Beethoven's Fifth. The differences in the performances are the natural consequence of the differences in the interpretations of Beethoven's Fifth by each orchestra. Neither of the performances represents Beethoven's Fifth – each is simply a different performance embodying a distinct interpretation

Now, this statement suggests an interesting distinction – namely that there is some object, some opus, called Beethoven's Fifth Symphony that exists independently of any particular performance. Some music lovers will speak of an abstract nearly Platonic object called Beethoven's Fifth; others will point to the written representation as the actual Beethoven's Fifth. [3]

This clearly does not exhaust the possibilities.

However you resolve that question, Chomsky proposed a parallel distinction for linguistics. He suggested that the actual utterances by individual native speakers were something like the individual performances of different orchestras. In particular, the performance at any particular moment by a native speaker patently does NOT represent the corpus or body of data to be described, analyzed and explained since it is flawed. In particular, it is flawed by being subject to temporary performance conditions that obtain at the time of the speech act. For example, a strict adherence to Bloomfield's criteria would require that the slurred, erratic and incoherent speech of an exhausted, inebriated or drugged [4] speaker should be included as part of the corpus. Syntacticians, therefore, would be required to develop grammars that generated these strings of words as well as other, more intuitively well-formed utterances. This has proved to be an impossible task. [5]

Chomsky took the position that the appropriate object for description, analysis and explanation for a linguist is the underlying competency of the native speaker. In any particular speech act, the native speaker may, given conditions such as those mentioned above (exhaustion, altered states due to chemicals in the blood stream…), utter sequences of words that are not legitimate productions of the underlying grammatical competency. These odd productions are the result of the underlying grammatical competency distorted as they are filtered through a set of performance variables. Further, he proposed that the proper domain of investigation for the linguist is the underlying competency and that all performance variables fell within the domain of psychology. In the linguistics vocabulary of that period, this difference was called the competency/performance distinction.

We offer the reader two examples of the confounding influence of performance and competency variables.

a) *The horse raced past the barn fell*

b) *The horse driven past the barn fell*

The first sentence (a) of this pair of sentences is unintelligible; while the second (b) is easily computed and understood. Notice that by the addition of the syntactic marker *that* – a remnant of a reduced relative clause - the unintelligible sentence (a) becomes perfectly intelligible, namely,

c) *The horse that raced past the barn fell*

The classical explanation for this difference (Thomas Bevers, personal communication, Rockefeller University, 1970) is that there is a perceptual strategy that we unconsciously use to process language in English wherein the first possible combination of subject noun phrase (*the horse*) with a matching verb form (*raced past the barn*) will be computed and therefore, perceived as the main subject verb combination for the sentence. In other words, there is a well-formed sentence,

d) *The horse raced past the barn*

Therefore, our unconscious linguistic processes of computation seize upon this sequence and parse it by assigning the main subject verb relationship to the sequence *The horse raced* so that when the final verb (*fell*) arrives, there is no position left for it to occupy. Given the parsing strategy involved, there is no possible successful computation. Since in the second sentence, there is no well-formed sentence (*The horse driven past the barn*), the assignment of the subject – main verb phrase does not occur until the final verb is reached and the computation is successful.

A second example of this competency/performance distinction is contained in the sentence, [6]

> *The cat the dog the horse bit chased ran away*

With the exception of professional linguists who train themselves in all manner of strange and wonderful competencies, this sequence is typically judged to be ill-formed – not a sentence of the language.

But consider the following sentences,

> *The horse bit the dog*
>
> *The dog chased the cat*
>
> *The cat ran away*
>
> *The dog that the horse bit chased the cat*
>
> *The cat that the dog chased ran away.*

and finally all together with the syntactic markers for relative clauses restored, we have,

> *The cat* that *the dog* that *the horse bit chased ran away.*

This may or may not be intelligible with significant effort by the reader. Such structures are called centered embedded structures – that is, structures where the main subject noun phrase (*the cat*) and its corresponding verb phrase (*ran away*) are separated by intervening material.

In this case, a subject/verb combination (*The cat ran away*) is split by a second subject/verb combination; namely, the intervening material (*the dog bit the cat*). A third subject/verb combination is interjected as intervening material – (*the horse bit the dog*) thereby completing the difficulty. Thus, center embedded sentences are said to be perceptually impossible although actually permitted by the internalized grammar. [7]

Notice that roughly the same meaning can be presented easily by selecting a non- center embedded syntactic form, namely,

> *Here is the horse that bit the dog that chased the cat that ran away.*

thus suggesting that the form or syntax is the source of the perceptual difficulty in understanding the center embedded structure, not the content or meaning of the sentence.

These are two relatively simple examples of what were considered performance variables at the time and were therefore assigned to psychology rather than forming part of the corpus to be described by linguists. The criteria by which linguists of the era decided that the examples offered were examples of performance variables and therefore the domain of psychology as opposed to linguistics were in hindsight somewhat self serving and tautological. They were self-serving in that they relieved the linguists of the responsibility to deal with them. They were tautological in that – in the case, for example, of the center embedded sequences – they were productions generated by well-established rule schema as grammatical and therefore, since they were unacceptable to native speakers, the difficulty must be in the performance variable.

Perhaps in hindsight, these disputes are best understood as examples of a particularly poor fit between the categories imposed on the world (f^2 transforms) and the actual structure of the processes in the world – in this case, the way that the various scientific disciplines carve up the world into special fields of research.

Intuition as a Legitimate Methodology

The acceptance of the competency/performance distinction simultaneously leads to a significant advance in syntactic patterning and into deeper epistemological waters. The actual contents of the corpus – the body of data that defines the linguist's task; the patterning that linguists are to describe, analyze and explain – depended in that era on precisely the ability to make the competency performance distinction. If all actual utterances are some strange mixture of competency and performance, how are linguists to decide which segment of what they hear is the consequence of the competency and which segment is the consequence of the performance variable or, indeed, some interaction between the two?

The simple answer is intuition: that is, the actual practice of a syntactician practicing his or her trade proceeds something like the following. There is some pattern that, as a syntactician, I am attempting to elucidate. Let us say, as a relatively simple example, I am attempting to describe formally the distribution of reflexive forms in American English. I note that there are sequences such as,

I shaved myself

You shaved yourself

She shaved herself

They shaved themselves

Now when I say these sequences to myself [8] and/or to other native speakers of American English and then ask,

Are these well-formed sentences?

their answer is affirmative, the sentences are well-formed.

In contrast, if I say the following sequences to myself and/or to other native speakers,

*She shaved myself

*They shaved himself

*You shaved themselves

*I shaved herself

and then ask the same question *Are these sentences well-formed?*, the answer is this time negative.

To offer a second example, if I offer the following sequence to native speakers of American English,

The woman looked at the man with binoculars.

and then ask whether the sequence is ambiguous – that is, has more than one meaning – the answer will be that the sentence could mean one of two things: either *the woman is looking at some man and that man has a pair of binoculars* or *the woman who is using a pair of binoculars is looking at the man.*

These judgments by native speakers are remarkably consistent and, importantly, are independent of formal educational levels. This last distinction is essential to ensure that such judgments on the part of native speakers are not simply reflections of prescriptive dogma developed by no doubt well-intentioned grammarians independently of the actual use of the language. [9]

Notice that these intuitions have a stability and consistency across individuals differing wildly in all respects except that they are fluent speakers of the language in question. Such a characteristic makes this set of intuitions ideal as the basis for modeling – for the development of explicit representations. This is, of course, the specific challenge for professional linguists. It is an open question whether there are other sets of identifiable intuitions with the same startling consistency as those we have about the language we speak.

Note that one consequence of establishing this distinction was to make explicit that the task of the linguist was to describe the rule-governed behavior that the internalized grammar represents. There was never any serious hope (at least at that time) that a grammar – a set of explicit formal rules for the generation and understanding of sentences in the language – could ever be explicated if the confounding influence of performance variables could not be sorted out from competency variables. Thus this distinction made possible a certain idealization in linguistics – not unlike idealizations in other disciplines. For example, any of the readers who in high school physics classes struggled to get the ball on an incline plane to perform within the acceptable limits of error will recognize the value of idealization. This is the intention behind the competency/performance distinction in linguistics.

These judgments about natural language are typically called intuitive: hardly a term to inspire epistemological confidence as the term itself is unanalyzed. While this is not the place to attempt to establish a sound epistemological foundation for linguistics, we will pursue the point slightly further to capture the methodological point – that is, how linguists actually practice their trade. [10]

One of the images most clearly fixed in my (JG) mind from my studies as a graduate student (1967-1970) is that of my major professor, Edward Klima, a superb syntactician, in the process of presenting some interesting syntactic pattern in an advanced graduate seminar. When challenged by a graduate student with a putative counterexample to the pattern under scrutiny, he would respond by listening intently to the example offered, take a deep breath, move his eyes up and while gently stroking his chin, make the internal visual search necessary for deciding whether the example offered constituted a genuine counterexample. Such searches, depending on the complexity of the point in question could vary from a few seconds to several minutes, during which the remainder of us, graduate students, would either make a parallel search or watch with fascination the efforts of this accomplished linguist to decide whether or not the challenge was a genuine counterexample, relevant to the pattern.

What was it that Professor Klima was doing? Here, I can only fall back on my own experience of some years of so operating as a professional linguist in the academic world. First of all, it is trivial in hindsight to appreciate how Klima was proceeding formally – the eyes movements described immediately allow any trained NLP observer to recognize that he was creating internal visual images as his primary search strategy – movements up indicate that the person is entertaining visual images. [11]

So, it is clear <u>how</u> Klima was going about the search to determine whether the proffered sentence was a legitimate counterexample - how, in the sense of the use of visual images. It is also quite easy for me to remember that immediately before announcing the results of his search, Klima would drop his eyes down to a position indicating that he was checking his feelings about the results of the search.

My (JG) own impressions of this process as a professional linguist is that when you ask me to decide, for example, whether a sequence of words in American English is well-formed or not – one of the most basic intuitions you have about your own language – what I experience is a very rapid internal access, typically, the repetition in internal dialogue of the sequence to ensure that I am beginning the search with the proper sequence, followed by a series of internal images, usually beginning with an abstract tree structure, and finally, a kinesthetic sensing of whether, indeed, the sequence has some neurological counterpart in what we have been calling the internalized grammar. In other words, I am attempting to sense whether the sequence presented corresponds to some legitimate computation of my internalized grammar (that is the question, *Is there a set of circuits activated by the sequence or not?*). [12]

We invite each of you readers to sample this process for yourselves– we present the following sequences and ask the reader to read each one, using internal dialogue or saying the sentence aloud, and then simply note how you go about deciding whether each sequence is a well-formed sequence or sentence in American English. In particular, note the differing sensations experienced when making judgments about the different sentences.

Who did Doug and Kathleen talk to?

*Who did Doug and talk to Cal?

Sharon told Katie to stop talking to herself in public.

*Sharon told Katie to stop talking to themselves in public

These sequences are presented to allow the readers to experience by direct contrast the most basic set of judgments linguists make as they ply their trade – answering the question whether some arbitrary sequence is or is not a well-formed sentence of their language.

There are significantly more sophisticated consistent judgments possible. For example, we invite the readers to ask themselves what is the difference between the following two sentences and to especially consider the way the term *Nicole* [13] is used

> *Nicole was eager to please*

> *Nicole was easy to please*

Cracking the Black Box

The point of the presentation of this portion of Chomsky's work can be summarized as follows: in pursuit of explicit representations of the patterning that characterizes regularities in natural language, the only relevant reference point is the source of the patterning itself – the human being. The grammar – that is, the linguistic competency of a native speaker of any natural language - is represented neurologically as surely as are the rules for the creation of three-dimensional visual images on the occipital lobe. The difficulty in both cases is that at present we do not have research tools adequately refined and non-invasive to permit anything approaching a direct sensing of such neurological representations. Therefore, we are faced with the task of formally representing the patterns of natural language using reports of native speakers – in particular, their intuitions about the forms in their language and in their visual field. The relevant yardstick is internal to our species.

How does one test to determine if our formal patterning is a useful representation of natural language? This is indeed an interesting epistemological challenge, as the minimum requirement for a test would be based upon matching the formal system of rules with the relevant reference point – and in this case the relevant reference point is the intuition of the individual native speaker.

Visual patterning work, as in the excellent research done by people like D. Hoffman (*Visual Intelligence*, 1998), will include the manipulation of various visual stimuli according to the patterning the researcher is exploring. As the manipulations are made, the researcher himself and/or some set of normally sighted people will make judgments as to whether, for example, they see two separate single points of illumination alternating with one another on and off, or a single point of illumination that moves rapidly from one position to the other. If the report by the human involved is that at a specified speed of alternation, the particular manipulation presented changes her perception from two discrete points of illumination to the experience of seeing a single moving point of illumination, then those reports then become the data point – the pattern to be described and explained. [14] How could it be otherwise?

The situation is quite parallel in the case of research on linguistic patterning regardless of the theoretical commitments on the part of the researcher. The linguist manipulates the syntactic, phonological, and semantic forms and judges and/or asks native speakers to judge whether the consequences are a well-formed sentence in the language, an ambiguous string or anyone of an array of numerous other possibilities. The relevant reference point by the very nature of the research is internal to the bearer of the internal grammar – the native speaker himself.

To put the matter in a somewhat different form, suppose that we succeeded in constructing an instrument that purportedly arrived at the same judgments for visual inputs as those possessed by normally sighted people.

How would we know whether the instrument worked?

The answer clearly is that we would accept the instrument as accurate if and only if the responses of the instrument precisely matched those of normally sighted people. In other words, we would calibrate the instrument by using exactly the same set of judgments (intuitions) reported by the people involved that we presently use in the absence of such an instrument. A parallel argument can easily be made for patterning in language with native speakers.

Thus in fields where the patterning under scrutiny is patterning of the behavior of human beings, the reference point and the source of the judgments will necessarily be the human being.

It is important to recognize that the task of the linguist in the TG tradition and its successors is an extended exercise in mapping intuitions onto explicit representations. Please note that this is precisely the definition of the core activity of NLP, modeling – the mapping of tacit knowledge (behavior competency with its attendant intuitions) onto explicit representations or models (see Chapter 2, Part I under *Terminology*).

Under the positivists' regimen, the competency/performance distinction is unavailable and the patterning we have been considering simply doesn't exist. In a deep sense, Chomsky succeeded in opening the black box – an accomplishment that puts many modern researchers deeply in his debt. We add that there were, as in any revolutionary shift in a discipline, precursors who were clear in their challenge to the prevailing winds of the time. In particular, the excellent works of Lashley, Tolman and Broadbent come to mind.

Consistent with the framing at the beginning of this section, we conclude that the use of humans as the reference point for research in human functioning and in particular the phenomenon of basing the data to be described and explained on the intuitions of native speakers has passed without challenge into the field of Cognitive Grammar as one of its operating procedures and a presupposition of its methodology.

More specifically, the trained NLP practitioner will upon reflection recognize that the strategy pursued by Grinder and Bandler in the creation and deployment of the meta model as a effective tool for inducing change in the context of therapeutic encounters, is thus firmly based on the ability of the agent of change (and subsequently, the client) to use the sets of reliable intuitions about the structure of natural language as a leverage point to induce change. This strategy is independent of whatever theoretical and hypothetical entities (e.g. Deep Structure, logical forms…) are posited at whatever stage of the development of the field of linguistics. The point is a methodological one – the use of intuitions as the reference point passed without challenge on to the successors to the Transformational Grammar of the '70s

The foundation of the meta model is the use of patterns of intuitions associated with our tacit knowledge of language structure. This is an operating procedure inspired by the methodology of the historical field of TG of the 70's. This methodology operates securely within the field of NLP and remains a powerful and viable model within that context. The black box is thus opened, allowing studies of excellence and the patterning that distinguishes the behavior of geniuses from "average" performers. Thus, an operating procedure generalized from the field of linguistics becomes the cornerstone of modeling as well as the basis for its actual use in applications.

Chomsky's Contribution to Neuro-Linguistic Programming

The Underlying Model for the field of NLP

A second aspect of Chomsky's historical work in linguistics offers a powerful lesson for modeling and research in NLP. We proceed by way of example. One aspect of this issue is how is the verification of NLP patterning to be done.

When a modeler detects and codes a pattern, how does a researcher verify that there is a pattern, what presuppositions are present, and how do these factors affect the outcome? Similarly, these remarks are equally relevant to an investigator who has done no part of the development of the patterning but who wishes to determine the validity of the proposals being made by that patterning.

Suppose that 100 native speakers of American English are presented with some sequence of English words and asked whether this sequence constitutes a well-formed sequence or sentence of their language. Further, let's say that 50 of them judge the sequence intuitively to be a well-formed sentence, and 50 judge the sequence to be ill formed, not a sentence. What will a professional linguist in such a situation do? Will she decide that there is no pattern involved? Will she expand the number of people in the study? Will she declare that the sentence is grammatical with a probability of 0.5 or that the probability of the sentence being grammatical is 0.5? While these are all understandable responses within the framework of a statistical model, the actual answer is: none of the above.

In fact, a practicing linguist will unselfconsciously declare that there are two separate dialects involved, each with its own intact underlying grammatical sets of formal recursive rule systems. She will immediately set about formally describing those underlying rule systems that differentiate the two intact grammars involved. She will attempt to discover, given the way she is describing the differences in the grammars, other linguistic phenomena associated with the differences predicted from the rule differences she is using to differentiate the initial two dialects. Her claim that there are two separate dialects involved will stand or fall on her ability to discover other linguistic patterning that justifies the original distinction between the two dialects that she proposes in her analysis. Her behavior is intelligible only in the context of the application of a discrete analysis.

The difference between the response of the linguist using the discrete model and the class of responses a psychologist using the statistical model would make to a similar situation is highly instructive. If a research psychologist is attempting to determine whether some behavior emerges from some specific (let us suppose) well-defined set of conditions and discovers that 50 out of a 100 people placed in these well-defined set of conditions manifest the behavior, and 50 do not, he will conclude that there is no pattern (the null hypothesis is confirmed) or that the probability that the behavior will emerge, given the conditions defined, is 0.5 or simply chance.

This is, above all, a paradigm issue – what is the appropriate underlying paradigm for NLP? We propose pushing hard on the assumption that the paradigm provided by linguistics (and to some degree formal studies as in certain fields of mathematics and formal logic) is, in fact, the most suitable of the paradigms we are aware of for the class of studies that NLP focuses on. However, please note that this is ultimately an empirical issue, not a preference. With the development of more refined analysis and evaluation studies, the question of the selection of a discrete underlying model or a statistical one for NLP will come to have significantly more substance than at present. It may well turn out that while a discrete model (for example, Automata Theory) is the more generally appropriate, we will be able to identify specific limited phenomena that play a significant role in NLP work that are best modeled by a statistical model. For example, it is our present best guess that certain aspects of anchoring phenomena may well be best analyzed and evaluated in a statistical form. [15]

Let's unpack this proposal carefully as the consequences are monumental and will, indeed, in significant part determine the effectiveness of the entire enterprise. We begin by identifying a portion of the paradigm current from TG at the time of the creation of NLP that maps cleanly across to the paradigm we are proposing for NLP. It is clear that within linguistics, there is a commitment to the following proposition:

Language competency is a rule-governed human activity [16]

By this, linguists understand that what they are attempting to explicate is a formal underlying system of rules that generates, among other patterns all and only the well-formed sequences of the languages under study – the sentences of that language. [17] This formal underlying system of connected and ordered rules is the language competency that is the base from which we generate and understand spoken language.

Move your attention back to the situation described above where the linguist has one half of the population classifying a particular sequence of words in the language under investigation as well-formed – that is, a sentence of their language – and the other half of the population classifying the same sequence as not being well-formed and therefore, not a sentence of their language. As stated, the immediate response of the linguist, without hesitation, is to declare that the language contains two dialects and will search for ways to justify the distinction between the two dialects proposed. [18]

Let's work up a matching example in NLP. One of the favorite patterns of NLP research to be subjected to testing by, no doubt, well-intentioned psychologists is representational systems (visual, auditory and kinesthetic) and, in particular, the eye movements that indicate which of the three major representational systems (visual, auditory and kinesthetics) is activated. Suppose that you as a researcher were interested in investigating the validity of the eye movements in a conventional scientific way. [19]

The Verification of Pattern

Let's say that we formulate – consistent with claims found in *The Structure of Magic* series or *Frogs into Princes* or *Neuro-Linguistic Programming*, volume I – a series of sentences which differ systematically by the presence or absence of predicates from one or another of the three major representational systems. Further we select only right-handed subjects to participate because of the claim in NLP that handedness – a measure of cerebral dominance – will interact strongly with the eye accessing patterns under investigation. Among these stimulus sentences, we find a prompt in the form of a question, [20]

> *What color are your mother's eyes?*

Suppose that we employ a video camera focused on the eye movements of the subjects involved and that we discover upon completion of the processing of 100 subjects that 80 of the 100 subjects when presented with this particular prompt, move their eyes to a position above the horizon and dilate their pupils prior to responding to the question. Further the remaining 20 subjects move their eyes down and to their left and then either dilate their pupils in position or then shift their eyes to a position above the horizon.

What are we to make of this? Shall we conclude along with the psychologists that the probability is 0.8 that when presented with this prompt, the subject (and the general population to which we presumably wish to generalize our findings) will move his eyes to a position above the horizon? And that there is a probability of 0.2 that the subject will look down and to his left and dilate his pupils or down and to his left and then to a position above the horizon?

It is possible to imagine contexts in which such probabilities might serve some purpose – the manipulation of eye movements in large groups of people (e.g. communication in print in mass advertising). However, to us as researchers, the conclusion is at best, amusing.

So what, you the reader will ask, is the proper response to the findings? What conclusions or further actions or analyses should appropriately ensue?

The experienced NLP trained observer ideally would continue the investigation of the 20 subjects whose response was at variance with the predicted behavior – that is, whose response was the movement down and to their left and dilated pupils; or, down and to their left and then to a position above the horizon – subject by subject. More specifically, the investigator would elicit with great care a description from each of these subjects regarding what his or her ongoing experience was at the time of the movements involved. What one would hope to discover thereby is that the subject was using internal dialogue to repeat the prompt sentence when in the down and left position and then formed a visual image of the mentioned person, either in position (down and left) or after shifting to a position above the horizon. Such elicitation would bring the behavior of all subjects into conformity with the anticipated behavior and would thereby simply regularize the data. Such a result would offer very strong support for the thesis under consideration.

To make the point perfectly clear, one of the presuppositions in linguistics that has an isomorphic counterpart in NLP is,

> Language behavior is rule-governed

This is typically understood to mean that the underlying language competence from which actual acts of speech (both production and understanding) can be most usefully represented as a formal system of well-defined recursive rules.

The counterpart of this methodological assumption of linguistics in the field of NLP, then, is

> Patterns of excellence in human behavior are rule-governed

What we are actually proposing here is that an effective and useful methodology for analyzing patterns of excellence in human behavior is to assume that the behavior we are observing in an individual is representative of an intact rule-governed system and to ask the question,

> *What set of rules would account for the behavior we are observing?*

This is typically understood to mean that the underlying competence from which actual behavioral acts emerge can be usefully represented as a formal system of well-defined recursive rules.

In parallel with its linguistic counterpart, we take this to mean that there are significant portions of human behavior – more precisely the subject matter of NLP, patterns of excellence - that can be usefully represented (or equivalently, modeled) by a formal system of well-defined recursive rules. If this is accepted as a fundamental principle of analysis and evaluation in NLP as in linguistics, then it becomes clear that the use of statistical tools

81

– in general, those methods of analysis associated with probability – as a strategy for description, analysis and explanation is entirely inappropriate. [21]

Interestingly, the generalization at present seems to be that if the patterning under scrutiny has as its elements, phenomena of different logical types (see Chapter 1, Part III under *Logical Levels and Logical Types* for a formal definition), the appropriate model is discrete. For example, in the patterning involved with representational systems, the visual, auditory and kinesthetic representations (the elements that compose representational systems) are of different logical types; there is no isomorphic mapping possible among them with respect to their essential characteristics. We propose that the appropriate model is discrete.

We point out also there seems to be a further correlation: if the patterning is clearly post FA, it is discrete. Further, if the patterning is within FA and is of the same logical type, statistical analysis may well be of utility.

There is a deeper point here – there are two great paradigms available to serve as the underpinnings of scientific description, analysis and explanation: the discrete paradigm, used in certain areas of mathematics such as algebra, formal logic, and in linguistics... and a statistical paradigm, found in theoretical physics (especially the physics of the very large and the very small), sociology, demographics... In fact, historically, Chomsky expressly selected Automata Theory as the appropriate base structure for linguistics.

We are proposing that this same universal discrete paradigm is the appropriate one for the modeling of patterns of excellence – the core activity of NLP.

The inappropriateness of applying certain of the statistical tools (for example, the mean) should be clear enough to any thoughtful observer. When analyzing a pattern in linguistics, and we propose equally so in many patterns within NLP, it is patently absurd to collapse the performances of a number of different subjects and average across their responses to determine whether there is a pattern. In fact, to collapse such performances and average them guarantees that any pattern that may be present will be obscured. As the linguistic example above demonstrates, the application of a discrete system strategy that treats each subject as an intact rule-governed system reveals a beautifully clear description (in the example above, the distinction between the two dialects) and yields an analysis of great utility. Such analyses then become the basis for further and more refined research.

Thus, along with the acceptance of the rule governed nature of the subject matter for NLP comes the commitment to a discrete analysis. The issue we have been working is how to analyze and/or evaluate a pattern. When engaged in such pattern detection (or evaluation), it makes precisely as much sense to talk about the probability of a solution to an algebraic equation being correct as it does to statistically smear the pattern of performance by individual subjects in an NLP study and then announce the probability that the subject is visualizing (given a specific prompt sentence which demands a response based on a visual image) as in the described experiment; namely, none!

Ideal Research in Modeling and Pattern Verification

We note, then, that the proper focus of an NLP modeling project will, in fact, be an individual unit – some genius or some team in a field of interest who consistently outperforms their counterparts in that field. All discussions of sampling theory, averages, coefficient correlations and other topics associated with probability and based on the continuous paradigm are hopelessly out of place in the practice of the discipline called NLP [modeling] and equally so in its evaluation. And, in fact, historically this is exactly what has occurred – in the Milton Model example (affectionately named for the man that inspired it, Dr. Milton H. Erickson, M.D.) presented in the two-volume work, *Patterns of the Hypnotic Techniques of Milton H. Erickson*, for, one finds a series of explicit descriptions (even instructions for how to construct the patterns being reported) of some of his behaviors, verbal and non-verbal. But nowhere will the reader of the two-volume work discover probabilistic strategies employed or even referred to.

All this is, of course, consistent with the study of excellence – the performer of excellence constitutes a unique opportunity to discover the answer to the core question for research in NLP [modeling],

> *Given some genius, what are the differences that make the difference between his or her behavior and the behavior of competent performers in the same field?*

Tossing the description of the patterning of behavior of a genius into a group of descriptions of patterns of other performers and averaging across them in order to attempt to validate a pattern is antithetical to the purpose of NLP modeling projects, as well as a guaranteed way for modelers to fail to detect the differences that are the essential focus of such studies.

It is an interesting question to us how in the field of psychology came historically to be such a complete and exclusive focus on average group behavior and patently not the exploration of the extremes of human performance (e.g. geniuses). Even in those strange tasks such as memorizing a list of nonsense syllables, it seems to us that the psychologists miss the entire point. Who cares how many trials on average it takes the mythical average performer to completely memorize the nonsense syllables? Of what possible interest is such a fiction?

Wouldn't it be more interesting, even in the context of this strange task of memorizing nonsense syllables to identify the subject who is significantly faster and more accurate in the task and model what she or he is doing? Further, if psychologists insist on making statements about the group or finds averages so tantalizing that they are unable to resist, they could measure how long, on average, it takes for them to transfer the strategy of excellence modeled from the best learner to the remainder of the experimental group. [22]

Such an attitude is clearly the appropriate choice for the modeling of excellence. It would be most enlightening if some of the leading researchers in standard psychology practice would reveal the underlying motivation for studies of the average as opposed to the commitment (as within NLP) to studies of extreme behavior – namely, genius.

There is a peculiar aspect to this way of thinking (NLP and the modeling of excellence) which we wish to point out to the reader. There is very little attention in NLP to prediction – a feature that we find prominent in traditional discussions of science and scientific activity. This absence of interest in prediction seems natural to us in the sense that the modeling of excellence and the presentation of the models of the differences that make the difference point one's attention to the creating the future rather than predicting it. [23]

What is the point of focusing on what will occur in the future, when the future contemplated is a projection based on the average performance of average groups? In fact, doesn't it make more sense to invest the time, money and attention necessary on the creation of a series of models of excellence and their transfer to interested parties? There seems to be only one area we are aware of where one can catch a glimpse of this kind of thinking, albeit in a rudimentary form – namely, in business. In addition to benchmarking, there is increasing attention (and the corresponding time and money) being devoted to best practices. The top work team, the highest performing manager, process innovators, the hot salesperson… are beginning to be recognized as a valuable asset not only in themselves, but one that could serve as the model for upgrading the performance of other members of the company, given a proper set of modeling resources. QUANTUM LEAP, the company in which your co-authors are principals, has conducted a number of successful programs applying the deep modeling principles of NLP to such challenges.

A Study in Pattern Verification

We pursue this point with an additional example. Imagine an NLP modeling project in which some academic skill that we have decided is essential for the educational system to develop in our children is modeled. That is, a group of highly trained modelers gains access to young people who, within their developmental peer group, exhibit excellence in learning and/or in the performance of a skill (spelling, reading, math....). The selected modelers could create a model of excellence from each young person. The result would be a robust set of multiple models for each skill to be placed in the hands of teachers. Since each explicated model would represent a specific learning strategy of one excellent young person, the challenge for teachers, then, would be two-fold:

> 1. To identify which one of the multiple strategies of excellence explicitly coded by the modelers' fits the individual child in front of them.

> 2. To adeptly create a learning context in which the teacher would lead classroom children, one by one, through the learning of a set of concrete strategies - models of excellence - that fits each of their particular needs for the academic skill involved.

Now, compare the positive experiences of the children who are being offered (guidance in) a model of excellence that allows them to emulate the performance strategies of the best performers in each of these academic requirements as compared with the educational institutes we presently have in the United States, for example. At present, in the US, we spend extraordinary amounts of time, attention, and testing of our children to discover only where they rank compared to some mythical average. Who gives a damn about the average? Are there really parents or teachers who are interested in achieving average performance? [24]

The objective, it seems to us, is to promote excellence. Imagine the difference such a program (one based on the modeling and transfer of excellence) would make in terms of the children's experience and subsequent competency, without mentioning the return on investment that would be achieved for each educational dollar spent.

Just imagine the trickle-down effect of achieving this educational objective. Perhaps in the future our daily newspapers (paper and electronic) would report the news at a higher academic level than the present norm (6th grade reading level) and just maybe the vocabulary used by journalists could actually be augmented beyond the present most common 1200 words – what could happen to *average*?

In this discussion of patterning, it is important to distinguish several different phases of research. At a first cut, let us differentiate between the discovery phase, the coding phase and the verification of patterning. The above example presents commentary about the discovery phase; the coding phase is treated separately (chapter 1, Part III. These phases have no known algorithms and are, at present, best considered artistry.

Let us assume that we have accomplished the first two phases of the project and have explicit multiple models of excellence for some academic task. Turning now to the verification phase, let's take an extended example to demonstrate how one might select and apply various methods, drawing from both the discrete as well as the continuous models available. We use as the example the evaluation of a proposal made in the field of NLP some decades ago – the NLP spelling strategy (this strategy was first presented in volume I of *Neuro-Linguistic Programming*). This spelling strategy was one of the first educationally oriented strategies proposed (through the NLP process of modeling excellent spellers) and is simple enough to use as the exemplar in this discussion.

The general context for the NLP spelling strategy is that in English and most languages (with some beautiful exceptions such as Spanish), educated people are required within the general requirement of writing their native language to master the mapping between the auditory (spoken) presentation of words of the language and the visual (written) presentation of words of their native language – the orthography. [25]

In other words, to be educated, one is required to be able to spell properly. The difficulty is that most languages, English included, have a reasonably complex set of mappings between their sounds and their orthography, with many, many exceptions.

sound   written
representations   representations

NLP practitioners [26], through the observation of excellent spellers, noted that there was a simple and consistent strategy employed unconsciously by such spellers and NOT by people who spell poorly.

The consistently effective spelling behavior of the best spellers is, of course, precisely that kind of systematic behavior of excellence that modelers seek with the attendant challenge of mapping this tacit knowledge into an explicit model for dissemination. One way for to represent explicitly this effective behavior is,

$$V^i \longrightarrow K^i \longrightarrow A^d$$

> where the V^i represents visual internal (that is, a image of the word to be spelled internally generated by the speller) while the K^i represents kinesthetic internal (a feeling that is an internal response to the preceding image – the image of the word to be spelled). Finally, the A^d (auditory digital – that is, language) represents the out loud spelling of word visualized and checked by feelings by the speller.

In words, then, the NLP spelling strategy consists of the speller following the succeeding steps: create an internal image of the word to be spelled, while viewing the image, check your feelings to determine whether the image being displayed is correct. If your feelings are congruent, spell the word out loud. If your feelings are not congruent, begin the process again with the image of the word in question spelled a different way.

Clearly, in order to be able to apply this strategy at all, the speller must have already seen the word to be spelled at some point in training.

Now let us put ourselves into the position of a well-trained psychologist, well-intentioned and interested in evaluating the validity of the NLP spelling strategy. We will assume that such an investigator would approach the design of an evaluation of the spelling strategy with several disciplined commitments among which we would find:

> 1. a willingness to master the strategy proposed itself as well as the more general intellectual context (representational systems and the eye movement patterning, for example) in which it is proposed as a way of ensuring that the testing is a testing of what is actually being proposed by the modelers of the NLP spelling strategy

> 2. a healthy skepticism, a systematic attempt to set aside the conscious filtering (belief systems, for example) that all too often accompanies approaching some new and revolutionary claim – that is, an active avoidance of the Rosenthal Experimenter Effect.

The express claim by the NLP spelling strategy is that people trained and skilled in the NLP spelling strategy will spell perfectly. A lesser-included claim would be that people using the NLP spelling strategy will spell more words correctly than people using either an explicit alternative strategy or no well-defined strategy at all.

Suppose that our disciplined experimenter settles on the following design: she will test the validity of the NLP spelling strategy and, in particular, its relative effectiveness when compared with a control group and a group trained in and utilizing an alternative spelling strategy – let's say, phonics – surely the most popular and wide spread well-defined alternative to the NLP spelling strategy. Thus, we have three groups:

NLP spelling group   the phonics group   the control group

Each group will receive a pre-training – the NLP spelling group will be trained in the NLP spelling strategy, the phonics group in the phonics strategy. The control group will spend an amount of time equal to the amount of time that the other two groups spent in their pre-training with the experimenter to control for contact time with the experimenter as a variable.

The experimenter will anticipate that the members of the NLP spelling group will spell all words perfectly. She will maintain a possible fall back position that any individual employing the NLP spelling strategy (that is, any member of the NLP spelling strategy group) will spell more words correctly than any member of either of the other two groups. Further at the level of group aggregate performance, she will predict that the members of the NLP spelling strategy group will, *as a group*, spell more words correctly that the aggregate performance of either of the other two groups. To enhance the effects (in other words, to create the context in which it is most likely that the differences between the groups will be made most manifest), the experimenter uses lists of words compiled by the association in the US that is in charge of conducting the national spelling contests that occur annually in this country. [27]

Our intrepid investigator conducts the experiment. She discovers an interesting mixture of results, including,

a. there are members of the NLP spelling strategy group that did not spell all words correctly

b. there are a few members of the phonics group and of the control groups that spelled more words correctly than several members of the NLP spelling strategy group

The NLP spelling strategy group *as a group* spelled more words correctly than either of the other two groups, *as groups*.

At first blush, these results seemed to indicate that:

1. the strong form of the proposal by NLP – namely, that the individual members of the NLP spelling group will spell all words perfectly – is falsified. The specific evidence for this rejection of the strong claim by NLP is two-fold: namely, the results listed above under a and b. Either one of these results alone would falsify the strong claim – both of them together apparently remove any question about the validity of the strong claim.

2. that there is a difference in performance between the groups, and in particular, the group using the NLP spelling strategy performed as a group better than either of the other two groups. Thus, the weaker included claim that the members of the NLP spelling strategy as a group would spell more words correctly than either one of the other two groups is validated.

Our understanding is that this is about where our intrepid investigator would normally simply publish these results and then roll up her tent and disappear into the shifting sands of research, seeking some other phenomenon to investigate.

We offer some comments about how ideally such an investigator would respond to these results. First of all, she would be intrigued: there is an effect at the group level that indicates that there is some advantage to the NLP spelling strategy when compared with either an alternative spelling strategy (phonics) or an uninstructed group (the control group). This indicates that there was a difference that was robust enough to survive the averaging of results that the statistical measurement called the mean represents.

Secondly, she would consider thoughtfully what the differences that did occur might represent, focusing especially on the strong proposal by the NLP modelers. Thinking along these lines, she would be particularly interested in certain classes of results. Thus, she would be especially sensitive to the least anticipated results and focus her investigations on them. She would, for example, review the videos of all individuals who spelled all words correctly, independent of the group they were in. During this review, she would be watching for the distinctive eye movements that indicate that the subject is visualizing - that is, spontaneously using the NLP spelling strategy. Ideally, she would discover that, indeed, all individuals who spelled all the words correctly used the $V \longrightarrow K^i \longrightarrow A^d$ NLP spelling strategy, either through applying the pre-training they received as a member of the NLP spelling strategy group or spontaneously (that is, without training). In the case of any ambiguity, the subject involved could be invited to return and be presented with a fresh set of difficult-to-spell words. During this second session, careful individual elicitation of the subject's strategy would provide confirmation or disconfirmation about which specific strategy this successful subject is utilizing.

Our investigator could do an error analysis - segment the list of difficult words with the simple meta model challenge - *"Difficult, how specifically?"* This would lead to a partition of the original list into those words that are difficult explicitly because of a discrepancy between the correspondences between the sound and orthography (spoken/written mappings) and other – that is, she would predict that the phonics group would do much worse on this subset of the list compared to the list in its entirety.

Next, our investigator could review the tapes of all individuals in the NLP spelling group who failed to spell all the words correctly and especially those individuals in this group who preformed worse than the average in the other two groups. Once again, ideally she would anticipate that any member of the NLP spelling strategy group who failed to spell all words correctly would demonstrate by their eye movements that they were not consistently following the sequence,

$$V^i \rightarrow K^i \rightarrow A^d$$

that represents the NLP spelling strategy. The subset among those performing less than perfectly that actually performed worse than the average for the other two groups would be particularly important to review, as an analysis of their performance should yield obvious deviations from the NLP spelling sequence. [28]

Even more compelling would be to demonstrate by the use of the videos that in each and every case where one of the members of the NLP spelling strategy group failed to spell a word correctly, the video would show that on that particular trial, the speller failed to follow the required sequence. Again, follow-up elicitation sessions could be used to disambiguate the situation and to determine which strategy the subject is employing when successful and when unsuccessful. [29]

Our investigator might decide to review the tapes of subjects, attending to those occasions when the subject misspelled a word – she would, given the strong form of the NLP modelers' proposal, predict that the strategy employed on all occasions when a word was misspelled was NEVER the NLP spelling strategy. In the cases of these individuals - trained in the NLP spelling strategy group who did poorly, our investigator would test through tasking and direct observation to determine whether, indeed, these individuals had in fact adequately learned the NLP spelling strategy and could visualize.

All this careful follow-up work is a way of investigating the gap between the strong form of the NLP modelers' proposal and the initial results. The claim itself establishes a reference point and all deviations from the performance predicted by that reference point identify precisely the set of differences to be more carefully focused upon. The point is to understand that set of differences. Note that all this follow-up work is conducted by using the initial set of differences as the points to investigate, and employs the use of individual elicitation to carefully appreciate the actual strategies being employed by individual subjects under varying conditions (both the initial correct and incorrect spelling as well as the more advanced types of testing – interference testing…).

What is implicit in these extensions of the experiment is the following kind of thinking: if the NLP spelling strategy works as its strong proposal states, then the results should be consistent with everyone who is using the strategy scoring higher than anyone in any other group. Indeed, any "errors" on the part of the NLP spelling group must be examined with great care as they approach a counterexample to the proposal NLP modelers are making. [30]

At the end of this follow-up work, the investigator will have a robust set of findings to present. She will be able either to confirm the strong proposal made by the NLP spelling strategy or to state with precision under what conditions that proposal fails to hold. Note that in this particular example, the only role that statistical tools (based on the probabilistic model) – the use of the mean and possibly some measures that characterize the type of distribution such as standard deviation – would have played would be to give the investigator some confidence that there was a pattern hidden in the amalgamated data (the group level results). Thus emboldened by this initial result, she could proceed to make a more refined study of the strategy and the strong proposals associated with it.

With the exception of this initial filtering for patterning through the use of statistical tools, the use of statistically based measures play no role. The question remains for us,

> Is there some other (other than giving the investigator confidence that furthermore refined investigation is likely to yield patterning) appropriate and useful role that statistical tools might play in the confirmation or disconfirmation phase of patterning?

We are uncertain what such other appropriate and useful role such tools might play. Thus, from our particular perspective, as modelers, the employment of such tools seems largely limited to the context described above – that of giving the investigator preliminary indication that there is a pattern lurking in the data.

Indeed, we can well imagine a purely qualitative study of this same strong claim for the NLP spelling strategy that uses no such tools without any loss of generality or validity. Simply instructing people in the NLP spelling strategy and then having them perform on a list of previously seen and difficult to spell words with the careful elicitation mentioned in what we called above the follow up studies would yield the same set of robust results described above. We would enjoy being instructed by investigators more experienced in such matters than us as to how tools based on a statistical model might add value to the analysis and evaluation of patterning of the class over which NLP modeling is defined. [31]

Summary of Chomsky's Contribution

We find that the method of discrete analysis typical of TG of the 70's continues to be applicable to the study of genius even as there is some movement within the linguistic field toward considering a non-discrete approach [32].

However the issue develops and is resolved in linguistics, in NLP, the patterns that are the focus (the differences that make a difference between the top performer and "average" performers) are based on the discrete analysis of individual systems – each of the geniuses who have served and will serve as inspiration for the patterning codified in NLP.

We look forward to a point where the vocabulary and coding of patterning in NLP [modelling] has refined itself such that arguments for a specific underlying paradigm for behavior more generally (that is, outside of the domain of language) can be then generated. Such arguments would then be used to demonstrate (as in Chomsky's classic arguments for language) where in the hierarchy of idealized computers or automata, the appropriate models for formalizing the patterns of excellence in human behavior reside.

Chomsky's work, and in particular his elegant formalization and critique of models of grammatical description prior to Transformational Grammar, gives us a glimpse of the mathematical base, specifically Automata Theory, underlying his thinking and processes of analysis found in his work – the study of patterning in natural language. We have stated that TG was the single most pervasive influences on NLP. We have offered two examples of how Chomsky's work deeply influenced the thinking and behavior of one of the co-creators of NLP (JG) and has continued to exercise a profound influence on the field of NLP:

1. The appropriateness of the use of human beings as the reference point for the patterning, both in TG and in NLP with its special niche – the patterning of excellence.

2. The selection of a discrete paradigm as the foundation for modeling, research and the verification of the patterning of excellence in NLP.

20th Century Contributions

Bateson

It is difficult to enumerate the myriad ways in which this intellectual giant has influenced NLP – albeit without his endorsing it. [33]

He, alone among the thinkers of his era that we are familiar with, has consistently demonstrated a style and quality of thinking that recursively breaks out of the intellectual categories that serve both as organizing principles for researchers and simultaneously as cognitive traps defeating their ability to think their way through to the advances they seek. It would be fascinating to have had a statement of the personal influences (family, early experience and especially descriptions of the activities that occurred in the contexts of discovery of his many contributions) [34].

In the authors' personal opinions, Gregory's work is best represented by the compelling *tour de force* of his early collection of articles, *Steps to an Ecology of Mind* – a work that will continue to stimulate researchers in all fields of study of human behavior including NLP for decades to come, so fruitful and full of possibilities it is. [35]

Bateson's ultimate concern was epistemology – beginning as a botanist sometimes he tracked this elusive beast through the study of intact non-western traditional cultures (e.g. Bali), at other times through the study of mental operations (schizophrenia, for example, at the Mental Research Institute of Palo Alto) and at others through studies in learning and communication. The breath and depth of his work is astonishing.

His influence on NLP takes a number of forms: first, his ability to synthesize work across disciplines inspired us to attempt such syntheses. In particular, we are thinking of his work on the relationship between conscious and unconscious processes, on logical levels in learning and communication, cybernetics ... We will challenge several of his key distinctions (see *Logical Levels and Logical Types*, chapter 1, Part III, for example). Indeed, Bandler and Grinder did make such a challenge in volume II of *The Structure of Magic* series. Secondly, his gracious personal support of the work of a couple of madmen (Grinder and Bandler) in their unorthodox challenge to professions such as psychiatry and psychology. He was the kindest of acquaintances and simultaneously the most demanding of mentors. An enumeration of the specific intellectual strategies and tools he developed that found their way into NLP patterning work would be enormous.

We mention one such strategy. Bateson used what he called logical levels to untangle a number of significant problems. He followed Russell's lead in employing this distinction although care must be taken here as Russell used the term *logical type* for what Bateson frequently referred to as logical levels. We will later propose additional distinctions and a reform of the terminology (see chapter 1, Part III under *Logical Levels and Logical Types*). Bateson's intrepid explorations of the application of this concept (or actually, this set of concepts) is so fundamental that in retrospect, it is difficult to imagine both how other thinkers had missed it and how anyone could possibly do effective work without its systematic deployment.

NLP practitioners who carry the dream of making a significant contribution will find inspiration in his work. Indeed, the drawing out of the implications of some of his thought will continue to influence the development of this field as well as others for a long time.

Erickson

Dr. Milton H. Erickson, the leading practitioner of medical and psychiatric hypnosis in the United States for decades, was the source of the patterning that constitutes the second model created by Bandler and Grinder in the field of NLP. His ability to influence the unconscious processes of his patients through official, as well as casual hypnosis, was legendary. He exercised exquisite control of his voice and spatial marking as well as commanding a wide array of verbal patterns in order to create the effects he achieved with his patients.

From the beginning of contact with Grinder and Bandler, Milton unselfishly offered full access and constant guidance to them (always in the form of metaphors, of course), greatly facilitating their work. Even though he constantly anticipated their needs as a true mentor, he refused to lead them; instead he waited for them to discover what they themselves needed in the way of material or background to continue the research. When asked for information, he would respond in his distinctive manner of speaking and would typically say,

> *"Having anticipated your request...* (pausing, as he reaches under his desk, he retrieves a reprinted bundle of articles he had written

94

over his lifetime to which access, he knew, was difficult), ... I have prepared this for you."

These materials in conjunction with direct observations made it possible to develop what Grinder and Bandler came to refer to affectionately as the Milton model.

His contributions to the understanding of the workings of the unconscious mind are enormous and obvious, a portion of which is detailed in the two-volume work by Grinder and Bandler (joined by Delozier in the second volume), *Patterns of the Hypnotic Techniques of Milton H. Erickson, M.D.* We shall not attempt to characterize these contributions in this book, as the patterns are available to the reader in those works. Again, as in the case of Bateson, Erickson graciously extended his personal support and was generous in his praise of the finished product – the two-volume work on his patterning. It is somewhat surprising to the present authors that such a large number of NLP practitioners have failed to generalize the patterns of unconscious functioning to officially non-hypnotic contexts and procedures. We will discuss this more fully in the discussion under *The New Code* in chapter 3, Part II of this book.

Erickson systematically explored the unconscious with subtlety and sensitivity, refusing to force the patterning into any conscious mind logic. His influence is particularly important in serving to balance the overemphasis found in western thinking and in particular, in the western educational system.

In particular, we (Bostic and Grinder) would propose that it is literally impossible for an NLP practitioner to function as a congruent agent of change unless he or she has cultivated an ongoing positive relationship with his or her own unconscious – the source of so many insights in the field of NLP. [36]

20th Century Contributions

Automata Theory

There is a relatively obscure and esoteric branch of mathematics known as Automata Theory – the study of abstract machines. The hierarchy of automata investigated by mathematicians in the specialty ranges from the simplest – finite state automata - to the most powerful - Turing machines.

The core issues in this field revolve around various questions of computability. Indeed, to say that a function is computable is equivalent to saying that there exists a Turing machine that can compute that function. The Turing machine is a well-defined mathematical model that has successfully served as a model for actual computers – in fact it is not a physical machine at all – but could be realized today in part in an idealized form of a modern computer. Turing machines were created by Alan Turing, a British mathematician, in 1936, long before actual computers existed in any form recognizable to present day users. Turing's formalization made possible some of the most striking computational achievements in the 20th century.

Underlying the field of natural language called Transformational Grammar is the model known as Automata Theory. Those readers already familiar with NLP patterning and its codification will recognize the significant borrowing from Automata Theory: in particular, the notions of the *6-tuple* (*The Structure of Magic*, volume II, part III), the *4-tuple* (*The Hypnotic Techniques of Milton H. Erickson, M.D.* volume II, pp. 17), *state descriptions* (ubiquitous in the original classic code by Grinder and Bandler), functions (such as the *c* and *r* operators in *Patterns of the Hypnotic Techniques of Milton H. Erickson, M.D.*, volume II)… As noted earlier, Automata Theory belongs to the class of discrete mathematical models as opposed to analogue or continuous mathematical models. This reinforces the distinction argued for earlier, a distinction that is critical in determining what is the proper epistemology for the field of NLP. [37]

But these borrowings while important and informative in their own right are only one point of articulation between Automata Theory and the field of NLP. We look forward to a point in the future where the vocabulary of NLP has developed with enough precision, the patterning has been coded with adequate explicitness…that equivalency mappings similar to Chomsky's classic argument about language but those between non-linguistic behavior and the hierarchy of Automata Theory becomes available in our argumentation. [38]

Informally a (deterministic, one tape) Turing machine (TM) is a hypothetical machine that has a finite number of states Q, a semi infinite tape that is delimited on the left by an end marker, $\}$, and is unbounded to the right, and a head that can move left and right over the tape, reading and writing. Surprisingly with this minimum set of elements as the start point, anything that can be computed can be computed by some one of the hypothetical machines in the Turing set.

Turing Machine

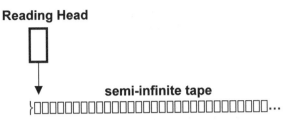

Think of the operation of this Turing machine as follows, the machine begins in its start state and reads the symbol written in the farthest left cell of the input tape. Within its set of formal rules (the transition function), it locates the instruction that says, if the machine is in state s^i, reading symbol a^i, then write symbol a^j and move left, right or stay in the same location, and change (or not) to another state s^j. Thus the machine works its way through the tape, following the rule set. If at the end of the computation the machine halts in the accept state, the input tape is said to be computable and accepted by that machine. If the machine ends up in the reject state at the end of its computation, this means that the input string has been rejected by that particular machine. Issues of acceptance and rejection can be (and were by Chomsky) mapped onto linguistic questions such as whether a particular string of words is a well-formed sentence or not in the language in question. [39]

There is even a representation of Gödel's amazing undecidability result within the domain of this field. In this context it is known as the halting problem: a situation in which in general it is not possible given some arbitrary well defined TM and an input tape to decide whether the machine will halt in its computation of that input tape after some finite number of steps.

While these results are astonishingly important and provocative in the larger context of the philosophy of science and mathematics more generally, they are not the point of the presentation here. We urge readers with requisite background and interest to consult any reference on Automata Theory to deepen their appreciation of these findings.

I (JG) find a great deal of my own thinking formally about behavior and its coding deeply influenced by the formalisms that defined by Automata Theory. Independent of the question of whether there are other significant borrowings from that field to be captured, the entire way of thinking about the decomposition of behavior in the study of excellence and the coding of its elements has been greatly enhanced by this accident of my personal intellectual background. I suggest that, indeed, a disciplined training in this field would clarify significant portions of the ongoing dialogues and ill-formed arguments that mix logical types and levels in the discussions presently occurring in journals purporting to represent work in the field of NLP.

Logic

While we are uncertain as to whether our position is controversial or not, it seems to us obvious that logic has its historical roots in the inherent logic of natural language. That is to say, the creation of formal systems, and in particular, logics (the formal systems of propositional, predicate and modal logics) are refined and sanitized extensions of the patterning found in natural language systems. If such a view is accepted, then it becomes clear that in addition to whatever contributions logic makes, it also represents a research wedge into the explicit modeling of some of the mappings that inform the f^2 transforms in natural language – an essential part of what the epistemology of the future will require.

We argue formally (see Part III, chapter 1, *Logical Levels and Logical Types*) that the underlying structure of language in both of the major categories typically distinguished by linguists (nouns and verbs) is a set of hierarchies defined by logical inclusion (logical levels). This logical inclusion ordering is typical of linguistic transforms and patently not so for many patterns at the level of FA – thus offering an important distinction in the selection of interventions in the application of NLP patterning to change work. For our present purposes, we note the following mappings between patterning in NLP, natural language patterning and formal logical systems.

In the most elementary of the formal logics, the propositional calculus, there is an attempt, originated by the Greeks, to define formally the rules of correct reasoning. The entire enterprise depends crucially on a set of definitions for sentential connectives – operators such as AND, OR, IF⟶THEN, NOT... The definition of these operators is accomplished by providing a set of truth tables. For example, the truth tables for the operator AND is given by the following:

Truth Table defining the operator AND

S^i	S^j	S^i AND S^j
T	T	T
T	F	F
F	T	F
F	F	F

(where T = true and F = false)

The table is read as follows: the two leftmost columns are the set of all four possible permutations of T (true) and F (false) for the individual sentences, S^i and S^j. The third column lists the truth value of the conjunction (the two sentences, S^i and S^j, conjoined by the operator AND). In summary, the truth table says that if we have any two arbitrary well-formed declarative sentences in our logical system, then the conjunction of those two sentences (the sentences conjoined by the operator AND) is true if and only if both S^i and S^j are themselves true and false otherwise.

The truth table for the logical operator OR is defined as,

Truth Table defining the operator OR

S^i	S^j	S^i OR S^j
T	T	T
T	F	T
F	T	T
F	F	F

This table is read in the same fashion and says that if we have any two arbitrary well formed declarative sentences in our logical system, then the disjunction of these two sentences is true, if, and only if, one or both of the individual sentences are true and false otherwise (the case in which both S^i and S^j are false).

These definitions by truth table align themselves well with natural language usage. If I say to you the following two sentences,

I am tired

You are wearing green.

and each one of the sentences are verified to be accurate (true in the vocabulary of the formal logical system), then the compound conjoined sentence,

I am tired and you are wearing green.

is taken to be accurate (true). In fact, if you ask yourself under what conditions you would accept this last sentence as true, you will be able to easily work out that you will accept it as accurate just in case both individual sentences are accurate. This accords perfectly with the formal definition of the logical operator AND.

In parallel, if I ask you under what conditions you would accept the disjunction,

I am tired or you are wearing green

to be an accurate description of your experience, you will arrive at a conclusion that perfectly matches the truth table for the logical operator OR. That is to say, you will regard the disjunction as accurate if either of the individual sentences is true. Now if both sentences are true, you will likely wonder about the point of the disjunction, but if forced to decide whether to classify it as true or not, you will ultimately assign the value *true* to it. Granted it is a decidedly peculiar communication under normal circumstances. So far, so good! The definition of NOT proceeds easily enough but the truth tables for IF——▶ THEN raise questions for many people.

These questions revolve around the vagueness or lack of precise definition of the terms *if x, then y* in natural language use. But this is precisely one of the critical differences between natural language and formal logics. A formal logic would be of no value in ensuring that its reasoning represented valid sequences of thinking if it were permitted to contain this lack of definition. We propose that indeed the formal logical system we are discussing was derived from natural language patterning by a prescriptive clean-up of the vagueness and ambiguity inherent in the corresponding natural language patterns.

It is important to appreciate that the propositional calculus is perfectly general: it is independent of the content of the individual sentences involved. No matter what the contents of S^i and S^j are, if we know their truth values, we know the values of the compound sentences formed by the logical operators. This gives great power for computational purposes – one of the profound advantages of any formal or syntactic approach, and a defining characteristic of patterning in NLP.

We note that in the second volume of the studies of the hypnotic patterning of Dr. Erickson, Grinder, Delozier and Bandler (*Patterns of the Hypnotic Techniques of Milton H. Erickson, M.D.*),

> *Linguistically, we have found it useful to distinguish three categories of casual relations or linkages,*
>
> > *(a) Conjunction, use of the connectives and, but (i.e. and not)*
>
> *… The most typical way in which a hypnotist uses these modeling processes is by linking some portion of the client's ongoing experience which the client is immediately able to verify to some experience or behavior that the hypnotist wishes the client to have.*

> > *Patterns of the Hypnotic Techniques of Milton H. Erickson, M.D.*, volume II, pages 147 – 148

In other words, the hypnotist forms an extended conjunct.

$$S^i \text{ and } S^{i+1} \text{ and } S^{i+2} \text{ and } S^{i+3} \text{ and } S^{i+1} \text{ and } S^{i+4} \text{ and } \dots S^j$$

> *where the sentences S^i through S^{i+4} are true, immediately verifiable expressions of the client's ongoing experience and S^j is what the hypnotist wants the client to experience…*

The client hears a series of statements that he can immediately verify as accurate (true) and, finally, after verifying a series of accurate statements all connected by the natural language operator *and*, he hears a sentence that he will make accurate (true) to preserve the truth value of the entire conjunction.

The natural language antecedent of the disjunctive logical operator OR can be discerned in change strategies as well. Recall that a series of statements connected by this logical operator will be said to be "true" if and only if one of the statements connected in the series is "true". Perhaps the most obvious of applications of this operator can be found in Dr. Erickson's work – more specifically, in the presentation of a series of alternatives from which the client is invited to choose. Typically, Erickson would fix the client's attention on a set of disjunctive alternatives and then have him select one freely for implementation. Dr. Erickson, of course, had generated the set in such a way that the previous (inappropriate) behavior was represented as one of the alternatives alongside more inappropriate options as well as the behavior or behaviors Erickson desired that the client actually engage in. For example, asked by the family of a young man who was displaying a deep identification with Jesus Christ to intervene – the young man's behavior was becoming less and less socially acceptable, Erickson instructed the young man to construct a large heavy wooden cross and on a scheduled basis, he was obliged to drag the cross through a residential area. Faced with the task of performing this clearly exaggerated (and quite taxing) behavior, the young man selected one of the relatively harmless options Erickson had included in the disjunction of options originally formulated by him.

The succeeding logic in the ordering of increasing complex logics, the predicate calculus, includes the study of the truth conditions that obtain when quantifiers are included in the sentences manipulated within the formal system. Representations such as the following are typical at this level of logic,

$\forall x$ *x is mortal*

$\exists y$ *y is yellow.*

The simplest translation into normal textual English is

For all x, x is mortal   or   *Everything is mortal*

For some y, y is yellow   or   *Something is yellow*

The symbol, then, $\forall$ represents the universal quantifier – in natural language terms, *all, every, each, everyone, everybody, everything, always (all time)...* while the symbol $\exists$ stands for the existential quantifier, *some, someone, something, sometime...* The interaction of the universal quantifier ($\forall$), for example, with negation (~) yields, *no one, none, nobody, nothing, never...* ($\forall$~).

In the first of the models created and coded in NLP, the meta model, one finds a specific challenge for universal quantifiers. The exchange below demonstrates the point,

Client: *Everyone hates me*

Agent of change: *Everyone? (with a rising intonation)*

Here the agent of change is usefully challenging a generalization by the client that constitutes one portion of his map that is presently operating as an obstacle to realizing his full potential and significantly improving his quality of life. The client's statement is of the form,

$\forall x$ x hates me

where the variable x is defined over the set of human beings

The challenge is a demand on the client by the agent to refine the map he carries, making distinctions where apparently previously there were none. Such shoddy thinking and expression are often the basis for obstacles to personal development as in general, choices not represented in the map of the client are not choices in the world for him.

Finally, as an example from a higher order logic, modal logic, we have examples such as,

It is necessary to wait until next week to process your request.

It is impossible to process your request right now.

With their translation into modal logic where the symbol $\square$ represents *necessary* and the symbol $\lozenge$ stands for *possible*. The compound $\sim \lozenge$ represents, therefore, *not possible or impossible*.

$\square$ ($\forall x$)   *x wait until next week to process your request)*

$\sim \lozenge$ ($\forall x$)   *x process your request right now)*

The conjunction of the modal operators of necessity and (im)possibility alongside the universal quantifier constitutes a particularly lethal set of representations in a client's map. The meta model challenges for these modal operators are,

Client: *It is necessary to wait until next week to process your request.*

Agent of change: *What would happen if you didn't wait until next week to process my request?*

Client: *It is impossible to process your request now*

Agent of change: *What would happen if you did process my request right now?*

There are other examples of contributions from these logics already coded for use in NLP. Our objective here is to point the interested readers to the intellectual antecedents of NLP in hope that they will examine these underpinning both to deepen their appreciation of the rich sources of these patterns and to invite them to search for additional contributions that would further enhance the patterning of NLP as these patterns have.

Summary

Each discovery and invention has a story. Behind that story are individuals whose education, interests and personal history come together within a context at an appropriate time to exploit an opportunity to create, invent, discover or develop something new. At the time of such an opportunity, the individual unconsciously falls back on their personal historical resources. These resources are, in large part, the unconscious filters through which he experiences the world. Those filters just happen to contain that difference that makes the difference between the filters of the guy next door who is satisfied simply to use that discovery – rather than to create it himself.

The purpose of this short excursion into the intellectual antecedents of NLP is two-fold:

1. to indicate to attentive readers where in particular they might investigate with the purpose of appreciating the roots of NLP.

2. to provide access to these sources so as to allow interested readers decide for themselves whether there are additional mapping, additional distinctions from these and associated disciplines that that were ignored or overlooked by Grinder and Bandler in their historical raiding parties.

The purpose, then, of this section has been to make explicit and available to the interested reader the intellectual currents of thought (in one of the co-creators - JG) that formed the context in which NLP was created.

The actual development and expression of this chapter and the succeeding one was initiated by a deep curiosity on the part of one on your co-authors (CB). This section is, then, in significant part is the result of the interaction that occurred between the two co-authors responding to that curiosity.

Good hunting!

Footnotes for Chapter 3, Part I

1. Your two present co-authors had the peculiar experience of participating as guests at a meeting in Vienna in 1997 at the Café Landtmann, the very Café that was the traditional meeting place of the Logical Positivists in the heady days of their formation in the 19th century. Fortunately, on this occasion, the topic was the creation of a cooperative effort among the German-speaking countries of Europe (with representatives from Germany, Austria and Switzerland) to achieve recognition by the appropriate authorities for Neuro-Linguists Psychotherapy. The consequences of a successful lobbying by the group would be that Neuro-Linguistic Psychotherapy would be recognized and registered as a legitimate form of psychotherapy and therefore available for payments by the medical and social security systems of the countries involved. Readers interested in learning more about this movement are invited to contact Peter Schultz at friendly@eunet.at or any member of the EANLP (European Association of Neuro-Linguistic Psychotherapy

2. Eric Robbie in an article published in *NLP World*, volume 7, No. 3 November, 2000 makes the following statement (based on his reading of Horrocks' *Generative Grammar*, 1987), quoting Bandler and Grinder in *The Structure of Magic*, Volume I, page 207

   > *We have an intuition that the Generative Semantics model will be the most useful in the area of Logical Semantic relations.*

   Robbie goes on to comment

   > *And he (Grinder) or they (Grinder and Bandler) couldn't have been more wrong.*

   Robbie is correct in his guess that the source of the opinion quoted from *Magic*, volume I, is Grinder but his conclusion (as well as that of Horrock's) is not. Indeed, Generative Semantics has long been abandoned and I (JG) would comment that just as in the case of the Chomsky's Standard Theory before it, it served extremely well as a precisely defined position that moved linguistic enquiry forward to the position we find it in today - the development of Cognitive Grammar. The development of the Cognitive Grammar and Cognitive Science depended precisely on the work that exhausted the possibility that Generative Semantics represented and freed the involved linguists to move past the paradigm. This is a natural and repetitive sequence in a rapidly developing discipline.

Our other comment is in respect to the form of the entire article by Robbie that is a strange mixture of logical types and logical levels. There are several aspects of this article that are symptomatic of what has to change if NLP is to take its rightful place beside other systematic studies of human behavior:

a. Robbie sets out to offer an ordering proof but nowhere is there an indication of what ordering he is out to prove (see Part III, chapter 2 of *Whispering* for contrast). Is the ordering he is proposing an ordering of application in the context of inducing change (that is, an ordering in real time application); or is it some sort of logical ordering among the patterns and grouping of patterns; or is it to be understood as a claim about the psychological reality of the grouping of patterning and their orderings with respect to one another...? None of this is explicated. Thus there is no coherent basis for joining in supporting and extending his proposal nor in offering counterexamples as a way of refining the discussion. This renders it impossible to use his work as a stimulus for making an advance in the development of the issue of ordering relationships within the meta model.

b. Proofs are very precise and explicit forms – either Robbie is unfamiliar with what a proof actually is or is using the term metaphorically. If he is using the term metaphorically, he bears the responsibility to so frame it. His failure to do so simply removes all credibility for readers who actually appreciate the formal requirements of proofs and in turn removes his study from serious consideration by mathematicians and linguists who are quite precise in what they mean by proof.

c. Robbie introduces and uses terminology without definition thereby removing all possibility of a serious attempt to appreciate whatever insights he is attempting to express – such minimal operational definitions are a prerequisite for opening a professional and interesting dialogue publicly within the field of NLP.

We offer this critique of Robbie's article simply as an example of the class of differences that need to be taken into account in reporting work in the field if NLP work if it is to be taken seriously and advances made.

Our own thinking is, of course, quite different and moves towards a reduced or minimal model - however one that is functionally equivalent to the full meta model. The fundamental point of modeling – mapping complex behavior onto a reduced set of learnable, efficiently transferable explicit variables – seems to have escaped him, as it has apparently M. Hall. This difference is independent of the critique offered immediately above and is an empirical issue.

3. An interesting thought to ponder: It could be argued that Beethoven's own written notations of his Fifth do not represent Beethoven's Fifth. The written notation in itself is merely a representation and an interpretation of a Fifth he himself composed in his own neurological circuitry.

   We also point out that the competency/performance distinction key to the discussion in the text has evolved over the subsequent years into a discussion in which the term *I-language* serves in its place. It is not entirely clear what the entire range of differences between the use of the terms *competency/performance* and *I-language* are. It is clear that Chomsky in part selected the new term to make explicit his objections to the analysis of language as a public construct of which individual speakers have partial knowledge. As far as we can determine, Chomsky's internalist position is consistent with the reading of the former competency/performance distinction presented here (see Noam Chomsky: *New Horizons in the Study of Language and Mind* , 2000).

4. If the reader doubts the point, we invite him or her to listen quietly to any actual conversation between two or more people whether alcohol, drugs or exhaustion are involved or not, and note how many of the utterances they would accept as well-formed sentences of English.

5. We would not like to mislead the reader, innocent of the practice of linguistics and especially syntax, into arriving at the belief that the exclusion of these intuitively ungrammatical strings of words from the corpus has lead to stunning success in describing the grammar underlying the performance of native speakers. As Paul Postal, surely one of the ablest of the syntacticians in Transformational Grammar tradition, once observed: *The life expectancy of a pattern without counterexample is approximately a minute and a half, except late on Friday afternoons, when it drops to 30 seconds.*

6. The NLP practitioner well-trained in the Milton model will recognize the center embedded structure as one of Erickson's favorite hypnotic conversational induction techniques. Erickson would begin a story, interrupt the story to insert a second story within the first, then a third story within the second (already within the first

story...(see chapter 2, Part II for another description). At about level three of embedded structure, Dr. Erickson's clients' conscious minds would either give up any attempt to keep the stories and their accompanying messages sorted out or become so fixated on some aspect of the unresolved stories that direct access to the unconscious mind was a foregone conclusion. Sometimes Dr. Erickson completed the center embedded structure by finishing each story in its appropriate order and sometimes he would simply leave the stories (and his clients) hanging.

7. One likely explanation for the difficulty associated with the center embedded sentence is that it exceeds most speakers' short-term memory capacity. It occurs to us that native speakers of German should then demonstrate a marked advantage in processing such structures. This occurs as the syntax of German involves a backwards stacking of all but the initial verb at the end of the sentence – a syntactic form partially analogous to the center embedded sentence in the example in terms or processing requirements.

8. The preferred method for establishing this specialized context of testing material against one's intuitions seems to be auditory although there are individual variations in this preference with some linguists preferring to actually see the sequence of words in question in a written form. NLP trained practitioners will recognize this as a representational system preference. Most linguists I (JG) have worked with also typically use a kinesthetic exit as part of their strategy for making judgments about sequences.

9. In linguistics, this distinction is captured by the terms *prescriptive* – dictated by fiat with no apparent basis in the actual internalized and neurologically expressed grammar of native speakers and *normative* - what native speakers actually judge to be well-formed, ambiguous, synonymous... sequences in their native tongue. The prescriptive grammar stance is a particularly amusing form of the map/territory epistemological error.

10. Fauconnier (1994) characterizes these traditional intuitive judgments of native or fluent speakers as the ability to construct "appropriate minimum contexts" (page xxvii of the preface to *Mental Spaces*). More importantly, his work along with others (e.g. Langacker) represents a paradigm break, with the dethroning of the sentence as the key unit of analysis and with a commitment to find a link to the cognitive structures we use as humans of which linguistic patterning is a consequence. We applaud his efforts.

11. NLP, of course, and, in particular, the codification of the eye movements and their significance had not yet occurred at this point historically.

12. Conversations with a number of professional mathematicians have revealed that during certain parts of their professional activities – for example, in the process of initially evaluating a formal proof – they experience process sequences very much analogous to what we are describing here.

   We also wish to point the reader to the discussions current in Cognitive Grammar (see Langacker, 1987, Fauconnier, 1994) about the nature of intuitions from a linguist's point of view – Fauconnier, for example, proposes that the intuitions are actually testing the ability of the native speaker who is making the judgments to generate a context in which the sentence being judged is acceptable. Langacker uses the proliferation of stars (the asterisk marking used in generative grammar and in this book) as an argument against the autonomy of syntax, proposing that there is a gradation of patterning of the lexicon and semantics through to the usage (the actual speech act) with no separate syntactic level (such as Deep Structure) distinguished.

13. For those readers who wish to compare their intuitive judgments against ours, consider the term *Nicole* as it appears as the apparent subject in both of the sentences. Its function in what linguists of that era called Deep Structure (something like the untransformed original version of a sentence before the application of various syntactic operations which map it onto what we actually say) is fundamentally different.

   Nicole was eager to please

   In the above sentence *Nicole* is the subject of the verb *please* – that is, the meaning of the sentence is that *Nicole* was the one who was eager to please someone else. In the second sentence,

   Nicole was easy to please

   the term *Nicole* functions as the object of the verb *please* – that is, someone or something else pleased *Nicole*. For example, one could say,

   Nicole is eager to please Gregg.

   but not

Nicole is easy to please Gregg.

14. We also recognize the extreme importance of experiments designed to detect unconscious perceptions of visual patterning as well as linguistic patterning. We leave aside for purposes of exposition here these additional research methods. Note that their inclusion would only strengthen the point we are making as the reference point once again is the representations and constructs of the human being. This initial and somewhat tentative exploration of the patterning of unconscious perceptions will surely become a powerful element in the future models of human cognition. As an excellent example of such research employing unconscious patterning, see Kurzban, Tooby and Cosmides in Proceeding of the National Academy of Sciences, week of December 15, 2001;

15. The specific variables that we have in mind in making this proposal are:

It has been observed for some decades now that the timing of the anchoring (actually establishing the anchor – state relationship) will strongly determine how effective the anchor will be in re-accessing the state. If, for example, the anchor occurs just prior to or just subsequent to the peak expression physiologically of the state to be anchored, it will be significantly less effective in re-accessing the state anchored then if it occurs precisely at the peak expression of the state – thus, the timing variable.

If the anchor is established in one of the three major representational systems (or input channels) and at the time of the anchoring, the client is entertaining other representations in that same channel, the effectiveness of the anchor will be significantly reduced. This is sometimes referred to as the purity variable – that is, how pure is the attention committed by the client to the state the practitioner is anchoring.

Now, both of these variables represent processes, ultimately neuro/physiological in origin, known to the practitioner solely through the physiological shifts that occur (that is, through calibration) associated with the state changes. Observations defined over our cumulative anchoring experiences (totaling some 50 years) have convinced us that anchoring is best understood (analyzed and evaluated) as a continuous process, not a discrete or categorical phenomenon. These comments cluster around observations that there is a gradation in responses to anchors as a function of the timing and purity variables managed by the practitioner.

Finally, the fact that anchoring – a core process in the practical application of NLP patterning - has to date NOT been systematically explored is a comment on the lack of serious systematic studies in our field. This cries out for a brilliant PhD thesis by some enterprising and well-trained practitioner of NLP.

16. One limiting case species-wise that we are aware of is Washoe, a chimpanzee raised by a couple at the University of Nevada, the Gardeners. They correctly recognized that one of the factors that could account for the chimpanzee's inability to learn language is the limitations of their vocal tract - that is, they are incapable of forming the sounds required as the physiological mechanisms involved simply do not permit it. Thus, any attempt to answer the question,

Are chimpanzees able to learn language?

by trying to teach them any spoken human language was corrupted by factors irrelevant to the spirit of the question. They, therefore, taught Washoe American Sign Language (ASL). The chimpanzee apparently mastered several hundred signs and demonstrated startlingly novel applications, including spontaneously making the sign for *flower* when looking at a picture of a flower in a magazine (does this mean that chimps are capable of map-territory epistemological errors as we are?). The Gardeners were then prepared to claim that Washoe had broken the language barrier, formerly believed to separate humans from all other species. My major professor at UCSD, Edward Klima was called in to analyze what it was that Washoe was doing. Klima, conservatively (and correctly to our minds), stated that the question as to whether Washoe had broken the language barrier depended in part on the answer to the question,

Is American Sign Language (ASL) a language of the same logical type as human spoken languages?

The answer it seems to us will revolve around demonstrating that ASL contains a fully developed syntactic system. More specifically, can researchers demonstrate that there is a pair of sequences of signs, composed of exacting the same set of signs but that differs in the sequence of those signs wherein the two paired sequences mean different things in the system under scrutiny. See Ursula Bellugi-Klima for studies on the question and in particular, the most recent comment by both Klima and

Bellugi-Klima with their co-author, Gregory Hickok in their article, *Sign Language in the Brain*, in Scientific American, June 2001, pages 58 – 65. In this article by Hickok, Bellugi and Klima, they state unequivocally,

> *But in truth, sign languages are highly structured linguistic systems with all the grammatical complexity of spoken languages.*

While we do not have access to the data to determine what the actual evidence for this conclusion is, we have confidence in these researchers, and look forward to examining the patterning they have uncovered.

17. This is only part of the task a linguist specializing in syntax has, but will serve adequately for the purposes of the presentation here. We remind the readers that since our objective in this section is the exploration of the intellectual antecedents of NLP, we are referring to the class of patterning in Transformational Grammar that was current at the time that Grinder and Bandler created NLP (the early 1970's). Much has occurred in the field and the readers are urged to acquaint themselves with current work in these fields that are identified as successors to TG (for example, Cognitive Grammar and Cognitive Science) as part of an effort to participate alongside other researchers in making significant contributions to the study of human patterning.

In particular in the case in point, the utility of the research strategy of making the performance/competence distinction – a keystone of syntactic work in the 60' and 70's – has been strongly challenged by Cognitive Grammarians. Their attempt to extend the patterning from the relatively isolated focus on syntactic patterning to include what formerly was considered the domains of semantics and pragmatics (the latter assigned originally as a task for psychologists) is to be welcomed. Ultimately, the use of language in any practical sense involves those areas now defined as appropriate research themes for present day linguists. Historically, the strategy was that the syntax could be autonomously patterned and that performance variables were relegated to an entirely different field (psychology). In hindsight this strategy served brilliantly to advance the field to the point where a paradigm shift became both appropriate and possible.

It seems to us that this is a natural progression in scientific disciplines that succeed – a model is developed using simplifying assumptions that lead initially to great success (as they simply greatly facilitate the patterning to be coded) and then hit the wall of proliferating counterexamples to the assumptions. These in turn leads to a paradigm challenge as has occurred in the last decade or so in linguistics.

18. This is not to say the linguists are always even-handed about these matters. There was a strong tendency in the '70s and '80s to focus syntactic and phonological studies in American English on the dialects favored in Ivy League and Eastern Universities – no doubt, an unintentional bias which has been or will be corrected.

I remember a high level conference in the world of transformational syntax back in 1970 hosted by the University of California, San Diego and attended by the best of the transformational syntacticians (Postal, Ross, Fillmore, Lakoff...) of the time (with the notable exception of Chomsky) at which G. Lakoff made a proposal that no language would allow a well-formed sequence of two or more contiguous modal operators. A graduate student (now a professor of linguistics) who co-authored a textbook written by one of your present authors (JG), Suzette Haden Elgin rose gracefully and commented,

You might could find such examples in the Ozarks!

The utterance was, of course, a counterexample to the claim promoted by Lakoff. What had happened was that there were simply very few linguists in the field who (as in the case of Elgin) came from, or were knowledgeable about, the dialects in that particular part of the United States.

19. Indeed, eye movements have been the subject of dozens of Master's and Doctoral studies in US and European universities over the last quarter of a century. Given the failure on the part of the researchers' to appreciate the methodological point we are developing here, these studies are typically flawed with about half of them demonstrating the validity of the eye movements and about half suggesting that there is no such pattern. We feel inclined to comment that it is not obvious to us what the intention behind such studies (other than the obvious objective of securing a degree) could possibly be, since, as we have attempted to make clear, NLP focuses on the study of individual intact rule governed systems. Clearly collapsing data across subjects as is typical in these flawed studies, significantly increase the probability that if there is a pattern, it will be thereby obscured. NLP is the study of single intact rule-governed behaviors in individuals who have distinguished themselves by consistent excellence in their field.

20. This question was the classic access question that was historically and in some cases still is used to provoke the subject to demonstrate the eye movements that indicate visual access. In retrospect it is interesting to note that if any evidence is needed to demonstrate the unconscious ethnic and geographical chauvinism of the origins of NLP

in general and representational systems in particular, the presuppositions of this question will serve. Imagine the utility (or even appropriateness) of such a question in a homogeneous group of people of Asian, African, Hispanic... descent.

21. This does not imply that all human behavior is best described by rule systems – for example as mentioned above, there are clearly analogue components involved in the practice of anchoring. The partition that distinguishes between those portions of human behavior most appropriately described by rule systems of a categorical type and those best represented by analogue processes at present requires much work. Indeed, Langacker offers an extended argument that language in certain of its aspects is not discrete but continuous. We invite the reader to review the argument directly (Langacker, 1987). We thus far find Langacker's analysis unconvincing.

22. Of course, the result would be a measure of the psychologist's ability to arrange an appropriate learning context as well as a measure of some sort of their modeling abilities – that is, making the elicited model an efficiently learnable one.

23. It is fascinating to us to note that there is currently a serious challenge being mounted by some scientists to what has for some decades been a set of presuppositions by those members of the scientific and philosophical communities who think about, write and comment about the activity called science. There are a number of aspects of this challenge. We mention two clear ones here:

    1. for some time, it has been noted that scientists, not unintelligently, have picked the lowest hanging fruit on the tree of patterning. More specifically, it is clear that the vast majority of patterning that has been done, effectively coded and verified has been confined to linear processes. More complex phenomena – those, for example, described by proponents of chaos theory, dynamic open systems - have typically been avoided as foci of research.

    2. In step with this ongoing emphasis, there is a well-recognized set of procedures for investigating and methods for coding such linear processes. As a natural consequence of this emphasis, there has (until recently) been little attention and effort expended to develop, refine and implement procedures for investigating and methods for coding non-linear, more complex phenomena.

At present, there are number of very able researchers who are calling for a shift in this emphasis. They have proposed a series of procedures and methods that initiate the great project of extending the de facto boundaries of scientific investigation to more complex phenomena.

The present state of NLP is so rudimentary that this challenge has, in our opinion, little relevance for ongoing work in the field of NLP. We would however be remiss not to mention the importance of this extension to more complex phenomena and the exciting suggestions about proper methodology and coding of them. Given NLP's focus on the modeling of excellence in human behavior, we have little doubt that these developments will make a powerful contribution at some point in the future when NLP can stabilize its fundamental vocabulary and procedure for investigation and coding of patterning of excellence. In particular, we recommend to the interested reader the following opening references: *Butterflies and Metaphors* by Gregory Bateson (a lecture taped at Esalen Institute just before Bateson's death, available through Esalen); *Dynamic Patterns: The Self Organization of Brain and Behavior* by J. A. Scott Kelso, 1995; *The Origins of Order: Self-Organization and Selection in Evolution* by Stuart A. Kauffman, 1993; *At Home in the Universe* by Stuart A. Kauffman, 1995, *Order out of Chaos*, by Prigogine and Stengers. We are again deeply indebted to Tom Malloy and Chris Mitchell for bringing this entire enterprise to our attention and to the fascinating conversations both face to face and electronically about its significance.

24. We wish to make clear that we understand that the upgrading of the performance of the children involved would by definition change the computed average performance – thus in the example, we are referring to some previously established average performance. The point under consideration is where to commit the available resources. Thus, we use the term *average* here in the same sense that Garrison Keillor (*A Prairie Home Companion*, Minnesota Public Radio) uses it at the termination of his presentation of the News from Lake Woebegone; namely,

> *"And that's the news from Lake Wobegone, where the women are strong, the men are good looking and all of the children are above average. "*

25. In Spanish the mapping between the orthography and the sound system is straightforward and therefore spelling is not even recognized as an academic task in, for example, the educational systems in Mexico.

26. Which of the initial group of NLP practitioners made the original observation is lost somewhere in memory – it occurred very early in the development of NLP – in the mid '70s. My memory (JG) is that whoever it was who first noted this simple and elegant strategy, Robert Dilts worked on this strategy, refining it and in particular adding the excellent

test requirement that a student employing this NLP strategy should be able to spell backwards with the same effectiveness and nearly the same efficiency as he could spell forwards. I remember working with Robert and David Gaster on creating a software package embodying this strategy as part of the commercial activities of Behavioral Engineering, a company then owned by the three of us: Grinder, Dilts and Gaster.

Much in the discussion of this example resulted from an ongoing discussion among the present authors (JG and CB) and Chris Mitchell and Tom Malloy (Department of Psychology, University of Utah), very close friends and most able researchers in their own right. Thanks!

27. Caution must be exercised here as it is likely that the words on the most difficult words spelling lists complied by such agencies will be highly biased to include precisely those words in which there is a maximum discrepancy between the auditory and orthographical representations. This would tend to exaggerate the effect (in a positive manner) of the NLP spelling strategy, as the mapping function called phonics is obviously useless for such words and the NLP spelling strategy is unaffected by this particular discrepancy, *assuming the spellers had ever seen the word in question.*

28. The inverse would not be particularly informative - that is, cases where a member of the NLP spelling strategy group spelled the word correctly without demonstrating the sequence of eye movements that confirm that that subject on that particular trial followed the required sequence. This is the case as the claim about the NLP spelling strategy does not propose that it is the only effective method for spelling – one can auditorily memorize words for spelling purposes – only that it is the most effective (100% correct performance) under the assumption that the word has been seen before and that it is more efficient than other strategies given that assumption.

29. There are other more advanced methods for testing for the presence or absence of a strategy such as interference testing, competing tasks, interruptions... These methods are discussed in detail in *RedTail Math: the epistemology of everyday life* (working title), Bostic and Grinder, 2002.

30. Note that the concept of a counterexample belongs to a paradigm of thinking and analysis that falls into the category of discrete patterning. Strictly speaking, counterexamples are not possible in a continuous analysis.

31. By the way, the initial results mentioned in this example are based on

an actual study conducted by a competent investigator who had an excellent grasp of the statistical tools and their limitations some years ago. The follow-up studies detailed in the text were, unfortunately not carried out. Further, nothing in what we have presented should be interpreted as denigrating the phonics strategy in general. Just as the NLP spelling strategy is irrelevant in those cases where the word to be spelled has never been seen by the speller, it is hardly just to criticize a method for not working effectively in precisely those cases it was NOT designed for. In that sense the two strategies – the NLP spelling strategy and the phonics strategy – are highly complementary – they occupy separate but complimentary niches. The NLP spelling strategy is absolutely inappropriate for words never before seen and the phonics strategy is inappropriate for precisely the class of words where there is a significant difference between the auditory and orthographic representations (as in the word *phonics* itself). Stated positively, the phonics strategy is of immense value for the activity of reading where one frequently encounters words never seen before while the NLP spelling strategy is equally valuable in the task of spelling just in case the word in question has been seen before. Indeed, we suspect that given this distinction, if it were possible to segment the words presented to the subjects by whether they had ever seen the words before, this information would be highly predictive for their subsequent performance.

32. See especially Langacker, 1988 for a discussion.

33. Bateson clearly found the original published work that established NLP (as contained in *The Structure of Magic,* volumes I and II) of great value. On the other hand, his initial response to the two-volume work he actually arranged for Grinder and Bandler to do was entirely different. His cryptic response to his initial reading of the first volume of *Patterns of the Hypnotic Techniques of Milton H. Erickson, M. D.* was simply,

   "Shoddy epistemology!"

The thinking behind this comment and the subsequent development of his thinking on this topic are fascinating but outside the scope of this book (see Joseph O'Connor's article by the same name, *Shoddy Epistemology* for one interpretation – an interesting interpretation although not one that is congruent with my (JG) understanding of what Bateson intended by the remark.

34. John Grinder and Gregory Bateson met initially as professional colleagues. Gregory was a professor at Kresge College at the same time that John was an Assistant Professor of Linguistics in the same college. During the writing of *Mind and Nature* (by Bateson), John

Grinder, Richard Bandler and Gregory Bateson found themselves neighbors all living on a piece of property in the Santa Cruz Mountains owned by the same individual, Robert Spitzer, owner of Science and Behavior Books. Gregory was also working on the manuscript *Where Angel's Fear* and John and Richard were working on the patterns that were the basis of *The Structure of Magic I*. As neighbors, the relationship between Gregory's family and John's family was casual – Nora (Bateson's daughter from his marriage to Lois Bateson) and Kathleen (John's daughter) near the same age, were playmates. From time to time, Margaret Mead (Batesons's previous wife) and Catherine Bateson would visit Gregory and wander about the property. Much of the relationship between John and Gregory was based on discussions of what each of the men was questioning or thinking about at the time - each available to the other. These exchanges could be characterized as *atypical* of a neighborhood gathering around the barbeque and more like a meeting of minds of two learned and very verbally precise individuals.

35. For those of you who have not read Bateson's work, we recommend it highly. The first time you read it, read as you would poetry for the pure pleasure of the experience – apologies Judith Lowe. Each time you read the work, just relax and be pleasantly surprised by how freely you will associate and generalize the nuggets of wisdom.

36. We would argue that the source of all pattern detection depends critically on the ability at the unconscious level to detect redundancy. Further, a positive relationship between unconscious and conscious functioning is a prerequisite for explicating the patterning already detected at the unconscious level – that is, the conversion of tacit to explicit knowledge.

37. A through grounding in Automata Theory therefore would prepare the learner for a deeper appreciation of both the methodology and the conceptual framework within which NLP was developed as well as the relevant research strategies to be applied.

38. Chomsky used the principles of Automata Theory to argue backwards that Bloomfield's limitations on the analysis of natural language were too severe. Thus, using the power of the formal well-defined mathematical object- finite state automata and their equivalence to finite state grammar – Chomsky was able to demonstrate that patterning found in natural language were beyond the descriptive power of the limited methodology proposed by Bloomfield. We have chosen not to explore in depth this part of Chomsky's work and the influence on NLP in this book. This topic is discussed thoroughly in *RedTail Math: the epistemology of everyday life* (working title), Grinder and Bostic, 2002.

39. More formally, a Turing machine is a nine-tuple,

$M = (Q, \sum, \Gamma, \}, \mu, \delta, s, t, r)$

where

Q is a finite set (the states of the machine)

$\sum$ is a finite set (the input alphabet)

Γ is a finite set (the tape alphabet including $\sum$ as a subset)

$\} \in \Gamma - \sum$, the left end marker of the tape

$\mu \in \Gamma - \sum$, the blank symbol

$\delta: Q \_ \Gamma \rightarrow Q \_ \Gamma \_ (L.R)$, the transition function

$s \in Q$, the start state

$t \in Q$, the accept state

$r \in Q$, the reject state, $r \neq t$

Chapter 4: Personal Antecedents of NLP

This is the one of most difficult sections of the book to write for two reasons: first, achieving a clear global perspective of any person is in itself a demanding task. When that person is yourself, even with the essential aid of my co-author with her provocative and excellent ability to tease out such material through her own unique, powerful questioning techniques and pattern detection skills as well as our ability to utilize NLP tools such as triple description... the difficulty of the task is compounded. Secondly, the man I, John Grinder, worked with in creating this technology, Richard Bandler, and I have been working separately for some twenty plus years and there is ample public evidence that there are major differences in the perceptions each of us carries about the historical events that took place during the creation of NLP. [1]

I will make use of this opportunity to make a statement publicly – one that I have consistently made both privately and publicly over the past 20+ years or so.

Personal Statement by John Grinder

> *The creation of Neuro-Linguistic Programming (NLP) represents a superb example of collaboration. I could not have created NLP by myself nor do I believe, could have Richard Bandler. Each of us brought specific talents and capabilities to the endeavor, not the least of which was the ability to work as a team. For some six years, we worked side by side as researchers, provoking, supporting, challenging and amusing one another in our efforts to codify excellence in terms that made it available to the rest of the world.*
>
> *Both as individuals and as a team, we followed the strategy of Acting As If impeccably and offered one another continuing challenges, stimulation and feedback as we developed the representations of the patterns that presently define the Classic Code in NLP. While it may be possible to distinguish partially the initial strengths of each of us, there was a deep cross-training that occurred in our collaboration through which we learned from one another how to carry out the extraordinary feats that have set the historical standard for NLP practice – both at the level of modeling as well as in its applications. I therefore recognize with pleasure the essential historical contribution of Richard Bandler as the co-creator alongside myself*

of the technology of NLP, and I specifically offer him even now my congratulations and best wishes in his continuing work.

Those readers in search of a model of excellent collaboration will do well to step past the present state of affairs between us and focus on the work accomplished by the two of us in the period 1973 through 1979. The descriptions that follow are designed to offer the attentive reader access to portions of the events involved in the creation of the field of NLP with special emphasis on the variables that defined the contexts and processes of discovery. Naturally the following description is uniquely from my point of view as one of the two co-creators of NLP.

We are aware during the last decade plus of a number of criticisms voiced with the implication that the "two great communicators", Bandler and Grinder, themselves are not *communicating effectively* – that they are failing to use the very tools they created. This seems to us to be an excellent example of a failure to distinguish between form and substance, process and content. From my point of view (JG) at any rate, Bandler and I are communicating perfectly. Neither of us has any further interest in pursuing either a professional nor a personal relationship and all the signals between us carry precisely this message - communication complete.

The evidence for this alleged failure to communicate typically cited (if any evidence is cited at all) is that Grinder and Bandler don't *agree*. This is absolutely correct – Bandler and I do not agree. And this is precisely the point. We are, however, communicating perfectly at the level of process. The ability to communicate never implies agreement. Anyone who is incapable of distinguishing between communicating and agreeing has yet to learn the most rudimentary distinction in communication. Indeed, some of the most striking breakthroughs in science and conceptual development occur in the context of such differences of opinion [2].

Characterlogical Description

Looking back from the vantage point of our present historical perspective (and from my personal point of view – JG) at the two men who created the field of NLP (Bandler and myself) at the point when they began to work together reveals a number of characteristics that I believe we shared:

Similarities

Arrogant

Curious

Unimpressed by authority or tradition

Strong personal boundaries – well-defined sense of personal responsibility for their own experiences and an insistence that others do likewise

Willingness to try nearly anything rather than be bored (or boring)

Utterly lacking in self doubt - egotistical

Playful

Full capability as players in the Acting As If game

Full behavioral appreciation of difference between form and content

However such adjectives carry very little information themselves and greatly exercise the circuitry of their receiver in interpreting them without any assurance of accuracy. As anyone trained in NLP will confirm, such characterlogical adjectives leave much to be desired – namely the entire set of contexts in which they occur. I therefore offer a brief narrative about myself to assist the reader in their interpretative task. Out of professional courtesy, I will leave a matching description about Bandler to Bandler himself should he choose to offer that material.

Extended Commentary on Key Characterlogical Descriptions

I was born the first of nine children to Jack and Eileen Grinder in Detroit, Michigan on 10 January 1940. I was raised and educated through my bachelor's degree in a Catholic educational context.

I remember clearly that strong approval for difference was characteristic of family life, including the ability to argue rationally and at the same time with passion. The typical way this framing was expressed was that the family blood connections among the family members created a context in which difference and expression of difference could be (and typically was) articulated with great passion without fear of rupturing the bonds of family.

While education was considered the key to furthering oneself and the portal to travel and adventure, we (the children) got the message that intelligence and education were independent variables. My parents made great sacrifices to ensure that each of us secured an excellent education –

typically, parochial schooling. I attended Sacred Heart Grammar school in Detroit through the sixth grade and then St. Bridget's Academy (Pacific Beach, California – suburb of San Diego) to complete grammar school, St. Augustine High School in San Diego (Augustinian order), bachelor's degree from the University of San Francisco (Jesuit order). Completing my bachelor's degree, I elected to enlist in the US Army with an assurance I would be sent to Europe – Europe was a dream I had cultivated since a small boy.

On a single eventful weekend in June 1962, I was officially inducted as a 2nd lieutenant into the US Army, married Barbara Marie Diridoni and graduated from the University of San Francisco. After training at Fort Benning, Georgia, I was assigned to the 24th Infantry Battalion in Augsburg, Germany from where I leveraged a transfer to the 10th Special Forces Group in Bad Toelz, Germany - and lived in the beautiful Alpine village of Lenggries, pursuing activities that can best be described as the all-American boy's adventure fantasies.

My first child, Michael (John Michael) was born in Augsburg in June of 1963. My daughter Kathleen (Barbara Kathleen) was born in June of 1965 in Munich. For a complex set of reasons, I resigned my commission as a captain in the fall of 1967 and returned to the US. I enrolled in the fall of 1968 at the University of California, San Diego as a graduate student in the department of Linguistics. I spent one academic year as a guest researcher in George Miller's lab at Rockefeller University (1969/70) in New York City where I shared an office suite for most of the year with Paul Postal, arguably the best of the syntacticians of the era. Other notables besides Postal and Miller included Tom Bevers, a most able psycholinguist. I took a position as assistant professor at the University of California, Santa Cruz in the fall of 1970 where I met Bandler, who was at the time an undergraduate student at Kresge College. Thus we began the joint adventure now called NLP.

I have sifted through the relevant historical time period with the following filter in mind:

> *What classes of experience in hindsight can I identify that were most instrumental in preparing and positioning myself to create NLP in collaboration with Bandler?*

I find myself focusing on the following:

1. a hypnotic fascination with competency/excellence

More specifically, beginning as early as my first memories, I recall spending long periods of time in what I now recognize as an altered state watching and listening to people who were excellent at what they were doing. The content of their activity was irrelevant - only the grace, effortlessness and sheer competency with which they did it was of importance to me. An example may serve:

I was walking home from Sacred Heart Academy (some mile and a half or so) one May afternoon, probably in 1949. I can still hear the sound of the bees and flies buzzing around me as I crossed a long athletic field – a field where I played Little League baseball then as a kid - engulfed in the smell of the recently cut grass. As I meandered along with no great desire to reach home quickly as there were chores waiting for me there, I became aware of a different sound – a rhythmic hammering, something like the sound of iron on iron. I decided easily enough that this was so unusual it deserved a thorough investigation. I followed the intermittent sound for about a half-mile until I arrived at the front of what had once been a large warehouse or barn. The giant doors were slightly ajar, and the sound I had been pursuing issued from them. Carefully with breath held, I looked around the edge of one of the doors and there in the soft, reduced light of a forge, I saw a man, stripped to the waist, sweating profusely as he went about his work. Time collapsed as I watched the movements in the choreography of his personal dance and listened to the accompanying song of his hammering and breathing. Each movement followed the one before as surely and as naturally as night follows day, as graceful as the flight of a falcon, as sure as the strike of a cat. There was no wasted movement, no hesitation, no misstep only the choreographed accomplished sequence of a master doing what he had chosen to do. Rudolf Nureyev would have understood completely.

2. a clean behavioral distinction between form and substance, process and content

There are multiple sources for this distinction – the dominance of style and form over content in the disputes that marked the normal course of a day in the Grinder household – my mother, Eileen, in particular, is gifted with a descriptive style of speaking that enthralled all of us as children. She is so articulate that when we offered statements that failed to meet her own personal requirements for precision, for example, she would insist that we reformulate the statement in more specific terms. Surely, much of my sensitivity to language patterning and portions of what later came to be known as the meta model find their origin in these exchanges.

The Jesuits are well known for excellence in argumentation – my experience of them at USF was what I imagined someone attending an advanced school of sophistry in ancient Greece would have experienced.

The Jesuits instructed me well not only in the valid forms of verbal exchange and thinking but critically how to evaluate the relationship between a proposal and putative evidence in support of that proposal. They prepared me well for the events to come.

My experience during the so-called cold war in intelligence work in Europe and in particular, the requirement to present myself as something I most assuredly was not (a member of a national and linguistic group other than American and in a context where mistakes could easily be lethal) sharpened the form/content distinction and taught me the value of behavioral flexibility. It also greatly refined my ability to Act As If.

Finally, the focused studies in syntax at UCSD as a graduate student in linguistics simultaneously accomplished two important things for me: first, it put the finishing touches on the distinction between process and content (what is called syntax and semantics in natural language systems) and secondly, a disassociation between myself as a person and the language I use to express myself, the direct experience of recognizing that what I say, what others say of me and who I am can be entirely different realms of experience. [3]

More specifically, I came to regard language as a tool – a sharp one but nevertheless a tool to be used to explore the world and my relationship to it. In this sense, NLP seems to me to be a natural extension of a methodology from transformational grammar to a larger domain – resulting in what might best be called the syntax of experience.

Indeed, this strategy of sharply distinguishing between process and content was already explicit enough that in a textbook that I coauthored with Suzette Haden Elgin written and submitted in 1969 (some years before meeting my future collaborator in the creation of NLP Richard Bandler) and published in 1973, I proposed,

>...*these same sets of rules* (of language), *this same set of categories, that structure perceptions as well. Specifically, these categories, or rather the distinctions presupposed by them, operate on the information being carried in the nervous system at the preconscious level, performing a transformation on this material, grouping, summarizing, deleting, and in general, introducing distortions, prior to the nervous system's presenting the resultant impoverished picture of the "world out there" to the conscious mind.*

>Grinder and Elgin, *A Guide to Transformational Grammar*, page 3

>....*if our earlier discussion is in any sense accurate, then the activity called linguistics will be the single most important activity in*

liberating one's head from the structure imposed by one's native languages. In the attempt to construct an explicit set of formal statements that reflect the structure of the language being analyzed, one becomes aware of the categories and distinctions inextricably interwoven in the fabric of the language system itself. This awareness or bringing to consciousness of the systematic distortion induced by one's language system gives one the opportunity to escape from the unconscious or preperceptual distortion mentioned...

Grinder and Elgin, *A Guide to Transformational Grammar*, page 8

3. a positive affinity for what others call risk-taking

Risk seems to be the name most people give to the possibility of failing. I would immediately insist on a distinction between risk taking where failure precludes further risk taking (that is, lethal mistakes) and failures that allow further risk taking. While there are a number of episodes involving potentially lethal risk taking in my personal history, they are not the issue here; rather the type of risk taking to which I am referring is of the second class and can be usefully captured by an example:

Frank Pucelik (the third man in the initial modeling and testing of patterning in NLP) was offering a demonstration before some hundred or so people at a seminar in San Jose in the mid 70's during which he was demonstrating some anchoring format – probably, phobia cures. He was approached by several people at the end of the demonstration and asked,

How can you take such risks?

In genuine bewilderment, Frank asked what risk they were talking about. They went on to explain that to do such a demonstration in front of all these people was to take a nearly (for them) unacceptable risk. At the end of their explanation, Frank was speechless and simply walked away. For Frank (given his Viet Nam experiences) and equally for Bandler and me (with our own personal histories of risk taking), such challenges were simply a welcome and required opportunity to learn what we could accomplish in various contexts. Frank was still incredulous about the question the participants had asked him when he returned from his work and recounted his experience to me.

I somewhere came to an understanding that if my purpose was to learn, the only risk was not taking the risk. In other words, to not accept the risk and act would be tantamount to failure. To engage in the risky activity never carried the possibility of failure – how could you fail to learn?

This perception of risk taking reminds me strongly of Bateson's comment about the levels of learning (see *Steps of an Ecology of Mind*). You may punish a rat with an electric shock for entering and exploring a certain section of a maze. And the rat will learn to avoid that section of the maze but the salient point is that the rat learned – an unqualified success. In the kingdom of learning, there is no failure, only consequences.

4. a recognition of the value of formalization and explicit representations

The distinction between form and substance, process and content, spilled over naturally for me into activities in formal thinking and the creation of formal representations of common experiences: language, behavior... The model of Transformational Grammar, especially for a syntactician, is an extended exercise in mapping from intuitions to formal representations that may then lead you to discover genuinely novel ways of appreciating what you are about.

Years of the kind of thinking characteristic of Automata Theory and other formal systems has convinced me that anything can be formalized – the more relevant issues are:

    a. the mapping that occurs during the coding phase of modeling is arbitrary: that is to say, there are no inherently principled rules for mapping from some complex behaviors in the world of perceived experience to an explicit representation of those behaviors. There are no discovery algorithms. Thus the coding phase of modeling remains at present an art. How the elements to be mapped are isolated in their natural context (how the modeler segments and imposes boundaries), the putative relationships between the elements isolated, what gets mapped from First Access onto the model and what does not, the selection of vocabulary both formal and informal... are names of sets of decisions that any modeler must make. These decisions are often made unconsciously. To my mind, this situation underlines the importance of carefully keeping clearly in mind the management of two points

        1) the importance of identifying and applying explicit evaluation criteria to the modeling process – in the case of NLP models, learnability (the time and effort measurement for people to learn the model) and effectiveness (the degree to which the behavior of the learner after mastery of the model approaches the original model's behavior in quality and time).

2) the explicit recognition that the domain over which the patterning of NLP is defined is representations and representations only, and that such representations are arbitrary in the deep sense mentioned above– that is, there are multiple descriptions, each of which has utility in some context, none of which represents that strange grail of misguided human endeavor, the truth.

b. At a higher level, there is the question of the domain of applicability of modeling. The question can be posed as follows,

What are the boundary conditions outside of which modeling (the translation of tacit knowledge into an explicit form) is inapplicable?

or equivalently,

In the face of what challenges specifically, does modeling simply fall mute and collapse?

The most obvious limitation, of course, is simply that if the patterning that I wish to model has no embodiment in a person or group – if there are simply no models available who display the patterning - there is nothing to model. This is both obvious and clearly the major limitation on the technology of modeling. Such cases also point to the possibility of approaching the objective through a design process.

At present, for example, there is no human who has achieved unaided flight. Therefore, modeling never gets off the ground; it is of no relevance.

There is, however, a more subtle limitation (self-imposed) to modeling, one best made metaphorically. I am reminded of the following story. I heard it first directly from Bateson in a casual conversation.

Isadora Duncan, one America's premiere choreographers and dancers of the last century had created and performed a brilliant piece of dance in New York (sometime in the '30s). The piece was received with enthusiasm by professionals, the public and even the critics. The response was unequivocally positive. Some days after its first performance, a controversy broke out among the critics about the meaning of the various symbolisms in Duncan's dance. One critic maintained that clearly the art piece represented the struggle between the capitalist class and the working class; another cast it in terms of a gender differences and a third as a conflict across the generational gap. Each argued for their interpretation, employing every critical, analytic and interpretive tool at his disposal. Finally, one of the journalists succeeded in securing an interview with Duncan and after expressing his admiration for the work, he asked,

> Journalist: *Isadora Duncan, there are a number of interpretations of your recent work. Could you please settle the differences between these competing interpretations? What does it mean?*
>
> Isadora Duncan: ... listening to the question attentively and pausing for a minute or so in obvious thought... *If I could say it, I wouldn't have to dance it.*

Now, there are several ways (in the discourse we are developing) to appreciate this story. For example, it can be understood as a warning to would-be modelers to use the experience of being in the presence of an exquisite dancer and choreographer such as Duncan as inspiration and an opportunity to learn through imitation some of the aspects of this extraordinary woman's work. However, any attempt to map from the direct experience into language will be unsuccessful except at some mechanical level (*three steps to the left and leap, landing on...*). In other words, the modeling process would be truncated - with the portion of the modeling process in which an explicit representation is developed deleted.

Or we could take this story to mean that there are experiences that are best left untranslated, in particular, not mapped onto language structures. Equivalently, the form of the expression (in this case, the dance itself) is an essential element in creating the experience. Since the form itself – the dance – occurs at the level of primary experience, its translation into language (equivalently, the imposition of linguistic categories) omits that essential element thereby changing the impact – the watcher/listener does not respond to the verbal description as they respond to the dance itself. But this brings to mind the NLP sound bite:

The meaning of the communication is the response it elicits.

Applying this principle, it is clear how the translation of an artistic expression from the form of a primary experience to a secondary representation (language) fundamentally changes the meaning. Thus we take it that Ms. Duncan as an artist was refusing to offer a translation as she possessed the wisdom to recognize that there was no adequate way to do so without significantly changing what she had originally intended to express.

The question is, of course, much broader than whether professional artistic work is best left untranslated. Take your most intimate moments with your children – you may tell a story about some specific part of such an incident but even as you do, you recognize that even the most attentive and sympathetic (second positioning) listener will respond differently to your *description of the experience* than you did to the *experience itself*.

Further, in matters of the heart, there seems to be great danger in attempting to explicate those special experiences of such depth and richness. It seems that at least in these two areas of human experience, there is a need for caution in deciding to impose linguistic categories. The reader has, no doubt, appreciated the phrase,

>   *...I guess that you just had to be there...*

at the termination of such ill-chosen attempts.

We caution readers here about a typical misunderstanding of what we are describing here. It is clear that language and formal systems are capable of representing any experience – the question is whether the consequences of such an explication are congruent with the original intention of the mapping.

There is nothing mystical about the difference – it is precisely the difference in a restaurant between seeing and smelling the richness of a buffet and ordering from a menu – the difference between an experience and a description of an experience.

Finally associated with this point are my minimalist tendencies – the drive to identify the minimum set of patterning required to accomplish some well-defined task. This, at least in my own case, pushes me to constantly review my own work (and that of others) applying the rule of parsimony, seeking a reduced set of patterns that will serve effectively to achieve some outcome. Thus, to achieve some valued outcome is the first move, but then comes the question,

>   *Can I achieve the same (class) of valued outcomes doing less (or equivalently, with fewer tools) while maintaining the quality involved and possibly reducing the time required?*

The exploration of doing more with less seems to me to be a healthy activity in that it challenges the assumptions of the patterning and sorts for superstitious behaviors hidden obscurely therein. As an example, see the section on the *Contexts of Discovery* (in chapter 1, Part II) where the original model of NLP – the meta model – is reduced to two simple verbal challenges without loss of generality or effectiveness and with a significant gain in efficiency. Thus in the hands of someone who has mastered NLP patterning, a significant reduction in the patterning required is possible – a search for the minimal set of patterns. This movement is quite common in the development and deployment of formal systems – thus quite possibly we have here the origin in myself of the minimalist tendencies that often characterize my work. [4]

5. a positive response to ambiguity and vagueness

The activity of modeling complex classes of behavior requires a positive response to or at least a tolerance for vagueness and ambiguity. Take the process of modeling that Bandler and I undertook in patterning Ericksonian hypnosis, for example. The strategy was initially unconscious imitation of the master and only moving to a conscious attempt to appreciate what he and we were doing subsequent to having demonstrated that we could replicate Erickson's work with our own clients. This requires a certain positive embrace of (or at least a tolerance for) what others typically describe as confusion.

Confusion was no part of my experience during such modeling, nor did I detect anything in Bandler's behavior suggesting confusion. It is clear that during extended periods of practice neither one of us knew what the hell we were doing in any coherent conscious cognitive sense – we could not have offered a representation of what we were doing.

Perhaps this is a misleading description. What is closer to the mark is that we actively refused to offer ourselves, one another or anyone else a representation of what we were doing until we had achieved the criteria of successfully replicating the behavior of the source. My understanding is that we both had and indeed exercised the choice of suspending the need to understand consciously what we are doing. The tremendous advantage of such a strategy is that the longer you can suspend the need to understand consciously (up to the criteria of replication of the performances of the model's behavior) the more complete (fuller and richer) the unconsciously (primary experience) generated maps of the transforms of the output at FA are. This significantly broadens and deepens the representation of "Korzybski's territory" (actually NOT the territory but rather the already transformed representations at First Access) from which you will ultimately map onto an explicit model (post FA) once you reach criteria. It also assists in defeating the strong tendency – a movement approaching a compulsion - we seem to possess as humans to classify new experience in terms of old categories of experience already registered in our maps.

Please note that this competency – the positive embrace of ambiguity and vagueness - is essentially an issue of state management.

> *Can you maintain a state of relaxed, non-anticipatory curiosity and congruity in a context where significant demands are being made on your ability to deliver serious value?*

It seems to me in retrospect that this positive response to ambiguity and vagueness with its accompanying development of the ability to choose and maintain a state such as I described above are prerequisites for acting effectively in the world during critical phases of the modeling process.

These have interesting consequences - if you have no conscious, explicit model for what you are doing, then you learn to ACT and act impeccably, AS IF you know what you are doing. This is an absolute requirement in many cases of modeling, especially during the unconscious assimilation phase when you are attempting to reproduce through imitation the effects that the model elicits. Note as a corollary to this, talking instead of acting is simply not a possibility. To talk about something implies that you have some (albeit miniscule) piece of the processes under discussion already explicated. But this was precisely what Bandler and I with discipline refused. Thus the only course of action left to us was the one we pursued: acting impeccably. Acting as a method for provoking the world into instructing us in what works and what doesn't work in which specific contexts. This strategy stimulates the world to offer us corrective responses. Such a strategy then becomes one of the dominant research methodologies in such a modeling environment prior to coding.

Implicitly this personal organization for research (in particular, modeling) follows a radically different course than much standard "learning" where emphasis is placed on left brain conscious understanding (see *RedTail Math; the epistemology of everyday life* (working title), Grinder and Bostic, 2002) for a fuller discussion of this critical personal organization point). In this sense, the modeling technology offers a second description of learning as a counterbalance to the entrenched conscious approach current in institutions of education in the west.

For those readers who work in the field of applying patterning from NLP (or any model, for that matter) in personal change work, consider the following question:

If you were offered a description of a client prior to actually meeting the client in a professional context, would you accept and read that description?

Now relate your response to the above discussion topic.

6. a sharpened alertness for unusual events

I am uncertain about others, but at least in my particular case, the positive embrace of ambiguity and vagueness carries with it a heightened sensitivity for the unanticipated, the unexpected, the out of the ordinary - the unusual events that may open the door to new patterning. Indeed, the history of discovery of patterning in NLP (and more generally, in any scientific discipline) is littered with such examples. We offer one such example:

> *In the mid to late '70s Grinder and Bandler formed a group of people they affectionately called the whiz kids. These were talented, intelligent young people, most of whom at the time were undergraduates at the University of California, Santa Cruz. The explicit purpose the two men had in forming the whiz kids group was two-fold: first, as an informal experiment to determine the effects of placing the collection of NLP patterns in the hands of a group of young people who had as yet made no commitment to a profession (and therefore had no professional commitments to any particular belief system about what was and was not possible), and secondly, to develop a set of well-trained practitioners with whom Bandler and Grinder could push the limits of the patterning thus far coded. The tasks and experiments preformed in this group ranged from the exquisite to the bizarre. The following experience occurred in this context.*

> *John was working in the group one evening pushing to discover the limits of hypnotic regression. The subject was Maribeth, an excellent hypnotic subject and a clever hypnotist/experimenter in her own right. At the time, Maribeth had a visual impairment (myopia – lack of distance vision). At the specific point where the narrative begins, she is seated comfortably in a chair situated facing a bookcase at a distance of some 12 feet away. John used classic Ericksonian patterning to induce the altered state and to make a series of specific suggestions about regressing to a younger age. His ongoing calibration of Maribeth's physiological responses indicated to John that she was responding quite adequately.*

> *John suggested to Maribeth that when she had reached the appropriate young age (note the lack of specificity), she was to*

133

indicate that she had arrived there by allowing her eyes (which had been closed during the induction) to open. When her eyes opened, John asked her what she could see (she was already capable of speaking without lightening her trance state, having learned to do this previously). While she displayed the typical regressed physiology, movements and speech patterns of a young girl, she also appeared somewhat distressed and seemed to having difficulty focusing on what was in front of her. Looking more closely at her, John realized that she was still wearing her contact lenses.

Chuckling in mild amusement at himself for his oversight, John rapidly delivered a set of suggestions for Maribeth to mark where she was presently and allow her eyes to close, finding again that sense of deep comfort and security as she moved back to the present. When she returned to something approaching her normal state, John invited her to remove her contacts and began the work again. However, on an intuition, before beginning the induction a second time, he asked her to read the titles of any of the books in the bookcase directly in front of her without her contacts. She spent several minutes attempting to make out any of the titles but without success. Now the stage was set for an adequate test of one aspect of hypnotic regression.

When Maribeth returned fully to the regressed state she had previously achieved, John asked her to open her eyes and to tell him what she saw. She replied among other observations that there were a bunch of books on the shelves in front of her at some distance. John then began to wonder aloud whether she really knew her alphabet. She replied saucily that, of course, she did, and that she could repeat the entire alphabet from memory, a competency she then demonstrated. John immediately requested that she choose any one of the books in the shelves in front of her and tell him what letters were written on its spine. Maribeth worked her way through an entire shelf of the bookcase, reading the titles, letter by letter with no apparent difficulty. Other objects were presented at more extended distances in an attempt to discover what if any visual impairments she retained in the regressed state. None were discovered.

Finally, John carefully offered a series of suggestions that had two intentions: first, to induce amnesia as he was unsure how Maribeth would respond consciously to the information that in the regressed state, she apparently had no trace of the myopia and had demonstrated that she could see with something approaching 20/20 vision. Secondly, he suggested that in all respects but one she would return to the present, feeling refreshed and pleased with herself for having done such a good piece of work. The one and only *respect in which she would continue to operate in the regressed state was that she was to leave her eyes young – specifically at the regressed age at which she had demonstrated her ability to see without impediment. When offering these suggestions, Grinder was aware that he had no idea what they might mean but relied on Maribeth's unconscious intelligence to interpret them in some interesting and effective way. The suggestions were repeated a number of times until John was satisfied that they had been understood at the unconscious level.*

When Maribeth aroused herself from the altered state, she reported feeling quite refreshed and pleased. Her attention was quickly moved to other issues not directly relating to the trance work. During the ensuing conversation in which she, John and other members of the group participated, she gave no indication of awareness of what had transpired. Of more importance was the observation that she showed no movement to put her contacts back on. She was casually handed a sheet of paper on which Grinder had written in relatively small letters a number of questions about her just-finished trance work with him. He asked her to fill out the form to the best of her ability and signaling the other members of the group to leave her alone, he moved to another task in another part of the room, watching carefully from a distance what Maribeth would do. With no apparent difficulty, Maribeth read and filled out the form and brought it to John.

With her permission, John re-induced an altered state and requested assistance from Maribeth's unconscious, More specifically, he asked whether the unconscious had any objection to making Maribeth consciously aware of what had happened. There was no objection and he and other members of the group watched and listened with quiet amusement to Maribeth's discovering what she had accomplished. Her ability to see clearly without artificial aid lasted some days before it deteriorated – it worked better during the daylight hours than at night. Arrangements for the return of the choice to see without artificial aids required something approaching what we now refer to as the heart of Six Step Reframing in which the positive intention behind the visual impediment was discovered and alternative classes of behavior were substituted for managing these aspects while leaving her free to see without impairment.

Thus, an amusing sequence of events consisting of:

a. an oversight on Grinder's part to note the presence of the contacts being worn by his subject

b. followed by Grinder's alertness in detecting the amazing "problem" the subject, Maribeth, was having trying to see through an artificial aid (contacts) but with regressed eyes that had no need for such aid

led to recognition that under certain regressive circumstances it is apparently possible to return to physiological states that are free of defects developed subsequent to the age the subject is regressed to. [5]

Summary

These personal antecedents represent a partial listing and first approximation description of certain personal strategies proven to be effective in the complex task of modeling (in my particular case) - the core activity that defines NLP. As stated, the list is partial.

Further and of more importance, there are no doubts in our minds that there are other constellations of strategies that may prove to be as effective or superior to this set of strategies. What these strategies may be remains to be seen as modeling activity in the field of NLP develops and refines itself.

Certainly the particular (and peculiar) personal history of one of the two creators of NLP merely represents an example of one personal historical path that has led to the development of these strategies. There are, no doubt, many other and quite possibly less tortuous paths that could lead to these same competencies. [6]

Footnotes for chapter 4, Part I

1. For example, up until the late 1980s both Bandler and Grinder both verbally and in writing acknowledged one another as the co-creators of the technology NLP. Sometime in the later 1980's verbally and in the early 1990's in print – see the cover jacket to his book *Design of Human Engineering* as well as statements on his website, Bandler began to claim that he was the sole creator of NLP. Apparently, this fiction served as part of the background for his filing a suit against Grinder in the mid-1990s. As a service to the interested reader, we have reproduced a document available upon request from the Superior Court of Santa Cruz where such fallacious claims are put to rest once and for all. This is the settlement document that terminated the lawsuits filed by Bandler against Grinder and subsequently, Grinder and Bostic among others (see appendix A). A number of practitioners have asked us,

> *Is this an example of the classic anchoring change technique known as Change Personal History without a containing ecology frame?*

We have no answer to this question.

2. There are a number of other inaccurate (and from my point of view (JG) inappropriate) comments that surface in public from time to time. We mention one such: in an article in an issue of *NLP World* in the late 90's published by an acquaintance, Lucas Dirks, the statement appeared:

> *Bandler and Grinder themselves have been quarrelling over the rights to NLP for several years now. Thereby harming its image. Numerous other pairs of NLPers have demonstrated their inability to heal their splits. All this made critics yell: "If even the founders can't cope with their issues, what is the value of NLP?"*

I spoke with Lucas face to face in Finland on the occasion of both of us making presentations there, about the historical inaccuracy of the statement and my concern that such a misrepresentation would pass unchallenged into the mythology of NLP. He listened with care and courtesy, did some research on the matter and in the succeeding issue published the following statement

> *"Bandler and Grinder themselves have been quarrelling over the rights to NLP for several years now."*

> *Some colleagues have indicated, that this statement was misleading, because it overlooked the fact that Bandler filed a lawsuit against Grinder (and several other members of the NLP community). And*

137

Grinder never attempted to assert any claim to the rights to NLP. It seems that a recent court decision brought this conflict to its conclusion. So we may see it as something of the past. The court ruling will prevent Bandler from ever again using alleged ownership claims to the rights to NLP.

3. I intend a distinction between commitments made verbally and other forms of verbal exchange – in such commitment statements, what I say has a direct bearing on my willingness to carry through on such commitments and therefore raises the critical issue of congruity. Other uses of language (other than commitment) seem to me to be best appreciated as stated in the text as a tool for exploration of possibilities.

4. I (JG) have received the comment from my siblings and co-author at various times that my minimalist tendencies have absolutely nothing to do with the issues raised implicitly here from a consideration of the methodology and the philosophy of science but simple laziness on my part: something like the law of least effort:

What is the minimum effort necessary to accomplish task X?

There may be some value in this observation.

5. This incident has apparently prompted an NLP practitioner by the name of Leo Angart of Hong Kong (leo.angart@ibm.net) to develop an entire treatment regime that incorporates this strategy alongside a number of others (some NLP based and some not) in assisting people in recovering the ability to see without artificial aid.

6. In looking back over my own (JG) personal history as part of the preparation for presenting these personal antecedents, I can identify people who have had quite similar experiences (not all the experiences represented here but some of them) and who have drawn radically different conclusions from such experiences. Thus, one variable left completely out of the description is the interpretation of the various experiences. There are experiences in my personal history that form the basis for some of the competencies described above that for other people, some of whom participated with me in some of these adventures, have had the net effect of reducing their interest and effectiveness in pursuing exactly these competencies.

Part II

The Eye of the Storm

The center of a storm is an illusion of calm and quiet. It is almost as if those in the center have learned to move with the same rapidity and unpredictability as the storm. By matching such aspects of the turmoil about them, they become part of that fearsome creature, indistinguishable from the storm itself and nearly always invisible to those who strive to remain unmoved by the forces driving the torment. These then surrender to the chaos and by so doing become an integrated element of its movement.

Chapter 1: Contexts of Discovery

It is a rare and somewhat humbling experience to witness the birth of a new field of human investigation, even more so to participate in such an event. Typically we learn about the history of such events through textbooks or popularizations. In such accounts, we are treated to a rational even compelling account of a relentless parade of events, each coherent in its own right, marching past us, linked by an impeccable logic, and leading inevitably to inspiring conclusions, smoothed out by hindsight, freed of the chaos and confusion inherent in any such enterprise.

You will not find in such accounts recognition of the role of the random, the unconscious cunning, the outrageous irreverence necessary to shatter old habits of perception, the awkward first steps, the unjustified and congruent acting As If, the bemused recognition of a wholly flawed hypothesis, the long, deep, quiet, desperate nights, the fortuitous personal friendships and connections, the quickening that accompanies powerful and wholly unexpected consequences, the camaraderie that holds the enterprise together, the dead ends, the leaps of logic, the irrational and unjustified assumptions, the accidents of personal history and not least, the gifts and accidents of unconscious metaphor – all of which in the end allow you to stumble over the distinctions that then become the fundamental variables of the new discipline because in the end against all odds, it does succeed.

This was the implicit complaint that I attempted to register in writing the preface to a popular account of NLP [application] called *Introducing NLP*,

> *These two men, O'Connor and Seymour, have set out to make a coherent story out of an outrageous adventure. The jungles through which Richard and I wandered are bizarre and wondrous. These fine and well-intentioned men will show you glimpses of an English rose garden, trimmed and proper. Both the jungle and the rose garden carry those own special attractions.*
>
> *What you are about to read never happened, but it seems reasonable, even to me.*

John Grinder, Preface to *Introducing NLP*, 1989

The kind of descriptions that you find in historical accounts of the founding of a discipline are reconstructions, whether found in popularizations such as the above reference or in textbooks. Such highly selective, sanitized, and tidy accounts are in part designed to promote the prestige of the field (and sell books); in part a marketing effort to stimulate, inspire and ultimately recruit the most able of the next crop of students from our finest universities as the researchers of tomorrow.

We have a quarrel with such mystification of process– it seems a grave mistake to place giants before us as inspiring figures that loom too large for us to emulate – well beyond our personal talents and reach. Science is not so fragile as to be shaken by an honest account of actual meandering and surprising accidents that nearly inevitably accompany an event as monumental as the discoveries that culminate in the founding of a new field of inquiry.

Each scientific discipline has its methodologies and properly so. As Kuhn has compellingly pointed out, these mopping up operations in the course of what he calls normal scientific activity are as domestic as discoveries are wild. [1]

To hide the accidents of discovery serves neither the scientific community nor the larger society that looks increasingly to this community for guidance when making decisions and allocating resources. Discovery has no algorithms; it proceeds by processes themselves thus far obscure and unmapped.

Philosophers of science distinguish what they call the context of discovery as a special topic in their studies. But it is people who make monumental, world shaking, paradigm busting discoveries – people like each of you and each of us. In *Personal Antecedents* (chapter 4, Part I) and in what follows we offer a narrative of a series of discoveries and the contextual elements that played various roles in those discoveries. It is our attempt to make transparent some of the contexts of discovery and the processes by which NLP was created.

Our hope is that by doing so, you will recognize that much depends on commitment as well as talent. It is our intention that the reader identify through these descriptions how specifically you might participate in this great adventure. The two men who created this field may have through accidents of their personal history acquired unusual skills and processes but *once made explicit, such resources come within reach of anyone committed to learning and willing to act impeccably.*

Thus, it is our hope that through a careful study of the following narratives, you, the reader, will be thereby emboldened and that these accounts will stimulate you to confront the chaotic and creative aspects of discovery.

Predicting the future can be done from the safety and comfort of an armchair; creating the future requires great effort, movement and exposure.

NLP's First Model: the meta model

It was a spring evening in the early 70's when an unexpected knock at the door pulled me (JG) reluctantly from my deep focus, reading a text (Monopoly Capitalism) which I was devouring in an attempt to deepen my understanding of economics – preparation for a course I was scheduled to teach in economics beginning in a few months for Kresge college at the University of California, Santa Cruz. Opening the door, I was surprised to find a fourth year undergraduate student, Richard Bandler, standing there. I invited him in, wondering mildly what the occasion for his visit could possibly be. It was not unusual for a student to drop by, as the newly founded college (Kresge) had instituted an integrated living/learning environment shared (in principle, at any rate) by students, faculty and staff.

I had met Richard some months before on the occasion of his having been assigned to be a member of a T- group (the so-called encounter group - a contribution in semantic ill-formedness by the people from National Training Lab – one of the original American sources for group therapy) for which I had the responsibility of serving as the faculty sponsor. The rapport between the two of us was immediate – each of us sensed quickly that there were a number of shared patterns between us – not least of which was a profound commitment to do nearly anything rather than be bored.

Up to this point, our experiences together had been relatively limited and while thoroughly enjoyable, had given no indication of the highly productive, even revolutionary collaboration that would ensue. These experiences consisted primarily of activities such as painting the windows on parking meters to make it impossible for the University of California campus police to issue parking tickets; playing strange mind games in the required T-group sessions; getting our fair share of abuse at anti-Vietnam war rallies and sampling local Santa Cruz herbs.

On this particular evening, Richard's conversation moved rapidly from one topic to another in his usual amusing and entertaining way without revealing what, if any, specific purpose the visit entailed. After we had passed a pleasurable 20 minutes bantering together, he abruptly rose to his feet and made to leave. I accompanied him to door where we both paused, and with an uncharacteristic show of self-consciousness, he hesitated and then asked me if I would like to go with him. He went on to explain that he and a friend, Frank Pucelik, were doing a Gestalt therapy group nearby and that he was inviting me to come along. He said that it might be interesting to me to observe the group. I was genuinely amused by the invitation. I thanked him and explained that I had no intention in participating in any therapy of any kind. Further, although I had absolutely no experience in these matters, it was clear to me that one of the primary consequences of therapy was to adjust people to the social, economic and political context in which they found themselves exploited; and further as a committed revolutionary it was obvious to me that such activity (therapy) was highly counter-revolutionary. I explained to him patiently that the adjustment of people to an inequitable system had the negative effect of reducing revolutionary potential. [2]

This ritual – a visit ending in an invitation to accompany him to the Gestalt therapy group – was repeated several times over the next few weeks until finally, I asked what it was that he thought my visiting the Gestalt group would accomplish. Haltingly, he explained that he had listened to me describe in detail, at great length and with precision, the processes of natural language (my doctorate is in transformational linguistics) and its relationship to the structure of the human mind. He described his frustration in the Gestalt group work saying that he and Frank were excellent Gestalt therapists; but their actual goal was to teach others to do what they did, and in this portion of their endeavor, they had thus far failed miserably. Richard stated that he had hoped that I might be able to figure out how to describe what they were doing so that they might accomplish their goal of training others in the art form of Gestalt.

With the challenge thus revealed, I found myself curious enough to accompany him to the Gestalt group he and Frank were doing. A single evening was more than adequate to capture my attention – it was clear to me that each of them, Frank and Richard, while engaging in strange and (to me) hilarious behaviors were superb at assisting others in making rapid and, as far as I could determine, profound personal changes, in which their clients succeeded in liberating themselves from the limitations they had imposed upon themselves. Their work was excellent. Indeed when I later compared their work with Perls' work presented on film and audio tape, I found Pucelik and Bandler's work to be significantly more effective than the model (Perls) they were imitating.

This is a puzzle we will return to consider subsequently.

I resolved to assist them in creating a description that would serve to make what they were doing explicit and therefore learnable by the group of interested people they had collected about them.

Relevant Background

My previous experience had prepared me perfectly for such a task. The focus in my doctoral studies at the University of California, San Diego was syntax. These experiences, along with four years of undergraduate experience at the University of San Francisco under the tutelage of the Jesuits had alerted me to the leverage point which in my opinion most cleanly differentiates NLP from other systems of change work – the unequivocal and complete focus on form as opposed to content.

I can recall spending hundreds of hours during graduate school at UCSD, sitting across from an acquaintance, apparently listening with rapt attention to them rattle on about some topic they found engaging. What I was actually doing was training myself to make internal visual images of the syntactic structure of the sentences they were using in their speech. I would sit there, evidently listening intently and looking with great interest at their faces with my pupils completely dilated, forming visually these complex tree structures, and from time to time, muttering some supporting sounds such as *Really! Great! And then what happened?* These responses were apparently sufficient encouragement for them to continue, thus allowing me to go back to what I in fact was doing – hallucinating abstract structures visually. Had they thought to ask anything about the content of what they were talking about, I would have been immediately exposed as a complete fraud as I hadn't a clue about the content of these one-sided conversations.

I had already achieved some fluency in Italian and German prior to entering graduate school, having learned these languages in the context of intelligence work in Europe. In the early phases of these experiences I was struggling to master some of the fundamental patterns of these languages. On occasions I even worked hard to present myself as something I demonstrably was not, namely; competent in the local language and even on occasion as a European – always from somewhere else, of course. All this activity brought into perfect focus a particularly valuable learning: namely that it is possible to act effectively in a non-native linguistic context without actually understanding very much of what Is being said. In sum, these experiences had taught me that *understanding is in no way a pre-requisite to acting effectively in the world* – this insight would subsequently be incorporated to great advantage in NLP patterning both as an essential element in the actual modeling of patterns of excellence as well as in the appropriate positioning of the NLP agent of change in the context of applications.

So, what is the point of this digression?

The point is that these linguistic activities were the background I referred to previously as the preparation for the creation of the first model in NLP. Indeed, this is a useful partial characterization of the first of the models of NLP – the meta model contained in *The Structure of Magic*, volume I

The narrative continues

I decided to respond positively to Richard's request for help in creating an explicit representation for the patterning which he and Frank were using in order to allow them to use this model to instruct their group in how specifically to do what they were doing. I determined to follow the same underlying strategy on which Transformational Grammar was founded. More specifically, I proposed to Bandler and Pucelik that I would accomplish the task in two phases: first, I would learn to do what they were doing until we all agreed that I was performing with roughly the same effectiveness and quality within roughly the same time constraints as they were. In other words, phase I would terminate at the point where I could produce the same responses in clients that they were producing. Then, in possession of my own intuitions about what I was in fact doing based on the circuitry I had developed through imitation and with a backlog of observations of the work that Frank and Richard were doing, I would begin phase II – the explicit mapping from the intuitions developed through the competency I had achieved to a formal representation that would have the qualities of being explicit and learnable. The result of this second phase was, of course, the meta model – the first of the models in NLP.

What ensued was what we referred to at the time as the Repeat Miracle group – I would attend a Monday night group and carefully observe the patterning used by Bandler and Pucelik and on Thursday nights I would conduct my own group during which I would attempt to replicate the miracles achieved by Frank and Richard from the previous Monday night –whether my clients needed those particular miracles or not.

Whatever the ethics of the Repeat Miracle group were (if any), the regimen worked well for our joint purposes. After several months, I was, indeed, able to reproduce the "same" miracles in my group as Frank and Richard were producing in their group. The project (phase II, specifically) was interrupted by other activities on the part of each of us – I was wandering about in East Africa on an endeavor combining the linguist study of KiSwahili (supported by a grant from the University of California at Santa Cruz) and pure adventure; Richard was in Cold Harbor, Canada attending a month long seminar for family therapists presented by Virginia Satir; Frank was in Oklahoma pursuing some personal and business interests. When I returned from East Africa, Richard approached me with a proposal. He related how he had come upon a new set of exciting patterns – the ones presented behaviorally by Satir and wanted to use the same strategy we had employed previously with the Perls patterns to create an explicit model of Satir's work. His enthusiasm was infectious and we began work immediately – specifically, the phase of my internalizing or unconsciously assimilating the Satir patterns as represented by Bandler.

Given the deep rapport between Bandler and myself and the set of non-verbal signals Bandler and I had worked out in the context of my learning the Gestalt material, it was relatively easy for me to come to a competency in the new patterns. By this time it had already become clear to the two of us that there were significant overlaps in the verbal patterning of the two performers (Perls and Satir). At this point, we decided to write a book (The Structure of Magic, volume I) in which we would make explicit both the Perls and the Satir patterning. We had the intuition (which subsequently events confirmed) that we could usefully code the verbal patterning of both performers in a single model.

A Fortuitous Decision: the Coding Issue

The decision to focus on the verbal patterning of the two performers was a fortuitous one – it significantly simplified the task in two important ways:

> 1. there already existed an explicit code for capturing verbal patterning: the descriptive and formal vocabulary for syntactic studies used by professional linguists.

> 2. Bandler and I were able to cleanly sidestep the issue of imposing a structure on the non-verbal components of the behavior of the two performers. This digitalization of analogue processes is an issue of supreme importance in modeling and one for which there exists no known useful explicit strategy – there is no known useful algorithm for such an activity.

Again an analogy may serve: suppose that we (Bostic and Grinder) had the task of creating an explicit model of the movements of some exquisite dancer to allow her to more effectively and efficiently transfer her skill and style to interested students. The art of dance is an example of an analogue process – that is to say, the movements of the dancer are a continuous sequence without any obvious inherent pieces or elements to it. Of course, trivially one could produce an explicit trivial verbal model of a dance by simply identifying three elements – the beginning of the dance (the posture and form of repose presented by the dancer prior to the actual beginning movements of the dance), the middle section (all the movements succeeding the beginning of the dance and terminating just prior to the end of the dance) and the end of the dance (the final posture and form of repose achieved by the dancer at the end of the dance). However, the gross granularity of this analysis precludes it from serving as a useful model as the novice dancers interested in reproducing the dance are essentially offered no useful information about the dance movements themselves.

A more granular analysis could be achieved algorithmically by the simple imposition of a Cartesian coordinate system on a video of the dancer's movements. Thus with a running time signature, we could describe the position of any selected part of the dancer's body at any point in time with arbitrary precision. The question is, then, would such an explicit model be useful?

We can imagine some uses it could serve. For example, if we were interested in showing the difference between the model dancer and an aspiring one, we could synch a video of each with an imposed Cartesian coordinate system and demonstrate convincingly where the two differed and precisely by how much. [3] However, if the purpose of the model was to capture the skill, style and grace of the original dancer, such a model would be of little value.

When we accept the challenge of modeling a series of complex behaviors such as those offered by the initial exemplars in the creation of the field of NLP, we are faced with a series of decisions about how to chunk or decompose the ongoing flow of interactive behavior between the model and their clients into segments. Even after explicitly giving up any claim to capture the "true" or "real" representation of what is occurring, the task is formidable.

Happily, we (Bandler and Grinder) were able to avoid addressing portions of this issue by focusing our modeling initially on verbal patterning of the two exemplars we selected – Perls and Satir.

The Narrative Continues

In the best traditions of scientific activity, the two of us along with Frank Pucelik spent months restricting ourselves to only those patterns we were attempting to explicate and test – we would choose a set of verbal patterns and strictly limit ourselves to the use of only these patterns to determine what the consequences of the systematic use of only these patterns were. After a series of such sessions, we would retreat to consider the results of having used these patterns; revise the set of patterns with which we would play and then return to the world prepared to test further the repetitive question,

What happens if we do only this set of patterns?

The three of us explicitly recognized that it was clear that our reputations and, even more powerfully, our use unconsciously of non-verbal patterns of influence with our clients constituted an obstacle to sorting out the impact of the verbal patterns we were modeling. We were inadvertently influencing our clients in ways that were confounding the research we were engaged in. The three of us (Bandler, Pucelik and Grinder) attempted to eliminate such variables in order to appreciate solely the effects of the set of verbal patterns we were testing. We went to great lengths in our attempts to remove the extraneous influence [4] of these non-verbal variables - even placing filters between ourselves and our clients.

One of the ways that we accomplished this last was by refusing to enter the room where the client was – sending one or more of our students into the room, well rehearsed and strictly instructed to limit their interactions with the client to the set of verbal patterns we were exploring and then to report back to us the results of the work. They would then be instructed by us to return and execute some intervention we determined to be relevant.

Months of such intense activities led finally to the production of the meta model published by two of us (Bandler and Grinder) in the first of the books that established the field of NLP, The Structure of Magic, volume I, first in manuscript form in 1974 and then in actual book form in 1975.

The meta model represents, as far as we (Bostic and Grinder) have been able to determine, the first complete syntactically based language model for an express purpose ever created. The thirteen (or so – it depends on how you count them) verbal patterns that constitute the meta model are a highly effective verbal model for use in the specific context of therapeutic change. They are designed for the express purpose of challenging the limitations in the mental maps carried by clients who seek professional assistance in changing themselves through the processes of therapy. Under the impact of the systematic use of the meta model patterns, clients are literally forced to expand and/or revise the mental maps that contain the traps, flaws and limitations that prevent them from shifting to more effective and congruent behavior.

Commentary on the Significance of NLP's First Model

The meta model is a recursive verbal model – a collection of syntactic patterns, pure and simple. There are always two components to each of the patterns:

1. the identification of a syntactic pattern used by the client

2. a challenge which is designed to create a context in which the client will expand his or her map of possibilities or discover they have no idea what they talking about – presumably, a useful first

step to changing the mental maps which contain the limitations that are the source of their dissatisfaction.

The meta model itself is a curious mix of patterning. The myth that has been perpetuated (in significant part by Grinder, Pucelik and Bandler's original students) is that the patterns in the meta model are patterns which Bandler and Grinder discovered through a thorough analysis of the verbal patterning of Perls and Satir. The actual history is significantly different.

Several of the meta model patterns were, in fact, common to the performances of Perls and Satir:

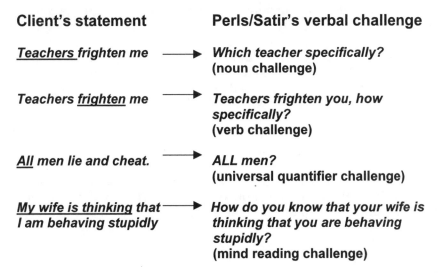

Client's statement	Perls/Satir's verbal challenge
Teachers frighten me →	*Which teacher specifically?* (noun challenge)
Teachers frighten me →	*Teachers frighten you, how specifically?* (verb challenge)
All men lie and cheat. →	*ALL men?* (universal quantifier challenge)
My wife is thinking that I am behaving stupidly →	*How do you know that your wife is thinking that you are behaving stupidly?* (mind reading challenge)

By saying that these meta model patterns were common to the performance of the original models, we are not saying that these performers used the challenges in a fully systematic way. What we are saying is that Satir and Perls used these patterns often enough that they could be identified as members of the set of behaviors which Bandler and Pucelik originally, and Grinder subsequently, reproduced in their imitation. What occurred, then, was that the three men, Pucelik, Bandler and Grinder during the imitation phase of their work, unconsciously biased their own behavior such that the frequency of use of these challenges was higher in their behavior than in the behavior of the original performers, Satir and Perls, who they were imitating. This biasing could be understood as a failure on the part of the three men to faithfully reproduce the behavior of the Perls and Satir through imitation or simply that they noted unconsciously that they obtained superior results by using the challenges listed above more frequently than the originators themselves did. Indeed, for us, these are roughly equivalent expressions, although we find the second formulation more enlightening [5].

Strategy for Achieving Competency in the Patterns to be Modeled

We find it most important to describe this process in a manner intelligible to the reader: imagine you are imitating one of the original models, for example, Perls. You have in front of you a real client, someone who is unhappy, dissatisfied with their life situation and looking to you for guidance and assistance in making a transition to more satisfactory life experiences.

On the one hand, you are committed to imitation of Perls (this is the research you are conducting); however, you simultaneously recognize a responsibility to the person in front of you. Since you have no conscious cognitive map for what you are doing (such a conscious map presupposes that you already have developed an explicit model – the very thing you are in the process of creating), so how do you decide moment by moment whether what you are doing is working?

The answer is alarmingly simple – calibration, your ability to note cleanly the voice quality differences, postural, breathing... muscle tonus shifts and even the words offered by the client as well as your ability to integrate these various forms of response to make a judgment about the congruity or incongruity of the client's response. If the responses you are provoking through the present form of imitation lead in the direction of what the client wants, continue. If they do not lead in that direction, pick any other one of the forms within the set of imitative behaviors available to you and shift to that one. This last principle, by the way, is the origin of the notorious NLP sound bite,

If what you are doing isn't working, do anything else!

If you think participatively about this complex form of feedback driven behavior (or even better, if you get off your butt and actually go out and do it), you will appreciate the difficulty of NOT unconsciously editing. In such a system, driven only by feedback and the outcome requirements of the client, you will, in fact, naturally drift unconsciously toward what works [6].

This is, in fact, an accurate description of the fundamental strategy used during the first phase – imitative behavior – of the models created in NLP in the classic era (1971-1979), and simultaneously provides us with the answer to the puzzling observation contained in the question.

How is it possible for people imitating a model to be more effective than the model himself?

Earlier in the narrative, one of your present authors (JG) mentioned that he noted at the time he began the modeling, which resulted in the first NLP model (the meta model), that the imitative behaviors of Pucelik and Bandler within their Gestalt groups were actually cleaner and more effective than Perls' behaviors as captured on film and tape. This unconscious editing process explains nicely the source of this initially surprising difference. If you were to succeed in finding some original audio tapes of the Gestalt work done by any one of the three men involved, Grinder, Bandler or Pucelik from these early days and compare the frequency of the use of these meta models challenges against a tape of Perls or Satir working (adjusting for the number of opportunities to legitimately apply the pattern), you would find that the imitators used them more frequently – significantly more frequently.

Satir also demonstrated in her behavior several other patterns that subsequently came to be coded as part of the meta model.

Client's statement	Satir's verbal challenge
My husband makes me crazy ⟶	*He makes you crazy how specifically?* (the cause-effect semantic ill-formedness challenge)
If my girl friend loved me, then she would always agree with me ⟶	*So, loving you is the same as always agreeing with you!* (the complex equivalence challenge)

So far, then, the myth is supported – with the peculiar caveat that the imitators were more systematic in their use of the patterns than the sources of those patterns. Counting the patterns thus far identified as inspired by the Satir and Perls, we have six of the meta model patterns. The question naturally arises,

Where did the rest of the meta model patterns come from?

We mentioned earlier the fortuitous decision made by Grinder and Bandler in selecting the meta model as their first explicit published model – namely there already existed an explicit code for capturing verbal patterning – the descriptive vocabulary for syntax used by professional linguists. By the time Pucelik, Bandler and Grinder had sorted out unconsciously the most effective of the verbal patterns used by Perls and Satir through the process of unconscious editing during imitation, it had become startlingly clear to Grinder –a professional syntactician – that these patterns were already very familiar to him. Indeed they represented well-studied, well-coded patterning in his professional field of expertise – the syntax of Transformational Grammar. The question immediately occurred to him,

In the well-developed, precise and large set of syntactic distinctions available to any well-trained transformational syntactician, what other syntactic patterning associated with the ones already identified might be useful in the context of processes of change?

The answer, of course, was an explosion of possibilities: nominalizations, agent deletion, multiple forms of negation, co-reference, comparative deletion, modal operators of possibility, presuppositions (33 syntactic varieties), modal operators of necessity, unexpressed performative verbs, referential index, object deletion, symmetrical predicates, transitive predicates, equivalence classes... [7]

A veritable feast of syntactic and logical patterning resulted – a smorgasbord on which to dine and dine they did! The ensuing months were characterized by a frenzy of activity as Grinder identified various syntactic patterns and the three men tested the consequences of the systematic use of these patterns in the context of change work- discarding some, retaining others until the meta model was complete.

Grinder and Bandler themselves explicitly recognize the additional source of the patterns of the Meta Model:

Since one of the ways in which therapists can come to know and understand their clients is through language, and since language is also one of the primary ways all humans model their experiences, we have focused our work on the language of therapy. Fortunately, an explicit model of the structure of language has been developed independent of the context of psychology and therapy by transformational grammarians. Adapted for use in therapy, it offers us an explicit Meta-model for the enrichment and expansion of our therapeutic skills and offers us a valuable set of tools to increase our effectiveness and, thus, the magical quality of our own therapeutic work.

The Structure of Magic, volume I, page 19

Focus of the Patterning Modeled: Form versus Content

Note that there is absolutely no attention given to content in the meta model. This absence of use of content becomes a key defining characteristic of NLP patterning in all the ensuing NLP applications models of the classic era. Roughly put, the position of an agent of change in serving as an effective guide in the change process is at a higher perceptual level than the client (what Jay Haley insightfully identified and usefully labeled as a meta-complementary position in his valuable description of Milton H. Erickson's work as a hypnotist in his *Strategies of Psychotherapy*).

Such a perceptual position is more inclusive in scope than the level at which the client is operating. From the perceptual position of the agent of change, it expressly covers both the client and a representation of the agent of change. More specifically, while the client focuses on the content of his or her experience, the agent of change focuses on a number of additional issues such as the relationship between the agent of change and the client, the mapping processes unconsciously employed by the client... By maintaining this large scope of perception and manipulating such processes, the agent of change's task is to create a context in which the client can discover appropriate alternative behaviors and patterns of action.

In other words, the client is fully committed to an exploration of the content of his or her life. The appropriate position for the NLP agent of change is to be the manipulator of the process through which the client explores this content and develops new possibilities. One of the ethics of NLP as applied to change work requires that the agent of change not involve himself or herself in the content issues being explored by the client. To do so would be to violate the special relationship between the agent of change and the client. More specifically, were the agent to comment on the content (positively or negatively, verbally or non-verbally), or offer alternative choices or in any way influence the client's ongoing exploration of content except for process manipulations, she would be betraying the special trust placed in her by the client. In fact, the complete focus by the NLP agent of change on the syntactic patterning of the client is one very precise way to meet this ethical requirement and avoid abusing this special relationship.

The ways in which an agent of change can influence his client are numerous and subtle. Freud, for example, after some initial testing of techniques involving hypnosis, cocaine and a highly participatory involvement with his clients (not all at the same time, thank god!) recognized that clients in the throes of the change process are highly suggestible and quite attentive to minimal cues from the agent of change as to whether they (the clients) are proceeding appropriately (from the point of view of the analyst). His solution was to minimize the influence of the analyst on the client by a manipulation of the physical context: facing the client away from the analyst (thereby removing visual cues); restricting the verbal responses of the analyst (at least, for some portions of the therapeutic session) to relatively non-informative prompts (*un huh, please go on, what else...* thereby reducing auditory cues) to indicate to the clients to continue with what they were doing; and placing the client on a couch while the analyst remained typically sitting (a kinesthetic restriction). Through these manipulations, Freud attempted to meet the special ethical requirements of the change process, protecting the integrity of the client. Specifically, the goal was to avoid imposing the beliefs and values of the analyst on the suggestible and vulnerable client struggling to change through verbal and non-verbal feedback.

The application of NLP to the process of change – the first context in which NLP models were developed – attempts to meet this challenge in a fundamentally different way. In the description above, we stated,

> *The appropriate position for the NLP agent of change is as manipulator of the process through which the client explores his content and develops new possibilities.*

The nominalization *manipulator*, derived from the verb *to manipulate*, is frequently a red flag among professional agents of change – we use it deliberately, with the intention of reminding all such agents of change of the special requirement their position entails. In particular, we use it in this context to point out that the strategy that NLP based change processes use to assure the integrity of clients is to restrict interaction with the client to the manipulation of process, and to leave the content entirely to the client.

In our experience, this is a quite liberating constraint – you do what you need to do to get the client what they want; as long as what you do is both ethical and is restricted to process. Let's say that you have a classic depressed client. In such cases, establishing rapport with the client and getting her into a responsive state are typically the first challenge that faces an agent of change. Given the remarks above, you simply do what you need to do to succeed at this first challenge. This could range from the classical mirroring strategy of early NLP work in which you carefully replicate the body postures, gestures, breathing patterns, voice intonation, vocal rhythms... of the client – a relatively benign and gentle manipulation; to making a meta-comment that you didn't realize how boring depressed people were; to bursting into tears and confessing that you have no idea of what to do with such an unresponsive person; to falling suddenly to the floor and faking a heart attack to secure her full attention; to accidentally spilling an entire glass of cold water in the her lap. These actions are all process manipulations, albeit with widely differing styles and consequences. This form or process versus content distinction was and continues to be critical to the development and rapid diffusion of NLP.

One of the more subtle ways in which agents of change inappropriately influence their clients – that is, manipulate them at the content level - is through *attempting to understand what the client's experience is*. Startling as it seems, the effort to understand another person's experience can be a highly manipulative act [8], independent of the positive intentions of the person attempting to understand.

We present a portion of a transcript in which an agent of change and his client are working – we invite you to attend to your own internal reactions as you attempt to understand to the verbal information offered by the client.

> Agent: *So, you're saying that there is something wrong in your marriage?*
>
> Client: *Yes, exactly, ...I'm not sure how to express this – let's just say that my husband is not behaving like what we promised one another when we first got married.*
>
> Agent: *OK, help me understand this not behaving congruent with what you promised when you first got married?*
>
> Client: *Well, you know, these things happen...after all, we have been together for over 15 years now. Things get a little stale, maybe – the grass is greener on the other side, you know...*(voice trailing off as if embarrassed to continue)
>
> Agent: *So, what are we talking about here?*

Reader, have you got the picture here? Do you see what this woman is talking about? Do you have a feel for what is and is not going on in this marriage? Do you understand? Note your response to these questions. We continue.

> Client: *It's a little hard to talk about – well, he is doing things with other people. Things that once we did only ourselves, and...* (voice breaking)
>
> Agent: *It's clear that this is affecting you emotionally in a very strong way. How do you feel?* (leaning forward and touching the woman gently in apparent support)
>
> Client: *I guess I just have to say it – even though I hate even thinking about it.*
>
> Agent: *Yes, you're in a safe environment here... go ahead, say it!*

Now, honestly decide what you the reader understand, from the point of view of the client, the issue in her marriage is.

We have several comments about the transcript:

1. the agent is obviously not NLP trained

2. he is fairly effective at not verbally hallucinating what the client is referring to. This does not mean he isn't speculating wildly about the content of the issue only that he isn't announcing his speculations

3. If he were NLP trained and were applying the meta model, things certainly would be moving along faster. For example, note what the immediate effect of applying a couple of the more basic meta model challenges would be,

First example:

Client: *Yes, exactly, ...I'm not sure how to express this – let's just say that my husband is not behaving like what we promised one another when we first got married.*

Agent: *What specifically did you promise when you first got married?*

or

Agent: *Not behaving like what you promised one another when you first got married, how specifically?*

Second example:

Client: *Well, you know, these things happen...after all, we have been together for over 15 years now. Things get a little stale, maybe – the grass is greener on the other side, you know...(voice trailing off as if embarrassed to continue)*

Agent: *No, I don't know, which things happen?*

or

Agent: *Which things get a little stale?*

Third example:

Client: *It's a little hard to talk about – well, he is doing things with other people. Things that once we did only ourselves, and...(voice breaking)*

Agent: *He's doing what things specifically with other people?*

or

Agent: *Which things specifically that once you did only yourselves?*

The point here is that if you attempt to understand someone in a context of change like this one, you will unconsciously and involuntarily activate your standard language meaning making processes at the unconscious level, the same processes by which you understand any sentences and words.

We ask the reader to visualize the following,

> ...a little kitten playing with a ball of yarn...

Now answer the following questions: what color is the yarn? What posture is the kitten in? What's the distance between the kitten and the ball of yarn? How big is the ball of yarn compared to the kitten? Is the kitten striped or a solid color, and what color...?

All of these images belong to you – you created them, you hallucinated them. The probability that those unconscious meaning making decisions, inherent in the language processes which allow you to understand, match the original image we had when we proposed the image exercise is exceedingly small. We're talking about a little kitten and a silly ball of yarn – not particularly highly charged emotional content.

To understand a word or phrase is to activate – sometimes consciously and *always unconsciously* – the set of images, sounds and feelings – associated with that word or phrase. This involves the accessing of a personal experiential base - a lifetime of associations - with the words presented. [9]

Note your understanding of the phrases:

> a. *my husband is not behaving like what we promised one another when we first got married*
>
> b. *after all, we have been together for over 15 years now. Things get a little stale,*
>
> c. *he is doing things with other people. Things that once we did only ourselves*

If the nouns and verbs in a phrase are non-specific and your intention is to understand, unless you are an extremely highly disciplined and well trained professional, you will hallucinate. Full stop!

> *Well, did you?*

Please note that the actual content of the nouns and verbs which were never challenged or specified by the agent of change could legitimately range from sexually infidelity – the hallucinations of the vast majority of people presented with this mini transcript – to the husband being involved in playing contract bridge with someone other than his wife (the client) and with a vast array of possibilities in between.

Now consider the implications of application of the verbal patterns coded in NLP – for example, the meta model. Clearly, you get to the specificity with something approaching optimal efficiency. But of more importance in the context of change processes, its application yields three extremely powerful advantages:

1. the agent of change introduces absolutely no content material. All content – all the words and their associated meanings - that are challenged for specification have their source in the client's spontaneous speech productions. The unspecified nouns and verbs are presented by the client, extracted by the agent and placed in the challenge frames, and re-presented to the client.

   > *Which _____, specifically?*   **for nouns**
   >
   > *_____, how specifically?*   **for verbs**

   This is entirely congruent with the ethics of the application of NLP to change work. This is also equivalent to saying that all the partitions over FA that occur in the interaction between the agent of change and the client are partitions (see chapter 2, Part III under *Sorting Functions*) created uniquely by the client. The agent of change is restricted in this context to the use of standard mapping operations of specification inherent in the structure of the language (a subset of the f^2 transforms).

2. The systematic use of such verbal patterning by the agent of change in the application of NLP to personal change work, if consistent and disciplined, protects the agent of change (and his client, in turn, is also protected) from the unconscious filtering created by the activation at the unconscious level of the processes of understanding in the agent – that is, the filters imposed by the activation of the images, feelings and sounds which are the meaning of the content material produced by the client in the change agent's mental map. At the verbal level, the agent focuses exclusively on detection and on the process of extracting and re-presenting to the client portions of her speech productions that are unspecified. The objective for the agent is to create a context in which, through the manipulation of process, the client arrives at a new, enlarged and enriched set of choices about her life experiences; not for the agent to understand anything. [10]

158

3. In the disciplined behavior of an NLP trained agent, the task of focusing on the syntactic structure of the client's speech patterns – that is, of identifying, extracting and re-presenting portions of the client's speech patterns in the form of a challenge - soon becomes a simple and unconscious act. This leaves the agent free to note and integrate all of the non-verbal behaviors being offered by the client. Such behaviors, largely unconscious, are nearly always a more powerful set of indicators about what is going on with the client. [11]

Evaluation Criteria for a Model

As we stated previously, the principal criterion for evaluating an NLP model is whether it works – this seems roughly equivalent to two issues:

1. *Is it is learnable?*

2. *Does it lead to the learner producing results congruent with the original source of the model?*

In the case of verbal patterning such as the meta model, the first criterion is clearly well met as any native speaker already possesses precisely the intuitions about the syntax of his or her native language that identify which portions of the client's speech are to be challenged – this is one of the contributions mentioned in the Intellectual Antecedents section as having its origin in the methodology of Chomsky's Transformational Grammar. It remains only to associate the specific challenges with the syntactic intuitions already present – a relatively simple task.

The second criterion is best left to the actual testing by the reader.

Many people find it extraordinarily difficult to focus purely on process. The content of the conversation beckons nearly irresistibly as a veritable siren on the lone rock in the moving sea of communication. The focus on content is, indeed, the cultural norm and nearly always a presupposition of what many people believe the purpose behind communication is. Now we have presented the case – in our opinion, compellingly – that, unless very special conditions [12] obtain, the natural language processes that allow us to act as if we understand one another will necessarily involve hallucinating or the creation of meaning on the part of the listener.

There is available a simple well-defined strategy that takes advantage of the natural tendency to hallucinate which is relatively epistemologically sound and nicely provocative. The source of the behavioral development of this particular set of challenges in a systematic form goes to Frank Farrelly, a gifted change agent. We offer the following narrative by way of introduction,

> On the occasion of being invited to be keynote speakers at a Frontiers of Psychiatry forum sponsored by Temple University in Philadelphia in the late 70's, Grinder and Bandler leveraged the opportunity by proposing to the forum director that he invite Frank Farrelly to work with an actual client on stage in front of the 300 psychiatrists attending the conference. The agreement was that immediately succeeding Farrelly's work, Bandler and Grinder would present an explicit representation of the key portions of what he had done – that is, they would model Frank's behavior, making his patterning explicit. Bandler and Grinder were already familiar with Farrelly's verbal patterning through his highly instructive, as well as amusing, book Provocative Therapy [13], and they had strong suspicions that they would find as well a number of non-verbal behaviors of excellence in his performance that they had already coded from their earlier research.
>
> Frank's demonstration was superb – to give a flavor of his verbal work as well as offer the reader an example of this hallucinatory strategy for specifying language, we reproduce several exchanges between Farrelly and his client.
>
> After a couple of minutes of relatively content free chatting between the two men (and during which it was clear, Frank was capturing the full conscious as well as unconscious attention of his client – typically referred to as rapport - primarily using the mirroring strategy coded in NLP), the following exchange occurred, [14]
>
> > Frank: OK, well, what do you want me to do for you?
> >
> > Client: Well, the thing that is bothering me is, well, my relationship with my wife.
> >
> > Frank: Oh yeah, I know what you mean - limited sexual positions in bed,
> >
> > Client (after a puzzled pause): No, I mean I just don't feel as close to her as I used to
> >
> > Frank: OK, I got it – the two of you are just not getting it on like you used to
> >
> > Client (again, a pause): No, that's not it – it's that we simply don't seem to talk about things together any more

Frank: So we don't talk about new ways to make it together

Client (again, a pause): No, I mean that we don't talk about the way we are raising the kids, or what we are going to do when we retire... (continuing to enumerate the specifics of what they don't talk about).

Farrelly's strategy for eliciting specific information, as the demonstration example shows, can be explicated as follows:

The Farrelly Model for Eliciting Specificity in Language

1. establish rapport

2. listen to what the client says he wants

3. select the noun or verb that seems key to the sentence and, of course, is at such a high logical level that it covers a vast number of possible specific experiences

4. deliberately invent some interpretation – that is, hallucinate floridly – some highly specific and provocative situation that technically the client could be referring to for which you have absolutely no evidence and indeed, that is highly unlikely. In Frank's work, both in this example and more generally, he shows a strong preference for using sexual content to accomplish this – however, any provocative misinterpretation will serve.

5. present this highly specific misinterpretation congruently to the client as if you believed that was what he was talking about.

6. listen carefully to the corrective response your highly specific misinterpretation provokes in the client

7. repeat steps 2 through 7 until the client (in desperation) offers you the specificity that you need to select an appropriate and effective intervention

A narrative representation of Farrelly's strategy would be to simply: get connected then select any important noun or verb offered by the client - some vague term that includes a very large set of possibilities in the world that the client could be referring to. From this set, select any highly specific and provocative interpretation that you suspect is absolutely off the mark and present it congruently to the client as if you actually believe it. Listen to the response and repeat the cycle until you achieve the specificity that you desire.

In introducing the Farrelly model, we (Bostic and Grinder) claim that it is a strategy that is:

a. nicely provocative

b. well defined

c. takes advantage of the natural tendency to hallucinate

d. *relatively* epistemologically sound

The adjective *relatively* modifying the phrase *epistemologically sound* refers to the fact the agent of change is introducing material on his own initiative rather than limiting himself to the verbal material offered by the client. Thus the contributions proposed by the agent of change clearly come from his own map and therefore may have potentially absolutely nothing to do with the experience of the client. As any experienced clinician will confirm, people struggling to change are quite vulnerable to content proposals from authority figures – a role that the therapist clearly occupies. Thus, the creations on the part of the agent of change in the Farrelly Model include the possibility of influencing the client inappropriately.

Countering this possibility is the deliberate act on the part of the agent of change to select through the process of hallucination something that is almost certainly wrong. This tends to provoke in the client a corrective response that restores the epistemological integrity of the process. Also it is clear that the agent of change is deliberately attempting (step 4) to selec something for which there is no evidence and is almost certain to miss the mark – thus, the agent of change has no investment in being right about the hallucination. This tends to correct the fact that the agent is contributing material that has its source in the internal maps of the agent himself.

The example makes it clear that it is provocative; the point-by-point strategy makes it both well defined and simple enough and it obviously taps into the ability (nearly a compulsion in many people) to hallucinate things that are not actually in the communication they are attempting to understand. We elaborate somewhat on the *relatively* epistemologically sound claim. Note that the instructions (the point by point strategy) contains phrases such as:

1. deliberately select some interpretation for which you have absolutely no evidence

2. present this highly specific interpretation congruently to the client as if you believed that was what he was talking about.

3. listen carefully to the corrective response your highly specific and provocative misinterpretation elicits from the client

All of these phrases contain epistemological instructions that are highly salutary in this context of application – you are instructed to hallucinate, recognize that you are hallucinating and put absolutely no value on proving that your hallucination is correct. The difficulty many people experience in this area are first of all, they fail to recognize that they are adding meaning which is not justified by what they actually are hearing (what we are calling hallucinating or filling in) and secondly, they invest themselves in the hallucination that they have created, attributing it to the speaker. Thus, by deliberately choosing to hallucinate, you gain certain amount of epistemological control over the inevitable unconscious processes of language. You know that you don't know what you are talking about!

The more general epistemological point is – especially as applied to patterning during modeling activities in NLP – when you find yourself personally convinced that you have discovered a pattern and you have formally coded that pattern, seek the counterexample. In particular, if the coding really is explicit (and meets the falsifiability requirement that any scientific activity entails), it is relatively short work to make precise what set of observations will serve as counterexamples. You need only then to congruently commit to creating experiences from the set of counterexamples. This epistemologically sound strategy is the inverse of the typical behavior we have noted – that is, the strong tendency once someone believes herself to have discovered a pattern is to exclusively seek additional confirming examples of the same pattern. This continuing investment in time and energy typically leads the discoverer to exercise herself greatly to prove that their pattern is correct, usually by a proliferation of examples. Further such a discoverer will typically work to demonstrate that alternative formulations of patterns covering the same ground are erroneous – with many unfortunate and unproductive exchanges as well as unseemly conflicts among researchers.

Commentary on NLP's 1st Model

These, then, are the salient points involved in the creation of the first of the NLP models, the meta model – that strange and wonderful set of verbal patterns which launched NLP and which has served as one of the chief tools in subsequent investigations, including their application in other modeling work.

It is important to be explicit about the appropriate role of the deployment of the meta model within the process of modeling. We propose that it is entirely inappropriate to apply these verbal distinctions directly with the model (the source). To do so is to confuse the respective roles of modeler and model or source. If you apply the meta model, questioning the source about their own representations of what they are doing, you are essentially asking them to model themselves – to accomplish the formidable task of making their tacit knowledge explicit. But this is precisely the responsibility of the modeler - not the model [15]

Thus we propose that the deployment of the meta model (or functionally equivalent sets of verbal patterns) in modeling activity has a specific and powerful application in the later portion of modeling – that is, after the modeler has demonstrated behavioral competency in the patterning to be explicated. In other words, the meta model is not typically utilized with the person being modeled but more productively applied to the modelers themselves during the phase of the mapping of the intuitions gained through effective imitation onto a formal or at least, explicit verbal representation of the patterns investigated and integrated.

NLP's Second Model: Representational Systems – an early breakthrough in NLP patterning

It was late one pleasant afternoon in the middle 70's when I (JG) picked Richard up at his place at 1000 Alba Road in Ben Lomond, a small mountain community up the San Lorenzo Valley some 8 or so miles from Santa Cruz. We were to begin a new group that evening – the first meeting of such groups is especially amusing and charged with expectations, as first meetings tend to be. We had little if any knowledge who the people who would show up would be, but we were certain that since they were from Santa Cruz, it would be at least amusing.

Richard asked me to stop at the Ben Lomond liquor store so that he could buy some cigarettes. As I sat in the car in front of the store waiting for him to complete his transaction, I mused over the events of the last few months as well as speculated where we were headed next. We had completed The Structure of Magic, volume I with the meta model and we were flying. The response to our work, both by local aficionados and professionals from around the country had been immediate and extremely positive [16].

We were jamming – we seemed to do little but eat, drink and sleep patterning - well, maybe there were a few other things. As Richard stepped back into the car, interrupting my reverie, he was laughing. I asked what was so funny. He said (more or less),

> You know, John, people say the weirdest things, the woman I was talking to at the counter. She said, " I see what you are saying."

He then relapsed into convulsive laughter. As I pulled onto Highway 9 heading for Santa Cruz, I watched him in my peripheral vision, wondering to myself what it was that made the statement so funny to him. After several moments, I said to him,

> Does the statement, "I feel that what you are saying is unclear." strike you as funny as well?

Bandler looked at me sharply, appearing to be simultaneously bemused and startled. We then began a very special and very typical game between us: as we drove toward Santa Cruz, we presented one another with example after example of the "same" pattern. Yet again, the game was afoot!

Please understand that neither one of us could have at that point defined what this pattern was that we were generating examples of. This intuitive opening gambit in patterning was very common between us. Both of us recognized that we were tracking a pattern and while at some point it would become useful to explicate the pattern itself, that that point still lay some distance in the future. In the interim, we were content to pursue the game.

The journey was hilarious as we continued amusing one other and ourselves with more and more outlandish examples. As we approached Santa Cruz, I pulled into the parking lot of a general store and several minutes I later emerged with a sheaf of colored paper, green, red and yellow.

When we got to the place where the group was meeting that evening (a private home), we positioned ourselves as was our custom at the front and watched and listened to the interactions among the people present while waiting for the last few to arrive. In those days in Santa Cruz, it was de rigueur to begin the first meeting of such groups by inviting each of the members of the group, one by one, to stand and present themselves, usually announcing their name and what idea, if any, they had about what they were doing there. This evening, however, as each member of the group finished their short self-introduction, either Richard or I would reach down, touch one of the three colors of paper lying on the floor in front of us. If the other one of us nodded, the one touching the paper would tear off a piece of that paper and present it meaningfully to the participant, naturally without explanation. [17]

We (Bostic and Grinder) offer several examples of typical presentations by participants to give the reader a taste of the process.

> Participant 1: *Well, good evening. My name is Linda and I feel really excited about being here with all of you. I'm kinda tingly and a little nervous. My hope is to really get in touch with myself and....*

> Participant 1 receives a yellow piece of paper

> Participant 2: *Wow! I'm looking around the group and I see a lot of shining faces. I'm George. The picture I'm getting is real focused. What I want to take a look at is my relationships with my girl friend and how I can help make our future even brighter...*

> Participant 2 receives a red piece of paper

> Participant 3: *I'm Paul. I've heard a lot of groovy stuff about these two guys here, Richard and John. Sounds to me like we gonna have a really cool time together. I was saying to myself that maybe here is the place – in other words, here is the group – where I can really tune into what's happening inside of me...*

> Participant 3 receives a green piece of paper.

After each of the members of the group had spoken and duly received their incomprehensible piece of colored paper, Richard and I gave them instructions to introduce themselves less formally to other members of the group. We instruct them that there was a particular and very important method (we acted as if everything was important in those days) to how we wanted them to accomplish this. For the first 10 minutes, they were to spend time conversing only with people who had the same color piece of paper that they had. We went on to explain that after 10 minutes, we would ask them to communicate uniquely with people who had pieces of paper of another color. We sat back to watch and listen.

The difference between the first and the second 10 minute periods was astonishing: During the first 10 minutes – the matching condition – the volume of sound in the room, the peals of laughter from different people, the animated movements of the participants, the eager and receptive postures as they connected... all spontaneous indicators of a group of well connected people.

The second 10 minutes, the mismatching condition, couldn't have been more contrasting – low volume, desultory fragments, pieces of conversation, extended periods of silence, minimal physical movement, wooden postures, minimal eye contact... As Richard and I observed the unmistakable difference between the sessions in the same group, we realized that we were tracking a very powerful pattern. We finished the group with some other material and exhorted the people in the group - who had noted the difference in the two sessions themselves – to figure out what the difference that made those differences was – obviously, we were giving instructions to ourselves as well.

Comment on the First Patterning of the Representational Systems

Although during the private debriefing session between the two of us – a ritual which was standard practice after a piece of work in which we would regale one another with stories about what had happened (and what could have happened) – we were quite clear that we had stumbled on the edge of a pattern that was quite powerful; the shape of that pattern was not yet clear.

We emphasize the importance of the style of playing with the pattern in this early phase even before we had any explicit understanding of the formal properties of that pattern. In the original game that occurred in the car traveling from Ben Lomond to Santa Cruz, the pattern – which at that time we were not competent to code was - synesthesia. Synesthesia is the name for the circuitry in the human cortex (although certainly not exclusively human) which links the various sensory input modalities and their primary cortical centers in such a manner that the cortical projection areas are cross wired. More specifically, approximately 1/3 of the visual cortex (occipital lobes) receives inputs from the kinesthetic and auditory sensory input channels, and again, approximately 1/3 of the auditory cortex (temporal lobes) receives inputs from the kinesthetic and visual input channel...

Among some of the more common experiences involving synesthesia you find listening to music with your eyes closed and watching shifting visual images (complete with color...) associated with the music (auditory to visual mapping: hear-see circuitry), the soothing feelings experienced when listening to a speaker who has excellent command of his or her voice and constantly uses tonality, rhythm, intonation contour... to enhance their presentation (auditory to kinesthetic: hear-feel circuitry), the feelings of exhilaration you achieve (especially if you have some previous experience in the particular art form and you mirror with micro muscle movements what you are observing) watching to a superb dancer or athlete perform exquisitely (visual to kinesthetic: see-feel circuitry)...

Some researchers use the term *synesthesia* rather more tightly – to refer only to those cases where the person who is experiencing the synesthesia does so involuntarily. In other words, in the above examples, the person having the synesthesia experience chooses to have the experience and is able, if they so decide, to terminate it. The clinical use of the term is sometimes restricted in use to a person who apparently has no choice about initiating or terminating the process. We use the term more generally as it seems to us that such experiences are a natural part of the legacy of being human. [18]

Now with this distinction, we can explicate the pattern implicit in the descriptions of the context of the two incidents: the game Grinder and Bandler had played on the car trip to Santa Cruz and the awarding of different colored pieces of paper in the initial group meeting. Note in the first instance, the examples:

> I <u>see</u> what you are <u>saying</u>

> I <u>feel</u> that what you are <u>saying</u> is <u>unclear</u>

Analysis: note the underlined predicates (verbs and adjective) are specified with respect to the sensory modality they presuppose. The following classification makes this explicit:

<u>Participant's predicate</u>	<u>Representational system indicated</u>
see	**visual**
saying	**auditory**
feel	**kinesthetics**
saying	**auditory**
unclear	**visual**

A diagrammatic representation showing the cross modality mapping, then, of the entire sentences involved would look like the following:

168

I see what you are saying

visual ————▶ auditory
(*I see*)   (what you are saying)

I feel that what you are saying is unclear

kinesthetic ——▶ auditory ————————————▶ visual
(*I feel*)   (*what you are saying*)   (*is unclear*)

Thus, what we were intuitively doing was generating examples of the set of well-formed American English sentences that reflected synesthesia linguistically as their defining characteristic. [19]

These synesthesia patterns play a part in a number of places in NLP patterning. In particular, we are thinking of their use in the sub modalities work (e.g. the Swish pattern) and in metaphors [20] where they serve as the neurological base for these classes of patterning.

The second group of patterns – the mini-presentations of the participants at the initial meeting of the new group – is actually significantly simpler than the synesthesia patterns. They are examples of the use by the speakers of predicates that are specified with respect to the underlying representation system activated and operating as the base for the person speaking. The examples previously offered were,

> *Well, good evening. My name is Linda and I <u>feel</u> excited about being here with all of you. I'm kinda <u>tingly</u> and a little <u>nervous</u>. My hope is to really <u>get in touch with</u> myself and...*

<u>Analysis</u>: all of the underlined predicates are solidly kinesthetically (feeling) based and indicate that at the moment, the speaker is using their kinesthetic representational system (feelings) as the base from which they are unconsciously selecting their specific words to communicate.

> *Wow! I'm <u>looking</u> around the group and I see a lot of <u>shining</u> faces. I'm George. The <u>picture</u> I'm getting is real <u>focused</u>. What I want to <u>take a look</u> at is my relationships with my girl friend and how I can help make our future even <u>brighter</u>.*

<u>Analysis</u>: the underlined predicates in this presentation are clearly visually based.

I'm Paul. I've <u>heard</u> a lot of groovy stuff about these two guys here, Richard and John. <u>Sounds </u>to me like we gonna have a really cool time together. I <u>was saying to myself</u> that maybe here is the place – <u>in other words</u>, here is the setting – where I can <u>really tune into</u> what's happening inside of me.

<u>Analysis</u>: The underlined predicates are resonantly auditorily based.

The selection of predicates under normal circumstances is an unconscious act – this makes it particularly valuable to the trained listener as the speakers are thereby revealing what their present ongoing underlying activated mode of thought and processing is, typically without any awareness that they are offering such information. It is relatively simple to develop significant states of rapport by the simple strategy of tracking (that is, following the lead of) the representation system preferred by the person you are attempting to achieve rapport with – as they shift from one representational system to another, you simply adjust your communication to remain in synch. [21]

Needless to say, such a formal manipulation facilitates the effective and efficient transfer of information as both parties are presenting their material in the same representational system.

The Narrative Continues

What ensued subsequent to our (Grinder and Bandler) initial analysis of what we had done at this group meeting is particularly interesting. For reasons now lost in the mists of memory, the next 5 or 6 days immediately succeeding the work in the group and the debriefing which followed hard upon it, Bandler and Grinder were separated physically. One or both of them were on a trip out of town. When they met again, nearly a week had passed since the group work and debriefing. Their encounter is highly instructive. Once again, with all respect to the actual exchange, something close to the following happened:

    Richard: Hey, what's happening!

    John: Hey, you know as well as I do!

    Richard: So, you've seen it!

    John: How could anyone miss it!

The non-referring pronoun *it* in the above exchange, of course, refers to what we now call eye movement patterns. The furious conversation that followed this somewhat enigmatic exchange revealed that each of the two men in the week that had passed since the work and debrief during which they had had no contact had had very similar perceptual experiences. More specifically, with the auditory filter for representational systems predicates cleanly in place, they had both been astonished by the regularity and obviousness of the associated eye movements – it was, as they say, as if the scales had fallen from their eyes. The astonishing part was not that each of the men had independently discovered the eye movement patterns – as one of them in the exchange says, *How could anyone miss it!* – but that they could have failed to notice this obvious pattern previously!

Grinder and Bandler coded their independent observations into what has now become known as the funny face:

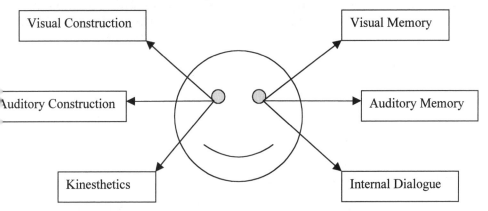

perhaps the most commonly recognized popular icon of NLP. They were struck with the simplicity of the pattern while sensitive to handedness (a common measure of so called cerebral dominance) as well as its robustness – independent of culture and language. [22]

This provided them with the opportunity to test whether others, given the original reference point – the predicates specified for representational systems – would find the same pattern. They then challenged a number of their students to find this pattern. This exercise proved highly successful as the majority of the students so challenged succeeded in finding the same set of eye movements that the Grinder and Bandler had originally independently discovered. [23]

There are few NLP patterns that can be justly claimed to be original discoveries by the co-creators of NLP (as opposed to modeling of patterning already present in the behavior of highly effective people albeit intuitively). The discovery of the eye movements represents one such original piece of research on the part of Bandler and Grinder. The majority of patterns coded by NLP are the result of the modeling of high performers (mapping from tacit knowledge (behavioral competency) to an explicit model; or borrowings from various fields such as linguistics, neurology and others. For example, subsequent to coding the eye movement patterns, Grinder and Bandler raided the Science Library at UCSC and educated themselves (as far as one can through a search of the literature on a subject) about the set of neurological studies that were in any way associated with their observations of the eye movements. Sure enough, there buried in the literature they found a set of studies conducted in the '50's in which neurologists had discovered that the movement of the eyes from a position at rest focused directly at the center of the field of vision to either side activated the contra-lateral hemisphere – thus, if the eyes move from center to the right in a lateral movement, the left cerebral hemisphere is activated, and vice versa. The identification of the significance of the vertical dimension and its coding apparently is an original piece of patterning and coding by Grinder and Bandler.

Commentary on NLP's 2nd Model

This second example from early NLP practice contains a number of noteworthy features of interest to the student of discovery processes:

1. the competency to suspend any conscious requirement for definition of what you are doing (or attempting to do) initially to allow a full and natural development of the patterning at FA.

2. the ability to generate intuitively (or unconsciously, if you prefer) additional members of the set under investigation without a rigorous representation of what precisely that set is.

3. the ability to act *as if* you know what the hell you are doing when, indeed, you have no conscious clue.

4. the ability to tolerate high levels of ambiguity and vagueness (two independent set of experiences) in the initial stages of investigation.

5. the ability to manipulate contexts in which the consequences of what you suspect is happening manifest themselves in ways that are unmistakable (e.g. the colored pieces of paper at the initial group meeting and the resultant difference in behavior of the people in the group).

6. the fixing of a reference point (the representational system predicates) that creates the illusion of stability in perception to facilitate correlating additional behavior with it as part of the discovery process (the eye movements patterns).

7. the deep value of collaboration – working in a team which allows cross verification of observations.

NLP's Third Model: The Milton Model

In 1975, Bandler, Grinder and Bateson all had their individual residences at 1000 Alba Road, Ben Lomand, California. The manuscript version of what would be published later that year as The Structure of Magic, volume I had been circulating among an excited group of people who had collected around the three men, Bandler, Grinder and Pucelik and who were assisting them with their research. Bateson had been provided with a copy of this manuscript some weeks earlier – Grinder and Bandler hoped that he would recognize what they had attempted to accomplish. Their hopes were more than met when they were invited by phone to come over to Bateson's place where they were treated to an intellectual feast – a remarkable and stimulating discussion with Bateson that lasted hours.

Gregory had a long wooden table in his dining room – one worthy of a mythical Norseman, rough-hewn of dark wood and sturdy. Gregory pointedly positioned himself at one end of this monstrosity as if conducting court and indicated to the two younger men to seat themselves immediately at his right (Grinder) and left (Bandler). The conversation that ensued was enchanting. It is noteworthy (and it seemed so even at the time to Grinder and Bandler) that Bateson's command of the patterning worked up in the manuscript was so complete that little time was spent on actually discussing it. [24]

Gregory offered a soliloquy, in large part reminiscences of the research he and his colleagues at MRI had conducted and then a strangely semi-apologetic rendering of (as he later clearly stated in his Introduction to The Structure of Magic) how he and his associates could have missed what we had, in fact, discovered and coded in the book – "how well the argument flowed from the linguistics, how confusing it had been to attempt what he had done starting with pathology and cultural patterns." He graciously offered to write an Introduction to the book and then, as if rousing himself from an old and repetitive dream no longer of relevance, he fixed each of us in turn with his deep intellectually unforgiving eyes glinting with curiosity and intelligence and said,

> *OK, boys, what you have done is very good, but I am certain that what's in The Structure of Magic happened some time ago – my question is what have you found since coding the meta model.*

We were enchanted – here was a man, easily recognizable as an intellectual giant, who understood well enough what we were about, to leap to the new sets of patterning that were obsessing us at the time.

Well done and...

Richard and I listened to his question in awe, looked at one another with perfect agreement, paused like cliff divers to mark the importance of that point of punctuation in experience before committing and then released a great wave of descriptions that flowed from us without effort.

Buoyant now, Gregory orchestrated us beautifully – he would sit listening intently to the two of us as we rushed forward into the patterning as if pursued. Sometimes one of us spoke, sometimes the other, sometimes both of us simultaneously as if attempting to fill his vast intelligence with our observations. He sat there between us, his eyes fixed at that special point above the horizon, processing thoroughly the reports of months of our work.

From time to time, he would freeze the cascade, breaking the spell, leaning back in his chair, dropping his gaze to point on the great table forward and to his left, shaping the question that would guide these two madmen into shallower water - the question that would complete the pattern that connects in his rich internal kingdom, assembled over 7 decades of participation with intelligence in the world about him, the answer he wanted to continue his incomprehensible process.

We were like two dogs, attempting to guide their master to where they believed he wanted to go, sometimes dashing on ahead, sometimes nipping at his heels, always attentive to his cues, always loyal to his intention.

The three of us arrived together then finally at the end of our long climb, exhausted and exhilarated. We sat back now, more thoughtful, no longer driven into the new, and presently curious about the now.

There was a new tone in his rich voice – one suggesting deeper emotions than thus far expressed. The sharp edge of his intelligence that had flashed brilliantly throughout the long climb was sheathed. No doubt, among the dozens of case studies, the life stories, each with its own compelling set of metaphors, something had stirred deep within him for the first time in a long time. He quietly recounted certain events from his youth, the loss of his dear brother John and of choices in Switzerland not pursued - all as if musing to himself, comfortable in our attentive, but passive presence. He worked it out finally then to his own requirements; and turned his attention once again to us.

His counsel now rolled softly from him to us, a reciprocal wave, but more refined and precise. He spoke of many things in this way – I will mention but two:

He asked how long we had been working together, collaborating. We responded, "Three years about" - He urged us to savor every moment as such productive and revolutionary collaborations were rare occurrences and often short lived. Richard and I caught each other's eye, confirming with a twinkle the confidence that only comes with certain knowledge of immortality and an irrevocably granted exception from the patterns other members of the species labored under. [25]

He asked who else we had presented these post Magic I patterns to – we replied, "To no one other than you." He indicated he was unsure of what positive steps to take but he finished his advice by pointing out that

> *....they burned Joan of Arc for less than you have presented me here this afternoon.*

One week after this remarkable meeting, Gregory again called us to his home and urged us to put our modeling skills in service of a dream he had carried for decades. In the '30's, married to Margaret Mead, and during the preparation for doing joint anthropological field work in Bali, the two of them had recognized the need to educate themselves on the fundamentals of altered states of consciousness. It had already been well documented that the Balinese officially enter trance states as a normal socially expected and accepted way of achieving the performance states involved in certain artistic activities such as dance. After making extensive enquiries, they learned of a renegade physician psychiatrist who had the reputation for being the most skillful of the practitioners of medical hypnosis, Dr. Milton H. Erickson. Their time spent with Dr. Milton Erickson had convinced Gregory of the man's genius in unconscious communication. Many years later when Gregory was heading up the MRI investigations, he dispatched a number of members of his research group including Jay Haley and John Weakland to Phoenix where Dr. Erickson lived and practiced his arcane arts. As Gregory said wryly during this conversation with a bemused look,

> *They all returned entranced by their experiences of the old man!* [26]

By this time, Richard and I had some familiarity with Erickson's through reading some of his published work and had already determined that we would seek access to this remarkable man. Richard immediately responded that he was prepared to leave now for Phoenix. Imagine my surprise to hear my voice uttering the words,

> *Thanks, Gregory, but I'm not ready to do the modeling of Erickson yet.*

We assured Gregory that we would do the model but not yet. Richard did not understand my hesitation – how could he, when I, myself, could not articulate it. I knew enough not to go... yet.

More than three months passed before I succeeded in sorting myself out and achieved a state of congruity about going to Phoenix. Richard was delighted – we called Gregory who likewise expressed genuine pleasure at the news. He confidently told us to go ahead and get on a plane – he would meanwhile call Dr. Erickson and make the arrangements. He instructed us to call as soon as we got to Phoenix. We arrived the following day in Phoenix, checked into a suite at one of the chain hotels there and called Gregory. To our dismay, he explained that he had spoken to Erickson and that while he was quite interested in meeting us, he had just finished the annual meeting of the Society for Clinical Hypnosis – a taxing event for him and that he was sequestered with his three closest students for the next few days. [27]

We finished the phone call, looked at one another and went to work. We took a copy of the bible (Advanced Techniques of Hypnosis and Therapy, a rich compendium of articles written by Dr. Erickson with Jay Haley acting as editor) and located a number of trance inductions inside various articles. We read these inductions to one another for the next hour or so until we agreed on how to extract from the patterning what we believed we would need for our purposes. We spent several hours analyzing these inductions, sorting through its various patterns until we thought we had a template. The distinctions in the meta model and the fact that Erickson's work is so well done made it quite easy to sort the content from the form. In all the content spaces we removed material Erickson had used to elicit the responses appropriate for the client involved and inserted variants of the two messages we wished to present to Dr. Erickson:

> *Make time now!*

> *See us now!*

And sometimes daringly enough even

> *Make time to see us now!*

We wrote out portions of the transformed version of Erickson's own inductions with the new messages embedded. We then flipped a coin. I won – I was the one who got to do the induction on the phone with Dr. Erickson. I insisted that Richard listen on the phone that was in the bathroom, out of my line of sight with a washcloth stuffed in his mouth. Doing this task would require all the focus I had – I neither needed nor wanted any distractions from Bandler – not in the form of laughter or even giggles.

I placed the call to the number that Bateson had given us – Richard picked up the other phone in the bathroom. After convincing Betty Erickson, Milton's wife, and a very good hypnotist in her own right, that her husband really did want to talk to me, [28] *I heard a deep riveting voice spoke into my ear,*

> *Yeeees, this is Dr. Erickson.*

I could clearly hear his breathing and I said,

> *Dr. Erickson, this is John Grinder – Gregory Bateson sent me.*

and without pausing, I began the induction. For two and a half minutes (we had timed it before the call), I moved through the induction containing the messages we had inserted, using to the best of my then quite limited knowledge the master's own patterns. I was greatly encouraged by the slowing of his breathing and his continued acceptance by his silence of the induction I was presenting. I finished the induction by slowing my voice and simply finally stopping. A good 30 to 45 seconds followed (an eternity for me), then there was a quickening in his breathing and he simply said,

> *"You boys come over here immediately!"* [29]

The succeeding 10 months were filled with strange and wonderful experiences – we would spend 3 to 4 days with Erickson in Phoenix watching, listening and modeling him with micro muscle movement as he worked with his patients. Then we would rush back to California to torture anyone who came within hearing distance with the patterning we were obsessively attempting to master.

Hours daily were devoted to disciplined practice, both in official contexts and in any context that presented itself – the waiter fixing the Caesar salad at our table suddenly found his feet were glued to the floor and was unable to walk away.

Then there was the woman who had the good fortune to occupy the center seat between the two of us on a flight to Phoenix. She began the trip sneezing and coughing and finished without a symptom and all we did was talk to one another past her quietly about the dry desert air and its healing qualities.

We arranged re-induction signals with our clients once we had convinced ourselves that we had mastered the induction phase of the hypnotic encounter to save time since we wanted now to focus on utilization of altered states. Everything was hypnosis, nothing was hypnosis, the roof creaked, the floor trembled!

We were quite disciplined in refusing to attempt any overt analysis – it had been clear to us even before meeting Erickson directly that some of the syntactic variables that informed the meta model were involved in some interesting way with the linguistic patterning of this genius. However, we rejected any explication until we were satisfied with our behavioral competency in eliciting the same responses from our own clients that Erickson had both unselfishly demonstrated to us in Phoenix and had so carefully detailed in his articles. We set out to reproduce every hypnotic effect in the bible (Advanced Techniques of Hypnosis and Therapy) as well as those we had observed first hand – we were flaming zealots.

As before, Richard was ready before I – three times he proposed that we write it – the first volume of what came to be known as Patterns of the Hypnotic Techniques of Milton H. Erickson, M. D. - and three times my response was, Not yet, bro'

Once I had achieved the internal congruency, the actual writing of the first draft of the book (volume I of Patterns of the Hypnotic Techniques of Milton H. Erickson, M.D.) by Bandler and myself was accomplished in a single marathon of some 36 hours - the subsequent clean up and polishing less than 8 hours.

Methodological Commentary

The model that captures some of the patterning of Erickson – the so-called Milton Model – was arrived at through a subtractive process. This process is so essential to the modeling of any complex system that it deserves at least an initial description.

We had assimilated Erickson uncritically during the unconscious uptake phase of modeling and demonstrated to ourselves, one another and our unwitting clients through imitation that we had mastered certain portions of his hypnotic patterning. The process of decoding ourselves took the form of challenging the superstitions we had temporarily accepted by suspending both belief and the requirement to understand consciously what we were doing in favor of experience driven by feedback. We had committed ourselves to a disciplined daily practice of reproducing Erickson's behavior with high fidelity. Our mark was to develop a reliable, consistent ability to elicit the same category of responses from our own clients that we had witnessed Erickson achieving with his clients in roughly the same time frame and with roughly the same quality. This criterion would ensure that we had captured behaviorally (in our own neurology) representations that were functionally[30] equivalent to Erickson's own behavior. The challenge that now confronted us was to sort out which behaviors (and the corresponding underlying circuits) were essential to the enterprise of inducing and utilizing the altered states of consciousness for which Erickson was so well known; and which behaviors were simply stylistic or purely idiosyncratic.

What is at stake here is the ability of determining the difference between a pattern and the noise in which the pattern is embedded. This issue contains an important methodological point.

In the standard design of medical, pharmacological or psychological experimentations, for example, the experimenter wishes to explore the possibility that the some treatment regimen or chemical substance has a certain effect on some identified population. The experimenter will assemble an appropriate representative group drawn from the population that is of interest. Either through random assignment of members of this population or through an assignment designed to balance the two groups with respect to the variables the experimenter suspects are of importance, she creates an experimental group and a control group. She then administers the treatment or chemical substance to the experimental group and expressly not to the control group. The control group in the case of a pharmacological study will receive a placebo (an alleged inert substance) or in a psychological study an amount of contact time with a professional equivalent to the contact time the experimental group is being offered. At the termination of the study, the researcher will use some measurement system to determine whether statistically the two groups differ greater than can be anticipated through random variations. If such a difference is discovered, the treatment or drug is declared effective for a specified percentage of the population.

Let us refer to this standard experimental design as additive. The experimenter is testing whether *the addition of some condition* (treatment regimen, drug…) produces a difference in what is accepted as otherwise equivalent population (the experimental and the control groups).

The methodology Bandler and Grinder applied in the coding of the set of differences which distinguished Erickson's superb performance from average practitioners of medical and psychiatric hypnosis can usefully be described as turning this standard design on its head – it is a subtractive strategy. The sequence of events that describe the modeling of Erickson (and the other studies of genius that created the field of NLP), was:

A Punctuation of the Modeling of Erickson

1. the identification of an appropriate model (Erickson)

2. the assimilation unconsciously of the patterning used by the Erickson through rigorous imitative practice over an extended period of time positively eschewing any attempt to understand consciously what we were doing.

3. the evaluation of ongoing results strictly through feedback

4. upon reaching criterion – the ability to behaviorally elicit the same set of responses from our patients which were typical of Erickson in the same time frame and with the same quality – the sorting of the behaviors mastered into two sets:

    A – the set of differences essential for eliciting the same responses

    B – the set of differences that was accidental or idiosyncratic to Erickson's style

5. the codification of the differences, mapping them onto a description which allowed an efficient and effective transfer of these differences to interested parties, using the same criterion as that mentioned in step 4 above.

6. the testing of the model through actual transfer with the attendant modification until the transfer was acceptably efficient and effective.

The point we are pursuing here is that contained in step four. Steps two and three of the modeling project ensure that the modelers have assimilated the essential patterns of the model with a minimum of conscious filtering (suspension of f^2 filters). Step four guarantees that the modelers are performing with approximately the same effectiveness as the original model or source of the patterning. Unfortunately, the modelers through the use of unconscious imitation have typically also assimilated portions of the model's behavior that are irrelevant to achieving the powerful results typical of the work of the model. The modelers may be said to be in a state of unconscious competency – that is, they are effectively reproducing the behavior of the model but they are still imitating and have no conscious understanding (no explicit model) of what they are doing. They can be usefully said to have tacit knowledge of the patterning that originated with the source of the patterning.

Step four is focused on the sorting of essential from accidental differences and is a non-trivial task. In particular, it requires a dance between the actual behavior and the way it functions in the larger set of differences being coded with special attention to the intention behind the various behaviors. An example will serve well here.

Erickson was partially paralyzed at the point in his life when Bandler and Grinder met him. This condition had given rise to certain behaviors that were clearly adaptations to his physical condition. For example, he had the habit of placing a small pillow on a retractable shelf which was pulled out from his desk (the one normally used for a typewriter [31]) and holding his right hand in his cupped left hand, he would lean forward resting his left elbow on the pillow to support the weight of both arms.

Further, except for very special occasions, he wore no prosthetics for his missing upper teeth and thus was largely toothless (although only in the strictly dental sense). This last condition resulted in a certain style of articulation when speaking.

Consistent with the disciplined non-cognitive assimilation phases (steps two and three in the above outline of modeling), both Grinder and Bandler spent months doing hypnotic patterning in an imitative mode including the reproduction of Erickson's characteristic posture (right hand resting in their cupped left hand) and his style of articulation in voice (the result of his missing upper teeth). After some ten or so months of diligent practice, both men were in agreement that they had achieved a mastery sufficient to consistently elicit the same class of responses with the same speed and quality – thus meeting the criteria for initiating step 4.

The specifics of the anti–superstition program are simple enough to describe. Grinder and Bandler would take two clients as close in problem presentation and style as were available. They would then do a piece of work with one of the clients using all the behaviors typical of Erickson's work which by now had been mastered by each of them as part of their disciplined practice. They would carefully calibrate the responses of that client. They would then take the second client and run the same set of patterns as in the first case *with the exception that they would deliberately leave out some single Ericksonian behavior [32] that they had included in the first case*. They would then evaluate the results, comparing the results they obtained with the two clients. The key question was,

> *Did leaving out the particular behavior that distinguishes the treatment offered to the two clients make a difference in the results?*

If the answer is yes, the behavior involved will be maintained as a conditionally essential part of the model. If no differences emerge, the behavior is apparently an accidental or idiosyncratic behavior that can be safely discarded without reducing the effectiveness of the model - so far, so good, simple enough.

Note all this sorting behavior presupposes several competencies not obvious in the behavior of the general population. Among these, we can identify:

> 1. a formal or syntactic frame of perception – it is our impression that the vast majority of people, professional or otherwise, when faced with the strong emotional content typical of therapeutic encounters do not respond by applying a perceptual filter which decomposes the experience into its elements. More typically they respond emotionally to the content. This formal, syntactic filter, then, is an essential element for modeling.

> 2. a command of behavior within oneself that allows you to segment your own behavior in a highly charged emotional context with grave responsibilities and consequences resting on your ability to deliver results. More specifically, you maintain the ability to decide which pieces of behavior to apply and which to leave out as part of the anti-superstition program being here described.

Continuing with this specific example, both of the men were certain that given their filter for decomposing Erickson's behavior into its component parts, they could safely discard both the posture (right hand held in the cupped left hand) as well as the characteristic voice quality which resulted from Erickson's lack of upper teeth. Each of them tested these intuitions with direct experience – that is, each of them ran double sessions with "matched" clients, in one case using the posture and in the second, leaving it out. The results, as anticipated, showed no detectable difference in the consequences obtained – so far, so good.

A Coding Puzzle

Imagine their surprise when they discovered with "matched" clients that dropping the characteristic voice quality produced by Erickson's lack of upper teeth resulted in a fundamentally different set of results. Did this mean that future practitioners of Erickson's patterning were condemned to reproduce the voice quality which were originally associated with his lack of upper teeth? Were Bandler and Grinder themselves now restricted in the use of their voices to this strange voice quality? How in the hell was such a result possible?

Fortunately there were other clues in the system. The solution to this modeling puzzle emerges naturally when the larger system is taken into account. The two men had noted that Erickson used two voices systematically although both were clearly influenced by his lack of teeth. At the end of a session with a client where he had used an informal induction, Erickson would shift the qualities of his voice slowly, articulating the words more and more clearly, slowly accelerating the speed of presentation in his voice, raising the pitch of his voice gradually… The result was that the client "spontaneously" aroused himself from trance, reoriented to the concrete external context and achieved something approaching a "normal" (for that particular person) state of consciousness.

The fundamental observation is that Erickson used two distinct voices systematically [33] – one voice that was used when he wanted his client go into or maintain a trance and the second when he wanted his client to maintain some consciousness in his presence. Thus the voice differences can be usefully thought of as dynamic anchors used expressly to inform the client's unconscious that state Erickson wanted them to enter or maintain as part of the ongoing relationship between them.

In the larger system, the contrast – the relationship between the two voices - was the point as it served to inform the client about which class of responses Erickson was requesting. Thus the relationship between the two distinct voices offered a resolution to the modeling puzzle confronting Grinder and Bandler (Erickson's voice quality), the two men asked the question,

> What is the intention served by Erickson's systematic use of two voices?

The answer that emerges is,

> To offer a signal (a dynamic anchor) to the unconscious of the client to inform him or her which state of consciousness or unconsciousness the hypnotist is calling for

As soon as they were able to make this explicit, Bandler and Grinder were able to generate a set of options – that is, other ways to offer a signal to the unconscious of the client to inform her or him which state of consciousness was being requested by the hypnotist. Clearly, other voice qualities, distinct from the missing teeth voice quality would therefore work as well or better than the original behavior – the imitation of Erickson's voice with the missing teeth - as well other dynamic anchors such as spatial displacement of the voice, change in intonation contour…

This extended commentary is designed to alert the reader to several coding issues. These include the utility of using contrast; of examining the larger system in which the behavior in question occurs; and making explicit the intention behind that behavior. These serve as tools to sort out during phase four of modeling those elements in the behavior of the model that are essential to the endeavor and those that may be dispensed with after behavioral mastery has been achieved by the modeler. Such a subtractive, anti-superstition program is essential to the modeling of excellence.

Summary of Chapter

We trust that the three examples just described offer the reader some insight into the contexts and processes of discovery that actually resulted historically in the creation of NLP. While we have offered commentary on certain portions of the descriptions of the contexts and processes of discovery themselves, the direct description contains many important points beyond our comments. We urge the reader both to study the descriptions directly and to seek out opportunities to put this class of patterning described into play to determine for yourself through action how to participate effectively in the modeling of excellence.

Footnotes for Chapter 1, Part II

1. Thomas S. Kuhn offers a series of brilliant studies on the sociology and philosophy of science. We highly recommend his work – see especially, *The Essential Tension* (1959), *The Structure of Scientific Revolution* (second revised edition, 1970), and *The Road Since Structure* (2000).

2. Such complete self-assurance arising from total ignorance was (and in some places still is) a sign of revolutionary fervor – ahh, the advantages of the clarity and the certainty of fanatical belief systems. This should not distract the reader from the actual point made- one that remains in full force.

3. Such programs have been in use for some time in the training of athletes at the professional level and more recently have been offered for amateurs in some sports. In golf, for example, an aspiring golfer can compare his swing with a model professional through such a synched overlay.

4. Extraneous only in the sense of confusing the research on the effects of the verbal model we were attempting to weave together. Under more typical conditions - where the sole objective of the encounter between agent of change and client is to achieve the client's goals - the influence of non-verbal factors is dominant.

5. Such unconscious editing is typical of all imitation we are familiar with. It even occurs, for example, in large social and ethnic groups. J. Delozier in her Bachelor's thesis (University of California, Santa Cruz, Religious Studies Program) in the late 70's pointed out that the likelihood that a religious group will fragment into various sects or subgroups is influenced deeply by whether the original group has an oral or written tradition for their belief systems. In the case of extra-somatic storage of dogma (written tradition) fragmentation is many times more likely than in the case of oral traditions (intra-somatic storage of dogma). The difference appears to be that in the case of an oral tradition (the within body storage), there is a constant editing of the corpus of beliefs (the group dogma) unconsciously as it is passed orally from generation to generation. This slippage or unconscious editing constantly updates the dogma, rendering it intelligible to the receiving generation, given the cultural and social differences that have arisen since its formation and reception by the previous generation.

6. You could well use this description as an argument that therapists would be more effective if they cultivated a disciplined state of non-reflexive consciousness (the disciplined know nothing state) for many aspects of the complex therapeutic context. From here it is not a very long leap to arguing that such a strategy is significantly more ethical than strategies

with a foundation in cognitive based states in the therapist with their attendant filtering by which they attempt to fit the client into some preset perceptual category in order to know what the proper intervention is. One of the most egregious examples of this kind of cognitive filtering occurs when the client refuses to adapt himself to (remains independent of) the categories of the therapist's cognitive model. This is typically the point where the therapist labels the client's behavior as resistance. There are no ethics in such a form.

7. We find it peculiar that there are people (Michael Hall, for example) proposing to add to the meta model additional patterns without justifying them. It seems to us that the entire point of modeling is exactly a movement in the opposite direction. Rather than expand a model already proven effective in securing some outcome, X, the task of a modeler is to attempt to reduce the model consistent with achieving X – that is, to demonstrate that X can be achieved with fewer distinctions or more efficiently...

Therefore, we would propose that anyone who wishes to argue for the inclusion of additional verbal patterning would accept the challenge of motivating their inclusion in the model. More specifically, such motivation would demonstrate that there are useful outcomes in addition to X that the inclusion of these proposed additional patterns allows that strictly speaking are not achievable through a congruent application of the original model. The only other motivation we can imagine would be a proposal to replace some or all of the patterns in the original model by some other set of patterns that are more efficient or more effective in achieving X.

Finally, we point out that Grinder published along with Michael McMaster (*Precision*, 1980) a pared down version of the meta model patterning in 1980 which reduces the set of syntactically based challenges to less than half of the original. This work also contains the first explicit coding in NLP of framing as a general pattern.

In our own work, it has become clear to us (Bostic and Grinder) that it is possible to achieve X, the same set of outcomes achievable by the meta model with only two of the original verbal patterns – the noun specifier and the verb specifier. We propose this as the minimum set. Further, we note as we argue in the text (see especially chapter 1, Part III), that there are competing requirements in the modeling of such phenomena – for example, while it is possible (according to our claim) to achieve every outcome that was achievable with the full original meta model with the reduced set of two mentioned above, it may be far more effective for training purposes to include patterns other than the minimal set.

However each trainer decides to approach the presentation of verbal patterning, we leave the challenge before the community: identify an outcome that is achievable with the original meta model that is not achievable with the reduced set proposed here.

8. We are speaking here of the special relationship which obtains in change work – attempting to understand a friend or acquaintance in some non-therapeutic context falls in the category of normal manipulation which, at least in California these days, is accepted as "caring" behavior.

There is a deeper epistemological question here as to whether it is ever, under any set of conditions, possible to understand another's experience. We will pass on this one and say only that if it is possible, it certainly requires a lot of time, skill and effort.

9. More specifically, any content word (as opposed to function words such as connectives, articles...) will access the set of experiences associated with that word. Thus, a word is simultaneously a partition on the product of the neurological transforms – what we have called First Access - and the *Open File* command for the set of all experiences filed under that term.

10. There are, of course, exceptions to this practice: patients in comas, under the influence of prescription drugs, in unusual altered states (OCD syndromes)... where the strict ethical rules regarding autonomy or independence of the agent of change are temporarily suspended until the client is able once again to take over the responsibility for the change process at the content level under the guidance of the agent of change.

11. It has been well said that the verbal patterns coded in NLP (take the meta model as an example) are what you as an agent of change do in the process of change while waiting for the muse or some magical demon to arrive.

12. It is useful to be explicit about what these special conditions are:

1. that all the nouns/noun phrases and verbs in the sentences presented have a specific reference known both to the speaker and the listener

2. there are no deletions present in the sentences or equivalently, all arguments of the predicates are explicitly filled with referring nouns or noun phrases

3. that there are no violations of the principles contained in the challenges such as Cause-Effect Semantic ill-formedness or Mind Reading...

By the way, such communication, except under exceptional conditions would be pedantic, tedious and flatly not very enjoyable. However it would have a chance in activating the appropriate language processes at the unconscious level without the necessity of the listener hallucinating or adding personal meaning. Note that even when these conditions are strictly met, only the denotative meaning (the actual referent of the word in question) would match up in speaker and listener – the connotative or deeper associations which are secondary and often experienced in western cultures as the feeling tone associated with the communication would be individually unique to speaker and listener, guaranteeing an ongoing difference between the two. This is nothing more than the recognition that the experiential base – in NLP terms, the portions of personal history (the 4-tuples) accessed in two different humans - will be associated with different experiences and therefore the emotional (kinesthetic) impact will vary as well as the representations in the other two major representational systems.

Please note that it is possible and not particularly difficult to train oneself to refuse to hallucinate in the sense we use here, and as we have described in the text with its attendant advantages. We are reminded when considering this question of an associated concept developed in an old science fiction novel *Stranger in a Strange Land* by Robert Heinlein – namely the Witness. A Witness was a person who was trained to resist the temptation to fill in or generalize from what they actually experienced. For example, if you and a Witness were looking at a horse in a pasture and you said,

> *Do you see that brown horse over there* (pointing to ensure referential requirements were met)?

The proper response by the Witness would be,

> *Do you mean the horse that is brown on this side?*

13. Indeed, they republished Farrelly's book through the publishing company they jointly owned at the time, Meta Publications.

14. I (JG) who was a participant in this event am not proposing that I am reporting the precise exchange verbatim between Frank and his client, only that it captures the spirit and method of his provocative approach to eliciting specific information – I trust that Frank would recognize it easily.

Like Satir, Frank has excellent rapport skills as well as many other licks. His performance was superb and his use of the provocative specification technique – described in the text – was simultaneously extremely effective and wildly disturbing to some of the psychiatrists present – so much so that during the modeling portion of the presentation – when Grinder and Bandler were presenting their explicit representations of Frank's behavior - one of the worthies present rose to his feet, trembling and outraged by what Frank had done, and in a very emotional voice said,

> How could you say those terrible, insulting things to your client, especially here publicly in front of 300 psychiatrists?

Frank, Richard and John looked at one another, then turned to the client who was listening to the psychiatrist in bafflement, and asked,

> Do you feel as if what Frank said to you was insulting?

The client reflected for a moment and then replied,

> No, I didn't …(pausing and accessing down and left - auditory internal - re-hearing some of the things that Frank had in fact said and then continued).… When I now think about some of the things he did say, they seem a little out of line, but I know that he was working to get what I wanted.

This strikes us as a brilliant example of two things:

> 1. the overwhelming effectiveness of rapport skills – Frank could say things publicly to his client under conditions of rapport that would have precipitated a disengagement if not a physical encounter under non-rapport conditions. By the way on this particular occasion, Frank demonstrated beautifully the classic code NLP strategy of mirroring, both visual (arranging portions of his body to match his client) and auditorily (modulating his voice to match certain aspects of his client's voice) to achieve this profound state of rapport with his client.

> 2. the perils of attending to content – the psychiatrist's response - and failing to appreciate the form or process, which was, in fact, highly effective – a point that the psychiatrist involved was apparently blind to, given his absolute commitment to content.

15. In addition, the personal metaphors of the source may be artistic but rarely do they offer any insight into how to usefully code the patterning. In this sense, they typically prove to be misleading. Further, it is often the case that the source finds such activity quite uncomfortable. Self-modeling is one of the most difficult tasks imaginable in our field of endeavor. The source of the patterning is being asked to make his own tacit behavior explicit.

Highly talented individuals (sources) often have strong if metaphoric opinions about what they are doing. Since the criteria for an effective model are learnability and efficient transfer of the patterning with the consequences that the learner demonstrates behavior approximating that of the original source, the particular metaphors of the source may actually inhibit this activity. They may constitute an obstacle to the development of an adequate model (as judged by the criteria just mentioned) or precipitate a rift between the model and the modeler over the questions of what the "real " model should be.

There is some value in presenting the source with meta model questions as long as the modeler appreciates the above point and explicitly recognizes that point of asking the meta model question is not to secure a useful verbal response to the question but to stimulate the internal, unconscious processes of the source, thereby creating an opportunity for the modeler to calibrate – that is, read the non - verbal responses of the source in order to appreciate the answer to the question at the non-verbal level. This can at times greatly facilitate further research by the modeler.

16. There were two exceptions to this response: one understandable (and quite predictable) and the second in equal parts, amusing and baffling. The first was a seriously negative and somewhat virulent response from psychiatrists and clinical psychologists. We can appreciate the source of the response.

Listen, if you had invested the amount of time and money in educating yourself to become a psychiatrist or a clinical psychologist that they had, it is completely understandable that you too would be outraged by these arrogant young unqualified amateurs proposing that they could achieve in a unbelievably short period of time therapeutic outcomes which you knew required years of hard, slogging work. It was even more alarming when they consistently publicly demonstrated they actually could do it.

If any of this surprises you, read Thomas Kuhn's *The Structure of Scientific Revolutions* as well as noting the economic consequences of what we (Bandler and Grinder) were proposing in respect to their professional practice of calendaring long-term standing appointments for their clients.

The second exception was contained in a quite amazing letter from Jay Haley to Robert Spitzer. Spitzer was a close personal friend of Bandler's – and the owner of the property at 1000 Alba as well as of the publishing company, Science and Behavior Books, which still publishes both volumes of *The Structure of Magic*. Spitzer was also Richard's employer. Richard worked part time as a warehouse man packing and sending off copies of books ordered by mail. Spitzer, cognizant of the strong influence Richard

190

had on his thinking and mindful of his responsibilities to select appropriate books for publication through his company, had sent Haley a manuscript copy of *The Structure of Magic*. He had asked Haley to serve as an impartial professional reviewer and to tell him (Spitzer) whether he (Haley) thought the book had value. Haley was well positioned to make such a judgment. In my own personal opinion at the time – with the exception of Gregory Bateson and Milton H. Erickson themselves - Haley was the author of the only books on psychotherapy that I had read that had captured my attention and respect. In addition, Haley had also been a member of the famous MRI (Mental Research Institute) of Palo Alto, headed up by Bateson (where Gregory developed his double bind theory of schizophrenia). Finally, Haley had studied directly with Dr. Erickson.

The recommendation made by Haley (at one point, Spitzer showed the letter from Haley to Bandler and myself) was to not publish the book. His comments included statements such as that he found the book interesting in some parts but that it was woefully naïve (probably correct) and most tellingly, it showed an absolute ignorance of Bateson's seminal work over the last few decades – this alone disqualified the book in Haley's opinion from being worth publishing.

It was only when Bandler and I showed the book to Gregory himself and he kindly read it and offered graciously to write the glowing endorsement of it which appears as an introduction to the book that Spitzer decided to publish it. I suppose that the portion of the introduction written by Bateson in which he states,

> *It is a strange pleasure to write an introduction for this book because John Grinder and Richard Bandler have done something similar to what my colleagues and I attempted fifteen years ago. ...Grinder and Bandler have confronted the problems which we confronted then...they have tools which we did not have – or did not see how to use. ...They have succeeded in making linguistics into a base for theory, and simultaneously a tool for therapy. ...This discovery seems obvious when the argument starts from linguistics...instead of starting from culture contrast and psychosis, as we did... May it be heard!*

> Gregory Bateson, introduction to *The Structure of Magic*, vol. I, pages ix, x and xi

proved somewhat surprising to Haley. We never heard from him again.

17. In this particular case, the paper was presented without explanation for the simple reason we had no clue consciously what it was that we were doing. This was and still is a very common experience during the initial

phases of modeling. It certainly was characteristic of our experience during this phase of our work.

18. Over the years, I (JG) have had a number of clients who experienced synesthesia in its involuntary form and have had excellent success in assisting them in developing choices about how to regulate its occurrence. Oliver Sachs, our sincerest compliments and send us your patients!

19. There is a significant assumption present here – one which permeates NLP practice; namely, that the syntactic structure of the sentences people use to express themselves mirrors the sequence in the underlying neurological processes. This assumption must at some point in the development of NLP be examined and justified. Consider, for example, the analysis of a language that is verb final in its surface structure – German.

Note that the linear order in which the representational system specified predicates occur in a sentence does not necessarily match up with the order of supposed internal representational events. Sentences in natural language have two dimensions – that is, they have internal hierarchical structure. Caution, therefore, needs to be exercised when mapping from the utterances of natural language to the underlying neurological events represented by the predicates involved.

Consider the second example in the text - the linear sequence (left to right) is unlikely to be the same as the sequence of the neurological representational system events. In this particular case, the linear ordering of representation of specified predicates in the sentence indicates the sequence:

feel...........saying........unclear

However, the syntactic structure itself involves an embedded sentence (*what you are saying*) that is actually subordinate. Subordinate in this sense means lower in the tree structure that represents the syntactic structure of the sentence than what succeeds it linearly (*is unclear*)). Thus, using the linear sequence alone would lead to a different analysis of both the sentence itself and the underlying events neurologically it purports to represent. We suspect that the correct mapping to the neurological events will turn out to be

feel (kinesthetic)... unclear (visual)... saying (auditory)

20. I remember with great pleasure introducing what we have presented here as mappings (in particular, isomorphic and homomorphic mappings) to David Gordon on a small blackboard after a group meeting at 1000 Alba in the mid 70's and urging him to explore in detail the neurological

literature in synesthesia as these two precise and powerful tools form an excellent opening base for describing the structure of metaphor. He used both to good advantage in his book, *Therapeutic Metaphors*.

21. It is useful to point out that this tracking strategy is independent of the content that you intend to express. The well-trained NLP practitioner, then, is capable of expressing any content in any and all of the primary representational systems (visual, auditory or kinesthetic). Note that this is yet another example of the advantage of distinguishing between the form and content – such a distinction in this particular case allows the well trained NLP practitioner to behave ethically – in particular, to present (re-present) the client's content while shamelessly manipulating the form – namely, the representational system in which the form is expressed.

22. With the well-known exception of the Basque whose patterning is consistent in the vertical dimension of the pattern (up for visual, side for auditory...) but not the lateral one – the one that signals which of the hemispheres is being activated. This difference is significant for the distinctions in the lower quadrants for the auditory (internal dialogue) and kinesthetic, and in the other quadrants, for the distinction between memory and composition in visual and auditory experiences. We are fascinated that among the Basque, there is (from reports – not personally verified) apparently a series of common and wide spread child-rearing practices that involve the systematic development of ambidexterity. This is worthy of further investigation as it is widely held that handedness and cerebral dominance are intertwined phenomena. The Basque are also quite distinctive in their blood type and the syntactic structure of their native language.

23. It has also led to the amusing situation where some of those original students who, given the representational system predicate distinction, were successful in meeting the challenge given by Grinder and Bandler by finding the eye movements patterns for themselves, have apparently come to believe that they actually were the original discoverers of this pattern (page 78, *NLP World*, volume 6, No. 2 July 1999).

24. My (JG) memory is that the only portion of the book (*The Structure of Magic*, Volume I) that Gregory was interested in discussing at any length was the syntactic processes underlying the syntactic processes of nominalization – the transformation of a deep verb into a surface noun (for example, *amuse* ⟶ *amusement*). His fascination is particularly understandable given his deep appreciation of the processes of reification and what these syntactically based transformational processes implied about how deeply logical levels are built into the structure of natural language.

25. He was, of course, correct in his prediction. On the other hand, we did pretty well – we got four more years, the next two better than the last two. It's not immortality, but it ain't bad.

26. In fact, there is a transcript which is the focus of an article in what is in our opinion the bible of hypnosis - the original Ericksonian patterning (a brilliant collection of articles written by Erickson himself) *Advanced Techniques of Hypnosis and Therapy* edited by Jay Haley) in which Haley and John Weakland are discussing with Erickson a specific induction Erickson did with a patient – the "conversation" between Erickson and these two researchers was essentially another induction utilizing patterning isomorphic with what Erickson did in the original work with the client, but this time focused on the two researchers.

27. If memory serves correctly, this group consisted of Kay Thompson. Marian Moore and Robert Preston (I am uncertain about Robert's last name – apologies if I have misspelled the names of these worthies).

28. Richard commented later, and I agreed, that it was harder for me to get pass Betty than to secure the desired response from Milton himself.

29. Now there are several interpretations as to what actually happened here. We could argue that we had captured enough of the patterning in our slightly altered version of Erickson's own inductions and further that who, more than the master of the patterning himself, would be more responsive to his own patterns. Therefore, indeed, what had happened was that this audacious young man had hypnotized Erickson himself, with his only feedback being his breathing pattern. Further, that the message had got through and the Erickson's response was, as he was fond of saying, most adequate.

Myself, I am inclined to think otherwise – I suspect that my delivery wasn't even close to what Erickson would have needed to hear to make a full response but that we nailed the patterning close enough that he was fascinated that without meeting him we had gotten a piece of it – the only question left for me was how it was that he chose to go into the altered state I detected through monitoring his breathing – as I got to know Milton, this option made more and more sense to me.

30. By qualifying the sentence with the term *functionally*, we intend to call the reader's attention to an important issue. The resultant model that is effective in allowing others to achieve the same results as the person who originally served as the source for that model leaves open the following question.

Is the resultant model, already proven to be effective, a faithful representation of what the source model originally actually did?

We are not certain whether this question is in any deep sense well formed. It may turn out to be the case that it is not and that the best response to the question is simply that the question is not epistemologically well formed. In other words, how could we know whether the model is a faithful representation of what the source of the model actually did? Or again, what possible evidence could we develop to decide such a question?

Happily, in any case, there is the weaker position available in response to the question; namely, any model that allows the practitioner to reproduce the results typical of the source in (roughly) the same time frame and with (roughly) the same quality is an effective model, independent of the question whether it is an isomorphic mapping of the source's neurology. This is the meaning of the term *functionally* in the referenced sentence.

This same issue will be familiar to students of Artificial Intelligence where it split the field some decades back. Some researchers took the path of attempting to model and reproduce in their software, patterns they believed to be isomorphic with the patterning present in humans when performing the same task as the software was to perform. Other researchers eschewed such constraints and simply worked to design software that was functionally equivalent in the sense that it produced results isomorphic with the results humans display when carrying out the task the software in question was supposed to produce.

Perhaps a simple personal example will serve. Sometime in the first year or so after Bandler and I had begun to work publicly outside of Santa Cruz, I was challenged in a seminar to present a model of how I remembered the names of large numbers of people who I had just met. The participants in the seminar were of the opinion that I did this very well and wanted the choice for themselves. I created and offered them the following strategy:

> 1. clear all internal representational systems – that is, no internal dialogue, no visual images not directly related to the immediate context, no feelings other than those associated with the immediate setting in which you find yourself.

> 2. When shaking the hand of the person who you are meeting for the first time, listen attentively to the sound of the person's voice saying their own name – especially, the non-verbal qualities of their voice

> *Hi, my name is _____.*

3. Make an internal recording of the person saying his own name and allow it to cycle several times.

4. As soon as you release the hand of the other person, move your gaze to their forehead and print their name on their forehead. Do this while moving the dominant hand with micro-muscle movements, printing the name. See it on their forehead as you do this. You have now captured their name in all three representational systems.

5. The next time you see the person, you will recognize their face ("You never forget a face"). As soon as you realize that you have seen the face before, look at their forehead and dilate your pupils, their name will "magically" appear – the face serving as an adequate set of contextual visual anchors to recall the name you put there.

6. Should you receive a phone call from the person whose name you have taken the time and care to store, the non-verbal qualities of his voice will trigger access to the tape previously made in which he announced his name. You may now surprise and delight him by greeting him by name before he presents it to you. This is particularly impressive in American cultures where little attention or value is typically placed on the non-verbal aspects of sound (apologies to my American musician friends).

The seminar participants did some rehearsals to master the sequence above and then tested their new skill, reporting a significant improvement in their ability to store and re-access a number of names.

I am quite certain that I do nothing of this kind – that is, I am certain that I do not use any such strategy. The strategy I offered to the participants who were then able to put it into play is the result of my design - not of any modeling activity.

By the way, I personally do not regard myself as having any advanced ability to remember people's names. I am, however, quite competent in reading nametags.

31. There may be readers who are unfamiliar with this ancient device – the typewriter. Seek counsel from anyone over 50 years old.

32. This phrase *deliberately leave out some single Ericksonian behavior* covers a significant portion of the art of modeling – more specifically, the ability to decompose complex behavior into useful component parts. Also see the *Coding of Pattern* in chapter 1, Part III of this book for a more refined representation of this point.

33. We simplify for purposes of clarity of explanation – Erickson had many more than two voices and he was exquisite in their systematic use.

Chapter 2: The Breakthrough Pattern

We pause in the historical narrative describing the development of the field of NLP to make explicit how NLP ^{application} in change work distinguishes itself from other approaches. The context of this portion of the book, then, is the *application* of NLP patterning to change – self-change or the induction of change in others. In particular we wish to make explicit how the application of the patterns of excellence coded in the Classic Code of NLP is different from other systems of professional change work purporting to address these same challenges. Once we have made explicit these differences and one of its ethical implications, we resume the historical narrative, describing the context and processes of discovery by which the breakthrough pattern, Six Step Reframing, emerged. We then turn to a critique of the classic code in light of the features of this breakthrough pattern.

We wish to signal clearly to the reader that in this chapter the focus shifts radically <u>from modeling to application.</u>

An Epistemological Characterization of NLP ^{application} Patterns

In chapter 1 of part 1 of this book, we developed a certain epistemological position and commented on some of its implications for NLP. We now offer a characterization of some of the most fundamental patterning in NLP from the point of view of that epistemology. While the epistemology presented in the earliest work (*The Structure of Magic*) is under-developed relative to what we have described here in *Whispering*, the two are compatible. The coding and presentation of NLP patterns are intelligible only in light of such an epistemology. It seems simultaneously startling and uncontroversial to state that the application of NLP patterning to change work has as its objective <u>*nothing more*</u> than the *manipulation of representations*:

> 1. the meta model is a set of epistemological operations designed to verbally challenge (e.g. through specification) the mapping (f^2) between FA and our mental maps as well as the internal logic of the language system itself (e.g. cause-effect relations) as it forms a base for the generation of linguistically mediated mental maps that guide behavior. A systematic application of this set of verbal patterns leads precisely and efficiently to the identification of the FA events (the reference experiences) that are the source of the representations to be changed to achieve the client's goals.

2. operations defined over representational systems and their sub modalities (e.g. overlap of representational systems, swish…) are a direct method for manipulating the FA representations of the client.

3. anchoring is a set of operations for bundling and manipulating otherwise undifferentiated groupings within FA (4-tuples) with the intention of bringing them into contact with other FA representations for purposes of differentiation or integration.

4. the various reframing patterns are operations in which a specific representation (e.g. a problem or challenge) is positioned within some larger representation (a context known as its frame) in such a way that its meaning shifts – all operations within the logic of the higher order epistemological mappings (f^2 or post FA).

5. the Milton model is a split level set of operations designed to shift representations at the level of the First Access without the necessity of mapping the elements of FA into the client's consciousness. Therefore, verbal (post FA operations) patterning is being used without bringing the representations being manipulated within FA out of FA. This model is said to be a split-level model in that it clearly uses post FA operations (verbal patterning) while working the material within FA (without the necessity of forcing the material into consciousness).
…

Perhaps the only thing odd about the initial statement is the phrase, *nothing more* in,

> …*application of NLP patterning to change work is <u>nothing more</u> than the manipulation of representations.*

In other words, given the epistemology that we have proposed here, what else could we be manipulating in the process of applying the NLP patterning to change work other than representations, since they are all that we have access to!

Making this point explicit, however, allows us to identify a number of consequences that the application of NLP patterning to change work entails that cleanly differentiates NLP [application] from other systems of change.

The Differentiators

1. the application of NLP to change work has clearly selected representations as the leverage point. Even those interventions that are manipulations of external variables such as behavioral tasking, imposed paradoxes, therapeutic double binds... are tactical decisions about how best to modify, extend, challenge... the client's mappings within and between the domains of the internal logics of FA and those of natural language. Indeed, a behavioral task is the manipulation of direct FA experiences to shift the mental maps of the client at that level (FA). The underlying presupposition that makes coherent all this activity is the proposition that if an agent of change can effectively manipulate these underlying representations (the so-called mental maps, either at the level of FA or post-FA) of the client, the client's behavior and quality of experience will shift as a consequence.

2. since the object of these manipulations is representations, any ethical method for effectively changing those representations will succeed in changing behavior *independently* of how such representations were developed in the first place – that is, the history of the formation of the mental maps of the client is irrelevant for the purposes of change. NLP patterning specifically eschews any archeological tendencies; as such we do not investigate the history of a problem or a challenge as an essential part of the change process. History, then, is irrelevant for purposes of changing the present representations. In addition, the recovery of history typically involves conscious re-accessing of historical events. But there is a great deal of evidence that such re-assessing is actually reconstruction. This observation (memory as a process of reconstruction) combined with the severe limitations of the carrying capacity of consciousness/working memory (the famous 7 ± 2 chunks of information) casts a somber shadow over the value of what is reconstructed when personal history is elicited through some conscious verbal process. We regard such productions as stories that clients tell themselves to make sense out of or to justify their actual ongoing experience.

3. given that the objective of an intervention is to change the client's representations, it is an empirical question whether consciousness should play any role in the process of change. This invites us to be explicit about what the goals of change processes are. If this set of goals includes developing the ability in our clients to talk about their problems and challenges, then consciousness is justified. On the other hand, if the set of goals includes ensuring that our clients have choices in their lives in precisely the places they formerly did not

200

have choices, then there is a great deal of evidence that there is no justification for attempting to achieve any conscious understanding of the client's problem or challenge: neither on the part of the client, nor on the part of the agent of change. Compare the difference in time, effort and quality of the changes secured through the judicious and respectful use of anchors with the results typically obtained in extended "talk" therapy.

Further, there is no justification for dabbling in content as mentioned previously. This is the basis of secret therapy or doubly secret therapy in which neither the agent of change, nor the client consciously understands what is being shifted.

4. neither the agent of change nor the client is required to believe any set of assumptions to utilize NLP patterning effectively.

Several of these positions on issues that differentiate NLP from other approaches – for example, that the root or original experiences where the client either suffered a trauma or learned to make some response that is not presently useful must be identified and made conscious for the client – seems to have come from the original work done by Freud. They have been uncritically incorporated into every other system of change work (with the behaviorist exception noted above) in western society that we are familiar with. Such a position is equivalent to insisting that we move further away from the client's current reality and the original reference experiences in order to effect change. There are many representations that constitute obstacles to achieving choice in life that reside solely within FA. To insist that these representations must first be mapped into the language domain is a statement about the skill set (or lack thereof) of the agent of change and is at least ethically questionable. In chapter 2, Part III under *Sorting Principles* (see the Iatrogenic Principle in particular) we will propose a more explicit way of managing this issue.

Allow us to offer an extended example of one of these differentiators: specifically, the fourth;

4. neither the agent of change nor the client is required to believe any set of assumptions to utilize NLP patterning effectively.

In particular, for example, there is no need to subscribe to the so-called presuppositions of NLP in order to benefit from an effective application of the patterns to some problem or challenge. Normally, these presuppositions [1] include statements such as,

Having choice is better than not having choice

All the resources necessary to make the change the client desires are already available within the client at the unconscious level

The behavior presently displayed by the client, no matter how bizarre, represents the best choice available at this moment in the representations of the client, given his perception of the context in which it is occurring

...

Further, *if the so-called presuppositions of NLP are to be taken seriously*, this decidedly odd collection of different logical types and levels are badly in need of revision and reorganization. Their defects, fortunately, need not trouble us at the level of application of NLP patterning.

The origin of many of these so-called presuppositions of NLP is somewhat obscure in my mind (JG). I believe that Robert Dilts played a strong role in their compilation. I recognize several of them (such as the three listed in the text) as statements I myself created or I created in conjunction with Bandler. They seem to be more or less the story we made up to satisfy the conscious mind question:

What would have to be true for the actual ongoing practice of NLP application to be coherent?

But surely all answers to this question will be rationalizations after the fact; some intellectual backfilling to justify and dignify actual practice. Somewhat more radically, we find the so-called presuppositions of NLP are, at best, a pedagogical device to assist people new to the adventure called NLP in making the required transitions in their thinking to the new forms of perception and thought implicit in the technology. Unfortunately presuppositions, like beliefs, are ultimately filters that reduce the ongoing experiences of their possessors. We personally do not find any value in the enumeration of such rationalizations (the so-called presuppositions of NLP). The enterprise called NLP succeeds or fails – works or doesn't work – based on actual performance whatever the musings about what the practice might suggest intellectually. This statement is, of course, nothing more or less than the application of the criterion already identified for a model – does it work?

A client/agent of change pair who congruently follows the sequence in a NLP pattern will achieve the positive results the pattern is designed to provoke, independent of their personal beliefs. The situation here is analogous to a number of non-western disciplines such as Tai Chi, Aikido, Yoga... In each of these activities, a person interested in the discipline may enter at the level of simple practice of technique (a First Access experience) or may approach their study of the discipline with a focus on the underlying philosophy or world-view of the discipline (a linguistic experience) or both. It is clear that the person who enters at the level of simple practice of technique will experience shifts in their internal representations driven by actual experience of the techniques while there is no guarantee that a person who elects to approach the discipline through a study of its philosophy will shift anything but their mouths.

This same point is quite relevant to the issue of how to intervene for change in the case of a person whose belief systems constitute an obstacle to change. [2]

There are any number of change of belief system patterns that have been proposed as NLP patterning. Whatever their status, the strategy preferred by the present authors is quite straightforward, simple and congruent with the above point:

Belief System Intervention (a special case of Behavioral Tasking)

1. Identify the change to be made – in this case, the limiting belief.

2. Design a direct experience (that is, FA experience) that would serve as a strong counterexample to the limiting belief.

3. Create the experiences identified as the counterexamples without revealing to the client at the level of consciousness, either the intention or the desired consequence of the experience that you have designed. This is most strikingly accomplished by burying the experience inside a task that the clients cannot recognize consciously as relevant to the outcomes they have come to achieve. The concrete example offered below will assist the reader in appreciating this point.

Notice in the above format that there is no mention of any attempt to understand the limiting belief; nor to discover its origin in the personal history of the client nor to bring any of this information to consciousness. The underlying assumption of this class of strategies (behavioral tasking) is congruent with the principle,

> ... if we can effectively manipulate the underlying representations, through the actual experiences (FA) of the client, that client's behavior and underlying belief systems will shift as a consequence.

We are proposing that changing the representations of the client (in this case, through a direct FA experience) – through a task, will allow a generalization both to behavior and to epiphenomenona: those classes of computations across representations such as consciousness and belief systems.

A Concrete Example: Belief System Intervention Format

In the early 80's, John Grinder was approached by a close friend who asked whether, as a special favor, he would accept as his client one of her associates, a woman named Susan. Susan had recently received a diagnosis of cancer with a suggestion that she had but months before the cancer would run its course and she would die.[3]

Grinder agreed. The initial interview revealed a number of possible leverage points ranging from a deep change in the marriage Susan was in to a radical reorganization of how Susan organized her own perceptions about what was important. But, most intriguingly, Grinder, employing a strategy called listening off the top, had detected the relatively frequent use of a phrase, marked unconsciously by Susan in which she stated directly,

> *For me to beat this cancer, <u>my entire world</u> would have to <u>turn upside down.</u>*

The underlined section of this statement identifies the portion marked by Susan each time she used the statement.

Listening off the top was a way of describing a specific auditory strategy Grinder and Bandler had developed during the period they were modeling Erickson. The two men had discovered analogue marking - one of the strategies Erickson used in conversational hypnotic communication to deliver to the unconscious a message without the conscious mind being aware that he was so doing. Analogue marking occurs when some non-verbal signal is systematically associated with specific portions of the verbal productions such that when taken together the non-verbally marked portions of the verbal message form a coherent separate message directed to the unconscious of the listening client. Erickson had a number of very sophisticated ways of doing this. The analogue marking could be as simple as a tonal shift each time he uttered a part of the "extra" message – thus, the unconscious of the client assembled the words and phrases so marked as an independent communication and responded to it – or as subtle as the physical position his head was in when speaking to the client.[4] Or again, the verbal material could be as simple as the sentence below (the underlined section is marked by tonal shifts),

People can, Mike, <u>feel deeply relaxed</u> when listening to a conversation.

or as sophisticated as a series of different stories, unassociated in any way except that within each of them a portion was marked in the same way so that the task of the unconscious was to assemble these disparate sections into a single communication, as suggested by the diagram below:

story 1   story 2   story 3...   story n

element a   element b   element c ...   element n

the marked elements (a) through (n) constitute a separate coherent story or set of messages to the client's unconscious

The unconscious identification of the separate but analogically marked portions of the series of stories allowed the unconscious to discover, accept and respond to the message so-crafted.

Once Grinder and Bandler had worked out Erickson's strategy for analogue marking, they were surprised and amused to discover that clients were frequently marking out special portions of their speech in an analogous manner.

These special signals from the client's unconscious to the agent of change (or for that matter, anyone who can listen in this way) can take any number of forms, including ambiguity. One of the simplest examples of this phenomenon occurred on the occasion of one of the impossible clients [5] brought to Bandler and Grinder by a Bay area psychiatrist – the client was experiencing, among other things, a kinesthetic hallucination in which she had the experience of insects crawling all over her body.

Within the first three minutes of the conversation about the client's hallucination that took place between her, Bandler and Grinder, she looked each of the two men squarely in the eyes and said,

My husband really bugs me!

Diagnosis complete!

The narrative continues:

Susan had marked this phrase "turn my world upside down" a number of times by voice shift, repetitive body posture and a distinctive facial expression. As circumstances would have it, at the time Grinder was training as an aerobatic pilot. He had the great fortune to have as his teacher David Gaster, an excellent aerobatic pilot (former member of the British aerobatic team, the Red Arrows) and a superb teacher. Grinder decided to use the special resources available to him at the time in pursuit of the therapeutic goal.

Susan herself was a proud person who insisted on finding a way to pay Grinder for his work with her. She had asked upon the occasion of their first meeting if there were any tasks that she might do to help pay off the cost of the work. Grinder called Susan and explained that he had made arrangements to meet with a representative of a British company that specialized in aerobatic aircraft but that an unanticipated emergency call from one of his corporate clients necessitated his being in Denver on precisely the day the representative was to arrive in Santa Cruz. He asked therefore that Susan take the responsibility of meeting with this representative and securing the information Grinder needed to decide whether or not to purchase the aerobatic plane in question. She was hesitant, as she had absolutely no experience in aviation and most certainly none in small planes in the aerobatic category. Grinder reassured her that he would provide her with a checklist and her task would be to simply interview the representative and secure the required information.

On the appointed day, Susan, dressed smartly for the occasion, met David Gaster at the agreed upon time at the Scotts Valley Skypark airport. Mr. Gaster expressed some consternation that he had come all the way from England for this appointment and Mr. Grinder was not even present. Susan succeeded in reassuring him that she would collect all the information Grinder needed to make a good decision regarding the purchase of the aircraft. Gaster then grudgingly accepted the situation and asked Susan what information she required. Susan dutifully worked her way through the checklist provided by Grinder (actually created by Gaster himself). Toward the end of the list, Gaster insisted that he explain to Susan the answers to some of her questions by showing her directly on the aircraft the differences she was enquiring about. Susan by now reasonably charmed by David acquiesced and they found themselves on the tarmac next to the aircraft, Gaster explaining the intricacies of the aircraft to a somewhat bewildered but attentive Susan.

As she completed her checklist, Susan thanked Gaster for his courtesy and patience in explaining everything to her and started to take her leave. As she turned to depart, Gaster rather abruptly asked where she was going. She replied that she had collected the information Grinder had asked her to secure. Gaster responded by pointing out that if Grinder really was an aerobatic pilot and a legitimate qualified buyer, he would insist on knowing what the feel of the aircraft was and that it was simply unthinkable to make a buying decision without that class of information. Before she could work her way out of this deep pattern interruption, Susan found herself wearing a parachute (a FAA regulation) and strapped into the front seat of the aircraft with a headset and speaker microphone on. The reader can work out what happened next. [6]

Susan herself, as they say, experienced a spontaneous remission.

The differentiators of NLP in its applications, set forth before the extended example, clearly distinguish it from all other systems of professional change work, with the notable exception of systems of change inspired by behaviorist psychology. NLP [applications] can be easily differentiated from these behaviorist systems in a number of ways.

The behaviorist, by the very constraints of the philosophy of science (logical positivism) from which his system is derived, is limited in his interventions to the manipulation of external, environmental variables. Historically, the focus on these variables under such titles as *reinforcers, contingencies, and schedules of extinction…* may, indeed, have been salutary and a welcome shift from the highly interpretive systems of so-called Insight therapies. However, the price is excessive. The black box is closed. More specifically, any system of change with this constraint is literally barred from taking into account the internal structure of the human beings involved in the change process (the clients). The behaviorists are, therefore, unable to explain how the specific perceptions and mental maps of clients (internal variables) lead to different responses to the same manipulation of environmental variables in different clients. Such systems will prove less ineffective than systems that are able to take into account such internal structures. Such systems are unable to respond intelligently to the common observations that the "same" experience defined in terms of the environment is followed by widely varying responses in different people subjected to it.

Effective change strategies recognize that there are two major categories of variables to be taken into account in the change process:

1. external, environmental variables such as those employed by the behaviorist. In NLP [applications], these can be seen as the variables being manipulated by the agent of change in such patterning as behavioral tasking, the use of consequences, contextual manipulations…

2. internal perceptual strategies and mental maps that influence the responses of the client – primarily and essentially all post FA mappings

The unfortunate exclusion of this second set of variables ties the hands of the behaviorist practitioner and seems to be inherently non-systemic. As we have argued, the leverage point for intervention in the application of NLP patterning is representations – whether addressed directly through language (the meta model, the Milton model...) or through non-verbal techniques (anchoring formats, for example) or indirectly, through behavioral tasking and contextual manipulation (as in the case of the above example of Susan's world turning upside down). It is amusing to us that these two systems (NLP [application] and Behaviorist inspired therapies), so divergent in their approaches and epistemologies, should find themselves in complete agreement, and in contrast to all other systems (known to the authors), in their position by refusing to investigate the "causes" of problems and denying the need for involving the consciousness of people undergoing changes processes.

An Ethical Consequence of the Differentiators

In the decisions associated with the issues raised in the discussion of the differentiators made by a practicing agent of change, there is an additional over-arching concern. The ethics of NLP [applications] surely includes an impeccable positioning by the agent of change to foster and develop the client's independence: both in general and specifically his independence of the agent of change. Thus somewhere in the treatment plan, steps must be taken to ensure that the clients recognize that they are the source of the resources and have the ability to participate fully in the processes of change initially managed by the agent of change. A judicious use of triple description (to be presented in the latter portion of this chapter) and especially, 3rd position is one of a set of excellent choices to accomplish this. The critical issue is *when* the client is to be invited to 3rd, aligning himself with the agent of change and beginning the process of forming a working relationship between his conscious and his unconscious minds. If this choice is used too early in the process, it can activate conscious mind patterning that impedes the creation of new choices. Thus, we again point with urgency to a responsibility without a present ability to offer some definitive solution. At present, then, this ethical requirement remains in the realm of art.

The Breakthrough Pattern

The historical narrative continues:

It was late on a Thursday afternoon when I (JG) arrived from Europe by plane at SeaTac (Seattle Tacoma airport). Although the work trip had been strenuous and the temporal displacement from Europe to the west coast of the US required careful management, I was looking forward to the next three days.

Several months before, I had presented a four-day seminar to the professional staff of St. Paul's Psychiatric Hospital in Vancouver, British Columbia. The training had been explicitly designed to offer precise patterns and strategies to the psychiatrists, psychiatric nurses and ancillary staff of this psychiatric Institute. The initial training had been well received and the agreement was that the participants would spend the intervening several months integrating the patterns presented into their work. I was to return to offer one day of demonstrations, working with chronic schizophrenics from the back wards, followed by two days of training – both to explain what I had done during the demonstrations and to assist the staff in cleaning up their own direct experiences of the last couple of months.

After renting a car at SeaTac, I drove to Vancouver and checked into the hotel. I sensed an imbalance and resolved to get a full night's sleep to begin work freshly the following day. When I awoke the following morning, I knew I was in trouble. I was running a fever of 104F and although only mildly congested, I recognized the symptoms of walking pneumonia. I rapidly assessed the situation and decided the most effective way through was to make a deal with my unconscious.

> *OK, I proposed, I need your help – here's the deal. I will put my behavior entirely in your hands. My request is that you ensure that we perform at the highest level of quality possible in the demonstrations, as surely these professionals as well as their clients deserve the best we can offer. In return, I promise as soon as the workday is finished, I will go directly to the hotel, down a couple of shots of brandy, fall into bed and sweat this fever out. [7]*

The day went quickly – as all days without consciousness do. I learned later through conversations with the participants that I worked with five different schizophrenics during the day and, at least in the opinions of the participants, with high quality results. I must

209

confess that to this very day, I have no access consciously to any of the events of that day with the exception of pausing twice during the day (a coffee break and the noon meal) when I managed to achieve some consciousness of my surroundings. I checked with my unconscious asking how we were doing. The response was immediate:

> *Hush up! I'm handling this.*

Keeping the conscious part of the bargain, I went immediately after the day's work to the hotel, popped a couple shots of brandy, collapsed into bed and sweet oblivion. I awoke in the morning feeling superb after thirteen hours of sleep and a good sweat out. During breakfast, I thought through the task before me for the day – namely, explicating the patterns I had used as part of the previous day's work with the chronics. It was at that moment that I realized that I had absolutely no conscious access to what I had done. [8]

I resolved therefore to arrive at the training facility early and to conduct an informal elicitation session with the participants, using questions such as,

> *Which of the demonstrations did you find most interesting?*

> *And what struck you about that particular demonstration?*

> *Which specific interactions between myself and the patient did you experience as most intriguing?*

> *You found them intriguing, how specifically?*

> *...*

While seeking these classes of information from the early arriving participants with casual desperation in the back of the training room, I noted my eyes wandering repeatedly to the front of the room and more specifically to the blackboard located there. Finally recognizing the familiar tug of my unconscious, I excused myself and walked to the front of the training room only to find myself standing in front of the blackboard on which the following was written in my own hand:

REFRAMING

1. identify the behavior(s) to be changed

2. establish a reliable involuntary signal system with the unconscious

3. confirm that there is a positive intention(s) behind the behavior(s) to be changed

4. generate a set of alternatives as good or better than the original behavior(s) in satisfying the positive intention(s)

5. get the unconscious to accept responsibility for implementation

6. ecological check

I stood before this pattern stunned by its simplicity – a direct production of my unconscious – a pattern that contains precisely the differences that would come eventually to distinguish patterns of the new code from patterns of the classic code. There is no doubt, nor was there any at the time, that this elegant pattern was the product of years of work by both Bandler and myself and represented a dazzling integration of the influences of Bateson and Erickson. Yet what a gift!

Further conversations with participants revealed that some of them had noted with great interest that at some point in the sessions with each of the schizophrenics I had treated the preceding day, I had run some or all of the points listed in the pattern (in varying forms). This was a pattern that none of them recognized from the previous four days training that I had conducted and one that had been effective in the extreme. At the close of the day, one of them had asked me to explicate the pattern I had been using. My response was the pattern that now appeared before me on the blackboard.

To this day, and with many experiences both personally and with thousands of clients over the years which repeatedly have demonstrated that the unconscious is capable of enormously complex and creative acts *when the proper framing and context have been established and the lead is released to the unconscious*, I remain awestruck by this experience – the presentation of a complete pattern for individual change, powerful in its consequences, elegant in its form and universal in its application. [9]

Critique of the Classic Code

We propose that this format – Six Step Reframing – illuminates with some precision certain characteristics of the classic code that we regard as questionable. Allow us to be more explicit:

In the classic code, there are a number of distinct natural groupings of patterns: For example, the meta model is a set of verbal patterns. Given the epistemology outlined in the initial section of this book, it is clear that this set of patterns focuses on manipulations at the level of the linguistic code. They are, then, patterns designed to change the representations through linguistic mapping, post First Access – what Freud referred to as secondary experience. Anchoring, in contrast, is a set of patterns that allow the practitioner of NLP to manage varying sized chunks of primary experience without the need to translate them into any linguistic form. In other words, anchoring is a set of processes defined over FA. Anchors are a set of procedures for isolating and moving pieces of primary experience around in different configurations without imposing any linguistic categories.

We will subsequently propose the principle that a minimum of translation is consistent with the ethics of change work as practiced in NLP ^{applications} and the set of patterns that involve anchoring as an application are precisely the procedures that allow the practitioner to be precise in their work with clients without explication (or even verbalization) of the content being managed by the client and practitioner. It is useful, if somewhat crude, to regard anchors as a rough and ready way of attaching handles to varying sized pieces of primary experience for the purpose of inducing rapid and profound change without entering into the content of the material being managed.

Pick any classic code anchoring format – for example, change personal history (re-imprinting) or collapse anchors (or knees). Note that in these particular formats, as in all the classic code formats, the following characteristics are always present:

Prototypic Classic NLP Anchoring Format

1. Identification (consciously) by the client of the change to be made (present state)

2. Identification (consciously) of the difference the client desires – this can take the form of identifying the desired behavior or state (future state) or simply the resource the client wishes to apply to the present state to change it.

3. Accessing of both the present and the desired states (typically both are anchored) – the sequence of accessing and anchoring depends on the perceived needs of the client and the style of the agent of change and is, in general, not critical.

4. Making the connection between the present state and the desired state or resource or new behavior, typically through the manipulation of anchors (sometimes referred to as future pacing).

5. Test the work for effectiveness (anchors, in the street...)

There are, of course, dozens of specific ways to accomplish each of these steps, resulting in hundreds of variations on the theme.[10] For example, in step 1, the practitioner has choices that emerge from distinctions such as, is the client to consciously identify what she wants verbally or non-verbally, if verbally, then literally or metaphorically; if non-verbally, through a dramatization or... As the client identifies what she wishes to change, what strategies are acceptable (Visual⟶Auditory⟶Kinesthetic versus Auditory ⟶ Kinesthetic...)? What degree of specificity is required in the identification – or equivalently, at what logical level is the identification to be made? Must all representational systems be activated and if so, in what specific sequence; if not, what are the minimal requirements?

Or again in step 3, the practitioner again has many choices for achieving what the step requires: the accessing can be achieved by the client himself or through actions on the part of the agent of change; it can occur in such a way that the client is conscious of what is occurring or is not conscious of what is occurring; the practitioner can provoke access through behavior (framed or not) or verbally or some combination of the two; the anchors involved can be self-anchors established and operated by the client or anchors established and operated by the practitioner or both; the input channel utilized by the anchoring party can be visual, auditory or kinesthetic; the anchors can be single or multiple anchors, dynamic or static, internal or external, consciously available to the client or covert. Such considerations are largely a complex interplay between the present capabilities of the client and the style preferences of the practitioner.

Whatever the specific variations on the classic anchoring change format are and whatever additional techniques are employed (playing polarity, dramatization, meta modeling, metaphors...), it will include the above five elements ordered as indicated above.

Flaws in the Classic Code

In this prototypic Classic Code anchoring format, then, we note that

1. The consciousness of the client is assigned the responsibility for the selection of certain critical elements: the desired state, the resource and/or the new behavior that will substitute for the behavior to be changed...

2. There are no constraints placed on the selection of the resource or new behaviors to replace the original behavior being changed.

3. There is no explicit involvement of the unconscious of the client.

4. The focus of the work is at the level of behavior.

We elaborate on these flaws:

1. At some point in the anchoring format and completely consistent with the ethics of NLP [application] (which requires that the NLP practitioner confine his or her manipulations to the process level and leave the content entirely to the client) [11], the NLP practitioner will ask the client to decide what the desired state (goal, objective) for the change work will be. Notice that this is a call for the client to make a conscious decision.

At some point further on in the format and equally consistent with the ethics of NLP [application], the practitioner will ask the client to decide what behavior or state or resource he or she would like to implement to replace the undesirable behavior. Once again, this decision is one made consciously by the client. These are important decisions and it is unfortunate in the extreme that the classic code assigns the responsibility for these decisions to the client's conscious mind – precisely the part of the client least competent to make such decisions.

2. Note in addition, that the classic code formats involve making these decisions not only consciously but also without explicitly identifying the context or frame in which the change will occur.

This can lead to such absurdities as a client choosing relaxation as the state they would prefer in place of a state of panic in the face of actual physical danger. Relaxation may indeed feel better to the conscious mind but hardly constitutes an adequate response state for dealing with and surviving unscathed the danger that presents itself. The experienced NLP practitioner will also easily recognize that such inappropriate decisions on the part of the client typically lead to nearly immediate "resistance" – this resistance is typically a signal from the unconscious that indicates disagreement with the

214

choice being made by the conscious mind. This "resistance" can take any number of forms – confusion, inability to access experiences that contain the state consciously selected, physiological symptoms…

3. There is no explicit place[12] in the format for the unconscious to participate - a resource that the client surely must engage in the implementation of the difference sought. Apparently, in the original coding, no thought was given to this critical feature.

4. Interventions in the classic code tend to occur at the level of behavior (as opposed to deeper levels of functioning – such as intention): the client is invited by the practitioner to select the behavior that they would prefer as opposed to their present behavior. The practitioner tends to use the presence or absence of actual behavior as the primary indicator of the effectiveness of their ongoing work. This tends to make the work shallow and unecological as the conscious mind is notoriously weak in its ability to appreciate what the function of a consciously undesired piece of behavior might be in the larger system of the person's experience.

The critique we offer, therefore, is that such classic code patterns are flawed. They fail to provide for any systematic framing (#2, #4) or access (#3) to the enormous potential of the unconscious. Further they make an assignment of responsibilities (#1) which can be called, at best, unfortunate.

I (JG) take responsibility for my personal involvement in being one of the two people responsible for coding and promoting these classic patterns. More bluntly, these flaws represent significantly unfortunate coding errors. We further propose that a close examination of the characteristics of the Six Step Reframing pattern, produced entirely by a rather astonishing unconscious process suggests the direction for correcting these flaws – a topic to which we now turn our attention.

A Comparison between the Classic Code and Six Step Reframing

It is instructive to compare these *flaws* with the structure of Six Step Reframing. To ensure that the reader's mental map is aligned with those of the authors, we offer an analysis of Six Step Reframing.

Six Step Reframing

1. identify the behavior(s) to be changed

2. establish a reliable involuntary signal system with the unconscious

3. confirm that there is a positive intention(s) behind the behavior(s) to be changed

4. generate a set of alternatives as good or better than the original behavior(s) in satisfying the positive intention(s)

5. get the unconscious to accept responsibility for implementation

6. ecological check

Step 1 is simply to verify that the client has identified some behavior that is concrete enough to apply the remainder of the patterning to. Note that no information about the desired state is elicited.

In step 2 the agent of change arranges the essential process that makes the rest of the pattern actually work. It is a respectful interactive dialogue within the client whereby he or she uses internal dialogue (talking to themselves) to present a series of prompts consisting of frames and questions to which he or she will then passively await the responses from the unconscious. It is the involuntary nature of these responses – physiological responses that cannot be reproduced by the conscious mind - that ensures that the pattern is not some arbitrary self-serving delusional and ultimately futile exercise.

The initial frames that the client presents to their unconscious acknowledges the conscious desire of the client (obviously prompted by the practitioner) to involve his or her unconscious intimately in the change process. While there are many variations on how specifically the process of actually establishing the signal system can be accomplished, the simplest and most transparent is to present to the unconscious in the form of internal dialog the following question,

Will you (referring to his or her own unconscious) *communicate with me?* [13]

After presenting this question, the client is instructed by the practitioner to wait passively with their attention focused on their kinesthetic system (body sensations) to detect the response from the unconscious. When a change in sensation arrives, the client simply validates its arrival (a touch on the portion of the body where the sensation occurred and a *thank you* (delivered through internal dialogue). The client next engages in a procedure to determine what the signal represents – after all, a body sensation is simply a sensation. The disambiguation procedure to determine whether the signal means *yes* or *no* as an answer to the original question posed, proceeds simply by presenting the following statement to their unconscious (again using internal dialogue),

If the signal just offered means yes, please repeat it.

The subsequent use of framing (explaining the need for a *no* signal in a frame and then requesting one) will yield the negative involuntary counterpart.

Now comes the *critical step*. Requesting that the unconscious remain inactive, the client is instructed by the practitioner to reproduce each of the signals, *yes* and *no*, consciously – that is, without entering into an altered state. If the client proves incapable of consciously reproducing the signals offered by the unconscious – that is, the signal(s) is involuntary, then step 2 is accomplished. If the client succeeds in reproducing one or the other of the two signals – the signal is voluntary and the client is instructed through the use of framing to request of the unconscious alternative signal(s) which are then subjected to the voluntary/involuntary test, until involuntary signals are achieved.

This, then, is an example of a much more general procedure, diagrammatically presented below:

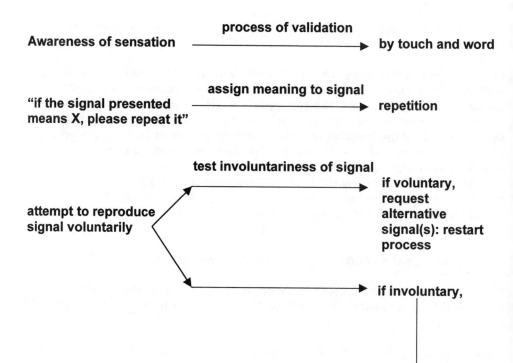

Awareness of sensation ——— process of validation ———▶ by touch and word

"if the signal presented means X, please repeat it" ——— assign meaning to signal ———▶ repetition

test involuntariness of signal

attempt to reproduce signal voluntarily

if voluntary, request alternative signal(s): restart process

if involuntary,

process complete

This process literally positions the unconscious in an appropriate way – one of the essential corrections to the classic code formats mentioned previously. Hopefully it also suggests to the trained NLP practitioner an entire generative class of formats to directly involve the unconscious in the change process. The procedure carries a number of advantages. One obvious one is that the unconscious is superior in its competency for accessing the long term and global effects of some particular change with respect to consequences. Consciousness with its limitation of 7 ± 2 chunks of information is ill-equipped to make such evaluations.

One less obvious advantage is to compare any pattern with this procedure (in whatever variant) with direct hypnosis. Hypnosis, especially in its deeper forms, typically implies a severe disassociation between conscious and unconscious. Indeed, one of the indicators that hypnosis is the treatment of choice is when the agent of change is presented with a client who is so filled with conscious requirements for understanding; has beliefs about the impossibility of change... that the agent of change determines these behaviors will greatly impede the client's ability to make changes. Thus, through hypnotic techniques that bypass the client's conscious mind entirely and therefore the obstacles that clients' conscious activities represent, a skillful hypnotist can stimulate the client's unconscious to make rapid and deep change in spite of such conscious patterns.

Please note, however, one of the ethical commitments of well-trained NLP practitioners is a sort of mental gymnastic whereby the practitioner makes a note of any disassociations she induces in her clients and ensures in the clean up phase at the end of the session that all such disassociations are reversed – that is, some corresponding association technique is required to re-integrate the portions of the client disassociated as part of the change process. Clearly hypnosis itself is disassociative in this sense, as consciousness typically plays no part in its application. Thus the hypnotist must accept the responsibility of making arrangements for a reintegration of consciousness and unconsciousness as part of the clean up after a piece of work. [15]

In steps 2 through 6 of the reframing pattern, all of which involved the use of this involuntary signal system, the client will be alternating between a "normal" state of consciousness (communicating with the practitioner) and an altered state of consciousness (usually a light to medium trance state).

Thus, we regard this class of procedures (the shifting altered state of the client during steps 2 – 6) as congruent with the position that Erickson held at the end of his career. When asked the following question,

> How deep an altered state should a hypnotist strive for with his clients?

Erickson replied,

> Only as deep as necessary to achieve the therapeutic goals desired [16]

In fact as we will explicate subsequently, the inclusion of some form of this involuntary signal system allows the conversion of any of the classic code patterning into new code in the sense of significantly correcting the flaws created by Grinder and Bandler in their original work together.

Steps 3 and 4 define conceptually the heart of reframing, and while they are best accomplished in two discrete moves, we will discuss them together here. The strategy is to identify what the positive intention behind the behavior to be changed is (step 3) and subsequently to generate a new set, namely, the set of behaviors that will satisfy this positive intention (step 4).

We present an example to assist the reader in appreciating how specifically this strategy (to identify positive intention and develop alternatives) works. Remember that in practice, it is typical that the practitioner will not know what the content of the change being effected is – secret therapy, one of the distinguishing advantages of NLP [applications] as applied by the agent of change to the change process. Indeed, while the client will know what the change being made is (as a result of having accomplished step #1) – in many cases he or she will not know consciously what the positive intention(s) behind the behavior to be changed is; nor will such a client consciously know what the new behaviors that will replace original behavior are - until such time as they actually enter the contexts where the former behavior used to occur. It is only at that point that they will discover what new behaviors were that were *unconsciously* selected to satisfy the positive intention.

Let's take as an example a man who has a drinking disorder – an alcoholic – or to people who desire to lose weight. It can be usefully applied to any addiction. In the typical case, an investigation of the client's past would reveal that he has succeeded in stopping drinking [17] for limited periods of time but then returns to the bottle. If we were to make explicit what the payoffs – secondary benefits or secondary gains – of this behavior are, we would discover one or more of the following:

> he drinks to relax

> he drinks to escape the pressures of everyday life

> he drinks to achieve a state of sociability

> ...

Suppose that we focus on the positive intention of achieving access to a state of relaxation. This positive intention is the name of a set – namely, the set of all behaviors that offer the client access to a state of relaxation. This set will, by definition, always include the original behavior.

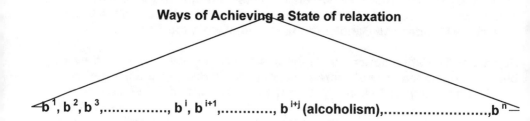

Ways of Achieving a State of relaxation

$$b^1, b^2, b^3, \ldots\ldots\ldots\ldots, b^i, b^{i+1}, \ldots\ldots\ldots\ldots, b^{i+j} \text{ (alcoholism)}, \ldots\ldots\ldots\ldots\ldots\ldots, b^n$$

In other words, within the set of *ways to achieve states of relaxation*, we find a large number of behaviors, b^1 (sports), b^2 (reading), b^3 (meditation), b^i (drugs), b^{i+1} (yoga), b^{i+j} (alcoholism), b^n (breathing exercises), (community service)... Once we have specified (partially at least) what the members of the set are, the change task is greatly simplified: simply select three or more behaviors from the set to replace the behavior in question – in this case, alcoholism.

In a classic addiction case, such as alcoholism, there is typically more than a single payoff or secondary gain involved. The practitioner is cautioned then to divide the change work into a series of sessions, one for each of the positive intentions and their associated payoffs. Thus, the application of this step leads naturally to the generation of a series of sets, each defined by each of the positive intentions behind the behavior to be changed.

It is interesting to note that these two steps (#3 and #4) need not involve conscious disclosure of content. More specifically, with the aid of a robust, involuntary signal system, the skilled practitioner can remain entirely content free in her approach. The more remarkable thing is that all this can be managed without the unconscious revealing the content involved – neither the positive intention nor the new behaviors. Thus, if the client chooses not to have a conscious disclosure of the content or the unconscious declines to reveal the information, the question presented by the client to his unconscious through internal dialogue in step #3 is:

Is there a positive intention behind the behavior to be changed?

Or, equivalently:

Can you, my unconscious, confirm that there is a positive intention behind the behavior to be changed?

In step #4, the request delivered by the client to his unconscious via internal dialogue is:

Develop a range of behaviors, all of which satisfy the positive intention you have already confirmed lies behind the behavior to be changed, and select three or more of these behaviors for implementation. When you have completed this task, please give me a positive signal.

This pattern guarantees that the client will not lose access to the payoffs the original behavior delivered. It has been our experience over some 35 accumulated years, that the major difficulty that confronts most therapeutic practitioners – resistance - simply does not occur.

Resistance, then, we propose, is a particularly important form of non-verbal feedback that carries the message that the change process being applied has not identified adequately the positive intentions behind the behavior to be changed or the alternative behaviors to satisfy those intentions are unsatisfactory. This is equivalent to saying that the behavior that the client says consciously he wishes to change has significant secondary payoffs that are not being respected by the change process presently being implemented. This is another way of saying that the person is engaging in a behavior that represents the best choice available at present within the limits of her own mental maps, given her perception of the context in which she finds herself. [17] In this pattern., More specifically, in steps #3 and #4, this principle is fully respected and resistance is obviated.

In step #5, the client then selects three or more behaviors from this set and asks that the unconscious take responsibility for implementing these new behaviors in precisely the contexts in which the original behavior being changed used to occur.

The final step (#6) is a request to the unconscious to verify that the new behaviors selected to replace the original behavior are congruent with the requirements of other parts of the person. Should it prove that there are objections to one or more of the new behaviors, the practitioner has two choices: either replace the behavior(s) to which there are objections with other behaviors from the original set generated; or use the objection as the starting point for another reframe, beginning with step #3 in which there is a verification of some positive intention behind the objection made. All this remarkably can be accomplished by a skilled practitioner without access to the content involved – a distinctive advantage of this application of NLP to change processes.

In summary, then, the four faults identified in the classic code are corrected by the reframing format that emerged in such a surprising way. [18]

The preceding discussion, and especially the explicit introduction of the positive intention as the method for defining the context in which the changes must occur, offers a precise way to determine which set of behaviors could serve adequately as substitutes for the behavior to be changed.

SUMMARY

This chapter is different than the ones immediately preceding it in the following ways: in form, it is a blending of our epistemological position with current and historical examples; in substance, it is a departure from modeling to an emphasis on application. It makes explicit how the epistemology is realized in the application of NLP patterning.

We began with a characterization of the epistemological positioning of NLP ^{application} with respect to other systems of change work, with special emphasis on the implications of the epistemology developed in Chapter 1, Part I. We pointed out that NLP ^{application} operates solely on representations, and rejects the necessity for an investigation into the roots of a "problem" or challenge in change work. Similarly, NLP ^{application} refuses the requirement common to nearly all other systems of professional change work; namely, that the person (or organization, in a business application) consciously understand the root "cause" of the behavioral "problem" and/or the processes of change employed as a necessary part of the change process. Such issues and the inevitable decisions that agents of change make are to be balanced within the larger frame of ensuring the integrity of the client or organization; in this discourse, primarily by insisting at appropriate points in the change process that the clients fully participate as responsible agents of change themselves.

We then offered a description of the breakthrough pattern with the historical emergence of Six Step Reframing. This pattern was dissected in some detail. The analysis was used as the basis for a critique of the classic code. Special emphasis was placed on how certain features in the structure of this breakthrough pattern illuminates specific flaws in the classic code.

Footnotes for Chapter 2, Part II

1. See an extended set of these so-called presuppositions of *NLP in Personal Strategies for Life* by Jules and Chris Collingwood of INSPIRITIVE or in the work *The NLP Field Guide* or in *A Framework for Excellence* by Charlotte Bretto.

2. It is also reminiscent of the asymmetry of the peculiar experiences Bandler and I had in our first work with professionally trained clients – clients who have extended experience in therapy. While remaining trapped in the patterns of behavior they stated that they desired to change, such clients were far more articulate than either one of us in describing the etiology of their problem and the form it took at that time. This demonstrates that it is quite possible (even common in some circles, among so-called intellectuals, for example) to achieve conscious insight into a "problem" without succeeding in developing choices about it. There are no examples of the inverse situation known to us: the situation in which the problem is solved – that is, a plethora of new effective choices are generated and successfully implemented by the client and the conscious articulation of the "problem" remain as fixed as it was when the client had the "problem".

3. Susan is not the actual name of the woman involved – I am happy to report that since she is alive and well today, I have changed her name in the presentation of her story to protect her identity.

4. We are exquisitely sensitive to the dislocation of sound sources, capable of detecting a difference of 1/250,000 of a second difference in the arrival times of sound waves at the two ears – a fact that Erickson used to great advantage.

5. For a period of time in the mid and late 70's Grinder and Bandler offered a special service to Bay area agents of change (psychiatrists, clinical psychologists, counselors, social workers…) in which if the professionals in question had exhausted their choices for assisting a client in achieving some therapeutic goal, they were invited to accompany their client to a session with the two men. The professional would observe how specifically Bandler and Grinder worked with his client and would be briefed by the two men at the end of the session to ensure that responsible follow up was available. In this way, the client got the choices she was seeking, the professional learned new strategies and Grinder and Bandler got some amazing cases to work with. The two men called this their *impossible practice*. Frankly, the impossible clients were in general easier to work with than regular clients as typically they were very well trained by their original agents of change.

6. Gaster was so skilled in aerobatic flying that once on a bet while demonstrating a Leer jet for a group of executives who were potential buyers, he executed a slow roll so smoothly and with such precision (maintaining a one gravity condition throughout the maneuver) that the executives in the aft cabin sipping champagne were entirely unaware that they were inverted until by chance one of them happened to look out the window and notice that the earth was above them.

7. Making such deals with one's unconscious is hardly an unusual experience although the specific strategies for doing so vary wildly from person to person. I note that Erickson, both in his personal communication with me and in several pieces of his writing mentioned that when confronted with a challenge where he had some question about his ability to perform, he would simply put himself in an altered state and trust his unconscious to manage the situation. Certainly for me, offering excellent demonstration work with the chronic schizophrenics at St. Paul's while sporting a temperature of 104F fell into this category.

8. We have found this pattern to be associated with other altered states that require a complete and tight focus of attention. For example, when climbing rock at or above the level of one's personal best; or flying extended complicated programs of aerobatics; or in situations where your survival, or that of someone to whom you are committed depends on your succeeding in taking a series of rapid decisions and acting flawlessly in their execution. Surely this is a characteristic of tightly, highly focused states of consciousness in which success depends on a complete release to unconscious processes. Regression to the experience hypnotically would offer a method for recovering such events, if desired.

9. In the summer of 1998 in Paris, I had the pleasure of catching up with Lynn Conwell, one of the original trainers of NLP taught and certified by Bandler and myself in the '70s. Lynn reminded me that something like a quarter of a century ago, I had challenged her and other members of the trainers training seminar to find me any personal change at the individual or small group level that could not be accomplished through a congruent application of the Six Step Reframing pattern. With her inimitable smile, she confessed that having attempted to find such changes over the years, she had to admit that thus far, she had found none.

10. It is regrettable that creating variations on such themes seem to be the principal focus of much activity in NLP as opposed to modeling of new patterns itself.

11. With important exceptions such as clients in altered states (comas, drugs or alcohol induced states...) that temporarily render them incapable of making such decisions. In such cases, the NLP practitioner makes the

minimum content decisions required to move the process along to a point where he or she can turn such activities over to the client.

12. This is not to say that the patterns don't work. They work, and they work brilliantly. However, the analogy for us is that of a high jumper who digs a hole just on the launch side of the bar and attempts to jump out of that hole over the bar. How much more effective such a performance would be without the hole!

It is important to understand how it is possible that these formats work despite these design flaws. We offer the following commentary based on decades of personal experience and observation of other practitioners. Clearly these formats in the hands of a skilled NLP practitioner will involve feedback from the unconscious – thus the importance of calibration skills, the most fundamental of all the NLP skill sets. The practitioner's ability while guiding the client through the steps specified in the format to detect, appreciate and incorporate the ongoing non-verbal feedback from the client's unconscious explains how this is possible. We shudder to think of the consequences of well-intentioned, enthusiastic practitioners applying the tools of NLP blindly following these classic code formats without either the requisite calibration skills or a deep appreciation of what the non-verbal signals indicate.

13. It is often helpful to have the client think about the new relationship they are about to build with their unconscious and to have the client choose a name for their unconscious that implies the type of relationship they think of when they want a partnership, for example; *my ally, my partner, my brother, my sister...*

14. A more radical approach to health and personal responsibility would propose that disease is precisely the result of ignoring the initial signals of imbalance and allowing the condition being signaled to persist and indeed to become increasingly more aggravated. Contrast this with the pill popping strategy mentioned in the text.

15. There are, of course, examples where a skilled practitioner will allow a disassociation to run over the course of a number of sessions to allow the changes arranged with the unconscious to be implemented and subsequently "discovered" by the client consciously. Only then will the practitioner take the necessary steps to ensure re-integration. There are, even in Erickson's work, examples of his arranging permanent disassociation. He refers to these cases as ones in which he choose to achieve "limited therapeutic goals" – in other words, to leave a form of disassociation intact as a way of re-organizing his client into a more functional status.

16. Erickson's position on this issue shifted many times during his career. At one point, he urged that the hypnotherapist train his subject (the client) to be competent in all the standard deep trance phenomena (e.g. limited vision, analgesia, time distortion, amnesia...) prior to beginning therapy. Bandler and I toyed with variations on this position – being minimalists, we finally decided that the successful implementation of this strategy actually required only that the client be trained and competent in one of the deep trance phenomena – namely, amnesia. We would then simply make the client amnesic for the problem he presented us with. Although there is little ecology in this strategy, it is surprisingly effective for a wide range of presenting problems.

17. By the way, defining the task as *stopping drinking* will ensure failure. There are two movements behind this provocative statement: first, It is literally nearly impossible to stop doing something that is your sole access or strategy for achieving highly valued states (or what is often called secondary gains or payoffs); secondly, as in the case of AA (with all the respect due to Bill X who gave hope to alcoholics when there was none), the phrase *stopping drinking* fixes the client's attention on drinking, or more specifically not drinking. Since the unconscious does not compute negation (the verb *stop* contains lexical negation) the phrase *stop drinking* rivets the attention of the unconscious on precisely that activity – in effect, a continuing fixation on drinking.

18. The only aspect of the entire adventure which I (JG) find in retrospect unsatisfactory is the name itself. The pattern would be better named *rebehaving*, albeit more awkwardly, as in fact, in the pattern, the frame (the positive intention and the set generated thereby) are held constant and the behavior is varied until satisfactory substitute behaviors are selected for implementation. As a matter of fact, the pattern we (Bandler and I) called contextual reframing – essentially a pattern in which the behavior is held constant and an appropriate context is identified (one in which the client recognizes that the behavior would be an appropriate response) – is prototypically reframing.

Chapter 3: The New Code

The Emergence of Design: a natural consequence of deep extended modeling and training activities

While the narrative below initially continues with the same sort of historical development that has marked the last several sections, it is important to frame the descriptions that we will offer ahead of time. With the exception of the last chapter, the main focus of this book has been modeling – the core activity that defines NLP. Here, with the presentation of the new code, we see the emergence of a new creature, albeit one whose origins are clearly identifiable as the result of the very modeling activity on which we have previously focused. This creature's name is *design*. The new code is a consequence of a sequence of design activities, not a modeling activity in the strict sense that we have defined it.

The immediate success and rapid diffusion of the initial models of NLP in the mid and late '70s created a ground swell of interest leading to a great demand for the presentation to and training of people who desired to become proficient in the patterning. This demand constituted both an opportunity and a distraction for Bandler and Grinder. The fascinating and fully engaging task of making explicit the complex behaviors of a number of extremely talented people (Satir, Perls, Erickson...) had a profound effect on the co-creators of NLP. While Grinder and Bandler had exercised themselves greatly in approaching each of the modeling projects in a disciplined know-nothing state (to be explicated below), it became apparent in the late '70s that the distinct models of excellence that had been coded had significant overlap.

In the case of the verbal patterning modeled, this is understandable. The two modelers had fortunately selected an already well-developed and relatively rigorous code for the language patterns modeled, the language of the transformational syntactician. It was understandable that the variables used in the description of the verbal patterning of different models would strongly overlap. This descriptive code, after all, is one that is based on the structure of natural language. It is, therefore, unsurprising that the same descriptive code for verbal patterning would turn out to be applicable and enlightening across independent modeling projects.[1] The point here is that the variables that describe the patterning known as the meta model, for example, overlap strongly with those that are required to explicate the Milton model.

The non-verbal patterning modeled, however, had no comparable initial stable code to utilize, as was the case in the verbal patterning. What seems to be a useful and accurate representation is that Bandler and Grinder arrived at a partial list of design variables inductively. This occurred in a process akin to the kind of unconscious assimilation of patterning, their deployment during imitation and the unconscious editing that spontaneously occurred (as described in detail in the modeling of Perls in the *Contexts of Discovery*). Further their extensive experiences in the application of the patterning and the design demands in the training context led naturally to a deep appreciation of the variables common to the patterns, partially explicit and partially tacit.

It was, for example, quite clear that rapport (between agent of change and client) was an essential component of any effective intervention in change work. Remember by rapport, we refer to the ability to capture the attention, especially unconscious attention, of the client, not the more common descriptions such as trust, confidence... But what is rapport other than a specific state? Thus the manipulation of state (both the state of the agent of change and of the client in a change work application) is seen to be common to all interventions, and simultaneously as an example of one of the members of the set of design variables that slowly emerged from these extensive experiences.

The incipient use of multiple perceptual positions implicit in the classic anchoring formats constitutes another example – another member of this set of design variables. Classic anchoring formats involve an identification and appropriation of some resource located in a historical experience in the client's personal history. When we ask a client to ...*remember a time when...* and then having located the relevant reference experience, we invite the client to step into the experience to recover the resource therein contained, we are implicitly creating an historical meta position (or as coded in Triple Description in the new code, an historical 3rd position) as an integral part of the intervention. But critically, this is a variable that is not explicitly coded in the classic code intervention format. This incipient movement emerges clearly into focus in the new code in the development of the explicit form called Triple Description. A third example of an implicit design variable would be the framing that occurred during classic code interventions (sporadic but nevertheless present in the uncoded behavior of the agent of change) in an attempt to intuitively address the issue of ecology.

As mentioned above the tremendous demand for training – initially, psychiatrists, physicians, social workers and clinical psychologists and subsequently, business people, athletes, students, musicians and pilgrims of all sorts of strange and bazaar shapes and beliefs - constituted both an opportunity and a distraction. It certainly distracted us from large scale, time consuming modeling projects such as the Erickson work. It simultaneously represented an opportunity – both financially and in the form of a challenge to design trainings to ensure a high quality, effective and efficient transfer of patterning thus far coded to interested parties in the form of books, tapes and especially seminars. It is important to note that this demand to train other people, sometimes in large numbers and with widely varying backgrounds and capabilities, played an important role in sorting out and refining our appreciation of these design variables. We constantly developed and tested new methods for making the transfer of patterning more effective and efficient. Sometimes, we accomplished this by creating a variation on one of the patterns actually modeled (tweaking the original pattern to discover a form equally effective but easier for our students to master). Sometimes the focus in facilitating the transfer of patterning took the form of discovering how to induce appropriate states of learning in the students – again, a manipulation of state issue.

We did made the adjustments, constantly experimenting with the question,

> *What happens if we do X?*

These adjustments represented steps in this inductive process of making at least partially explicit the set of design variables underlying the classic code patterning.

All this activity left the two co-creators of NLP with a partially explicated set of design variables. It was about this time that these two men decided to separate their interests. Looking back now with the advantage of hindsight, it is apparent that each of the two co-creators of NLP subsequently pursued their personal preferences. The form that the exploitation of the partially explicated set of design variables took in the case of Bandler is what he refers to as the Design of Human Engineering [2]; while in the case of Grinder, it took the form of the New Code.

I would be remiss in my presentation if I were to fail to point out that certainly in my own case (I invite Bandler to explicate his own experience in this matter), the systematic use of the partially explicated design variables that resulted in the new code can be understood to be a certain kind of self-modeling.

I am most pleased when my experiences run well in advance of my ability to consciously and explicitly represent the effective patterning in my own behavior. Such experiences – I refer to such periods as running before the wind - are an indicator that I am developing new patterns that I will have the pleasure subsequently of explicating. But note that this is a distinct form – one that shares certain characteristics with modeling but still is quite distinct in other aspects. There is no identifiable external model to imitate; I arrive at new patterning by a partially conscious and more importantly by an unconscious manipulation of certain design variables; I use feedback to determine what is worth pursuing until I reach some criterion – that is, until I am satisfied that I have achieved the results I wanted to achieve. Then and only then, do I attempt in a disciplined manner an explication of the patterning that I have designed.

The above narrative is an attempt to indicate to the reader the processes by which design activities emerged as a natural consequence of the modeling activities and simultaneously as a response to the demands of transferring the product of NLP modeling effectively to the world in the training context.

The Context of the Creation of the New Code

The historical narrative continues:

> In the early to mid 80's, I found myself in a somewhat peculiar position. As I looked about the world of NLP that Bandler and I had created, I noted several things of serious concern to me.
>
> > 1. There were a number of extremely well-trained practitioners of NLP who were themselves clearly capable of miracles (relative to the capabilities of other systems of change work) with clients; however it apparently had never occurred to them (or perhaps, they simply had chosen not) to apply the patterning to themselves – that is, self-application of the patterning. Thus, my perception was that many of them were incongruent in significant contexts in their lives – there were portions of their personal and professional lives that showed absolutely no presence of the choices they busily assisted others in creating in their lives. I was not happy with this situation.
> >
> > 2. Many of these same people were focused on the task of creating applications of the NLP patterning (what I perceived to be minor variations of the original patterning) but gave little or no attention to the core activity of NLP – modeling.
> >
> > 3. The focus of attention for many of these same people was reactive problem solving where the problems they focused on were defined by whatever issue the client happened to walk through the door with. There seemed not to be much, if any, concern with larger-frame issues such as aesthetics, ethics or social and political challenges, nor could I detect any movement toward a pro-active approach to such larger issues on their part.

I resolved therefore to develop what has come to be known as the new code in NLP. [3] Judith Delozier participated in some aspects of this endeavor.

In particular, I set myself the goal of designing patterning that could be effectively presented in training if and only if the presenter was himself congruent with the deeper principles of choice that are the key issue in any application of NLP. At the same time, I recognized that this re-coding of NLP [applications] offered me the opportunity to correct some of the design errors which Bandler and I in our great rush of enthusiasm for codifying the classic patterning had committed.

In hindsight, I seemed to have failed utterly in my attempt to achieve the first goal – there are plenty of incongruent people making a living "teaching" the new code. Time will tell whether I succeeded in the second.

Independent of the original objectives I had in designing the new code, from my present point of view, the new node represents a natural although radical extension of certain variables embodied in the classic code. In particular, there was from the beginning of the coding of the classical code a number of constant practices:

1. an insistence that putative changes had to be verified through calibration for the agent of change to be satisfied that change had occurred;

2. the consistent use of experiences of the past as the source of states of high performance to be used as resources in change work;

3. the deliberate avoidance of content as an important part of the process of change;

4. the use of contextual cues as anchors to ensure appropriate re-activation of the resource state involved (future pacing) and

5. a relative lack of concern with conscious understanding on either the part of the client and the agent of change with respect to the content of the changes being made. This translates to refusing to indulge in investigations into the origins of the behaviors to be changed - in other words, an avoidance of all archeological activities.

The new code, then, takes these variables to their extreme values. For example, in the new code, the so-called resource states are created directly through the participation of the client in an activity - often a game - that itself creates a high performance state but one, curiously enough, that has neither history nor content to it. [4] It is simply a game but a game that activates neurological circuits that serve as the base for changes in the context selected previously by the client. The structure of the game itself is designed to ensure that certain characteristics that are typical of high performance states are present. But once again this occurs without any particular content and without reference to any historically experienced states. The technical requirements of the new code compared with the classic code are sharply reduced, lowering the skill threshold for people desiring to participate.

One of the fundamental strategies behind the new code was to develop a set of activities or games which lead naturally to the activation in the player of a content free, high performance state. The implicit assumption behind this strategy is what has come to be known as the chain of excellence:

The Chain of Excellence

Respiration

Physiology

State

Performance

This ordering can be usefully read from the bottom up and is explicated in narrative form in the following three sentences: Performance in the world is a function of state; therefore, to optimize performance in the world, select a state that gives you access to the enormous resources already available at the unconscious level. The most effective and straightforward way to activate such a state is through a manipulation of your own physiology. One of the most efficacious means for manipulating your own physiology is through the modulation of your breathing pattern.

This chain, then, is an ordering of ascending leverage points [5] that can be utilized to optimize performance – as well as a class of other activities as we shall develop below. The set of leverage points that make up the ordering expressed by the chain is generated by successive answers to the question,

What leverage point allows me to shift this portion of my experience?

To us, this chain also represents a commentary on a number of important issues:

First, the chain proposes that the simplest leverage point available is the manipulation of breathing; as in turn a shift in breathing leads to a corresponding shift in physiology and subsequently in state and performance.

Secondly the proposition that underlies the chain is an explicit rejection of Descartes' original sin - the split between mind and body. In effect, the proposition says that there is no such valid distinction – that the words *mind* and *body* as referring to separate entities are fictions or worse. A way to think about this is to take, for example, any two cancer patients diagnosed with the same form of cancer and in the same stage of development: one of whom dies within the statistically approved time period and the other who achieves a state of grace known technically as "spontaneous remission" and lives a full and complete life. Where will you draw the line between mind and body in each of them? Where does their personal response to their diagnosis touch upon the physical reality of cancer and what part does their attitude play in selecting their future? Indeed, these words (*mind* and *body*) are simply terms that refer to two facets of the same diamond – they are the results of the kind of filters we identified and discussed in the introductory epistemological remarks - the linguistically based filters - distortions introduced by the obsessive naming function of our species. And we argue that this distinction – the subject about which library shelves are burdened with learned books – is not only <u>not</u> useful, it is positively devastating in many of its applications to human experience.

Thirdly, observe that world class athletes, actors, actresses, negotiators, musicians... indeed anyone whose success depends on consistent high quality performance under pressure, develop rituals. These rituals are designed by these high performing individuals to allow them to voluntarily enter into or maintain high performance states. All of us intuitively attempt to accomplish this – getting pumped for a sales call, rehearsing for an important meeting, preparing "mentally" for an anticipated challenge... That favorite bracelet or tie or that special way of entering a room - all are personal dynamic anchors for re-accessing some favored state within us for performing some particular task or responding to some challenge with excellence. Thus, we can readily observe in ourselves and in those around us the use of rituals as a spontaneous utilization of naturally occurring iconic anchors to re-access highly valued states of high performance.

But we already know a great deal about such processes in NLP applications. At various points in this book, we have commented that calibration is the most fundamental NLP skill without which it is literally not possible to do high quality work in the field of NLP - regardless of whether we are referring to modeling, application or the teaching of the methodology.

Fourth: But what is the chain of excellence if not a simple explication of the mechanisms behind calibration? The chain of excellence proposes that our ability to perform with excellence has certain associated states and each such state has associated with it a specific physiology. This connection between performance/behavior and underlying states with their own associated physiologies is, in fact, the fundamental observation about how we communicate non-verbally and identifies that which makes calibration possible.

We "know" that our spouse or close friend is not in a mood to consider positively an offer to dine or go to the theatre by the tone of voice, or posture, or breathing pattern or more likely, by the Gestalt or overall physiological pattern he or she presents to us unconsciously and which we typically detect and respond to unconsciously. If, in fact, we have calibrated accurately and are not presently hallucinating (projecting) our own emotions, such calibrations serve as the basis for successfully reading the people around us. The chain of excellence is simply the recognition and aggressive utilization of these commonplace observations: a careful drawing out of the implications of the fundamental process of calibration.

Fifth: the chain of excellence is a strategy that recognizes and systematically exploits the power and wisdom of unconscious processing. The clues had been around in NLP practice for nearly a decade at the time of the development of the new code. Since the modeling of Dr. Erickson in the mid '70s, the systematic use of his powerful hypnotic patterning had deeply influenced and informed the practices of both of the co-creators of NLP. These patterns placed great emphasis on avoiding conscious barriers to change such as beliefs, not by the paradoxical activity of focusing on such limiting beliefs [6] but by simply circumventing such obstacles and inducing change at the unconscious level.

Further, these patterns had in common a deep trust that unconscious processes *when properly organized and constrained* would produce deep, long term ecological changes in spite of, for example, a client's declared conscious beliefs that such changes were impossible. The limitations of consciousness, the 7 ± 2 chunks of attention available in working memory, makes understandable the inability of the consciousness to successfully select desired states, appropriate resources or specific new behaviors with any degree of competency. This limitation applies, however, only to conscious processing and not to unconscious processing. Thus, as you would expect, given this difference, the ability of the unconscious to assess the longer-term consequences and then, based on this assessment, to make such selections (desired state, resource or replacement behavior) greatly exceeds that of the conscious mind.

In the critique of the classic code we identified design flaws that the new code corrects. These flaws contrast maximally with the Six Step Reframing format that we are proposing creates the bridge from the classic code to the new code. In the new code, we find that:

1. The unconscious of the client is explicitly assigned the responsibility for the selection of the critical elements – the desired state, the resource, or new behaviors;

2. The unconscious is explicitly involved in all critical steps;

3. There are precise constraints placed upon the selection of new behavior(s); more specifically, the new behavior(s) must satisfy the original positive intention(s) of the behavior(s) to be changed;

4. The manipulation occurs at the level of state and intention as opposed at the level of behavior.

Further, experiences with these patterns of unconscious access seem to lead to what we have come to call the disciplined *know-nothing state*. [7]

The know-nothing State and some Implications

We begin the discussion of the know-nothing state by analogy. Those readers who have extensive experience in competitive activities, in situations where lightening quick responses to actions by their opponent are the measure of success, will recognize this highly valued performance state - a disciplined no-know-nothing state. In any martial art, tennis, racquetball, handball, squash, baseball, soccer, football... there are significant portions of the competition that depend on such responses -

lightening quick responses that spring forward without language – they are just there.

Our favorite example is competition in martial arts – Aikido, for example. In such a competition, suppose we decide prior to beginning the competition through an analysis, let's say, of the strengths and weaknesses of the opponent that she is likely to open with a certain maneuver X, and we bias our position (balance, muscle tension…) to respond to X. If we are facing a worthy opponent we have, in effect, already lost the match. She will detect the bias (unconsciously) and select (again unconsciously) an opening that exploits the bias we are expressing and the match will be over quite quickly, and most definitely in her favor.

Entry into this know-nothing state consists in eschewing any expectations, a refusal to anticipate what will occur in favor of putting yourself in a balanced resource state with no bias toward any specific course of action, freed of internal representations in all channels, your attention cleanly committed to sensing externally what is occurring and with all the response patterns of the game equally accessible. Such a state (sometimes called "being in the zone") releases to the unconscious the right and responsibility to select whichever of the many patterns practiced over long periods of preparation is optimal in response to what your opponent is doing. This occurs without the involvement of the conscious mind. This greatly accelerates the speed of the response and guarantees that the performer will display the most appropriate of the choices available at the unconscious level. [8]

More concretely, this know-nothing state strategy is exploited strongly in the new code as will become apparent subsequently. We would like you to recall at this point, however, our discussion of six step reframing beginning (Part II, chapter 3). When one applies step four of six step reframing, in essence, one is relying upon a know-nothing state (the assignment of the task at hand to the unconscious) to generate alternative behaviors to satisfy the positive intention of the behavior to be changed. In the majority of cases, the clients are unaware at the successful conclusion of the application of this change format what specific new behaviors they will experience when next they enter the context where the original behavior occurred. They only know that they have received an involuntary signal from the unconscious that the unconscious has generated a set of alternative behaviors from which will emerge the actual new behaviors. This is what the clients will experience automatically when they enter the context. Our impression is that the client when entering the context the next time is essentially in a disciplined know-nothing state and that the unconscious at that specific point activates the set of alternatives anchored to the auditory and visual stimuli that define the context of change. Further it is at that point that the unconscious actually makes the selection based on the positive intention of the person and the set of alternatives generated during the previous change work, choosing the most appropriate of the new behaviors given the actual context in which the client finds herself. This is a reasonable description of the advantages of the know-nothing state.

There is a number of other applications whereby the know-nothing-state has excellent application and numerous advantages.

> *I, (CB), was the Director of Mergers and Acquisitions for a major American corporation and for other entities for a number of years. In addition to the actual negotiation and final purchase of a proposed asset, my responsibilities typically included the due diligence preceding the negotiations. I considered the due diligence phase an integral element in negotiation. As such, I was quite systematic in making use not only of the standards required by such due diligence, but also by tapping less traditional sources of information about the potential asset, such as: disgruntled employees; customers who had defected to competitors; suppliers who had voluntarily terminated their supply contracts ... I considered all this information not only essential to establish a purchase price which would meet the parameters my company had set for growth, but to prepare me for the next phase – negotiation.*

> *I commenced each negotiation with an explicit strategy to purposely set aside the months of investigation and preparation the moment that I arrived at the site of the negotiation. I would enter the room in a know-nothing state – having cleared myself, at the conscious level of functioning, of the very information I had so diligently developed. I marked this know-nothing state for myself, by ritualistically locking my briefcase that contained the documentation, putting it safely beyond temptation. This know-nothing strategy enabled me (as if an Aikido master) to optimize my ability to detect and utilize the information being presented both consciously and unconsciously by the individuals sitting around the negotiating table.*

This ability to suspend conscious filters without losing the benefits of the preparation is another example of the advantages involved in the development and deployment of the know-nothing state. This same know-nothing state played a critical role in creating the initial model of NLP (see chapter 1, Part II, *Contexts of Discovery*) – the meta model. It was especially important during the period of disciplined practice that occurred while assimilating the patterning from the source of the patterning as well as the imitative practice that led to mastery of the patterns.

In the new code change pattern, clients are induced into a know-nothing state by the explicit assignment of certain key responsibilities to their unconscious minds.

The new code based in significant part on the deep mechanisms which underpin the most fundamental of all NLP skill sets - calibration - focuses on the development of content free, high performance states and their connection to the stimuli that define the context in which the client desires that the change occur. The responsibility for the selection of the desired state, the resources to be applied to the challenge, the specific new behavior that will replace the behavior to be changed are all reassigned to the unconscious, thereby correcting some of the design flaws in the classic code.

A Partial Listing of New Code Patterning

The following is a partial listing of patterning contained in the new code:

1. Multiple Perceptual Positions especially Triple Description (1st, 2nd and 3rd position)

2. Explicit Framing (outcome, intention, consequence with relevancy challenges)

3. Ordering relationships including hierarchies such as logical levels

4. Timelines (developed initially as an exercise in a joint seminar presented by Grinder and Dilts in the early '80s

5. The Verbal Package with reduced questions, explicit framing and the more refined verbal distinctions such as those named by the terms, *description, interpretation* and *evaluation*.

6. A single format for change in four steps with a variable 3rd step (the high performance state inducer – the games). These games include The Alphabet game, the NASA game, variants of Roger Tabb's [9] trampoline exercises...

7. Stalking (shunts, automatic movement to privileged states)

8. Multiple forms of involuntary signals between conscious and unconscious

9. Characterlogical adjectives

We select a couple of the above patterns for more detailed presentation to offer some flavor of the new code: the single change format with a new code game and some applications of Triple Description.

New Code Change Format

The new code as applied to change work clearly reflects my (JG) minimalist tendencies. In place of a plethora of formats, the change format in the new code is a single ordered sequence consisting of four simple steps:

The Change Format for the New Code

1. select from 3rd position some context in which you experience some behavior you wish to change/influence

2. Localize physically this hallucinated context and the image and sounds of yourself in that context performing the behavior you wish to change/influence and step into the position of the image of yourself (1st position) without attempting to change anything – self-calibrate. This is also the opportunity for the coach to calibrate your present state response to the context in question.

Separator State

3. Play the game (1st position) or equivalently, enter into the content free, high performance state (e.g. The Alphabet game, the NASA game...)

Spend 15 minutes playing to allow full activation of the circuits underlying the performance in the game. [10]

4. At the end of the play (15 minutes or until the circuits are fully activated), the player (1st position) without hesitation and most importantly *without attempting consciously to influence in any way his experience* steps back (into 1st position) into the physical space where in step 2 occurred – that is, the physical space (on the floor) where he had located the hallucinated context in which he wanted to change something.

Please note that step 3 contains a variable – specifically, the variable is what specific game the player will engage in during step 3. In effect, this opens the door for the design and incorporation of as many different games as you can design that meet the well-formedness conditions contained in the reference games (Alphabet, NASA, and trampoline work...)

and which have the effect of inducing within the player a content free, high performance state.

Of great importance in the application of the new code format is the principle that states:

> *The quality of the player's state during play will determine the quality of the changes that the player will subsequently experience when he steps back into the context within which he wanted to make the change.*

While a complete verbal representation of the finer points necessary to the deployment of the skills of the new code format are well beyond the scope of this book, it is important, given this principle, to comment briefly on the importance of the role of the coach in these formats.

The coach has varying responsibilities, depending on the particular game selected for step 3 but there is one task, and in our opinion, the most important one, which is always assigned to the coach in this set of games – that of serving as the guardian of the physiology of the player. [11]

We have noted a tendency – especially among highly competitive players to try to perform the game faster, more accurately... as if there were some reward for such characteristics. The only reward is negative – *trying* for most people involves more than a whiff of failure. The difference between the two statements:

> *I will try to stop eating chocolate.*

and

> *I will stop eating chocolate.*

In addition and most relevant to this play context, *trying* involves the introduction of inappropriate physical tension into the body of the player, reducing the natural grace, coordination and speed of the player. Most telling, of course, is that if the coach allows the player to *try* to play the game, these attributes (reduction in the natural grace, coordination and speed of the player) will transfer unconsciously to the context in which the player desires to change his experience – the context selected in step 1 of the format. This is precisely antithetical to the entire point of the new code format. This is the meaning of the generalization presented above:

> *The quality of the player's state during play will determine the quality of the changes that the player will subsequently experience when he*

steps back into the context within which he wanted to make the change.

Thus in carrying out her function adequately, the coach will interrupt the player should she detect (again, through calibration) that the player is playing in a less than optimal state. She will use separator states and any other techniques (e.g. pattern interruption) required to shift the state of the player until she is satisfied that he is playing in something approaching an optimal state.

An Example of a New Code Game

We select and present now an example of the type of game used in step 3 of the new code to activate the circuitry underlying a high performance state. Again we wish to recognize the essential contributions to this application by Roger Tabb. The game consists of a chart that contains the first 25 letters of the English alphabet [12] written in five rows of five letters each. The following is an example of such a chart:

a	b	c	d	e
l	r	t	t	l
f	g	h	i	j
r	r	t	r	t
k	l	m	n	o
l	r	t	l	r
p	q	r	s	t
l	t	l	l	t
u	v	w	x	y
l	l	t	r	t

Note that immediately beneath each of the first 25 letters of the alphabet is written one of the three instructions (l, r, t), standing for r = right, l = left, t = together. The player stands in a relaxed (no excess physical tension in the body), balanced and flexible posture approximately a meter from the chart that is affixed to a vertical surface (typically, a wall) in front of the player. There are three fundamental conditions for the player.

Condition one consists of the player beginning at the letter *a*, saying the name of the letter aloud and simultaneously, raising the hand and arm indicated by the letter written below the letter whose name he is speaking – in the case of the sample chart above, saying the name of the letter *a*, moving the left hand and arm forward and up a couple of feet and then allowing that hand and arm to return to the normal relaxed position at the player's side. The player works his way through the chart terminating at the letter *y*. This process is repeated several times until both the player and the coach are satisfied that the player is correctly executing the game – saying the name of the letter and simultaneously executing the instruction written below the letter. All of this is to be accomplished with only the body tension required to actually execute the movements indicated.

Condition two consists of the player doing exactly what condition one required. However, this time the player is working from the bottom right of the chart, beginning with the letter *y*, moving backwards through the alphabet towards the letter at the upper left hand of the chart, ending with the letter *a*. In other words, the only difference in condition two is that the player starts with the letter *y* and moves backwards through the alphabet and ends with the letter *a*. The coach is constantly monitoring the physiology of the player to ensure that the game is being played with optimal physiological characteristics, coordination, balance, grace, minimum effort, rhythm... [13] The player spends approximately 2 minutes in each of the first two conditions.

Condition three is equivalent to condition two with one addition – as the player works his way backward through the chart, saying aloud the names of the letter while carrying out the movement instructions written below that letter, he will also simultaneously lift the foot and leg on the *opposite* side of the body. Thus, while saying the name of the letter *s* in the chart above, the player responds to the instruction *l* written below the letter by both raising his left hand and arm and his right foot and leg. The instruction *t* in the third condition implies then, a small jump. The player spends approximately 10 minutes playing this condition. Players typically report a tingling, an activation of their nervous systems within several minutes of playing condition three. This is to be expected as part of the activation of the high performance state. By the way, any particular chart is useful for approximately a half hour of play, after which the unconscious has to a large extent memorized the chart and its ability to serve as an adequate challenge to stimulate the player's nervous system is compromised. [14]

The importance of the actions of the coach cannot be overemphasized. The coach serves as the guardian of the player's physiology (state) and has the primary responsibility of insisting (pattern interruptions, separator states…) upon an optimal physiology during play. The coach will also monitor the player's performance with respect to his execution of the indicated movements but this is of secondary importance. This emphasis is congruent with the principle presented previously,

> *The quality of the player's state during play will determine the quality of the changes that the player will subsequently experience when he steps back into the context where he wanted to make the change.*

The player moves directly (without hesitation and never with a separator state) into step 4 of the New Code Change Format to connect the high performance state activated with the stimuli that define the context of change selected in step 1. The very stimuli that formerly activated the resource less state in the player originally will now serve as dynamic anchors to ensure that the next time the player enters that particular context or one with similar stimuli, the high performance state achieved during play will be automatically re-activated.

We point out that the player usually experiences many differences (e.g. spontaneous sub modality shifts) in step 4 when he re-enters the context of the change to be made compared with his experience of entering that context the first time in step 2. Most frequently, the player does not know consciously what the specific differences in behavior in the context in which the change is occurring will be at that point, only that something enormously interesting has occurred. [15]

This design produces something close to a know-nothing state in which the person having played the game correctly will subsequently enter the context in which he chose to make a change and only then will he discover in his own behavior the differences effected by the format. This is a significant advantage as the actual context may contain elements that were not well represented during the application of the format and/or the player may have intentions distinct from those originally present during the use of the format. Thus, the know-nothing state permits the unconscious to select the most appropriate of the behaviors available in the player's repertoire, given the perceived requirements of the context upon entry into that context. Further the player will experience a number of behaviors rather than simply those he imagined during the change work as in the classic code, and these will vary from instance to instance even in the same context.

Many adults have requested instructions about how to use games such as the alphabet game with children of different ages. [16]

In general and assuming that the adult involved knows the child well, we recommend simply that the adult think through where in his experience the child needs to upgrade their performance – say in math class or on the soccer team or in specific circumstances in family life. The adult will then identify stimuli that are uniquely (or nearly so) associated with those contexts where in the judgment of the adult, the child needs improvement. Then go directly to the game. When in the calibrations of the adult acting now as coach, the child has entered into the high performance state, the adult will mention the stimuli (for example, the questions below) as the child continues to play. For example, the adult desiring to assist the child in improving performance in math class could at the point where he sees and hears that the child is in the activated state, simply ask all or any of the following questions,

Where exactly do you normally sit in math class?

Does your math teacher have a ponytail/mustache?

What kinds of questions does your math teacher ask the class?

Note that any of these questions will force the child, whether she overtly answers the question or not, to unconsciously form representations that are associated with the context in which the adult desires that the child improve her performance. This connects (future pace) the activated state with stimuli that define the context in which the change will emerge. The three questions above entail kinesthetic, visual and auditory representations respectively. It is useful to include at least one question or statement for each of the three major representational systems. The adult coach must, of course, be particularly alert for any deterioration in the performance of the child's play when he (the adult) presents such stimuli, as they will tend to elicit the less than resourceful performance behavior he is attempting to improve. Should the adult detect any loss of quality in the child's performance under the impact of his questioning, he will use pattern/state interruption, reorientation of the child's attention... to restore the quality state of the player and continue with the game. Should this occur, the adult is thereby warned that he will have to present the stimuli that define the context of application in smaller chunks to avoid a repetition of the loss of quality of the child's state.

The adaptations described above for the application of this new code game for children then collapses step 4 into a parallel process that occurs naturally as the child plays the game. Step 1 is the sole responsibility of the adult and is accomplished prior to initiating the game while step 2 is deleted.

The alphabet game, then, represents an embodiment of a certain set of design variables whose aim is to activate in the player a high performance state that will then serve as the resource for something approaching a know-nothing state in the context in which the change will emerge naturally. There are a number of other games created for use in the new code that are also built on these design variables.

Multiple Perceptual Positions

We turn our attention, then, to a second pattern that finds explicit form in the new code – the pattern called multiple perceptual positions. In the creation of the new code, the patterning (formats) that confers the ability to occupy multiple perceptual positions is made explicit. It is important to appreciate what this ability represents epistemologically and how it provides leverage points for choice.

In the epistemology developed at the beginning of *Whispering* and in other places throughout the book, we have made the point that what we normally refer to as the world is a fundamentally transformed set of representations (FA). Prior to our gaining access to it, the data streaming in from our receptors has been modified by the neurological transforms that define the human nervous system. We captured this point by making the provocative statement that Korzybski was too conservative: not only is the map not the territory, but his territory isn't even the territory. We went on to argue that after First Access, we typically apply a second set of transforms that are linguistic in nature (or derivative of linguistic mappings).

We are now asking you to recognize a further filtering or transformation of our experience, unique and specific to each of us as individuals – here we are pointing to the cumulative effects of what we call our personal history.

How, then, are we to understand the term *personal history* in this context? What is clear is that every natural language offers a rich set of transforms that can be applied to FA. However, at the point when we master the fundamentals of our native tongue, we have no appreciation of any of these facts. What in fact happens is that we intuitively model the linguistic competencies (or lack thereof) of the major influential figures in our life at this point – usually our parents and members of our family of origin. This is equivalent to saying that out of the full set of transforms offered by our native language, we unconsciously adopt a smaller subset – more specifically, those of our models. This implies that we rarely (without great personal discipline and supporting tools) come to a mastery of the full array of choices offered by our native tongue. The situation here is analogous to the unconscious modeling that results in each of us developing an unconsciously preferred representational system.

This early unconscious modeling of linguistic competencies also explains how the meta model functions to create choice - as it is an explicit method for challenging and expanding the set of linguistic competencies of the individual, client or user. The cumulative effect of unconsciously and systematically applying our personal limited subset of linguistic transforms to our experience (FA) over years is what we call our mental maps or models of the world. In turn through the process of feed-forward, these mental maps become an additional set of filters on our experience. Thus, our personal history is best represented by the mental maps that are the generalizations that we have made over our lifetime, using whatever set of linguistic competencies we happen to have developed.

Many students of NLP, especially in their initial enthusiasm for the effective use of the patterning, seize upon an epistemologically peculiar (and impossible) goal. The task they set about to accomplish is to free themselves from all perceptual filters, often stating that thereby they will appreciate the world without distortion. Such a naïve project is surely incoherent. A significant part of what it means to be a member of our species is precisely defined by the set of filters that we identified as the f^1 transforms. It is difficult to know what it might mean to actually free one's self of such filters.

Although, it is not possible to free one's self from all filtering of the world around us, it is possible to manipulate the distortions resulting from specific f^2 transforms. We direct your attention once again towards our previous point, namely, that we as children selected (from the array of linguistic patterns available to us as mapping functions) a limited subset normally those of our family of origin. The cumulative effects over a lifetime of that unconscious selection lead to the development of our mental maps. Focusing our attention on the f^2 transforms, a coherent possibility presents itself; namely, that one can train oneself to be excellent at deliberately shifting filters – indeed, to genuinely enter into another perceptual position is synonymous with shifting perceptual filters.

When an individual deliberately trains himself to master the art of shifting perceptual filters, he expands his world of choice. Equipped with a process to systematically offer to himself an array of choices that were previously unavailable, the ability to generate new behaviors in old contexts manifests itself. A natural consequence of creating multiple descriptions of the world – hence more choice - is more flexibility about how specifically one may act in any given context.

Among the simplest methods to create more choice - a leverage point for flexibility - we can identify the following:

1. shifting attention – more specifically, deliberately selecting new portions of the world of experience to attend to as well as how specifically we attend to them.

2. adopting the characteristics and perceptions of some identifiable group. As an example to give the reader a taste of this, imagine what a well-aged hunk of cheese represents from the point of view of:

    a. a mouse

    b. a cow

    c. a starving student

    d. a lactose intolerant patient

    e. a marketing executive

    f. a lawyer

    g. an accountant

    ...

3. systematically shifting perceptual position from one to another of the three privileged perceptual positions specified by Triple Description. We would like to note here that number 2 above could be classified as a generalized 2nd.

4. developing and deploying with discipline the art of multiple description through the explicit manipulation of the linguistic competencies available. In particular, we are suggesting that the reader use the differences proposed by the processes of description, interpretation and evaluation.

Note that within the potentially limitless set of perceptual positions we can learn to occupy, there is a privileged set that we call Triple Description, listed as number 3 above.

Triple Description

One of the differences between the classic code and the new code is the aggressive exploitation of the power and wisdom of unconscious processing – when properly organized and framed. We exploit precisely this property of unconscious functioning with respect to the application of Triple Description and its consequences. Among the formats of the new code, Triple Description, in its application, is one of the ways in which a shift to reliance on unconscious processing and an explicit format for shifting perceptual filters takes form. Triple Description is fundamentally an epistemological format.

Triple Description was originally inspired by Bateson's notion of double description (see *Steps to an Ecology of Mind* as well as *Mind and Nature,* e.g. page 235) – a statement about the inevitability and the attendant wisdom of perceiving any particular phenomenon from more than one perceptual position. Bateson pointed out that this movement toward achieving a double description occurred from the most fundamental levels of neurological organization – for example, the unconscious saccadic eye movements that we are all subject to that guarantee that we are, in fact, perceiving what we see from two constantly shifting perspectives – to even higher levels of organization (the system of checks and balances within modern western European and North American political systems).

Triple Description also owes much to Castaneda's definition of a warrior as a person who collects multiple descriptions of the world (without any movement to resolve the question of which of these descriptions represents reality). Such a position is fully congruent with the epistemology developed in Chapter 1. The question is NOT

What is real?

But, rather

How many ways can we appreciate what surrounds us?

Triple Description itself is the ability to enter into three distinct and highly valued perceptual positions: namely,

1) 1st position: the perceptual position of the person himself – that is, he is seeing through his own eyes, hearing through his own ears and in contact with his body. The person is fully present.

2) 2nd position: the perceptual position of the other person(s) involved in the context under consideration, seeing the context (including you yourself as an actor in that context) through the eyes (and perceptual position of the other person(s); hearing the context through the ears of the other person(s); and feeling what the other person(s) is experiencing kinesthetically in the context under consideration.

3) 3rd position: a perceptual position from which you are able to see

and hear clearly and cleanly that which is occurring in the context under consideration including a representation of yourself as one of the actors, from this privileged outside perceptual position. This privileged position is sometimes referred to as a meta position, director [17] or observer position. See expanded explanation of 3rd position after the example below.

The example that follows is a story that enfolds from each of the three perceptual positions enumerated above. The narrative describes a specific situation involving a person (Angela) who planted a garden and the person (Geraldo) who was hired to maintain that garden. The dialogue moves from 1st position (I - Angela), to 2nd position (he – Geraldo - other person involved in the context), and, finally into Angela's 3rd position (meta, observer, director or consultant position). Please note that in this specific example that after entering 2nd and 3rd positions, Angela always re-enters 1st position (I – Angela). This repetitive re-entry into 1st after entering each of the other positions is highly effective and represents one of the sets of variations about how to operationalize Triple Description. The intention for offering the following detailed example is to provide the reader with an explicit application format for using triple description on an individual basis.

A Concrete Example

Dialogue from 1st position (I, Angela):

> I am in a dense garden of wild flowers bounded only by natural grasses, oaks, Madrones, and valleys tumbling down to the deep open ocean for as far my eye can see. I breathe deeply pulling in the fresh sea air and enjoy the coolness of the air as it enters my nostrils. I look at the flowers, I notice as my eyes scan the panorama, that I am fixing my attention and lingering a little longer on those flowers and colors which I find most pleasing. I enjoy the fragrance of some of the flowers and not others – as I feel my nose wrinkling to emit a forceful sneeze. I chuckle. I am listening now to the sounds of the bumble bees –a little twinge in my body reminds me of the time I was stung and I become completely alert as an insect lands low on my ankle. Hmmm, just a beautiful butterfly attracted to my red toenail polish.
>
> I walk with purposeful steps careful not to step on any of the plants or brush up against a busy bee or to disturb a visiting humming bird; I feel the sun on my face, my arms, and the soft moistness of the fertile ground giving way under my feet as I move through the various shades of lavenders, yellows, blues, reds, and oranges. I am in the garden – I am one with the garden in this moment - alive with

the riot of colors, the buzz of activity, the sensations and the array of fragrances – unconsciously alert to any danger – and totally present with the garden in the moment.

The Narrative Example Continues

Geraldo, the person Angela hired to maintain the lawn without destroying the wild flowers, arrived this morning with his crew and equipment. He has just told her that the job for which she has hired him is not possible. Based on Gerald's report about the garden, Angela has the information she needs to be able to step into the perceptual position of Geraldo to experience the garden from his eyes, ears, feelings, questions and professional filters.

Angela has stepped out of 1st position, shakes off the wonderful experiences of being part of the garden and moves into another special location where she steps into the perceptual filters of Geraldo. Dialogue from 2nd position (he - Geraldo)

> *The task Angela has assigned to me is to maintain this lawn without disturbing the wild flowers. As I drive up and look at the area from the road, I don't see a lawn. I see many varieties of tall and medium sized flowers - some annuals and others perennials – covering approximately 1 acre of terrain falling off over gentle slopes which terminate in a valley.*
>
> *As I walk into the planted area, I see for the first time small grassy foot trails scattered with Alyssum and short ground cover flowers. In other places I see narrow over-grown grassy paths surrounded by an abundance of wildflowers. I glance at the cutting blade of my lawn mower, as it is being lowered from the truck. I can hear Angela telling me that she wants this lawn mowed and her warning rings in my ears, "Be careful", don't mow down the wildflowers".*
>
> *As I follow the small over-grown grassy trails through the flowers, my foot in some places, feels the soft moistness of the ground beneath me, in other places my toe catches in a hole where an apparently hungry gopher has pulled a whole plant down into its run; yet, in other places I see rocks deposited in mound like fashion – surely the excavation of the industrious gopher.*

Angela steps out of 2nd position keeping this perceptual position separate. She accomplishes this by shaking the experience off and moving back into the location of her 1st position. In 1st position, she then reports to herself with the following dialogue:

Even though my experience of my beautiful garden was fundamentally different when I used Geraldo's eyes, ears, feelings and professional filters, and I now appreciate his report that mowing the lawn footpaths is impossible. His mower is huge. I still want something to happen, today. Everything is here to make it happen - Geraldo, his equipment and his crew.

Angela recognizing at this point that she is emotionally involved in the situation and as such has reached the edges of her resources in this moment. She is torn between the time and effort she has put into the project, her strong attraction to the flowers, the people and equipment waiting, and some goal that she wants to make happen now. She needs fresh, eyes, ears and resources – the counsel of an outside perceptual position which is disinterested, one not emotionally involved with the same issues confronting her in this moment. She steps out of 1st position and moves over into 3rd (observer) position to take advantage of the wisdom of her director position (3rd position - observer, director). Angela continues the dialogue from 3rd experiencing the voice, eyes, ears and the feelings of her director, as follows:

I see her standing among the wildflowers beside Geraldo. His crew is standing near the equipment, chatting and idly tossing stones into the canyon below. I see her twirling around with arms wide-open and I hear her exclaiming to Geraldo how very much she loves the wild randomness of this garden. I hear Geraldo explain how it is not possible to accomplish the task that she has hired him to do, and asks her what she would like him to do instead, as he glances at his crew and checks his watch. I hear her say to Geraldo that he has performed miracles in other contexts for her and that she's confident he can once again.

Director question (3rd):   *What does Angela (over there) need at this time?*

Angela's response (1st):   *Some ideas about how to utilize Geraldo and his crew today*

Director response (3rd):   *You can ask the crew to hunt the gophers so that Angela (over there) can cook them for lunch; or have the crew pick all the flowers for bouquets and then mow the whole area; or just tell them to go all go away and come back on another day;*

Angela's response (1st):   *Very funny! Now that you have made me laugh, tell me how your suggestions fit in with my objective to have wildflowers growing outside not*

*in vases inside? Your suggestions are for a lawn.
Lawns are so boring.*

Director response (3rd): *Now, I find that quite interesting, if you didn't want a lawn, what was your intention for planting grass and then hire Geraldo to mow it?*

Angela's response (1st): *My intention all along was to have wildflowers scattered randomly throughout the area. I only planted the grass as a backup.*

Director questions 3rd): *Does Geraldo know that? What specifically does he need to know?*

Angela's response (1st): *Interesting questions. I don't really know the answer to first and I'll think about the second.*

Angela steps cleanly out of 3rd position and re-enters 1st position, from 1st position she looks over in the direction of her director and continues with the narrative:

Thank you, you have offered me some interesting options. I'll pass, however, on your suggestion to cook the gophers for lunch. On the other hand, the question I could not answer has provided me with a next step.

Angela, in 1st position, walks over to where Geraldo is patiently waiting. She clearly communicates her intention in the following conversation with him:

I just realized that I have never really explained to you how this garden developed and what I had intended when I planted it. After the topsoil was in place, I scattered as many different varieties of wildflower seeds that I could buy. Since, I had never planted wildflower seeds before, I didn't know which varieties would grow in this environment. After weeks of watering, the flowers began sprouting, in small little clumps. So, I threw a couple varieties of grass seed into the barren patches. Suddenly, everything started to grow. I was delighted, until the grass started to choke out some varieties of flowers.

My intention was to be able to drive up to my office and see a riot of colors. I wanted to create a context outside of the office so that while I worked I could look out, enjoy the butterflies, birds and deer that would be attracted to the flowers. I wanted something active. Lawns are just so passive.

Geraldo responded appropriately with a paraphrase of what Angela had said:

"If I am understanding you correctly, you wanted the grass merely to cover the areas not covered by flowers, but now, the grass is growing tall and infringing on the flowers. You really don't want grass at all. Is this correct?"

Angela concurred with Geraldo's paraphrase:

Correct, the grass was simply a back-up!

Geraldo in response to Angela:

Now I understand. Everything seems to grow very well here. Hmmm, I can see some decorative, yet very natural looking footstones that will provide you with pathways through the flowers. Today, while I sketch up a plan and order the materials, I will have my crew, water, weed, pull out grass, as well as, repair and hunt gophers. The footstones can most likely be delivered tomorrow. Will you accept this as a miracle?"

Angela responded:

Miracle accepted!

What has happened here is that the judicious use of Triple Description enabled Angela to be explicit about what she wanted and the necessity of communicating that intention to Geraldo. Even though Angela came to appreciate how the situation looked, felt and sounded to Geraldo, the man who was to carry out the work, Angela never gave up her position that she wanted something to happen, right then and there. This is an important point, often times individuals step into 2nd position and abandon the intention they hold in 1st. This occurs as they fail to re-enter 1st and use the information gained from 2nd positioning to consider how their initial intention could be concretely realized. Unfortunately, continued failure throughout a lifetime to use 2nd positioning as an information gathering tool, rather than a way of life, becomes a trap for some individuals and many, over time, lose the ability to know what they want as themselves from 1st position. What is the "empty nest syndrome" if not an example of this pattern, anyway?

The next important point in the example was the recognition [18] on Angela's part that she had reached the limits of her resourcefulness, either because of her emotional involvement in the situation (state), not being clear to herself about her intention or a failure to communicate that intention to the other side of the loop. This is where the magic of a very clean 3rd position occurs – the ability to take information from 1st and 2nd and put it over there and adopt the filters of an outside observer – in this case director to appreciate the information with fresh eyes, ears, and feelings of an observer, who is interested, and whose only agenda is finding a solution to the situation. This is a key point in the judicious use of 3rd position – it is important to make explicit the point that 3rd position is not a disassociated position in the sense that there are no kinesthetics involved in 3rd position. A well-formed 3rd position always involves strong kinesthetics – the difference is that the strong kinesthetics in 3rd are those selected previously by the individual (are typically, states that correspond to nominalizations such as resourcefulness, curiosity, creativity [19] ...) and most importantly, the kinesthetics of 3rd are by definition NEVER the kinesthetics of 1st or 2nd. [20] Note that 3rd position is at a higher level in the hierarchy than 1st and 2nd position as it expressly includes the representation of the other two perceptual positions: 1st and 2nd.

The preceding example is not too dissimilar to what occurs within the culture of a business enterprise. Over the last 13 years in their company, QUANTUM LEAP, Inc (QL), [21] the authors have focused their attention on the modeling, coding and design of patterning of excellence in larger systems – companies, institutes and sometimes, governments. Readers who work in business have experienced situations in companies where a person is summoned by a superior or called into a company to perform a function; and find themselves scratching their heads. The person instructing or hiring this individual asks him to do something that borders on the incoherent. Many times the person giving instructions to the person hired is not clear about his particular objective. Sometimes that person (the one giving the instructions) is experiencing a conflict of objectives, other times he simply may not have thought the situation through and knows only that he wants something to happen, but is not specific about what it is, or what the boundary conditions are.

Those readers, who have experienced QL's services within a company, are smiling at this point. QL's processes for provoking a clarification of the objectives that a company or a leader purports to have is outside the scope of this book. However, the purpose for explicating this point is to offer a very simple expression of the application of the process called Triple Description in situations that are not particularly problematic. In such situations - the wild flower garden - makes transparent the effectiveness of Triple Description in refining mental maps, improving communication, helping to clarify objectives and could result in some creative outcomes.

When a person is wrestling with a situation that is problematic or in a situation where the person feels stuck (without options) the process carries even more value.

We would like to focus our attention more specifically at this point on some of the important aspects of 3rd position. Preceding the flower garden example, in the definitions of the three perceptual positions that are the components of Triple Description, we offered a reasonably explicit representation of 3rd position – we repeat number three for the reader's convenience:

> 3. 3rd position: a perceptual position from which the individual is able to see and hear clearly and cleanly which is occurring in the context under consideration from an outside perceptual position – sometimes referred to as a meta position, director or observer position

Note the variable mentioned in the definition,

> *the context under consideration*

The specific context under consideration in the definition and ensuing flower garden example is the context in which the individual has already experienced 1st and 2nd position, and then brings all that information (largely tacit) to 3rd position to consider what choices there are. We point out that 3rd position is a variable, and as such is not restricted to any particular context.

Therefore, to take a 3rd position with respect to *the context under consideration* is to move to a meta position with respect to that *specific* context. The key element is to escape the real time pressures of performance by moving to 3rd in order to appreciate the situation from outside (a new perceptual position). Once freed of the real time pressures (thus, in a highly resourceful state), to intelligently access and develop a full set of choices from which a re-entry into 1st to deploy the behavior selected will follow. Note, however, that the definition allows other contexts to serve as well as other movement into and out of 1st and 2nd position simply by filling in the variable, *the context under consideration*, with some value other than 1st and 2nd position. One such context is the position of the individual already in 3rd position with respect to 1st and 2nd positions. In other words, if the individual *is able to see and hear clearly and cleanly what is occurring in the context under consideration from an outside perceptual position*, then one such context is the original 3rd. This example makes explicit that 3rd position is definitely a variable. Thus, one additional 3rd position an individual could develop is the 3rd of the original 3rd. Presumably, such a move would have the motivation of checking from an outside position (a 3rd) what is occurring in the context under consideration – that is, the original 3rd. This would constitute a strategy for the individual to verify that he is performing well in his original 3rd. This would seem to be what Dilts (4th position) and Hall (meta meta position) are talking about when they attempt to extend the ordering of perceptual positions past 3rd position. Our own preference is to simply note that 3rd is a variable and one need only specify *the context under consideration* to make explicit how it applies. To say that one is in a 3rd position is an incomplete statement. To be intelligible, we must specify that the 3rd involved is a 3rd with respect to some particular context under consideration (and possibly some specific set of perceptual positions). [22]

The attentive reader will have noted that we are discussing an ordering relationship – in particular, an apparent hierarchy. We point out that this hierarchy is generated by scope. As a common example of scope, take a contractor in a construction project: he will ask the subcontractor (for plumbing) whether the delivery of the plumbing equipment to be installed falls within the scope of his contract. This is equivalent to asking whether the contract with the subcontractor *covers* the delivery of the equipment. A second common example occurs a number of times within this very book, *Whispering*, in the phrase,

> *...is beyond the scope of this book*

meaning that whatever is in the position of the ... will not be *covered* in this book.

Roughly, scope is equivalent to asking what elements lay within the domain or influence of what other elements.

Scope is a well-studied phenomenon in linguistics.

Take, as an example, the sentence

> *The girl chased the boy without shoes.*

This sentence is ambiguous and more relevant to the point; its ambiguity is a consequence of the scope phenomenon. The sentence is typically understood by fluent speakers to mean either:

> *The girl who was without shoes chased the boy*

or

> *The girl chased the boy who was without shoes.*

The ambiguity arises as the phrase *without shoes* can be understood either as applying to the subject noun phrase (*the girl*) or to the object noun phrase (*the boy*). Equivalently, in linguistic terminology, we say that the ambiguity arises as the phrase *without shoes* has two possible scopes (the two noun phrases involved). In slightly more user-friendly language, the ambiguity occurs as we cannot decide whether the phrase *without shoes* covers only the subject (*the girl*) or only the object (*the boy*). [23]

The scope of the original 3rd position (in the initial definition and example) covered 1st and 2nd positions. The scope in the extended explanation of 3rd position – the one where the intention of the individual involved is presumably to check on the effectiveness of his original 3rd - is 1st, 2nd and his original 3rd position. Thus the hierarchy in question – triple description (and its extension in the above explanation) - is generated by the ordering relationship of scope.

Revisiting the classic code

Given the wide-spread use of the classic code and the critique presented in chapter 2 of Part II, *Critique of the Classic Code*, the question naturally arises how a practitioner, well trained in and accustomed to the classic code patterns might utilize the differences identified between the classic and the new codes. The adaptation of the classic code patterning, in order to take advantage of these differences seems straightforward enough. Let's take the Prototypic Classic Anchoring Format as an example of the entire class of anchoring patterns in the classic code.

Prototypic Classic NLP format

> 1. Identification (consciously) by the client of the change to be made (present state)
>
> 2. Identification (consciously) of the difference the client desires – this can take the form of identifying the desired state (future state) or simply the resource the client wishes to apply to the present state to change it
>
> 3. Accessing of both the present and the desired states (typically both are anchored) – the sequence of accessing and anchoring depends on the perceived needs of the client and the style of the agent of change and is, in general, not critical
>
> 4. Making the connection between the present state with the desired state or resource or new behavior, typically through the manipulation of anchors (sometimes referred to as future pacing)

It seems to us that the adaptation of the classic code pattern will involve awarding the client's unconscious a full and powerful role in the processes of change. In particular, we would urge the practitioner to develop within the client some form of an involuntary signal system between his conscious and unconscious. The preceding analysis of the Six Step Reframing format offers one such method for accomplishing this. There are many other options for creating such a system whose critical element is the involuntary nature of the signals issuing from the unconscious processes of the client.

Assuming then that the practitioner is adequately skilled to make these arrangements, the subsequent adaptation of the classic pattern is clear enough. In the initial step wherein the client selects the change to be made, the practitioner will simply invite the client, once he has decided consciously on the change he desires to effect, to submit his conscious choice to the his unconscious. The unconscious, through the systematic use of the involuntary signals, then participates directly in this step by indicating its acceptance or rejection of the change selected consciously.

Before proceeding to the subsequent step – the selection of the desired state (what the client wants to have at the termination of this change session) or the resource (that will generate the new choices) – the practitioner will create a context within which the change will occur. This will ensure that the new choices (behaviors) or the resource selected will be constrained so as to satisfy the original intention behind the behavior to be changed. One explicit method for accomplishing this is described in step 3 of the Reframing format wherein the request is made to the unconscious to verify that the behavior to be changed has behind it a positive intention, whatever the actual consequences are. The personal style of the practitioner involved and the perceived requirements of the client will dictate whether this positive intention will be made conscious or simply accepted – having been identified and verified by the involuntary signals from the unconscious mind.

The actual selection of the new choices (or the resource to generate them) may be left to the unconscious of the client as it is in many cases in 6 Step Reframing or there may be an interaction between conscious and unconscious process to determine what these choices will be. Any number of possibilities could occur as answers to the question of *how specifically this is to be accomplished*. Whatever method the practitioner employs, she is advised to insist that the interactions include a validation by the unconscious of the choices to be implemented, however they are developed. At a minimum, the practitioner will insist that the new choices must be contained within the frame established by the positive intention behind the behavior being changed,

Depending again on the personal style of the practitioner and the client's needs, the practitioner may wish to include some formal ecology check. Our experience, however, indicates that once the unconscious is positioned to actively participate as we have indicated, the ecology issue is mute. If there is any objection to the choices under consideration, that objection will manifest itself in a quite obvious form. With these adaptations, any one of the classic code patterns can be adapted so as to take advantage of the features first made explicit in the remarkable discovery and coding of the Six Step Reframing format. In the succeeding part (III, chapter 2), we will present a sorting principle to assist the NLP practitioner in knowing how, given a presenting problem, to select the appropriate pattern for an effective intervention. The reader will note that the above suggestions about how to convert a classic format into a form that takes positive advantage of certain design features of the new code simultaneously transforms the classic code format into a 2nd order change technique.

Summary

In this chapter, we have described a certain historical context – the historical motivation for the creation of the new code. Given the critique of the classic code in the preceding chapter, we have indicated how we think that the patterning can be shifted by a practitioner of the classic code to take advantage of the insights that occurred originally in the Six Step Reframing format and embodied subsequently in the design of the new code.

The new code itself represents a natural although radical deployment of the design variables, partially explicit, partially implicit, present in the activities of modeling, applications and transfer activities (training, books, tapes…) of the co-creators of NLP, Bandler and Grinder. It obviously also reflects some of the personal preferences of Grinder – for example, his minimalist tendencies. Several patterns from the new code were offered in enough detail to give the reader some sense of how it works in the context of change work and how they are a representation of the epistemology underlying the entire endeavor. The description of multiple perceptual positions and the extended example of the application of Triple Description are presented. These represent years of experimentation and fine-tuning by the authors in their trainings across many different cultures and in several different languages.

Footnotes for Chapter 3, Part II

1. Perhaps the most obvious example of this sort of overlap was the relationship between the meta model and the Milton model. The meta model, as we have detailed in earlier text, is a syntactically-based system of verbal challenges designed to force the recovery by the client of underlying reference experiences through the systematic use of challenges that either:

1. demanded specificity (or a reconnection with the reference experiences in FA) such as *which ____ specifically?*; *_____, how specifically?...*

or

2. challenged connections (mappings) proposed by the client among various portions of their experience (primarily between FA and linguistically mediated mental maps) such as *My teenager makes me crazy! My spouse believes that I am incompetent...*

When we examine the code required to explicate Erickson's verbal patterning, we find precisely the same distinctions that occurred in the meta model. However these distinctions are here employed to create a movement away from FA toward less specified representations. These provide for the client, who is listening carefully to the hypnotically presented verbal Rorschachs of Erickson, the structure onto which they can project their own requirements preparatory to changing them. Thus the meta model and the Milton model are often presented as inverses.

2. I confess that I have been unsuccessful in discovering any new patterning in the published work that has appeared under the title of *Design of Human Engineering*. What should be clear to the informed reader of these documents is an extended mixture of classic Ericksonian hypnotic patterning and the manipulation of sub modalities. An e-conversation with Denis Bridoux confirmed this. At the same time, he (Denis) offered a description of a clever skill-installation strategy that apparently functions without mapping the tacit knowledge of the model onto an explicit representation – one that was accomplished through the manipulation of these two sets of variables. Perhaps Bandler's oral presentations in seminars contain some genuinely new patterning or applications.

3. Parts of the new code were developed in conjunction with Judith Delozier – the book *Turtles All the Way Down* co-authored by Delozier and me captures a portion of this joint endeavor. *Turtles all the way Down* is a written transcript of a recording made during a live seminar called *Prerequisites to Personal Genius* presented by Judy Delozier and John

Grinder in March, 1986. The manuscript was edited to fill in the voids – the non-verbal and visual information which was available to the presenters and the participants – which could not be captured by an audio recording of the event.

Further, readers are invited to read Delozier's account of the new code – see *NLP World*, March, 1995, volume 2, number 1, pages 5 - 19. The particular characterization of the new code offered by Delozier differs significantly from mine. Some of these differences arise, no doubt, from the fact that I have continued to develop and refine the new code in collaboration with Carmen Bostic St. Clair with whom I have been working since 1989. Delozier and I stopped working together in 1988. Some of the differences are due in part to the particular emphasis each of us had and continue to have as to the relative importance of aspects of the new code.

I confess that I am somewhat confused by the taxonomy Delozier proposes in the article referenced especially in the overlaps and redundancies I detect in it. In particular, her categories of perceptual positions (page 10), filters (page 14) and multiple descriptions (page 15) seem to me to be different terms for the same patterning. Perhaps her intention is a presentation for pedagogical purposes rather than elegance.

4. One of the (usually) minor nuisances of using previous experience in the client's personal history as the source for resources is that the anchor drags along with it not only the resource state or behavior the client desires but a bundle of irrelevant history of no utility in the application in the new context. While this is normally just a nuisance, it sometimes takes a strange form that has no appropriateness for the client. Indeed, there are cases where the selected previous experience while containing positive aspects carries along with it negative associations which tend to reduce the effectiveness of the work or even have a negative overall effect (for example, self-sabotage).

5. It is important to note that the same leverage points within the chain of excellence that are used to attain high performance states are conversely also leverage points by which we inadvertently (often times driven by a habitual response to some trigger) access a state that is less than optimal for performance – the manner in which we breathe and the characteristics of our physiology during those instances of non-excellence, if maintained, can perpetuate a state of low quality. A common example is the *scared rabbit syndrome* – the strong tendency of people to hold their breath when frightened.

6. In the case of AA and its epistemology, attention is focused on the issue (either drinking or not drinking). This simply strengthens the demon and maintains these phenomena (the focus on drinking/not drinking and the

associated beliefs) as the focal point of the person's experience. AA's strategy thereby commits the individual to organizing his behavior around these inappropriate reference points rather than allowing them to get on with their lives. See Bateson's brilliant exposition of the contradiction between the intention of AA and its actual consequences in *The Epistemology of AA* in *Steps to an Ecology of Mind.*

7. A disciplined know-nothing state is to be sharply distinguished from the type of know-nothing states you can find, for example, on the mall in Santa Cruz. Such undisciplined know-nothing state representatives can usually be distinguished by vacant gazes and verbalizations such as *Gee, I don't know, man* to the most common of questions.

8. This in part accounts for the fact that at the highest levels of performance (the Olympic games, for example), where the difference between achieving success and failing to place is rarely determined solely by the actual physiological competencies of the performers but by what is erroneously referred to as the mental state of the performers involved. Although this way of talking about the experience is an example of the acceptance consciously (inappropriately, in our opinion) of the Descartes' original sin, the phenomenon itself is strong evidence, indeed, for the unity of mind and body achieved by such performers in competition.

9. Roger Tabb of Portland, Oregon (RTabb464@aol.com) is an optometrist with whom I had the pleasure of working. Roger introduced me to a series of exercises that greatly influenced the development of the form of the new code.

10. The 15 minutes is, of course, a statistical approach, to be dispensed with either through self-calibration or calibrated by a trained observer. Replacing the statistical guide (15 minutes of play) with calibrating the activation of the high performance state is, of course, another example of the use of a discrete underlying model for NLP.

The 15 minutes simply represents an "average" amount of time within which when playing congruently an "average" person will succeed in entering into a high performance state. This is equivalent to saying that after observing hundreds of people over the years, the majority of people who are congruently playing the game will succeed in entering into a high performance state within 15 minutes of play. However, it is not unusual for some people to reach the same result in 10 minutes or less and some people may require up to a half-an-hour.

11. The set of games mentioned here (NASA, Alphabet, trampoline...) all require a coach capable of calibrating the physiology of the player. This is an essential characteristic of the application. A player attempting to play

any of the games in this set by himself is, at best, wasting his time and the results will be variable. This leads to the question of self-application. One particular highly recommended practice in NLP is to ensure that practitioners are well trained in self-application but the requirement of having a coach removes this possibility. The alert reader will have already worked this out for herself. There is a set of games that you can substitute for the set presented here in which the most and critical function of the coach is replaced by a structural element in the game itself. The design of such auto-application games presupposes an explicit set of design criteria and is beyond the scope of this particular presentation.

12. The adaptation to other languages is trivial – for example, in French, German and Spanish respectively, the corresponding instructions would be:

g = gauche;   l = links;   l = izquierda

d = droit   r = rechts   d = derecho

e = ensemble   z = zusammen   j = juntos

Obviously adjustments can be made in the sequence of letters in the chart to reflect more closely the alphabet of the particular language.

13. Each player begins, of course, with a different level of development in these qualities – this is a positive aspect of the design as there is no competition in this game except with yourself. Thus, everyone can play at his or her own appropriate level. Further, there are no premiums for going fast. All these remarks need to be placed cleanly in the context of the appropriate relationship between coach and player. As in the case of an actual athletic coach and player, the task of the coach is to demand the highest quality performance possible from her athlete. The upper level on this demand is precisely the point where the coach detects the beginnings of trying, usually in the form of excess muscular tension in the shoulder, the jaw, around the eyes... Such signals are indicators to the coach to reduce the demand slightly until the signs of tensions disappear.

14. The construction of additional charts follows the following simple rules:

1. write the first 25 letters of the alphabet on a large piece of paper

2. write the instruction r beneath the letter l, the instruction l beneath the letter r and the instructions t beneath the letter t.

3. distribute the instructions *l, r, t* beneath the remaining letters with the constraint that no more than two adjacent letters in the sequence may have the same instructions written beneath them.

The instructions and the letters should be indistinguishable from one another except by position – i.e. written in the same color, font, case, size... as one of the points of the exercise is to challenge the player to make the distinction within their own neurology not by manipulating the external representation (the chart). Readers will appreciate the constraint specified in step #2 of the rules of construction after playing the game as they will discover that if there are errors in the play, they typically will occur on precisely those points. What is occurring is that the game played well demands a parallel processing of the incoming visual stimuli that splits the two visual systems we have as a species, with the foveal visual system focusing on the letter whose name is to be pronounced, while the peripheral visual system mediates the instruction to be acted upon. This parallels the typical organization of these two visual systems in which foveal vision feeds consciousness and speech while the peripheral vision feeds the unconscious and quite often motor reflexes.

15. The differences that players report upon concluding step 4 are typically whole scale alterations of the various sensory modalities – with many reports containing spontaneous sub modality shifts. The precise connection between the reported shifts in representational systems and associated phenomena such as primary representational systems remains to be explicated.

16. In the case of children who haven't yet mastered the alphabet, a colleague from Guadalajara, Mexico, Alfonso M. Munguia Calderon (e-mail Muncar@hot mail.com), has made an adaptation of the standard alphabet game. In this adaptation, the letters of the alphabet are replaced with pictures of animals whose name the child knows or can learn quickly enough while in the place of the instructions (*l, r, t*), each letter has beneath it, a splotch of color (red, green and blue). Splotches of color are also made on the back of the child's hand, green on the back of the left hand, say, and red on the back of the right hand with smaller marks of blue on both hands. Thus the child says the name of the animal pictured while noting the color presented below the animal and moves the corresponding hand and arm (marked by the same color), adding the opposite foot and leg in condition #3. It will be interesting to note the long-term effect of introducing children to such high performance games at such as early age.

17. In making presentations in some cultures, I (CB) have coined the term *consultant* instead of the term *director* when assisting participants in creating 3rd position. The connotations of the word *director* in some cultures brings with it some anchors from an authoritarian culture (i.e., the

director directs him to do X – rather than supplying options from which to choose in order to do X.) For most individuals in these cultures, the word *consultant* carries with it a new set of perceptual filters, and the notion of choice.

18. The ability to recognize that one has reached the limits of his resourcefulness is another topic in and of itself, it involves the use of a variety of NLP [application] tools that are not the topic of this section or book.

19. Creating resources for 3rd position is an important component of the Triple Description pattern. When assisting groups in creating resources for their 3rd, I (CB) find that groups typically report the inclusion of resources such as: intelligence, curiosity, creativity... into their 3rd. I accept their choices and direct their attention to additional possibilities though various exercises that are designed to stimulate inclusion of other classes of resources. These resources often include, for example, freedom from the boundaries (or rules) that characterize their behavior when they are in 1st position. Even if their consultant offers ridiculous, outrageous options, the message received is that options are available, limited only by some set of particular filters. If the individual, when in 1st is surprised by her response to an outrageous option, such an emotional response represents, at the least, the opportunity to shift attention and subsequently behavior to parts of the world that she normally does not attend to.

20. We have been astonished to discover with alarming frequency an interpretation of 3rd position in which participants in training programs are being instructed that 3rd has no kinesthetics. Little wonder those participants find it difficult to operate effectively from their so-called 3rd position.

21. QUANTUM LEAP was founded by Carmen Bostic St. Clair in 1987: its focus includes the design and implementation of programs to achieve sustainable competitive advantages, the coaching of the formal and informal leadership, the design and implementation of strategies to convert companies into learning organizations, the development and exploitation of knowledge management systems, succession strategies, mentoring programs, leadership development, ISO and QS 9000 series certifications... QL has some 17 associates worldwide specialists (finance, technology...) who participate on a contract-by-contract basis with the principals, Carmen Bostic and John Grinder, in delivering high quality consulting work. The two offices for QL in California are

QUANTUM LEAP
3000F Danville Blvd., #368
Alamo, California 94507

QUANTUM LEAP
245 M Mt. Hermon Rd., #277
Scotts Valley, California 95066

QL also presents public seminars in various topics such as Modeling, New Code, The Construction and Delivery of Metaphor, Unconscious Processes, Tapestry – weaving the fabric of your life...

22. This solution – obviously one that we find elegant – is strongly reminiscent of Hegel's famous pattern:

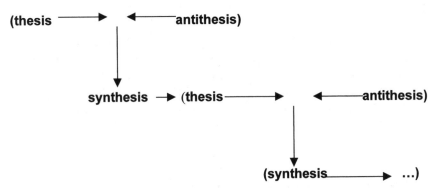

In words, Hegel proposed a process pattern historically in which each thesis (concept, idea, political system, economic system...) is opposed by its antithesis. After extended contact between the thesis and its antithesis, some integrated form emerges called the synthesis – one that contains elements of each of its predecessors (the thesis and the antithesis). This synthesis in turn historically becomes the next thesis, to be opposed by its antithesis. This new pairing (thesis and antithesis) integrates to form a new synthesis that in turn becomes the next thesis...

Those practitioners with some years of experience, especially with extended experience in self-application of the change patterning in NLP practice, will also recognize Hegel's process pattern as an excellent format for continuous personal development over time. In other words, today's optimal set of states, strategies, intentions and behaviors (today's synthesis) becomes tomorrow's thesis to be opposed by some new antithesis ...

Further, it is not altogether clear to us what advantages accrue by extending the hierarchy of perceptual positions past the original 3rd. If the individual in question has constructed a clean, robust 3rd, then it remains only to verify its effectiveness in practice. It seems that to extend past the original 3rd by whatever name, 4th position, meta meta position or with our own terminology (3rd of the original 3rd or 3rd with respect to the context in which the original 3rd is found) is very much like creating a document, then creating an executive summary of that document (original 3rd), then a summary of the executive summary, then a summary of the summary of the executive summary... It does have wide spread ensuing confusion as a possible advantage.

23. Take as an additional example, the phenomenon of scope and negation: the difference between the following two sentences;

John Conrad said that he wasn't making up words again

John Conrad didn't say that he was making up words again.

These two sentences differ significantly in meaning, truth values... The difference detected is a function of the scope of the negation. In the first sentence the scope of the negation (the *n't* contracted form of *not*) covers only the embedded sentence, namely, *he was making up words again*, and the assertion by John Conrad is that he wasn't doing that. In the second sentence, the negation has the entire sentence (both the main sentence and the embedded sentence) as its scope and the assertion is that he (John Conrad) didn't take a position on whether he was making up words again or not. The scope is the domain to which the negation operator applies, with the resultant differences in meaning, truth values...

Part III

A Steady Sea Breeze

The birds, smaller mammals, an extraordinary array of insects... emerge slowly from the secret places tentatively, probing to determine whether the storm has indeed passed. The trees, plants and flowers cautiously uncurl and stretch themselves once again beneath the drying, warming, life-giving gaze of the sun. The clouds run before the steady sea breeze. The world is fresh; the possibilities are limitless.

Whispering in the Wind has up to this point used the form of a quasi-historical narrative in presenting the creation and development of Neuro-Linguistic Programming. The remainder of the book represents a break with this form: rather than continue a historically driven narrative, we present a number of issues whose sole common thread is that if the distinctions proffered and the principles presented are operationalized, they will clarify portions of NLP, in its modeling activity, in its applications and in its teaching/training as well as improving the quality of practice in all these activities. We present here an overview of the three chapters of Part III.

Chapter 1

1. Coding Issues including the tension between elegance in modeling and effectiveness in pedagogy

2. Ordering Functions: both linear and hierarchical including an analysis of Dilts' Neuro-Logical levels

3. Logical Levels and Logical Types: beginning with a brief look at the original use of the term *logical type*, the two distinct notions, here called *logical level* and *logical type,* contained in its usage and conflated historically are teased out. Explicit representations are proposed for the deployment of these key concepts.

Chapter 2

1. Sorting Functions: how to know, given a particular presenting client in professional change work, which class of patterning to apply (1st and 2nd order change and their corresponding levels of intervention).

2. Chunking and Logical Levels: beginning with the description of a classic training exercise, the use of logical levels, as defined above in *Logical Levels and Logical Types*, is demonstrated in several important NLP application contexts.

3. Form and Substance; Process and Content: the opening of a discussion concerning perhaps the single most distinctive characteristic of NLP application, namely, the process/content distinction. This distinction is explored with practical suggestions about how to manage it and thereby assure the integrity of clients in NLP application.

Chapter 3: Recommendations: A series of concrete suggestions as to how the enterprise of NLP can be refined to ensure a process that will position it in its rightful place as a scientific endeavor contributing to the study of human functioning – in particular, the patterning of one of the extremes, human excellence.

Chapter 1: Key Issues in NLP ^{modeling}

The Coding of Pattern

The definition of modeling offered in chapter 2 (Part I) is the mapping of tacit knowledge into explicit knowledge. The resultant product is usually referred to as a model. A phase-by-phase description of modeling - the core activity that defines NLP - was offered in the commentary immediately following the narrative of the work that Bandler and Grinder did with Dr. Erickson (see *The Milton Model* in chapter 1, Part II).

One important issue in that process concerns coding: the processes of mapping tacit knowledge acquired through an unconscious uptake during imitation of the original model onto an explicit code as well as those issues surrounding the verification that such coding of patterning is effective. In Part II in *Contexts of Discovery*, we present certain comments about the task of discovering and coding patterns lurking in the imitative behavior of the third phase of modeling. Allow us to remind the reader where in the modeling process this issue arises. Suppose that we have already achieved criterion. In other words, we have assimilated the patterning of the model through unconscious uptake and disciplined imitative practice. We can do what the model (the person who is the source of the patterning) can do. We are in a state of unconscious competency – we have personal tacit behavioral knowledge.

We are now faced with the task of making that tacit knowledge explicit. As a prerequisite for such a mapping, we are to discover through some process which portions of our imitative behavior is essential to creating the excellent results that both the model and we ourselves can consistently obtain. Those portions of the imitative behaviors not so characterized are then understood to be stylistic or idiosyncratic and may be discarded without loss of effectiveness.

Note that at this point, we, as modelers have two data points:

1. the behavior of the original source of the patterning – the original model

and

2. her own behavior (after all, she has reached criteria).

This means that we are actually engaging in modeling of the source of the patterning as well as self-modeling. The fact that we have already achieved criteria confers on us intuitions (based on the successful replication of the results obtained by the source) that are enormously useful in finding a useful coding of the patterning mastered.

The fourth phase in the modeling process is identified as the point where this explicit mapping of the patterning of excellence occurs. The intention of the modeler/coder in this phase is to make the patterning accessible in some form (typically verbal) that renders this patterning transferable in a relatively efficient manner. The issues surrounding coding are numerous and quite complex. We offer below a number of comments to alert the reader to these issues.

A. In any coding exercise, it rapidly becomes clear that there is an arbitrarily large number of different representations of a complex behavior that could potentially serve as a description. A classic example of this is the set of three representations immediately below – a binary number, a decimal number and a phrase in English:

101101011010010000

186,000

the velocity of light

In fact, these three representations are equivalent – they are simply three distinct codes for the same information. Note that the example makes explicit that *information is independent of the code* selected for its expression.

B. We frame the next portion of the discussion by the question:

> *In what code (vocabulary) can we report the patterning of the excellence modeled in such a way as to make its transfer effective?*

Bandler and Grinder focused on the specific behavioral differences that distinguished certain well-known therapists Fritz Perls, Virginia Satir and Milton H. Erickson from the average practitioner of the art of therapy - the pursuit of the differences that make a difference. Grinder and Bandler discovered to their surprise and delight that they were indeed able to identify with some precision a set of answers to this fundamental question.

In casting about for an appropriate method for reporting the results of what they had found in their initial modeling, they had come to a recognition that there was at the time no standardized vocabulary for the description of patterning in the field of psychotherapy. Each school - Gestalt, Family Therapy, Hypnotherapy, Transactional Analysis, Rogerian psychotherapy, psychoanalysis... - had developed a specialized vocabulary which was unrelated to (and in the opinion of these two young men, incommensurable with) the basic terms which formed the universe of discourse in the other schools of professional change work.

Grinder and Bandler were alert enough to appreciate that the choice of terms in this new universe of discourse for the meta discipline NLP had to meet certain criteria. First of all, these terms had to be relatively transparent to the user. [1] Secondly, if they were to use terms already associated with some of the phenomena in psychology and more specifically, in clinical psychology, they would drag along with them unwanted and undesirable associations.

For example, we would be hard pressed to argue convincingly for the term *anchoring* in lieu of the term *conditioning* except for precisely the unwanted and undesirable theoretical baggage the term *conditioning* has attached to it.

Grinder and Bandler's solution was the creation of a vocabulary (in some cases) wholly unassociated with previous work to allow a fresh perspective on the patterning being coded. History will determine whether this was an effective solution to the issue they confronted.

C. The next issue associated with the coding question is deeply epistemological. It seems to us obvious that the ideal vocabulary for such coding of the patterning of excellence would be a set of sensory-grounded descriptions. This, of course, raises the question whether it is indeed possible to develop such a sensory-based vocabulary – one that allows the clear reporting of patterning resulting from modeling studies. Fortunately, this question – at least in its general form – has a long history of investigation in the philosophy of science.

The answer that emerges from a review of such investigations is a resounding *No!* We urge that the reader explore this area of investigation for her or himself. In particular, we recommend the clear and precise presentations on this issue by Carl Hempel (see bibliography for references).

We personally find Hempel's critique of the possibility of a complete sensory based descriptive vocabulary compelling. We can, however, avoid the full force of Hempel's critique. We suggest that an adequate response to this issue could be made simply by applying the epistemological insights first presented in this book - more specifically, to move the focus of reporting patterning from a post-FA level to something approaching FA. This could be accomplished to a significant degree thereby offering a representation in all three major natural coding systems. One way to do this would be by creating a library of videos that would serve as reference points for the patterning we are working with. Consider the difference between a purely verbal written description of some pattern and that same pattern presented by a video tape (visual and auditory representations) accompanied by some verbal written description. Such a library thereby sidesteps significant portions of the excellent critique offered by Hempel while simultaneously providing access to all interested investigators. We will elaborate more precisely on this suggestion in the last chapter of this book, *Recommendations*.

D. The large set of distinct potential representations can be effectively reduced if the purpose of the modeler/coder is made explicit. Further, the purpose or intention of the modeler/coder interacts strongly with the selection of an appropriate vocabulary for coding. For example, anyone who has ever taken seriously the task of communicating (effectively transferring) a model to interested, uninitiated participants will recognize that there is a strong tension between one of the criteria typically used in scientific work – elegance or presentation of a pattern with a minimum set of terms – and the pedagogical requirements of creating a context in which the participant will learn effectively – that the participant will *get it*.

Perhaps a couple of historical examples from NLP itself will serve:

1. In the book that established the field of NLP, *The Structure of Magic*, volume I (1975, page 14), the reader finds the authors (Grinder and Bandler) making the statement:

> *The most pervasive paradox of the human condition which we see is that the processes which allow us to survive, grow, change and experience joy are the same processes which allow us to maintain an impoverished model of the world – our ability to manipulate symbols, that is, to create models. So the processes that allow us to accomplish the most extraordinary and unique human activities are the same processes that block our further growth, if we commit the error of mistaking the model for the reality. We can identify three general mechanisms by which we do this: Generalization, Distortion and Deletion.*

Wait a minute – either Grinder and Bandler are incapable of the modicum of clear thinking here or we have an example of the difference we are attempting to elucidate. We refer here to the development of inelegant coding but one that facilitates the reader's arriving at an understanding useful to the purposes of the authors – that is, the use of a vocabulary or code which is pedagogically effective.

<u>Analysis</u>: The apparent claim by Grinder and Bandler is that the processes by which we construct our mental models (largely unconsciously) are marked by three systematic processes that create flaws in its product (ways in which the resultant mental model will differ from the reality). These three are:

Generalization   Distortion   Deletion [2]

But this is analytically absurd! Let's begin with Generalization. How, in fact, do we move from different experiences to arrive at a generalization over those experiences? While any generalization from only two cases is highly suspect, the two-case situation provides simplest of all possible examples for analytic purposes. Given any two direct experiences, we can achieve a generalization about them if and only if either

they are identical

or

we agree to ignore the differences between them and focus instead on the similarities.

But to agree to ignore the differences is precisely the process of deletion. Thus, we may conclude that deletion is one specific process for moving from different experiences to a generalization about those experiences – that is, deletion is an operation that can result in generalization. Or, in other words, one process that allows us to achieve a Generalization is Deletion.

Note, furthermore, that when we delete, or equivalently, when we generalize through the process of deletion, we are deliberately creating a difference between the things themselves (more carefully said, FA – the closest we get to the world, namely, our direct experiences) and the representation or model of those things (our linguistically mediated mental maps – post FA). In normal parlance, this is usually called a Distortion of the original direct experiences.

Therefore, we may conclude that in fact, the three operations touted by Grinder and Bandler are either unequivocal evidence they were out to lunch or an attempt to develop a useful pedagogical code. Such devices are designed to make presentations less dense and more passable to the reader struggling through the dense intellectual underbrush. While the epistemology represented by these three processes is underdeveloped and its coding is strongly biased toward an effective pedagogical presentation, it is generally compatible with the epistemology developed by Bostic and Grinder here in *Whispering* - representing a significant extension and refinement of those original remarks.

2. NLP is characteristically defined in popular writing as the study of subjective experience – indeed, there are a number of books on NLP co-authored by myself and others (e.g. *Neuro-Linguistic Programming*, Volume I) where this description occurs. But consider the phrase – *subjective experience* – what could this possibly mean? Is it intended to contrast with objective experience (surely, an oxymoron!) or what? We have argued in the epistemology presented in chapter 1, Part I that first access (FA) is the first point at which we can experience the world around us. But FA is a point in the human neurology by definition at which the incoming data stream from the world has already passed through the initial series of neurological transforms of the human nervous system (f^1). Since these neurological transforms are known to change the data that streams through in their movement to FA, the representations at FA are, by definition, subjective – having been operated on by the structure (the neurological transforms) of the human nervous system in ways as yet undefined.

Thus, again, either the expression (subjective experience) is absurd – in this case, confusingly redundant - or it is being used pedagogically as a code to provoke a certain understanding in the participant.

3. Finally, we offer an example of how coding enterprises can go awry. In the early NLP publications (and trainings) Grinder and Bandler made extensive use and reference to Ashby's Law of Requisite Variety (roughly): [3]

> *In any connected system, the component in the system with the widest range of variability will be the controlling element*

This is something Bandler and Grinder lifted from Ashby's excellent work on cybernetics This law as usually interpreted in NLP practice – for example, in change work – is understood to be the requirement on the part of the NLP practitioner to continue the learning process well after she achieves initial success in handling the full range of challenges that walk through the door of any professional change agent so as to add additional effective patterns. This ensures that she has multiple ways of succeeding in achieving the class of outcomes the client brings to the encounter. Some additional noises are typically made about the agent of change needing to have more choices about inducing change than the client has about rejecting change.

In hindsight, there are a number of difficulties with this formulation. The characterization of the agent of change having to have more ways of inducing the change than the client has of resisting the change carries a presupposition antithetical to good NLP practice. The presupposition is that the client and the agent of change are operating at the same level of experience. In fact, the appropriate relationship between an agent of change and her client is quite different. In his excellent book on the underlying strategies employed by Erickson (*Strategies of Psychotherapy*), Jay Haley is precise in identifying that one of the systematic contextual manipulations perfected by Dr. Erickson is the development of a meta-complementary relationship with his clients. A meta-complementary relationship is one in which the agent of change positions herself as an advisor, a facilitator creating a context in which the client may choose to change. The *meta* portion of Haley's descriptive phrase indicates that the agent of change is to operate at a level that includes the level at which the client is operating. Such a position would preclude the kind of contest between the agent and the client implicitly proposed by the application of the law of requisite variety to the processes of change driven by NLP patterning.

The second difficulty we detect is the use of the phrase, *controlling element*. Surely, if there is one thing all of us who have extended experiences inducing change with human beings (ourselves included, of course) through the application of NLP patterning can agree upon, it is the futility of thinking in terms of controlling anything in the realm of human activity. Control is a fiction - a seductive illusion – choice is the point. These are fundamental distinctions in the life vocabulary of any well-trained NLP practitioner.

Finally, there is the brute fact that the most difficult of all classes of clients in our experiences and those of many other practitioners we have conferred with is NOT the client with great flexibility in their behavior; one who has a chameleon-like quality to his psychological movements. In fact, the inverse - the client so fixed, stuck, locked into a repetitive pattern (e.g. obsessive compulsives, schizophrenics with stereotypic ritualistic behavior...) that he displays but a single repetitive pattern of behavior – turns out to be the most difficult. This seems to suggest either a reformulation of the law of requisite variety or its interpretation as applied to NLP practice is in order.

Nevertheless, however these refinements are to be made, there is much to be said in favor of any program of continuous learning (whatever its original motivation) – the constant addition of new patterning to the set of patterns already mastered by the agent of change.

E. In the commentary on the modeling of Erickson and the coding of his patterning (Part II, Chapter 1, *the Milton Model*), we introduced what we called the *subtractive method*. By this, we refer to a strategy that appears to be the inverse of standard experimental design in psychology, pharmaceutical research... In these standard designs, two groups are distinguished: an experimental group and a control group. These groups are by design or by random assignment taken to be equivalent in all relevant respects – indistinguishable for the purposes of the experiment at hand. The control group is given a drug, a treatment, some regime... whose effects we are interested in discovering. The control group is offered some seemingly innocuous regime that we believe has no effect (such as the presumably inert sugar pill – the placebo). The research question is whether the addition of the specified regime given to the experimental group will result in some desirable effect in the behavior, health... of the members of the experimental group.

In the modeling of pattern through the subtractive method we proposed relevant for NLP modeling and its coding, the sequence is reversed. Through imitative modeling, we get the result that we are interested in – the desirable effect - by throwing everything we have at the situation (the set of imitative behaviors). Once we have demonstrated that we can consistently secure that desirable effect, we begin to leave out or *subtract* certain behaviors that were present when we succeeded in eliciting the desirable effect. In describing the application of this method to the modeling of Ericksonian hypnotic patterning, we used the phrase,

> ...*deliberately leave out some single Ericksonian behavior...*

to indicate an example of this subtractive method. The point is that if the presentation of the putative pattern to the client without this *some single Ericksonian behavior* has no discernable effect on the quality of the client's response, we conclude that the single Ericksonian behavior under consideration is not essential for the pattern and may be safely discarded.

Frank Tall has observed in his usual impeccable manner that the subtractive method we describe here: the one being appealed to by the phrase – *deliberately leave out some single Ericksonian behavior* - is significantly more complex than we indicate in the example in the text. Suppose in attempting to code the model's behavior, we have already decomposed her behavior into some set, (A, B, C, D... N) of distinguishable behaviors. We now apply the coding strategy containing the subtractive method in its simplified form as presented in the text with actual clients in order to test the coding we are considering.

Representing the task somewhat more formally, suppose that we have observed that the desired results (some set of client responses) occurs whenever both A and B are present in the behavior of the modeler. We now apply the subtractive method in the form presented in the text – that is, we leave out either A or B (actually each in turn) to determine whether they are essential to obtaining the desired results. Suppose further that it turns out that in our testing that whenever we leave out either A or B, the desired result (the positive client response) does *not* occur. The question is,

> *May we legitimately conclude that the sequence (A and B) is an essential configuration of behaviors constituting a pattern?*

The answer is negative. Consider the following possibility: suppose the actual pattern was,

$$(A \wedge B) \quad \vee \quad (\sim A \wedge \sim B)$$

> where $\wedge$ represents logical *and*
> $\vee$ represents logical *or*
> $\sim$ represents logical negation, *not*

In words, suppose that the actual pattern we are attempting to discover is (A and B) or (not A and not B). The subtractive method as presented in the text would never uncover this possibility. Frank points out that the class of examples beyond the reach of the subtractive strategy as presented in the text is far more extensive than this single example. Consider, for example,

$$(A \wedge B \wedge C \wedge D \wedge E \wedge F) \vee (\sim A \wedge \sim F)$$

As a possible candidate for the simpler of the disjunctive patterns, consider one of the points made in *Whispering* where we proposed a sort of mental gymnastics on the part of the agent of change whereby she keeps track of any disassociations used in the work in order to ensure that during the clean up phase at the end of a session, there is a reintegration of each and every one of the disassociations employed. Suppose further that the desired result in the client is a state of congruity. If we did a disassociation during the session and failed to do a reintegration, the result would be an incongruent client at the close. It is also quite possible that if there had been no disassociation during the session and we attempted to do a reintegration at the close, we could create an incongruent client. However, if we did neither a disassociation nor a reintegration during the session, we could end up with a congruent client (depending on what else occurs during the session). This seems to be an example of this first disjunction,

$$(A \wedge B) \quad \vee \quad (\sim A \wedge \sim B)$$

It strikes us that examples of the more complex case presented

$$(A \wedge B \wedge C \wedge D \wedge E \wedge F) \quad \vee \quad (\sim A \wedge \sim F)$$

could be constructed from certain hypnotic patterning – consider, for example, the use of center embedded metaphors, one of Erickson's favorites.

The fact that we used the verb *constructed* in the preceding sentence does not disqualify the examples nor should it distract the reader from the possibility that they could actually occur naturally. Indeed, they may have occurred as part of the complex set of activities of coding during some historical modeling work, but how would we know? Clearly, a more sophisticated version of the subtractive method needs to be developed to handle these possibilities.

If the reader ever needed an example of the extraordinary advantages and clarity that formal thinking and formal representation offers the researcher, here is a superb example. Frank's observations represent precisely such a point of articulation between formal representation and down in the dirt modeling and coding of pattern.

It now should be perfectly clear to the reader that much work is required to refine the issues that revolve around the question of coding. A more extended development of this important aspect of modeling is offered in *RedTail Math: the epistemology of everyday life* (working title), Grinder and Bostic, 2002

Ordering Functions

It seems to us altogether natural that within the history of NLP – the art of modeling those complex differences that make a difference between a top and an average performer – we find the same obsession with naming, classifying, categorizing… that occurs in the general activities of our species. What is, then, somewhat surprising is that so little effort has thus far been devoted to an explicit appreciation of what orderings we use and what the implications of these orderings are.

Linear Orderings (partially or totally critically ordered)

An enumeration of all of the examples of the different orderings found within NLP would itself be a formidable task, but clearly it would include all patterns codified within the field as these patterns contain a partially or totally critical ordering within their description. We know of no patterns proposed by NLP researchers that are unordered listings of operations to carry out. Even patterns as elementary as rapport are reported in an ordered sequence: some quite elaborate:

Achieving Rapport through Mirroring

1. For the first 30 seconds, slowly move the bottom half of your body into the same position as your client. Continue to adjust this portion of your physiology to maintain a match with your client should he move during the exercise.

2. During the second 30 seconds, subtly arrange the upper portion of your torso in the same position as the upper torso of your client. Continue to adjust this portion of your physiology to maintain a match with your client should he move during the exercise.

3. In the third 30 seconds, position your head with the same tilt both side to side and front to back as your client and imitate certain aspects of the facial expressions presented by your client. Continue to adjust this portion of your physiology to maintain a match with your client should he move during the exercise.

4. During the fourth 30 seconds, match the frequency, depth and timing of your client's breathing with your own. Continue to adjust this portion of your physiology to maintain a match with your client should he move during the exercise.

5. Test that you have achieved a relationship of rapport by slowly shifting any portion of your physiology into a new position. If the client shifts to that position without conscious awareness of the shift, you have the evidence that you require to know that you have achieved rapport. If not, return to step 1.

Other rapport formats are quite simple:

Achieving Rapport through Crossover Mirroring

1. Sway your body subtly in unison with the rhythm of the client's breathing.

2. Once you believe you have achieved rapport, subtly change the

rhythm of your body sway and note whether the client's breathing shifts accordingly. If so, you have achieved rapport. If not, return to step 1.

In the first pattern, there are some elements that are totally ordered with respect to the other elements and some that are not. For example, you can achieve the same quality of rapport in the same time frame by doing step 2 before 1 or step 3 before 2... The critical ordering in the first format is simply that steps 1 through 4 must be accomplished before performing the 5th operation. The second pattern is totally ordered – you have to perform the operations to establish rapport prior to testing for its existence. Thus, the ordering involved in the presentation of these two patterns is a simple linear sequencing: in the first case, the sequence is a partial ordering: perform steps 1 through 4 in whatever order you prefer and then step 5. In the second case, the ordering is total – step 1 must occur before step 2.

A convenient form for representing graphically this class of linear sequences is a flow chart.

Step 1➔ Step 2 ➔Step 3 ➔ ...➔ Step n

There are also (at least implicitly) branching flow charts: for example, take any anchoring format. Typically, the "problem" state (the behavior to be changed) is accessed and anchored prior to the selection of a new behavior or resource state. Within the domain of anchoring intervention patterns, it makes sense to explicate what is to be changed before attempting to select the difference the client desires to experience [4]

We reproduce the Classic Prototypic Anchoring Format here for convenience:

Prototypic Classic Anchoring NLP Pattern

1. Identification (consciously) by the client of the change to be made (present state)

2. Identification (consciously) of the difference the client desires – this can take the form of identifying the desired state or simply the resource the client wishes to apply to the present state to change it

3. Accessing of both the present and the desired states/resource (typically both are anchored) – the sequence of accessing and anchoring depends on the perceived needs

of the client and the style of the agent of change and is, in general, not a critical ordering

4. Making the connection (e.g. integrating, sequencing, stacking, chaining...) between the present state and the desired state or resource or new behavior, typically through the manipulation of anchors.

5. Test the work for effectiveness (anchors, in the street...)

Step 1 → Step 2 → Step 3 → Step 4 → Step 5

Within this prototypic sequence for anchoring patterns, steps 1 and 2 are totally ordered with respect to step 3 and 4 while steps 1, 2 and 3 are totally ordered with respect to step 4. Steps 1 through 4 are totally ordered with respect to step 5.

Now suppose that down inside step 2, the agent of change in pursuit of the resource or new behavior to replace the behavior her client wants to change instructs the client as follows,

Make an image of what you want to occur where the behavior you want to change presently happens!

Suppose that the agent of change initially failed to note that the presently activated representational system the client is using is kinesthetic as opposed to visual, the one identified in the instructions offered by the agent. Demonstrating her calibration skills, she notes the mismatch between her instruction and the client's presently activated representational system. She now exercises her flexibility as she smoothly shifts to a kinesthetic instruction, something like,

Feel what you would want to occur where the behavior you want to change presently happens!

The alternative paths through step 2 of the pattern can be easily represented by a branching node in the linear sequence that moves into step 3 no matter which of the branches in the transition between steps 2 and 3 is taken.

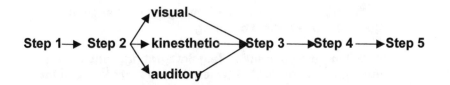

Another frequently branching structure that occurs in the prototypic classical code anchoring format involves the identification of a specific behavior to replace the one the client desires to change. Typically, the agent of change will cue the client with something like,

> **Agent:** *Now search for a time when you experienced the behavior you would rather have in place of the behavior you want to change.*

> **Client:** *Well... I have never actually had the experience I would like to have in this situation.*

> **Agent:** *All right, think of a person who you respect who you have seen and heard do this behavior you want to experience.*

The agent then guides the client through some sequence of events in which he first sees and hears someone who serves as a model perform the behavior, then replaces the model's image and voice with his own and finally steps into the edited video strip with sound track and experiences it kinesthetically as well as visually and auditorily (in 1st position). The larger pattern then may proceed. Such a branching sequence can be accommodated in a branching flow chart like this previous one:

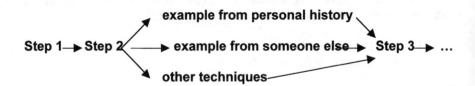

All of this seems clear enough – the generalization is that the ordering of events sequentially enumerated in an NLP pattern corresponds to their positioning in time. If any event, e^i, occurs before any other event, e^j, in some sequence, e^i is to be executed temporally prior to e^j.

Hierarchical Orderings

We note also in NLP a proliferation of orderings of a different logical type than simple linear sequences, namely, hierarchies. We take it that hierarchies are a set of orderings that can be represented in a vertical dimension – a set of graphic representations utilizing a spatial metaphor (the vertical dimension). For those readers familiar with branching flow charts, we invite you to think of the collection of orderings called hierarchies that we present here as branching flow charts rotated 90°. Somewhat more technically, hierarchies appear to be directed sets. A directed set is a partial order in which for any two elements, there is some third element that is larger than both of them. The simple operator ≤ (greater than or equal to) will serve as an example. The relationship ≤ is a partial order if

1) $x \le y \le z \Rightarrow x \le z$ (transitivity)

2) $x \le y \le x \Rightarrow x = y$ (antisymmetry)

A partial order is said to be directed if it also satisfies

3) $\forall\, x, y \;\; \exists\, z$, such that $x \le z$ and $y \le z$ (reflexivity)

        where $\forall$ is the universal quantifier *all*
        and $\exists$ is the existential quantifier *some*

We will examine this set of orderings with care as it has come to play an important (and increasingly contentious) role in NLP patterning.

In linear sequences, the ordering left to right corresponds clearly to when the event described is to occur in time with respect to the other events enumerated by the description: the question remains, what events in the world correspond to the top to bottom orderings in hierarchies. What are we to understand is implied by the vertical ordering we call a hierarchy? We begin by examining examples of hierarchies.

An organizational chart within a company or institution typically is an ordering of the certain relationships among company members. The organization chart is induced by the relationship *is accountable to* or *is in charge of* – depending on whether your preference is to read the chart from the bottom up or from the top down respectively.

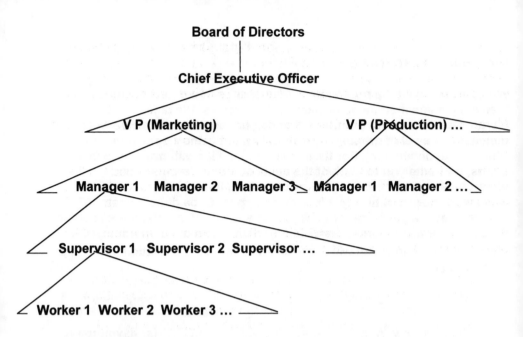

The structure of military units is a hierarchy generated by the relationships *commands* or *reports to* (again depending on whether you read the hierarchy top to bottom or vice versa). Religious groups such as the Catholic church and governmental organizations appear to have hierarchies isomorphic with the military.

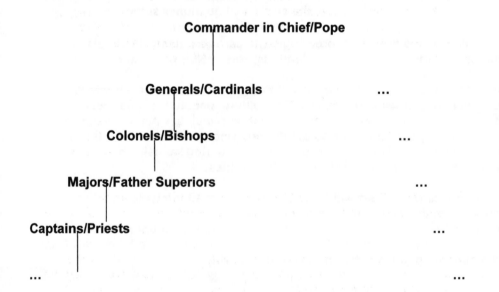

There is even evidence that certain cultural groups have structured their family units to be isomorphic with this common pattern. Certainly, within certain economic and social classes in Latin America, there are many examples of highly traditional families that reflect these structures.

A tennis ladder is a hierarchical ordering generated by the relationship *has recently beaten* (or inversely, *has recently been beaten by*).

Some hundreds of years ago, the great taxonomist Linnaeus created the hierarchy that to date organizes the observations of biologists beginning with kingdom, phyla, family... [5]

We turn our attention now to the field of NLP; a partial enumeration of the uses of hierarchies would include the following:

> The meta model: a set of operations defined on language inputs typically from a client and having as its output challenges by the agent of change with the intention of enriching, extending, modifying or challenging the client's mental maps as represented by the original verbal inputs of the client. In this case, the word *meta* implies that the meta model is a model about a model. The meta model is said to be a model (the meta model) of a model (the client's model of the world as represented by his linguistic productions). In this case, the term *meta* – the *about* or *scope* relationship – points to a set of operations defined on the domain of the client's language productions. The principle, then, by which the hierarchy is created is the relationship, ...*covers/establishes scope over* ... (downward) or ...*is covered by/is within the scope of* ...(upward). The prototypic scope relationship is that shown in the succeeding figure:

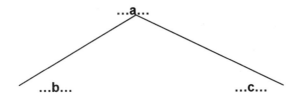

> Thus, in the figure *a* is said to cover or have in its scope the elements *b* and *c* or equivalently, the elements *b* and *c* are said to be within the scope of *a* .

> Meta commenting: a low level therapeutic maneuver in which the agent of change notes a communication, usually incongruent, by the client. The agent then comments, describing or at a minimum

referring to both the verbal and non-verbal components of the client's communications and requesting that the client assist the agent in understanding what the communication represents – a challenge to the client's incongruity. In this case, the meta or about relationship is equivalent to *contains a description of* or *a reference to* – the agent is describing or referring to communication by the client. A meta comment is a verbal communication that comments on and includes either a description of or a reference to some other communication act that it is said to be a comment about. Thus, given a meta comment A, commenting on some previous statement B, we say that A *is about or covers* B or B *is within the scope of* A. These various characterizations of the meta relationship in terms of the *about* relationship, scope or coverage are presented as equivalents in their application in this book.

<u>Meta states</u>: literally states about states, states within the coverage of other states or states within the scope of another state. In its actual usage, it is sometimes very difficult to understand what the author who is proposing the *about* relationship intends. For example, M. Hall's gives the impression that he finds great value in a riotous proliferation of ever "higher" levels of meta states although we find it difficult to imagine what advantages might accrue from such activities. We invite M. Hall to make explicit the answer to the simple meta model challenge,

> *Meta states are states about other states... about, how specifically?* [6]

One explicit use of a meta state is 3rd position as it occurs in Triple Description. This is a state in which the person involved positions herself perceptually such that she is entertaining representations of herself as an actress/player in the scene that represents the situation she wishes to influence. This is variously referred to as the coach, the observer, the consultant, the director, 3rd position or the meta position. In this particular use, the meta position or 3rd is a perceptual position that *includes or covers in its scope* a representation of the representing party. The ordering principle that generates the difference in levels is ...*contains/covers a representation of...* (downwards) or *is included in/covered by a representation of...*(upwards). In this usage, as we mentioned earlier, the descriptor *meta* is roughly equivalent to the phenomenon of scope. If A is meta to B, then B falls within the scope of A, or A covers B in its scope. The standard 3rd position, then, covers or has 1st and 2nd position within its scope – it covers them in the sense that those two perceptual positions are represented within the scope of representations that the individual in 3rd entertains.

TOTEs: originally developed by Miller, Galanter and Pribram in the 1960 work, *Plans and the Structure of Behavior*, as an alternative to the Stimulus⟶ Response work of B. F. Skinner (especially after Chomsky's devastating critique of such proposals as adequate models of human behavior - and in particular, verbal behavior), this schema has found a home in NLP. The most frequently occurring example is the *driving the nail* subroutine

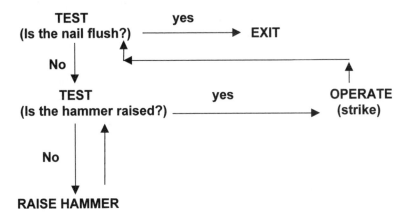

TEST (Is the nail flush?) — yes → EXIT

No

TEST (Is the hammer raised?) — yes → OPERATE (strike)

No

RAISE HAMMER

The subroutine *driving the nail* is itself, of course, part of a larger TOTE such as (for example) *fixing the planks* which in turn is part of a larger TOTE, *putting siding on a house* which in turn is embedded within a larger TOTE such as finishing the outside of a building which in turn... These nesting dependencies appear to be part/whole relationships.

Six Step Reframing (step 3 especially): here we find a movement from one level of experience and activity to another – from a specific behavior to the intention that behavior satisfies - the intention is said to be at a higher level and diagrammatically is presented as such. The ordering relationship that generates this hierarchy is the complex predicate ...*satisfies the intention of*... (reading upward) or ...*whose intention is satisfied by*... (reading down).

Dilts' Neuro-logical Levels: We will return to this topic subsequently in an effort to appreciate what this hierarchy might represent.

New Code's Chain of Excellence: the chain of excellence identifies in ascending order the leverage points through whose use, it is possible to effectively and efficiently shift the state of the entity/entities below that leverage point in the chain. The ordering is that of leverage points – or the relationship ...*can be altered by a change in...* (reading upward) or *a change of which promotes a change in...* (reading downwards).

Chunking: a language based drill to alert practitioners to the fact that language itself is structured in levels. We will explicate this ordering in the succeeding section (*Chunking/Logical Levels* – Part III, chapter 2) and will in fact propose that this process generates precisely the class of hierarchies that are embedded in the underlying structure of natural language itself. Indeed, we will propose that this prototypic hierarchy is the reference of the, until now, loosely used term *logical levels.*

Framing: the verbal presentation of a part of the mental map of the speaker adequate to allow the listener to understand the context in which the communicator is operating. It defines for the listener the boundaries of relevancy for the exchange that is occurring. The hierarchy can therefore be generated by a downward series of partitions that reduces the scope of the exchange. The predicates ...*is occurring within this universe of discourse...* (for the upward movement in the hierarchy) or... *sets the boundaries of relevance for...*(in the downward read).

Representational systems and sub modalities: The sub modalities in each of the sensory channels and their corresponding representational systems are the variables that form the set of elements from which experience in each of these channels and representational systems is composed. The visual representational system includes elements such as motion, color, shape, size, orientation... Continuing down the hierarchy, the element color is composed of variables such as saturation, hue... While hue is decomposed into either partitions of wave lengths or as we more commonly say, the names of those partitions of wave length – the names of the visible color spectrum in English, green, red, yellow... Thus the product of imaging will be said to contain a specific value of some or all of the sub modalities that make up that image in a descending order of elements. This is easily represented as an ordered hierarchy:

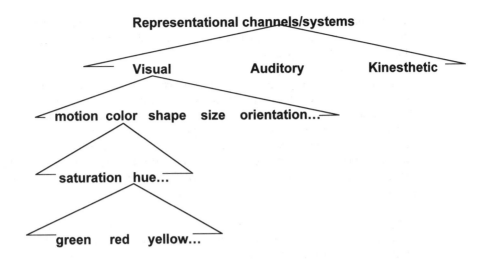

The elements that constitute the sub modalities themselves can be decomposed into their various elements (*color* ➤ *saturation, hue...* whose elements are in turn decomposable. Thus the hierarchy represents the relationship...*is composed of...* (the downward movement) or...*are the elements that constitute...* (reading upwards).
7

Practitioner/master practitioner/trainer/modeler: an administrative or marketing device that is designed to guide an aspiring NLP type through four levels of competency. Each prior level is taken to be a prerequisite to enter the succeeding level beginning with practitioner. This hierarchy can be generated by the predicate *...has already spent X dollars on seminars...*

While this brief tour does not approach exhausting the multiple uses of hierarchies in NLP, it does give a flavor of its many meanings.

Logical Types and Logical Levels

As mentioned in the text immediately above, there has been little or no attention until present given to making ordering relationships explicit within NLP practice. Without such an explicit discussion, work in NLP is significantly flawed – thus, the care with which the issue, for example, of hierarchies was presented. In that discussion as well as in Part I, *Epistemology*, we developed the notion of several possible ordering relationships operating in hierarchies: more specifically, part/whole hierarchical orderings and what we referred to as logical level hierarchical orderings.

The text of this book itself up to this point has alluded to a critical distinction between logical levels and logical types albeit without offering an explicit representation for the two key terms, *logical levels* and *logical types*. Congruent with the commitment to make such distinction explicit, we offer the following discussion.

We are quite aware that we are at variance with the historical use of the terms *logical type* and *logical level* in our presentation. We here intend to make explicit our reasoning for purposing this non-standard usage and the attendant linguistic reform.

Historically, it was Bertrand Russell who proposed the term *logical type*. Initially in his work entitled *Principles of Mathematics* (1902), Russell came upon a set of paradoxes that now bear his name – Russellian paradoxes. To give the reader a sense of the Russellian paradox, consider the following.

> We begin with a well behaved set: suppose that we agree that a class is defined by the extension of a property, i.e. given a property, e.g. "weighs more than one kilogram at sea level on the planet earth", we can form the class of all things that weigh more than one kilogram at sea level on the planet earth, written as {x: W (x)}, where W is the property "weighs more than one kilogram at sea level on the planet earth", and the expression is read as the class of all x such that x weighs more than one kilogram at sea level on the planet earth. This is, of course, equivalent to the set membership rule or equivalently, an intensive definition and in particular, the structure of natural language (more specifically, the relative clause). So far, good enough!
>
> Now consider S = {x: x is not a member of x} (read *S is the set of all x such that x is not member of x*). There are two possibilities: either S is a member of itself (a member of S) or S is not a member of itself. We consider each case in turn:
>
> > Case 1: assume that S is a member of itself. But by definition, S = {x: x is not a member of x}. Therefore S is not a member of S. But if S is not a member of S, it must be a member...
> >
> > Case 2: assume that S is not a member of itself. But then (again, by definition) S must be a member of S. But if S is a member of itself, it must not be a member of S...

This recursive cycling on truth values demonstrates that each of the logical possibilities – the two cases presented - leads to contradiction.

We offer a somewhat more user-friendly example to make the point. Consider the following objects (courtesy of Frank Tall):

The bibliography of all bibliographies that don't list themselves.

The barber who shaves all those who don't shave themselves.

The postman who delivers mail to all those that don't deliver mail to themselves.

If you take the time to work it out, you will discover that none of these objects exist.

The origin of the difficulty is the so-called unrestricted comprehension (or abstraction) axiom in naive set theory. This is an axiom, first introduced by Georg Cantor, to the effect that any predicate expression, $P(x)$, containing x as a free variable will determine a set. The set's members will be exactly those objects that satisfy $P(x)$, namely every x that is P. It is now generally agreed that such an axiom must be either abandoned or modified.

The resolution of this paradox at the present is simply to note that not all properties determine sets, i.e. not every class determines a set. The resolution is legislative – that is, we set down axioms asserting that certain sets exist; these axioms (if selected properly) do not allow us to construct such a set S.

Russell's own response at the time to the paradox is contained in his theory of types. His basic idea is that we can avoid reference to S (the set of all sets that are not members of themselves) by arranging all sentences into a hierarchy. This hierarchy will consist of sentences (at the lowest level) about individuals, sentences (at the next higher level) about sets of individuals, sentences (at the next higher level) about sets of sets of individuals, etc. It is then possible to refer to all objects for which a given condition (or predicate) holds only if they are all at the same level or are of the same "type". Although Russell first introduced the idea of types in his *Principles of Mathematics* (1902), the theory found its mature expression six years later in his 1908 article *Mathematical Logic as Based on the Theory of Types* and in the work he co-authored with Alfred North Whitehead, *Principia Mathematica* (1910, 1912, 1913). This later work was the most ambitious of the lot – carrying the intention of creating a solid foundation for all mathematics – namely, logic.

The entire issue of the Russellian "paradoxes" is no longer troubling in present work in set theory. As Frank Tall, a friend and professor of mathematics at the University of Toronto with a specialty in Set Theory describes it,

> *Russell's paradox shows that we cannot naively (naïve set theory) use the unrestricted comprehension axiom. The accepted resolution is that instead we postulate as axioms various principles that tell us that certain sets exist and that new sets can be constructed from old ones, (e.g. given two sets, the set consisting of both of them exists). In this context, there is no need for Russellian type theory. However an analysis of these axioms reveals that we are indeed postulating that sets exist in a hierarchy of levels. The difference between Russell's types and Zermelo's levels is that the levels are cumulative- sets at the nth level are also at the mth, for $m > n$.* [8]

Bateson, in his treatment of levels of learning and communication and in his analysis of double binds both in *Steps to an Ecology of Mind* and *Mind and Nature*, offers a number of fascinating informal examples of his understanding of Russell's distinction. It was his work that first captured Grinder's attention and alerted him to the importance of working out with some precision what was being proposed as well as its potential applications.

So much for the history of the term. We propose now the following definition: we shall use the term *logical level* to identify the levels presented in any hierarchy generated by logical inclusion.

Logical Levels

> For any two (or more) arbitrary elements in a tree structure (hierarchy) generated by logical inclusion, *a* and *b*, say, element *a* will be said to be at a higher logical level than *b* just in case *a* contains *b* in one of its partitions below *a* in the hierarchy.

Logical inclusion itself is a well-defined ordering relationship specified by the two properties of constriction and inheritability (see Part I, *Epistemology* and Part III and *Chunking/Logical Levels* for a fuller presentation):

1. constriction - reduced coverage under each successive partition induced by relative clause formation

2. inheritability - the preservation of the set membership criteria under partition by relative clause formation

This usage seems to accord well with the conventional use of the word *level* with its accompanying suggestion of a visual display – namely, a vertically oriented ordering – a hierarchy. [9]

Note, now, that this leaves the term *logical type* undefined. We propose, then, that henceforth the term *logical type* will be defined as follows:

Any two (or more) sets, s^i and s^j will be considered to be of different logical types just in case there is no isomorphic mapping between s^i and s^j that preserves all the essential characteristics of each set.

Any two (or more) sets, s^i and s^j will be considered to be of the same logical type just in case there is an isomorphic mapping between s^i and s^j that preserves all the essential characteristics of each set.

By isomorphic mapping, we are referring to a one to one mapping between two sets, s^i and s^j, such that the relationships among elements in set s^i are preserved in the relationships among their counterparts in s^j under the proposed mapping.

An example will help clarify the intention behind this distinction, in his gracious preface to the *Structure of Magic*, volume I, Bateson writes,

There were a few beginnings from which to work: "the logical types" of Russell and Whitehead...they (Grinder and Bandler – JG and CB) develop a general model of communication and change involving the other modes of communication human beings use to represent and communicate their experience. What happens when messages in the digital mode are flung at an analogue thinker? Or when visual messages are offered to an auditory client?

We did not see that these various ways of coding – visual, auditory, etc. – are so far apart, so mutually different even in neuropsychological representation, that no material in one mode can ever be of the same logical type as any material in any other mode.

Gregory Bateson, Preface to *The Structure of Magic*, volume I, Introduction, pages x – xi

295

It seems to us that Gregory got this one just right. The implication is that there are essential characteristics of each of the modes of representation and communication (the representational systems) that distinguish them from one another in deep and fundamental ways. For example, kinesthetic representations have characteristics for which there are no corresponding counterparts in visual representations and vice versa. More specifically, for example, visual representations may contain contradictory representations (or better, representations of contradictory information) in a stable form (without any *spontaneous* movement to integrate) while kinesthetic representations that contain contradictory representations will be unstable and the contradictory representations will (except under conditions of extreme disassociation such as long established multiple personalities or sequential incongruity) *spontaneously* integrate. This *spontaneous* movement to integrate simultaneously presented kinesthetic representations (different feeling states) is the basis of many of the integration patterning in NLP's anchoring formats.

In other words, a well-trained agent of change will choose to put the contradictory representations in the kinesthetic system through the use of anchors just in case he or she wants their clients to *spontaneously* integrate the contradictory parts of themselves. That same agent of change will select a simultaneous display of contradictory parts in the visual representational system just in case he or she does NOT want the parts to *spontaneously* integrate. [10]

Thus, this characteristic that differentiates visual and kinesthetic representations – that is, whether they *spontaneously* integrate (kinesthetic representations) or not (visual representations) - is precisely an example of a relationship in one set (the set of kinesthetic representations with the spontaneous integration of two differing kinesthetic representations), r^i, that is not preserved – that is, has no counterpart relationship - under the mapping onto the other set (the set of visual representations).

Applying this more refined and grounded representation to kinesthetic and visual representations, we may note that in the context of an agent of change selecting an appropriate system into which to map the representations of conflicting parts of the client, these two sets (visual and kinesthetic representations) are clearly and solidly different logical types.

Further from the point of view of a person presenting the general concept of mental maps and their varying representational possibilities (visual, auditory, kinesthetic…), these two sets are obviously of the same logical type.

In summary the decision as to whether any two (or more) sets are of the same or different logical types requires the specification of the mental space determined by the intention carried by the classifying agent with its attendant *essential* characteristics.

This is the definition of different logical types offered above. Further this concrete example calls our attention to the unfinished definition of logical types as we are proposing it here.

The wild card in the definition of logical types is contained in the phrase

...all the essential characteristics of each element...

Until this phrase is grounded, the definition is vacuous and cannot be considered adequate. The difficulty is that what constitutes *all the essential characteristics of each element* for any particular element varies as a function of the intention of the person doing the mapping.

Let's take a very simple example – in colloquial American English, there is a common expression, often heard in exchanges between people in the context of working to resolve difference:

No, that is unfair – you are comparing apples and oranges!

In particular, note the implication of the use of the idiom *apples and oranges*. The commonly understood meaning of this is that there is something incomparable about the two sets of objects named by the terms, *apples and oranges* that renders the comparison invalid.

So, consider the two sets of objects in the world named by *apples* and *oranges*. Are these two sets to be classified as the same or different logical types? Now a gap in the original definition reveals itself with clarity. Consider the following descriptions of intention:

> From the point of view of bureaucrat with the intention of preparing a report on agricultural productivity of various parts of the country, when tallying the total production of fruit from some region of a country's agricultural resources, apples and oranges are of the same logical type. They are both fruits and will therefore be lumped together for purposes of determining that region's contribution to the total production of fruit.

> From the point of view of a chef, with the intention of preparing a delicious dish that uses fruit as one of its ingredients, there are critical differences between apples and oranges. *Canard aux Pomme* (if indeed it exists) would be decidedly distinct from *Canard a L'Orange*.

So what is going on here? We propose that the critical variable is the intention of the person doing the classification. This intention defines a mental space in which an isomorphic mapping occurs or fails to occur.

There are features of the two sets involved in this example that are shared characteristics: both grow on trees, both contain significant amounts of certain natural vitamins, both are offered as snacks and dessert dishes, both are important commercial crops grown, for example, in the USA...

There are also features of these two sets of objects that are quite distinct: they are attacked by different agricultural pests, members of one set (apples) are typically eaten with the skin on while members of the other set (oranges) are not, they have quite distinctive flavors, their chemical analysis is distinct...

Therefore to determine whether two sets (or more) of objects are of the same or a different logical type requires the person proposing the classification to first specify their intention. Their intention thereby defines a mental space. Implicit in their intention (and explicit in the mental space so generated) will be a focus on certain characteristics of the members of the two (or more) sets involved – the difference between the bureaucrat and the chef. This is the operational meaning of the adjective *essential* in the originally flawed phrase, *in all essential characteristics*.

We may then conclude that apples and oranges are of the same logical type if the characteristics that are considered essential from the point of view of the intention carried by the classifying agent map isomorphically, or equivalently in the mental space generated by the intention of the classifying agent, and otherwise not.

This same issue occurs in a number of places in NLP practice where the use of logical types occurs. We mention two such examples. Those NLP practitioners trained in metaphor will recognize this patterning. More specifically, when mapping from a presenting situation with a client or group to some metaphoric space (the story that the practitioner will present to the client), the technique generally requires that the intervention be presented to the unconscious without the client being conscious of what the intervention is. This is typically accomplished by entirely changing the nouns while holding the verbs (or relationships) constant. If, as a crude example, we have two co-owners of a company that are fighting over control, we might speak of two humming birds fighting over a food source. Notice in the simple example, the following correspondences obtain:

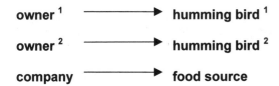

owner [1]	⟶	humming bird [1]
owner [2]	⟶	humming bird [2]
company	⟶	food source

In other words, we have changed all the original nouns by mapping them onto a new set of nouns. This is typically sufficient to confuse the conscious mind as to which entities in the metaphor correspond to which entities in the actual situation (remember, we are using a particularly transparent example here for instructional purposes). Isomorphic mappings used in metaphors may be as transparent as this or as obscure as the agent of change desires.

The way that the unconscious mind recognizes the cast of characters (that is, who is represented by whom) is accomplished by ensuring that the relationships that obtained among the original nouns are preserved in the relationships among the counterpart nouns in the metaphoric space. As an example, consider the relationship between the co-owners of the company. It is exactly the relationship that obtains between the humming birds; the relationship between the co-owners of the company is precisely the same as the relationship between the humming birds and the food source. Through these mappings that preserve the fundamental relationships the unconscious easily unpacks and successfully interprets the metaphor without the conscious mind understanding what is occurring. But note that the fact that one of the co-owners of the business is married and the other not, is not captured by the mapping – this is congruent with the description above. Practitioners desiring to use an isomorphic mapping between the actual presenting situation and the metaphor that will serve as the intervention have no intention of ensuring that all characteristics of the original cast of characters are mapped onto their metaphoric counterparts. Their intention is to select only those characteristics they judge to be relevant to a successful intervention.

A second place in the practice of NLP where this requirement to define a mental space in which the mapping is occurring is in the set of chunking exercises, ubiquitous in NLP trainings. It is typical in some portions of our NLP seminar work to offer the group – typically as a circuitry warm up exercise – a short drill in chunking. For example, suppose that we begin with the word *boat*.

boat

a downward chunking (i.e. toward more specificity) might yield *yacht, canoe, rowboat*...as an adequate down chunk while for an upward chunking (toward more generality) would yield *maritime surface vessels*. In descending order of generality we have a chain of sets:

Maritime surface vessels

Boat

Yacht

Thus yachts are members of the set of objects called *boats* while the set of objects called boats is included in the set of objects named maritime surface vessels. The underlying process we are applying is essentially given *boat* to make downward chunk, so we ask

What is a member of the set of objects designated by the variable boat?

and we obtain, among others, the response, *yacht*. If we start with *boat* and wish to chunk upwards, we ask

What set is boat a member of?

yielding, among other possibilities, the response *maritime surface vessels*

The request for a sideways chunking is more complicated – suppose we begin again with *boat* and request a sideways chunk. In order to respond, we will have to decide (at least unconsciously) in what context or mental space we are operating. We could respond *plane* or *car* or *motorcycle*, and most people would intuitively respond affirmatively – *yes, that's a legitimate sideways chunk.*

We could, however, respond with *pumice* or *obese people* or *Styrofoam* or *hippopotamuses with their lungs full of air* but we are surely less likely to secure immediate agreement. What is going on here?

We believe that in the case of the set *boat* that maps across to *plane, car, motorcycle*, it is relatively easy to find a set at a higher logical level implied by the set of objects (*boat, plane, car, motorcycle*) – they are all examples of means of transportation although in different mediums (water, air, land and land respectively). In other words, in order to chunk sideways we are mapping by identifying a set at a higher logical level (the mental space) that contains the beginning prompt (*boat*) as a member and then by selecting other members of the identified set. Thus mentally, this sideways mapping is a two-step process:

1. identify a superset (a set at a higher logical level) that contains as a member the beginning prompt (*boat*)

means of transportation

↑

boat

300

2. respond with any other members (*plane, car, motorcycle*) of that set that occurs at the same logical level as the prompt (boat)

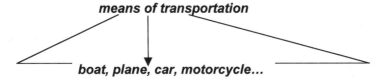

means of transportation

boat, plane, car, motorcycle...

The only difference between the two sets of responses to the prompt *boat*: the set - *plane, car, motorcycle* - and the set *pumice, obese people, Styrofoam, hippopotamuses with their lungs full* is the super set we arbitrarily select.

Applying the two-step process, we have step 1,

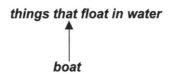

things that float in water

boat

and step 2,

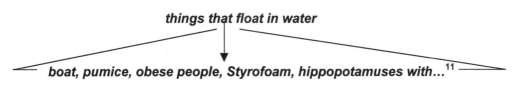

things that float in water

boat, pumice, obese people, Styrofoam, hippopotamuses with...[11]

We offer then a more refined version of the definition of logical types by incorporating the reference to the mental spaces generated by the intentions of the classifying agents as follows.

> *Any two sets, s^i and s^j will be said to be of the same logical type for some mental space, m, if and only if there is an isomorphic mapping available between s^i and s^j within m, and otherwise not.*

> where *m* is the mental space defined by the intention of the classifying agent

In (slightly) more user- friendly English, two collections of objects are to be considered of the same logical type if there is some way of associating the members of one collection to the members of the other collection so that the relationships among the members of one collection also occur among the matching counterparts of the other.

We propose, then, the terms *logical levels* and *logical types* as defined here be adopted as a useful common vocabulary to facilitate communication about models, patterning and the processes by which these activities are conducted within the field of NLP.

Dilts' Neuro-logical Levels

In the last decade or so, Robert Dilts, considered to be one of the leading representatives of NLP, has developed and promoted several work products that appear to us to be problematic. We offer an analysis of these as a way of indicating how NLP might improve the quality of its patterning and to distinguish among the various types of ordering relationships. The inclusion of some as yet undefined nominalization such as that pointed at by the term *spirituality* is one such example. The partition, *spirituality*, is apparently a partition of great interest and importance to many people.

If spirituality is taken to be a human phenomenon to be modeled, then, of course, it secures its place alongside other complex patterning such as *excellence, flexibility* and *creativity* as a legitimate focus of modeling. Insofar as it is incorporated into NLP as an unanalyzed partition that occurs in NLP patterning, it represents an excursion into content and personal preference in self-organization. We have no particular quarrel with anyone desiring to pursue any theme on a personal level but we urge that such enterprises be framed cleanly as such and not be passed off as a legitimate part of the field of NLP.

A second problematic issue, and one more to the point in the present discussion is the question of a hierarchical ordering proposed by Dilts. The question, then, that we wish to pose is

> *What is the ordering principle that generates the vertically arranged sequence of nominalizations presented by Dilts under the title of Neuro-logical Levels?*

The answer to this question takes on an urgency when we discover other authors making comments [12] such as

> *The model of "Neuro-Logical" Levels of Robert Dilts has so fully entered into the very fabric of NLP that most of us think about them when we think of "NLP" or "logical levels"*
>
> Michael Hall, *Greater Flexibility Using the Other "Logical Levels"*, NLP World, page 1

We will argue that it is clear that the so-called Neuro-Logical levels Dilts has proposed is patently not an example of logical levels. We demonstrate that the ordering principle that generates the Dilts' sequence is neither of the ordering principles defined here: namely, neither that of logical inclusion (and therefore, logical levels) nor that of part/whole relationships.

A definite answer to this classificatory question would assist in determining whether this sequence is a formal or a content object and therefore whether it is appropriately included within the field of NLP or not.

Clearly, Dilts seemed to be presenting some sort of ordered relationship in a vertical dimension in his model. While there are some minor variations in the presentation, the most common representation is an ordered chain of nominalizations as follows,

Spirituality

Identity

Beliefs/Values

Capability

Behavior

Environment

One way to pose the question is,

By what ordering principle is this hierarchy generated?

Responding adequately to this question is made particularly difficult by the lack of definition (explicit set membership rules) that specify the partitions induced by each of the various nominalizations that appear in the hierarchy. We shall proceed both by inviting Dilts to offer his own partitioning criteria and by temporarily assuming common definitions for the presently undefined terms unless and until Dilts offers different ones.

We have already made two members of the set of hierarchical ordering principles explicit – logical inclusion and iconic (part/whole) relationships. Hierarchies generated by logical inclusion have two formal properties:

Inheritability

Constriction

If Dilts' model were, indeed, a hierarchy generated by the mapping known as logical inclusion, then any characteristics (set membership rules) that define the sets higher in the hierarchy must also serve as set membership criteria for those sets lower in the hierarchy. We pass over without comment the top nominalization – *spirituality.* We are simply not comfortable commenting as it is too vague a term to discuss without direct input from its creator (we are here referring to Dilts). *Identity*, then, we take to be the highest nominalization we are willing to use in this discussion – the top partition in the hierarchy. We take it as uncontroversial that the set membership rules for partitioning FA into the set called *identity* and its complement set will include the notion of a physical body - whatever else you might like to include. The concept of personal identity without a physical body seems ill formed at best. [13]

We may, then, legitimately ask whether all the sets subordinate to *identity* include this characteristic (a human body) as part of their set membership rules.

We find it difficult to imagine how having a physical body could possibly be a requirement for any of the sets below except behavior - in particular, the set *environment* is problematic in this respect. While this may be a failure of imagination on our parts, we do not understand how this requirement can be satisfied by the putative hierarchy presented. Similarly, applying the second of the two formal properties yields a negative result. We fail to understand in what sense the set called *environment* could be a more restricted set than the set called *behavior* as would be necessary if the hierarchy were a hierarchy of logical levels generated by logical inclusion. Thus, the hierarchy cannot be understood to be a hierarchy generated by the ordering relationship of logical inclusion and therefore is clearly not an example of logical levels.

We attempt, then, the application of the iconic or part/whole ordering principle. More specifically, we ask

Is identity part of spirituality?

There seems to be individuals who represent this possibility. In general, the prototypic member of a religious order – Muslim, Christian, Jewish, Buddhist… are likely to claim that their identity is subsumed under their spirituality. However at the same time, more secular-oriented people would be more likely to claim that their identity includes their spirituality. The difficulty is how to understand the claim implicit in the hierarchy. But what is clear is that both orderings actually occur in different individuals. This would appear to be formally contradictory.

It appears that the hierarchy presented is neither a hierarchy generated by logical inclusion nor part/whole relationship. It is again difficult to be certain but we doubt that Dilts would want to sustain the claim that, for example, the environment is part of behavior – an implication of applying the part/whole relationship to Dilts' hierarchy.

Thus, when evaluated by the formal characteristics of hierarchical orderings of logical inclusion and of part/whole relationships, the vertical sequence presented by Dilts, is demonstrated to be a hierarchy generated by neither of these two orderings. We conclude then that his hierarchy is generated by some principle of hierarchical ordering as yet unidentified.

We value Dilts' intelligence and invite him to make explicit the ordering principle by which he generated the alleged pattern, and simultaneously request that *he make an unambiguous statement that, his Neuro-logical levels are not intended to represent logical levels* – one of the key defining hierarchical ordering principles upon which the structure of natural language is based.

We have taken the time and care to carefully present this critique of Dilts' Neurological levels as it has caused considerable confusion in the field of NLP practice with a significant number of practitioners erroneously identifying it with logical levels. Such a confusion results from the failure to make precisely the set of distinctions we have proposed, with a number of negative epistemological consequences. We have demonstrated that it is clearly NOT an example of this ordering principle of logical inclusion and therefore is NOT an example of logical levels. The answer to our invitation to Dilts to specify the ordering principle behind its structure will determine whether, indeed, it is a legitimate formal pattern or a content model, possibly *useful but clearly not within the domain of NLP.*

This *useful but clearly not within the field of NLP* comment requires elaboration. We proceed by way of example. Virginia Satir had a procedure that I (JG) witnessed many times in her excellent work in family therapy. I describe the sequence.

> Satir is working with a family; both the husband and the wife are present as well as a number of offspring. At some point, the husband erupts in anger, face contorted, fists clenched and pounding on the arm of the chair in which he is seated, voice high, shrill and loud and with the words,
>
> > You all really piss me off – I work my ass off to provide...
>
> Satir moves quickly to a position besides the irate man, aligning her body with him (facing in the same direction), watching and listening carefully to his performance. At some point when the man pauses for breath, Satir enters the fray. More specifically, she expresses herself emphatically imitating the voice qualities of the man, duplicating with great force initially as well his postures, expressions and movements. Indeed, her behavior is recognizable (unless you fall into the content trap) as an exaggerated version of what he has just

done. She continues thusly for some period of time, calibrating the reaction of the husband in her peripheral vision. When she detects a shift in his posture, expression... she begins to alter her voice qualities, expressions and movements. Over the period of some minutes as she reiterates the verbal productions of the client, confirming them,

> *George works his ass off to provide the quality of life that he believes his family deserves... and he is one angry guy because what he is feeling is a sense of lack of recognition for his tremendous efforts...*

As she is working her way through this litany, her voice shifts little by little, arriving finally with an astonishingly soothing, supportive, almost intimate voice quality – her posture modifies itself until it is non-threatening, almost conciliatory, her expressions become those of concern and apparent understanding of the man's ongoing experience while her words gently shift to phrases such as,

> *...and I sincerely hope that each of you (pointing at each of the members of the family present) has the same healthy choice of both feeling what you are feeling and having the ability to express those important feelings*

She is supremely attentive to the man as she makes these shifts in her non-verbal and verbal behavior to ensure through calibration, that the man is tracking (following her lead), having been adequately paced by her initial exaggerated outburst. If she detects a hesitation on the part of the man to follow her lead, she moves in the direction of the emotional expression of anger previously demonstrated by the man. If he is following appropriately, she continues leading him toward the states described above.

As she recognizes that he is responding appropriately to the state she is inducing, she stretches out her arm and places her hand immediately above the abdomen of the man at a position approximately 2 to 3 inches above it, moving her hand in a slow clockwise motion. Her body is now supple and attentive; her gaze fixed squarely on the captured eyes of her client; her voice has entered a low register, suggesting a very private conversation between her and the man and she says:

> *...now that you have adequately expressed the anger you genuinely felt (note the past tense of the verb), are you willing to talk about the deep feelings of hurt that lie behind them?*

The response by the man at this point is typically a collapse into an emotional state marked by tears and confessions of hurt feelings that surprises everyone in the room (including the man himself); everyone except, of course, Satir.

What has occurred here? The presupposition of Satir's statement is that beneath every expression of anger are feelings of hurt. She also believed that it was useful to vent or give expression both to the anger and to the hurt feelings that she assumed to be their base. These presuppositions were, indeed, part of her mental maps.

And, most importantly for the point we are making here, she has imposed this presupposition on her client. Given the man's altered state induced by Satir's exquisite ability to pace and lead him, she has engaged in content hypnosis. She has utilized an altered state in the client as an opportune moment to introduce her presupposition:

expression of anger ⟶ feelings of being hurt

But, wait a minute, you say.

Doesn't the fact that the client breaks down and confesses to hurt feelings with appropriate emotional affect proves that she was correct – that there were unexpressed feelings of hurt beneath the anger?

The answer is clear enough - the behavior offered by the client is as valid a way of demonstrating that there were unexpressed hurt feelings in the man as the fact that a stage hypnotist can get his "volunteers" to cluck and run around like chickens demonstrates that the volunteers actually had unexpressed feelings of being chickens. The effective use of content hypnosis does not prove anything except that the client or volunteers are capable of accepting and responding congruently to the suggestions of a competent hypnotist.

Check your own mental maps as a reference point. Have you ever discovered hurt feelings behind an expression of anger? Yes, of course. Have you also expressed anger that had no feelings of hurt behind it? Yes, many times! Thus expressions of anger do not justify assuming an underlying substratum of hurt feelings.

For us, the critical issue is the same one Freud wrestled with well over a hundred years ago.

How do you protect the integrity (beliefs, values, preferences...) of a client who is vulnerable to suggestions by virtue of being in an altered state typical of the states experienced by people undergoing significant change?

Freud's response to this issue was the well-known constraints he imposed on the behavior of the analyst (listen with minimum input to the free associations...) and the physical arrangements (couch facing away from the analyst to avoid visual cuing...). In the practice of NLP (especially in its applications to individual and small group change work, the response to this question is to partition the problem into two domains: the content of the exchange between client and agent of change and the processes of the change – the formal characteristics of the sequences by which the content is manipulated. Indeed, the current practice of NLP demands that the practitioner make the content/process distinction and leave the content entirely to the client while manipulating the process shamelessly, effectively, and hopefully, artistically.

A significant part of the ethics of NLP practice, then, depends on the practitioner's ability to make the distinction between process and content and his or her ability to confine their manipulations to the process level.

In all the cases but one where I (JG) witnessed the Satir procedure described above when done by Satir, the family member involved accepted unconsciously the presupposition we have explicated and complied, demonstrating the emotions appropriate to her suggestions. [14]

In other words, the procedure worked – in the sense that it led to a next step enroute to a piece of effective family therapy. The fundamental observation is that Satir was effective in inducing change. However she engaged in content hypnosis in inducing such change – an unethical practice. The fact that some procedure works does not mean that it is a legitimate pattern, either in the field of NLP or elsewhere. Indeed, it may be said that clients in a typical altered state induced during the process of change are so suggestible that they display amazing flexibility in interpreting otherwise incoherent proposals from their authority figures (agents of change) effectively. Thus being successful in such endeavors is a necessary but hardly a sufficient condition for proposing that a sequence of actions is a pattern in the sense that we have defined here for NLP. Unless you are well trained to calibrate the physiological signals of altered states, there is little protection for the client unless this process/content distinction is consistently employed. [15]

Footnotes for chapter 1, Part III

1. Any NLP practitioner, familiar with such *transparent* terms as the *4-tuple*, is, no doubt, convulsed with laughter at this point. We agree. So Grinder and Bandler blew it on certain choices. Clearly, the 4-tuple is one of the major user-unfriendly examples of this naming exercise – thus, the linguistic reform proposed in this book – *First Access* instead of the *4-tuple*.

2. My (JG) major professor, Edward Klima, pointed out this difficulty with the so-called three major mapping processes of Generalization, Deletion and Distortion to me in his usual gentle and incisive manner on the occasion of a lecture I presented at UCSD in 1976.

3. I accept responsibility for importing this law of requisite variety – here argued to be inappropriate – into NLP practice.

4. The new code embodies an alternative strategy which essentially relegates the identification of what is to be changed to the status of serving as entry point into the context that defines the set of stimuli that will subsequently serve as the trigger for reactivating the high performance state developed during the exercise. Thus, when in the text we state *that it makes sense to explicate what is to be changed before attempting to select the difference...* we are restricting the comment to an environment in which classic code for anchoring patterns apply – one which contains an assumption challenged by the new code: namely, that the client needs to participate consciously in the selection of the new behaviors and resources as an integral part of the change process.

5. The advent of DNA analysis and the movement to reformulate this hierarchy in terms of either of overlap of DNA or clades simply mark recent challenges to the particular hierarchical ordering relationships implicitly used by Linnaeus in constructing his taxonomy.

6. A special flexibility challenge to M. Hall – write an article (even a paragraph) that does not use the term *meta* - smile, Michael!

7. This hierarchy, then, is a classic example of a part/whole hierarchy. To appreciate the bewildering confusion that can result from a failure to make explicit the ordering principle that generates a hierarchy under discussion, read M. Hall and B. Bodenhamer's recent proclamation in *Surprising New Discoveries about Sub modalities,* NLP World, Vol.5, No. 3, November 1998. We agree that the article is surprising.

8. Frank's reference is to Ernest Zermelo's 1908 axiomatization of set theory and to its most common modern form – namely, Fraenkel's

modification of Zermelo's original work. The distinction between naïve set theory and set theory is whether the theory accepts Cantor's assumption – those that do are labeled naïve. We are deeply grateful to Frank Tall for his many comments and patient tutelage in these matters. He is, of course, absolved of all responsibility for our interpretations.

9. Notice, for example, the number of times the term *level* occurs in the paragraph presented in which we introduced Russell's way of defining logical type (italicized in the following paragraph reproduced for the reader's convenience):

> His (Russell's) basic idea is that we can avoid reference to S (the set of all sets that are not members of themselves) by arranging all sentences into a hierarchy. This hierarchy will consist of sentences (at the lowest *level*) about individuals, sentences (at the next lowest *level*) about sets of individuals, sentences (at the next lowest *level*) about sets of sets of individuals, etc. It is then possible to refer to all objects for which a given condition (or predicate) holds only if they are all at the same *level* or are of the same "type".

This last condition (*it is then possible to refer to all objects for which a given condition (or predicate) holds only if they are all at the same level or are of the same logical "type"*) is the ad hoc constraint placed on Russell's logical "types".

Our understanding is that the class of hierarchies created by Russell in his ad hoc solution is at present used as a measure of complexity in set theory – not a characteristic particularly relevant to NLP at this stage of development.

Further, we note by way of justifying this shift in terminology that natural language contains precisely this class of hierarchy as an inherent part of its structure – generated by relative clause partitions on higher-level sets. We also point out that given the epistemological position we have developed here – namely, that all formal systems (logic, mathematics, formal artificial languages…) are derivative of the inherent logic in natural language, we find this linguistic reform quite satisfying. We remind the reader that we use the term *derivative* in two senses: in the historical sense where we are proposing that the first component of human nervous system developed that has been modeled as finite recursive rule system is the syntax of natural language. The second sense is that formal systems such as logic still retain obvious connections with natural language as do the most fundamental branches of mathematics – arithmetic, for example (see Part I, chapter *Intellectual Antecedents of NLP* under *Logic* for specific examples).

310

Thus, logical levels are precisely those various levels in any hierarchy generated by the ordering relationship of logical inclusion.

10. There is an extended discussion of these somewhat technical issues in Part II, pages 27 – 96 in *The Structure of Magic*, volume II. We note that to the best of our knowledge, there is as yet no thorough definitive investigation of the various characteristics of the different representational systems along the lines of the discussion in the text. This is a powerful piece of work waiting to be done by some competent practitioner.

The italicizing of the term *spontaneous* in the associated paragraph is our way of calling the reader's attention to a descriptive distinction that flows from a command of perceptual positions. From the point of view of the client or an outside observer untrained in these matters, the process seems (both visually and auditorily) to be spontaneous. However, from the point of view of a well-trained NLP agent of change, such spontaneity is a structural part of the ongoing manipulation by the agent of change at the process level.

Please note that in anchoring formats where visual representations are used as the integrative medium – the so-called visual squash, for example – the client must actually do something to force the integration of the contradictory parts – in the example of visual squash, the bringing together of the hands, each of which begins by holding a visual representation of the contradictory parts.

11. Our responses to the prompt *boat* and the instruction to chunk sideways could as well have been the set, *nail file, toilet paper, backhoe and the Eiffel Tower*. But this is nearly impossible to understand. What super set includes all these objects as possible legitimate mapping? One answer would be that the super set involved is simply things that we were thinking about this morning. But such a strange sideways chunking would have little value in NLP applications and borders on the oxymoron of private language.

This two-step process mirrors perfectly our definition of logical types. Translating then from the two-step process, we have:

1. through an examination of the intention for the classification, or equivalently the mental space generated by the intention of the classifying agent, determine which characteristics of the set to be mapped are essential.

2. decide through inspection whether all essential characteristics are preserved under the proposed mapping.

If the inspection reveals that all the essential characteristics in the mental space so generated are preserved under the mapping, the sets involved are said to be of the same logical type.

12. The reader may wish to consult *NLP World*, volume 6, no. 1, pp 32 - 69 where a number of comments on Dilts' Neurological Levels appear – in the majority, in a negative critical mode.

13. Or it presupposes a particularly virulent form of Descartes original sin. A perusal of Dilts' most recent and quite ambitious project (in association with Delozier), *An Encyclopedia of Systemic NLP*, under the title *Neuro-Logical Levels*, pages 866 – 868) reveals a series of predicates as follows:

> *relates to*
>
> *is associated with*
>
> *is made up of*
>
> *relate to, physiologically relates to*
>
> ...

in the portion of his presentation of *Neuro-logical Levels*. While these predicates may be suggestive, they do not constitute definitions and are hardly adequate to allow interested parties to participate in an intelligent discussion of the utility. Less sophisticated readers will be misled by such sleight of mouth into believing that the hierarchy presented is well defined.

When the reader turns to the entry in this same document under *Logical Levels*, pages 667 – 671 whatever coherency that might have existed is lost entirely. In particular, the hierarchical arrangement of question words as representatives of the various levels moves the discussion further into confusion. How (by what ordering principle), for example, could one place question words (*why, who, what, how, when, where...*) in a hierarchy?

What does remain clear from all this is Dilts' intention to find a relationship between a set of nominalizations and their physiological and neurological correlates. The attempt to link actual behavior and neurology/physiology is the basis of the new code – calibration. This is laudatory and, in fact, is what we are suggesting in Part I, *Epistemology*, when we propose that future effective epistemological research will be most likely conducted by interdisciplinary teams including neurologists and linguists. But by beginning the investigation with undefined nominalizations is to position the work on a content base. We have argued ad nauseum in *Whispering* for a commitment to the creation of formal, process models as the distinguishing characteristic of the endeavor known as NLP .

14. The results of the use of this procedure in the hands of people other than Satir yielded very mixed results. My judgment was that other practitioners were far less congruent and forceful in their presentation than Virginia herself.

In the single case I (JG) witnessed where the family member rejected the presupposition described in the text, maintaining that he was genuinely angry but had no feelings of being hurt, Virginia gracefully shifted her strategy and did not insist on her presupposition. We intend this statement to be a compliment to Satir – one that indicates to us that she maintained behaviorally the sensitivity to such possible differences in mental maps. This behavior contrasts favorably with the late work of Fritz Perls who in our perspective succeeded with clients just in case they accepted his presuppositions (or perhaps, more accurately, just in case, the problem they presented fit the presuppositions Fritz used). All else was typically labeled by him as resistance and was dealt with severely by him. See Pucelik's *Disassociative State Therapy*, for a more adequate treatment of this topic.

15. I (JG) still remember the experience when under the tutelage of Erickson, I came to an appreciation of those physiological indicators of altered states – especially, ones that occur spontaneously in the normal course of conversations. I came at that point to realize that therapeutic techniques such as guided fantasy or statements laden with presuppositions, strategic planning sessions or even "normal" conversations where one party was presenting information in a representational system other than the one preferred consciously by the other person were all occasions for the development of significantly altered states. Since such altered states occur even under circumstances where the professional agent of change has no intention of inducing them, the only safeguard in my opinion is a thorough training to ground oneself in the identification of those physiological signals that indicate the presence of such significantly altered states. The construction of perceptual filters riveted on these physiological indicators certainly changes one's appreciation of what others refer to as religious practice, the behavior of politicians, education, entertainment...

Chapter 2: Key Issues in NLP application and training

In this chapter, we turn our attention to issues of importance to NLP in its application and training. We treat three such topics:

Sorting functions

Chunking and Logical Levels

Form and Substance; Process and Content

Sorting Functions

Within the area of NLP application, there is any number of formidable challenges facing a practitioner applying NLP patterns of excellence. When such application is directed to the process of change, at the level of individual, small group and self-application, the specific form the challenge takes is to know, given a presenting situation, which specific pattern or intervention to select as an adequate response to effecting the change she has as her objective. This corresponds to the third of the three elements (selection criteria) proposed by the authors as part of a standard format for reporting patterning in NLP modeling (see the *Presentation of Pattern* in Chapter 2, Part I, *Terminology*).

Selection criteria: the identification of the conditions or contexts in which the selection and application of this pattern is appropriate.

We will propose in the following sections two principles for answering the question of how a practitioner can respond adequately to the challenge of intervention selection: 1st and 2nd order change and the Iatrogenic principle.

Part III, Chapter 2, Sorting Functions

1st and 2nd Order Change

Any NLP practitioner with some years of experience in applications will be capable of recounting stories where they succeeded brilliantly in creating a context in which their client was able to make rapid change, only to discover some weeks or months afterwards that the client had regressed to the original behavior. The client who had successfully given up the habitual pattern of smoking, drinking or a co-dependency relationship finds himself reverting to the old habit. Such cases indicate clearly the point we are working towards – namely, that the patterning in NLP is powerful enough that even when an inappropriate intervention is selected, positive results are obtained, although they are typically temporary.

This observation, it seems to us, places a rather significant responsibility on the practitioner to come to an explicit appreciation of how to select the proper pattern to ensure, not simply immediate results, but results that endure. We once again caution the reader with respect to the verb *endure* - both logically as well as in terms of our direct experience. When a client makes a change congruently using the patterns of NLP, there are a number of consequences, one of which is that the client will return to the context where the behavior that she has changed originally occurred. Since the client is now back in this context but is offering new behaviors, the other people involved in that context will be stimulated, through the client's new behaviors, to shift their responses. Over a relatively short period of time, this double shift will redefine the original context – in many cases to the point where the new behaviors selected in the original change no longer represent optimal choices.

Thus, the client, recognizing that the original context has shifted, applies appropriate NLP patterning to select a new set of behaviors to optimize her experience in this particular context. And so the cycle continues. This constant updating of choices with its repetitive upgrading in the quality of the client's experience is to be anticipated and greeted with pleasure. This is a cybernetically sound process as it provides the client with a continuous improvement loop and ecologically meets the objectives of the practitioner. Relax, Maslow, there is no full realization of human potential, only an ascending spiral of differences and change.

If the application of an inappropriate pattern yielded little or no immediate results, it would be trivial to note that the practitioner had made a pattern selection error and an immediate correction would be forthcoming. We acknowledge the succinct way in which our associate in Guadalajara, Jalisco, Mexico, Dr. Edmundo Velasco Flores of Desarrollo Estrategico Integral articulates this point,

> *!La PNL es tan buena que hasta mal hecha todavia funciona!*

or in translation

> *NLP is so good that even badly done, it still works!*

Indeed, without some explicit method for sorting the classes of presenting problems and the associated appropriate responses to these presenting problems (matching the intervention to the problem), the process of intervention selection is intuitive or trial and error. We are not proposing that there is anything wrong with intuitions as long as the practitioner involved has great intuitions – intuitions are in fact an essential part of any discovery process and certainly played an essential role in the discoveries made by Grinder and Bandler in the original modeling work which established the field of NLP. Nor can there be any doubt that intuitions presently play an important role in the applications of NLP patterning. However, well-developed intuitions are the result of experience - fundamentally trial and error learning - the basis for continuous learning. Intuitions (at least the consistent and effective ones) are simply knowledge in a tacit form. [1]

Trial and error is what we do when we have yet to develop effective intuitions and have no explicit model to guide us. It is clearly the strategy by which we typically begin the adventure of learning in the absence of an explicit model, both in the sense of an exemplar to imitate and in the sense of explicit knowledge of the area we wish to master.

The difficulty is double:

1. Until a practitioner accumulates some robust set of actual experiences, they have little in the way of tacit knowledge – they are actually using trial and error to acquire such knowledge. This leaves open the ethical question of what happens to the clients they work with during the process of acquiring the tacit knowledge that will ultimately serve as the basis of effective behavior on the part of the practitioner.

2. Tacit knowledge is not easily transferable [2] saying something is *tacit* is equivalent to recognizing that there is a lack of explicit representation. Thus, a demand is being made on the learner that essentially insists that he accomplish a number of things. He must first gain access to someone who has such tacit knowledge. Having gained access to the model, the learner must then accept the responsibility for modeling those behaviors that are specific examples of the tacit knowledge he seeks and then generalize those specific examples into a pattern – essentially acquiring the knowledge through a mentoring/apprentice relationship. The difficulties that most frequently arise occur either in finding an adequate model or in the learner's lack of experience/ability in learning in a context of massive ambiguity and vagueness.

While such modeling mechanisms for the transfer of knowledge are perfectly valid, they are hardly efficient for most people and not everyone finds the task of modeling either enjoyable or a learning style at which they can succeed. While modeling is unconsciously ubiquitous, given the fast pace of present western life and the lack of recognition of modeling as a legitimate form of learning, it is often considered to be a less desirable form of learning. Given the choice between learning from someone who can both do what the learner wants to learn and describe explicitly how he does it, and a second person that can do this same thing but lacks the ability to describe what he is doing, nearly every westerner will select the former as a preferred teacher.

It is very interesting to note that in business as well as in certain artistic endeavors that there is a resurgence of interest in modeling – typically in the form of mentoring in business and apprenticeships in art. This is perfectly understandable, as typically the material to be learned in each of these contexts has no explicit model available for its transfer. QL has participated in a number of successful programs in corporations involving the development and roll out of such programs.

Refocusing the discussion on the immediate issue of how a practitioner can effectively select the appropriate intervention, given the presenting problem, we propose two explicit principles (the distinction between 1st and 2nd order changes and the Iatrogenic Principle). These two principles will, we hope, initiate a lively, good natured and intelligent public discussion refining the issue of how we can best manage this responsibility – that of the selection by the practitioner of the class of appropriate interventions, given some presenting problem.

The Distinction between 1st (unbounded) and 2nd (bounded) Order Changes

In the epistemology in chapter 1 in Part I of *Whispering*, the example of asking a child to sort a pile of toys into natural grouping was offered. We proposed that the child would sort this pile of toys using criteria that were naturally present in FA; color, size, shape... In somewhat more formal terms, in the activity of sorting the original pile of toys into different groupings, the child is applying a specific operation to the pile – one that is referred to as a partition.

> Partition: a partition is an operation defined on a collection of elements that sorts or divides the collection into multiple groupings (or subsets) in such a way as to satisfy two conditions:
>
> 1. each member of the original collection is assigned to one of the groupings or subsets of the original collection – by satisfying this condition, the assignment is said to be

exhaustive. Thus, every member of the original set appears as a member of one of the resulting subsets.

2. each member of the original collection is assigned to *only* one of the groupings or subsets of the original collection – by satisfying this condition, the assignment is said to be *exclusive* – each member of the original set is assigned *uniquely* to one of the groupings.

We could say then that if the child sorting the original pile of toys placed each toy into some one grouping or subset (exhaustive assignment) and only one such grouping (exclusive assignment), the actions of the child could be usefully described as performing a partition on the original pile.

The issue to be addressed then is: how does a practitioner faced with the presenting problem of a client decide what member of the set of all interventions is appropriate? The answer to this question depends first of all on how the set of all possible changes is itself partitioned.

We propose, then, that the practitioner sort the set of all possible changes into two groupings or subsets: what we have historically referred to as 1st and 2nd order changes. The set membership criteria for the set of 2nd order changes are as follows: a 2nd order or bounded change is any change that falls into any one of three classes of presenting problems:

1. addictions (drugs, alcohol, tobacco, co-dependencies...)

2. physical symptoms

3. behaviors that have associated significant secondary gains or payoffs

Now that we have identified the members of the set of 2nd order changes from out of the set of all changes, we simply label all remaining members of the original set of all changes as 1st order changes. Equivalently, we define 1st order or unbounded changes as the complement set with respect to the set of 2nd order changes – that is, all changes in the set of all changes possible that are not 2nd order changes by partition are defined as 1st order changes.

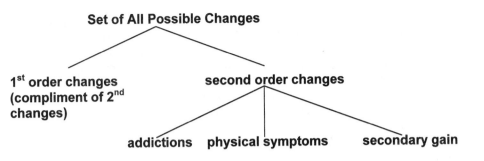

Set of All Possible Changes

1st order changes (compliment of 2nd changes)   second order changes

addictions   physical symptoms   secondary gain

The first two of these three categories of 2nd order changes are well defined. It is not difficult for a practitioner to determine that an addiction is present (although a formal definition of addiction has not as yet been satisfactorily developed – as a brilliant start, review Bateson's remarks both in the *Epistemology of AA*, an article in *Steps to an Ecology of Mind* and in his lecture about addiction on the Esalen tape series). Nor is there much difficulty in noting the presence of a physical symptom. The third category, however, requires some further explication and much refinement.

The difficulty with the third category is contained in the modifier *significant*. How are we to discover whether any particular behavior has significant secondary gains associated with it? By what specific interactions or analysis are we to draw the line between significant and non-significant secondary gain in the life of a client, or in our own case for that matter? We could always ask the client questions designed to address this concern, such as,

> *How would your life be different if you suddenly simply didn't do pattern of behavior X (the behavior in question)?*

Or slightly more provocatively, we could challenge the client as follows:

> *Convince me that you are better off, that your life is fuller and richer by keeping this behavior than by eliminating it?*

Both of these maneuvers are worth considering and with the competency to calibrate in a refined manner, the agent of change may, in fact, detect in the client's response to these provocations some incongruity which when developed further could identify a significant secondary gain or payoff. Both, however, suffer the same defect – they both depend on the client's conscious ability to identify and articulate things that are typically available only at the unconscious level. Once again by presenting the client with these verbal demands, we are directing our communication to precisely the part of the client least able to respond appropriately – the conscious mind.

There is a stopgap methodological solution to the dilemma – this solution exploits a certain asymmetry between changes of the 1st and 2nd order. More specifically, 1st order changes can be easily handled by patterns designed to make 2nd order changes; however as to the converse, patterns designed to make 1st order changes will not serve (over any significant period of time) as adequate techniques for making 2nd order changes. Therefore, the methodological solution is simple enough - when in doubt about whether you as the agent of change are facing a 1st or 2nd order change, select a 2nd order change pattern.

Another way to appreciate this point is to compare the difference between what we call *the cowboy* and *the anthropologist* strategies. The cowboy strategy is quite easy to describe: simply assume that all changes you wish to induce are 1st order changes; select whatever 1st order change pattern you prefer and have at it - with a full commitment to scan for, recognize and respond to any signals of resistance. We are urging the would-be cowboys and cowgirls to search with great care for any such signals of resistance or incongruity in the client's response to the 1st order change work you are doing. If such signals are detected, shift to a 2nd order change pattern.

This is, of course, simply a way of provoking the unconscious of the client to successfully resist the inappropriate application of a 1st order change pattern to a 2nd order change. Such a strategy requires well-developed calibration skills and the flexibility to change what you are doing in the face of non-verbal feedback from the client.

The anthropologist's strategy, on the other hand, is the inverse of the cowboy strategy – the anthropologist assumes that all changes are 2nd order changes. Since 2nd order formats handle 1st order changes anyway, the anthropologist is simply electing to be conservative. The tradeoff is that the agent of change will be somewhat less efficient than optimal, but will never fail to achieve the change the client requests.

Such a stopgap solution, while adequate for our immediate practical purposes, is hardly a satisfactory principled solution – it essentially says that we are, for the moment at least, able to make only partially explicit the distinction between 1st and 2nd order problems as they are presented and that we are simply adopting a strategy that guarantees effective interventions. This difficulty is a statement identifying a significantly unexplicated portion of NLP patterning and practice that, no doubt with time and further developments, will be resolved into finer distinctions.

A note about terminology – the names, *1st and 2nd order change*, are unfortunate in that for the reader with some logical and mathematical background, they suggest associations that are inappropriate. To such readers, we offer our apologies and request their forbearance. The difficulty is that many years ago, I (JG) selected these terms without an appreciation of their use in formal systems and there are a significant number of practitioners trained in their use. What is clear is that the essential differences between the two classes of change are partially explicated by the intensive definition for changes involving addictions, physical symptoms and behaviors with significant secondary gain (2nd order changes) versus changes without these identifying characteristics (1st order changes). We suggested in parenthesis above the alternative terms: *unbounded* and *bounded*. Our thinking is as follows: given the intensive definition offered above for the two categories of change, it is relevant to demand of the authors a characterization of which NLP intervention patterning corresponds to this distinction in changes.

Knowing how to classify changes into the two categories suggested without knowing which patterns are appropriate interventions for the two distinct categories of changes is useless. Therefore we offer the following characterization: the distinction on the other side of the loop (within the patterns of interventions available) is whether the pattern identifies the set of new behaviors from which the new behaviors of the client will be drawn (bounded/2nd order) or simply introduces changes without such specification (unbounded/1st order). In the most familiar case we have presented – Six Step Reframing – this refers to the use of the positive intention behind the behavior to be changed as the basis for generating the set of alternatives.

Remember steps 3 and 4 in the Six Step Reframing pattern. In that pattern, the positive intention of the behavior being changed is discovered and a set of alternative behaviors, all characterized by being adequate to satisfy the original positive intention is specified. From this set so defined, substitute behaviors are selected and implemented in place of the original behavior. Thus, when the set of behaviors that could serve as adequate replacements for the behavior to be changed is specified, the change in the client is contained or *bounded* – that is, the new behaviors are drawn exclusively from the set of behaviors that are as effective or more effective in satisfying the positive intention of the original behavior. In the classic anchoring formats of NLP applications, there are no boundaries placed on what new behaviors the clients will experience subsequent to the work – this is the unbounded case or 1st order case.

Thus, any intervention or applied pattern that includes the specification of the set of behaviors at the level of intention that will serve as adequate substitutes for the behavior to be changed is a bounded or 2nd order change format – otherwise the applied pattern or intervention is an unbounded or 1st order change pattern. Clearly, as mentioned above, the bounded case is the more conservative and typically more ecological intervention.

A Second Sorting Principle f ^{1} and f ^{2}

In the first World Congress on Psychotherapy held in July of 1997, Grinder gave a keynote address in which he proposed that practitioners of psychotherapy accept as one of the ethical standards for their work the following principle:

> any change intervention must be selected to be congruent with the level of representation (FA or higher) at which the "problem" exists.

By this, he argued, if the client before us has a "problem" that is coded at the level of primary experience (FA), then the set of appropriate, ethical interventions must occur at that same level of coding – namely, primary experience. Further, he proposed, any intervention that requires the mapping of the "problem" onto a different level of representation is at least questionable as it introduces additional distortions (the f ^{2} mappings) that are not originally part of the "problem" presented by the client but arise uniquely through the actions of the agent of change. This he referred to as the Iatrogenic principle.

This was intended as a critique of therapies (classic psychoanalytic practice, for example) that required that the client achieve conscious, verbal understanding of their problems, whether the "problem" is coded neurologically at that level or not. It also serves as a method of selecting effective interventions. We refer here to this principle as the:

> Iatrogenic Principle
>
> > *Interventions in change work will be selected to effect change at precisely the level of representation at which the representation of the experience to be changed is coded: the most fundamental distinctions being primary experience (FA) or secondary experience (the mental maps resulting from f ^{2}).*

Note that that the Iatrogenic Principle expressly does *not* mean that the practitioner or the client is confined in their actions to the same level of representation as the one at which the "problem" is coded; it means only that the intervention is to be selected so as to operate at that same level. Nearly every case known to us requires maneuvering at many levels to create the context in which the clients will achieve the changes they seek. [3]

Consider the following case as a concrete example:

A woman of thirty something was brought to Grinder by a Bay area psychiatrist who had done his best to cure her of a phobia; a very peculiar phobia – a phobia of the sound of people chewing gum. None of the traditional methods available to the psychiatrist involved had proven effective in assisting the client in achieving the cure she sought. Naturally, when she arrived at the office in the company of her psychiatrist, Grinder met her at the door chewing gum. In those days this behavior on the part of the change agent was referred to as testing the phobia or gaining access to the "problem" state. [4]

The woman demonstrated that indeed, she was phobic of gum chewing. As Dr. Erickson used to so succinctly put it,

> *Her response was most adequate!*

After she had recovered her state, Grinder initiated a procedure he developed with Bandler that allowed both the testing of the effectiveness of the content free approach to solving therapeutic problems as well as the option to subsequently investigate the formation of the problem for purposes of appreciating what, if any, contribution the original experiences made to the current presentation of the problem. The first session (beginning with the special greeting at the door of the office) proceeded without incident and by using primarily an Ericksonian technique of conversational induction and utilization, arrangements were made by Grinder with the client's unconscious that she would be free of the phobia. Rousing her from the trance state he had induced, Grinder dismissed her. While clearly still confused and obviously consciously doubtful that anything of consequence had occurred, the woman departed, promising to return in two weeks for a follow up appointment.

When she arrived for her second appointment – this time without her psychiatrist – she laughed at Grinder when (yes, as you guessed it) he again met her at the door chewing gum. Clearly, she had achieved her primary objective – to rid herself of the necessity of making a phobic response to the sound of people chewing gum. She literally bubbled over with accounts of other experiences – the so-called secondary changes (that included a spontaneous ride on a motorcycle – she had been phobic of that experience as well although she hadn't mentioned it in the first meeting - and a growing confidence in her ability to handle aggressive older men) that she had noted in herself over the last two weeks. Grinder listened for a short period and then using cues (hypnotic anchors) established during the first session, quickly induced a satisfactory altered state with her. Having assured himself that he had satisfied the requirements of his client, Grinder proceeded to explore the circumstances under which the phobia had been established. He accomplished this by instructing the woman to speak while remaining in the altered state with its attendant amnesia. It turned out that this phobic woman's father carried a strong if misguided commitment to ensure that his daughter developed a full set of resources to cope with the difficult world about her. In particular, on the specific occasion when the phobia was established, the father had noted while traveling on a train with her that his young daughter (she was 4 or 5 years old at the time) had showed signs of fear when seated in a regular train compartment looking out the window at the passing countryside streaming by at high speed. Consistent with his commitment, he immediately carried her to the open platform between the car they had been seated in and the adjacent coach. Explaining to her that she mustn't be afraid, he lifted her and held her outside of the platform so that she literally was suspended outside the body of the train above the ground that raced by below her at high speed. And, yes, as you would predict, he was chewing gum at the time.

So, what are we to learn from this case? Questioning both by the psychiatrist and by Grinder had revealed that the woman had no conscious or linguistic access to the original experience. The experience where the woman learned to respond to people chewing gum was coded at the unconscious level of experience; that is, at the level of FA primary experience – without any imposition of linguistic categories. As the experience was represented at this level and following the Iatrogenic Principle proposed above, the appropriate intervention would effect the change without forcing the experience into the client's consciousness through the use of linguistic patterning. Indeed, the intervention consisted of the use of Ericksonian patterns with direct access to the unconscious and the employment of linguistic variables (relative clauses – devoid of content, to be filled in by the client's unconscious such as *...those experiences where you learned to respond so strongly to the sound, sight and smell of chewing gum, the new responses you are capable of, those specific changes in the ways you perceive people chewing gum...*). Some of the phobia cure formats (variations on single or multiple disassociations) would have served equally as well.

What is key here is the absence of content. The agent of change did not request a verbal description from the client (equivalent to inviting her (the client) to push the experience through the language filters). Nor did he offer her any content. The entire change process was conducted without the experience being forced into her consciousness and without it ever being verbalized. [5] The change in representation at the level of FA occurred without conscious involvement.

Let's be more precise about what occurred. When we say that the change occurred without the conscious involvement of the client, we mean that although the conscious resources of the client were activated and utilized by the agent of change for some portions of the interchange, they were not applied to the content of the experience whose representation needed to be changed. There was no imposition of linguistic categories – neither the client nor the agent of change attempted to describe the experience verbally, and certainly there was absolutely no attempt to understand either the problem (other than its identification) or its origin (until, of course, the changes had occurred and then only on the part of the agent of change). The representations of the original experience were accessed at FA and activated through the application of Ericksonian patterning, but not processed through the client's language system and her conscious processing.

Yes, of course, the agent of change initially utilized the client's conscious resources during purposeful conscious communication with the client. Critically, however, all elements in the actual change of the client's representation occurred at FA. The sound of chewing gum – the auditory portion of the original experience stored at level of primary experience - was an icon that had come to represent that entire experience. That sound (icon) served as the trigger point or anchor to re-access the state she - *the now phobic woman* - had experienced as a young girl during her father's misguided but, as usual, well intentioned effort to teach her something of importance.

Further examination of the client's reports of other spontaneous shifts in her experience during the two-week period between the first and second sessions,

> *...literally bubbled over with accounts of other experiences – the so-called secondary changes (a spontaneous ride on a motorcycle – she had been phobic of that experience as well although she hadn't mentioned it in the first meeting - and a growing confidence in her ability to handle aggressive older men)*

reveals other remnants of the original experience – the spontaneous ride on a motorcycle (consider the overlap between the air streaming past her in the original train experience and the experience of the air in a ride on a motorcycle). The shift in her response to older aggressive men is likewise perfectly intelligible once the original conditioning experience is identified and changed. The woman also reported that she had no difficulty traveling by car, plane or train but preferred not to sit next to a window. Again the cluster is a set of *icons* that reflect the structure of the original experience.

How the unconscious mind selects some elements of the original experience to serve as iconic trigger points for entire experience remains a mystery greatly in need of investigation. However accomplishing the change for which the agent is responsible is independent of any understanding of this process of unconscious generalization.

It is useful to mark the fact that the generalizations that occurred spontaneously at FA are consistent with the partitions that occur at that level of coding – natural partitions and their resulting natural sets defined over the domain of representation, FA, produced by transforms, f^1, operating on incoming stimuli. The generalizations that occurred: the sound of chewing gum, the rush of air streaming by at high speed, the response to older aggressive men are all generalizations at FA. The young woman experienced no corresponding difficulties with other authority figures (females), or with written communications even when aggressively expressed and having their source in older men. Had the client had such additional problems, they would have indicated that the experience had been coded at the level of linguistic experience and that generalizations of the problem had occurred at this linguistic level of coding as these are not natural partitions (that is, partitions at FA) that could connect the original experience with these last experiences.

The specific manner in which certain elements of the representation of the experience generalized themselves is a fundamentally different issue than how to effect a change. The patterns that led to a shift in the representation and subsequently to behavioral options not previously available did not require conscious understanding, either on the part of the client or indeed on the part of the agent of change.

We noted in presenting the sorting principle for partitioning changes into 1st and 2nd order changes that there is an asymmetry in the application of this sorting principle – namely, that if the agent of change is uncertain whether the change the client is requesting is a 1st or 2nd order change, assume that it is a 2nd order change and proceed accordingly. This is an effective rule of thumb that makes use of the asymmetry that the applications of 2nd order change techniques to both 1st and 2nd order changes yields satisfactory results while the application of a 1st order change technique to a 2nd order change typically yields only temporary effectiveness with a subsequent regression to the original behavior. Again, when in doubt, select a 2nd order change intervention pattern.

There is a corresponding asymmetry in the sorting principle presently under discussion. If the client's representation of the experience that they want to change is coded uniquely at FA, then an intervention at that same level will congruently serve. However, a linguistic, conscious level intervention is questionable, both practically and ethically. Conversely, if the representation of the experience that needs to be changed is coded at both levels, FA and linguistically, then either level of intervention will serve. Thus, in parallel with the rule of thumb for 1st and 2nd order changes, the selection of the intervention based on the Iatrogenic principle dictates that when in doubt, select an intervention at the level of FA.

It may give a practitioner some satisfaction to come to an appreciation of the connection between the so-called secondary changes and the elements of the original conditioning experience as it did Grinder in this case. Please note, however, that the critical point is that the change work itself was entirely accomplished in a short period of time with excellent results without conscious knowledge on either the part of the client or on the part of the agent of change. There was never any demand on the part of the agent of change to force the imposition of linguistic categories on the experience stored at the unconscious in primary experience. No new distortions of the experience were generated by the encounter between the client and the agents of change - the Iatrogenic principle was respected.

If the Iatrogenic principle had not been respected, the likely course of treatment would have involved the following steps: first, a struggle to bring the representation of the original experience into consciousness with the unconscious "resisting" – that is with the unconscious signaling that the material was inappropriate and difficult for the conscious mind to deal with. Secondly, once through persistence and the "breaking down" of the unconscious resistance, the material was made available to consciousness, there would have ensued a relatively lengthy period (weeks, if not months) during which the client prompted by the agent of change would have attempted to force some linguistic representation on the experience. One likely path would have involved attempting to understand the intentions of the father. This is likely to have generalized to an inventory of the relationship, past and present between the woman and her father...

What justifiable purposes can be assigned for all of these steps and this excessive amount of time? What is the intention of these processes? Is it the intention to build conscious, linguistic representations so that these representations now can be used to shift the representations of primary experience? Is the practitioner's objective to achieve conscious understanding of what happened in the past? If this is so, what possible positive intention could an agent of change have for imposing this additional set of transforms on the representation at the level of primary experience? These questions also touch upon the issue of secret therapy – one of the characteristics that sharply distinguishes the practice of NLP in change work from other systems of change.

Summary

Two partially explicated principles to aid the practitioner in her selection of appropriate patterning for effective interventions are proposed. The first of these principles requires the partitioning of the set of all changes into 1st (unbounded) and 2nd (bounded) order changes. The second principle requires the practitioner to respect the level of coding at which the problem exists. Elements of both of the sorting principles proposed are in need of refinement in order to make explicit the conditions under which the agent of change selects the interventions based on them. In the meantime, exploiting the asymmetries involved gives us a way of proceeding effectively.

Chapter 2: Issues in NLP application and training

Chunking/Logical Levels

The term *chunking* refers to a class of manipulations of natural language developed by Grinder and Bandler in the very early days of NLP: their primary intention at the time was in training trainers to be effective in utilization techniques in the training context – the rallying cry at the time, as Anne Linden of the New York NLP Institute reminded me,

> *Chunk and sequence!* [6]

In a training context, we frequently give participants an exercise to call their attention to a deep structural pattern in natural language. We proceed inductively; if I give you the word *boat* as a starting point and ask you to chunk down, you may legitimately respond with any of the following words:

> *kayak, sailboat, canoe, tugboat, yacht, ski boat, ocean liner, tanker...* [7]

Implicitly, you are exercising one of the deepest patterns in the structure of natural language. Each noun (or indeed, as we shall see, verb) is a partition on the set of products of the neurological transforms (FA). That is to say, the noun *boat* partitions all the events that are the output of the neurological transforms into two sets: boats and non-boats. Again we warn the reader to be precise about the domain over which this partition *boat* (or any noun or verb for that matter) is defined – the domain is not the world but the transformed version of the world, FA, produced by the operation of the neurological transforms, f^1.

There are two ways to specify a set: [8]

1. A list or enumeration of the contents, the members of the set involved

2. the set membership rules – a procedure that allows you to move through the world and classify the events you encounter as being within the set *boat* or within the complement set *non-boat*

An enumeration of the set of all boats would be a tedious and lengthy process. Further since even as we begin to compose a list of each and every boat, there are new boats being built; old boats being destroyed; the task is open ended. On the other hand, the intensive definition offers a reasonable task – we need only specify what the set membership rules to be a member of the set *boat* are and we are finished. Thus armed with this set membership rule, anyone who was interested could move through the events in the world (FA) available to them and decide effectively whether the event before them is a boat and therefore a member of the set or not. Whatever the full set membership rule for the set boat is, it will surely include something like the following,

Membership Rule for the Set *boat*

Any event possessing the following characteristics shall be a member of the set *boat*:

a) it floats – when placed in water; the object must displace a volume of water that weighs more than the object itself

b) ....

Placing the events previously identified into a hierarchy, we have,

boat

kayak, sailboat, canoe, tugboat, yacht, ski boat, ocean liner, tanker...

Examine each of the sets that these new terms refer to. Ask the question,

Does the set membership rule (partially) specified above apply to the set membership rule for each of the new sets?

You will conclude affirmatively that each of the new sets named by the new terms – whatever they are - will have as an essential part of its own set membership rule the (partially) specified set membership rule for the set *boat* – namely something that floats.

Note that the set *boat* itself is a member of a number of higher-level sets such as [9]

> artifacts produced by humans

> means of maritime surface transport

> things that float

> ...

We can imagine an ordering of levels mapping upward ordered by minimum differences in the set membership rules as the variable defining the distance between levels in a hierarchy.

The set *boat* can be positioned as a part within the hierarchy subordinate to other sets,

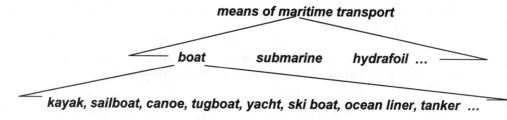

There is an additional characteristic of this type of hierarchy that begins to emerge clearly in this example; namely, that there is a decreasing coverage of the events in the product of the neurological transforms as you move downward in the tree. There are fewer boats than there are means of maritime transport just as there are fewer kayaks than there are boats. Each successive level in the hierarchy further restricts the partition, achieving less coverage and simultaneously more specificity.

There is no ambiguity about this characteristic; each proper subset of a set fails to contain some member of the original set - by definition. But critically, this is not simply a fact about the construction and definition of sets in set theory, but rather this is a fact about the very *structure of natural language*, and on those occasions (quite frequent for most people) when we think in natural language, a fact about how we as a species think. This formal characteristic identifies a powerful hidden presupposition in the structure of natural language. [10]

Nouns and verbs are partitions defined over the domain generated by the set of neurological transforms culminating at FA. The ordering principle that generates such levels is the relationship known as logical inclusion. Such partitions result in what we call logical levels. The two formal characteristics of hierarchies specified by logical inclusion are:

Inheritability: any set, s^i, lower than s^j in a hierarchy generated by logical inclusion will include the set membership rule for s^j among its set membership rules

Constriction: any set, s^i, lower than s^j in a hierarchy generated by logical inclusion will have a reduced scope relative to s^j (that is, will have less coverage of the events of product of FA – will have fewer members).

Therefore, we arrive at the following conclusion:

The Connection between Logical Levels and Natural Language

The partitions on the product of the neurological transforms (FA) generated by repetitive acts of naming for both of the natural language categories *nouns* and *verbs* result in a hierarchy of logical levels generated by the relationship of logical inclusion.

We have identified and defined one of the most fundamental of all hierarchies: one that is implicit in the very structure of natural language and thinking patterns based on natural language – logical levels generated by the ordering relationship of logical inclusion.

With this reference point in hierarchies established, we are now in a position to look freshly at other types of hierarchies. We have noted that inevitably when participants are working in chunking exercises, certain classes of disputes occur. At first, this puzzled us. After doing an analysis of the contentious examples, we recognized the pattern involved.

Whenever there was a dispute, it implicitly revolved around which ordering principle to use to generate the hierarchical relationships. For example, using the same noun partition to initiate the process, *boat*, some participants would argue that a legitimate response to a request to chunk down would be the word *hull*.

331

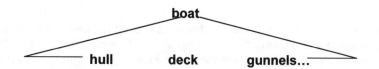

Implicitly the participants were applying a distinct ordering principle to generate the hierarchy; that of iconicity or the part/whole relationship. Note that parallel to the logical levels – those defined by logical inclusion, the part/whole ordering principle permits a continuing specification of levels in the hierarchy.

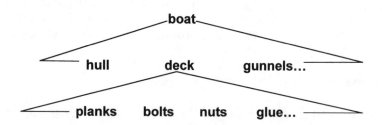

This hierarchy is explicated by the part/whole relationship, a fundamentally different ordering principle than logical inclusion. Apply the formal characteristics we presented for logical levels to this hierarchy. More specifically, the questions,

> *Are the set membership rules that define sets higher in the hierarchy inherited by the set membership rules for sets subordinate to them in that hierarchy?*
>
> **(the inheritability criterion)**

> *Do the subordinate sets that occur lower in the tree structure have fewer members than those above them?*
>
> **(the constriction criterion)** [11]

The answers are clearly negative. The answer to the first question is a mixed result: affirmative in some cases (*hulls, planks...*) and negative in others (*gunnels, bolts...*). The set membership rule for *boat* does not systematically occur as part of the set membership rules defining sets subordinate in the hierarchy. Hulls and planks float, but not (necessarily) gunnels and bolts.

332

The answer to the second question is exactly the opposite of that we obtained in logical levels. There are more bolts, nuts, planks, glue, hulls, decks and gunnels in the world of FA (the product of the neurological transforms) than there are boats. Thus the part/whole ordering principle generates hierarchies that fail to meet the formal criteria that define logical levels.

Hierarchies formed on the part/whole relationship are very different creatures than hierarchies generated by logical inclusion. The reduced scope principle – constriction - seems to be inverted – that is, in general, the further down a hierarchy specified by the part/whole relationship you go, the larger the scope, the greater the coverage of events by the sets enumerated. Sets lower in the hierarchy have more members than those above them. There is no clear generalization with respect to the inheritability requirement that we have been able to formulate. It seems that when it does occur, it occurs without any pattern; certainly any pattern presently transparent to us.

Consider the hierarchy defined by the TOTE:

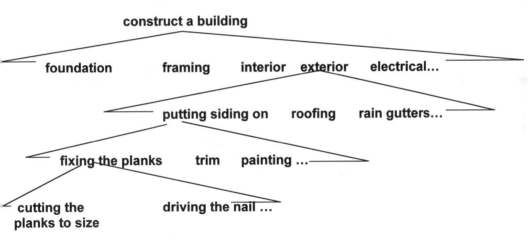

A cursory examination of the TOTE supports the claim made earlier that TOTEs are examples of part/whole hierarchies.

Our purpose in this section has been to open a dialogue concerning the hierarchical orderings currently used in NLP patterning and applications. We have offered a precise formulation of two of the most commonly occurring such orderings as a stimulus inviting careful consideration on the part of NLP practitioners when developing and reporting patterning.

The art of thinking when based on linguistic patterning will surely require an explicit appreciation of these ordering relationships.

Form and Substance: Process and Content

Substance is the stuff out of which physical objects are composed. Form is the shape or organization that informs or makes the substance involved what it is. The statue in the Palace of the de Medici's in Florence, Italy known as Michelangelo's *David* is distinguishable from other statues not by the quality of the marble that Michelangelo used but by the exquisite form he conferred on it. One human being differs from another less by the substance – the flesh, blood, bone and sinew – and more by his individualized shape or form. We see something in the distance approaching – at some point, we suddenly recognize it as a human being – at some closer point, we identify it as the form of a particular friend or acquaintance.

This is the distinction that differentiates NLP applications from applications of other systems of change and, in our opinion, accounts in significant part for the tremendous success of certain applications of NLP and their rapid diffusion to nearly all parts of the planet.

The distinction in question is not trivial to define: we therefore begin with a number of very clear examples of the distinction and then consider, for contrastive purposes, both work that simply does not make the distinction or work that purports to make the distinction but, in fact, does not do so.

One of the clearest examples of this distinction is the meta model. The meta model, the first model (collection of patterns) created in NLP is unwavering in its attention to this distinction. The meta model is a purely syntactically based set of questions that has as its purpose the specification or challenge of verbal utterances – more specifically their connections to the reference experiences in FA they represent. The natural consequence of the rigorous use of this model is a series of verbal challenges to those impoverished portions of the mental maps of the client who finds himself without adequate choices to create the quality of life he is seeking. For example, if a client in the appropriate professional context produces a sentence such as,

A lot of people don't trust me!

the parsing of the sentence reveals one noun *people* and one verb *trust* that are so unspecified as to be uninterpretable without the listener (or indeed, the speaker) hallucinating what, in fact, they might refer to. The classic application of the meta model dictates that the proper verbal responses [12] to the sentence are,

> *Which people specifically (don't trust you)?*

and

> *Don't trust you, how specifically?*

If these meta model challenges are properly applied (that is, recursively and in the order of specifying nouns to criteria first and then subsequently defining the verbs), they will have the consequence mentioned in the framing to this section – the expansion of the impoverished portions of the client's mental maps as part of the process of creating the options he requires to achieve the quality of life he is pursuing.

As mentioned in the earlier description of the meta model, the challenge questions are perfectly general.

for unspecified nouns   *Which _____ specifically?*

for unspecified verbs   *_____, how specifically?*

the blanks represent the unspecified nouns and verbs

These challenges apply to any noun or verb *independent of the content the nouns or verbs refer to.* Substitute any appropriate (in context) noun for *people* (*men, women, children, people of East Asian origins, entrepreneurs, dogs, geckos, creatures with webbed appendages...* or any appropriate (again, in context) verb for *trust* (*like, pay attention to, listen to, help, respect, support...*). Note that the question-challenge pair remains equally effective, independent of the changes in meaning as you substitute the various different nouns (or verbs) into the slot in the challenge frame. In the field of linguistics, the distinction is captured by the difference between *syntax* and *semantics*, respectively the study of the structure of the language and the study of meanings of the language. Thus, we can conclude that the effectiveness in the model is invariant under changes of meaning. It is a purely syntactic exercise and in absolutely no way depends on the content involved in the exchange.

Our second example comes from formal logic. A logician will point out that the validity of the patterning of the prepositional calculus again is invariant with respect to meaning. By this, she will be referring to the fact that if sentence, S^1, is true and sentence, S^2, is also true, then the conjunction of S^1 and S^2 (literally, S^1 *and* S^2) Is likewise true. Further if one of the two sentences is false, then the entire conjunction is false however, if the two sentences are connected by a disjunction (the form, S^1 *or* S^2), this form remains true if one or both of the sentences are true. All of this occurs independently of the content of the sentences referred to by the variables, S^1 and S^2.

We draw on the field of two-dimensional or plane geometry for a third example: there is a set of objects in geometry known as circles. This geometrical object – the circle - can be defined as any object where all points on its perimeter (those which define the shape of the object) are equidistant from its center. The algebraic definition of a circle is given by the general equation,

$$r^2 = x^2 + y^2$$

Note that all this is independent of the size of the circle, the color of the circle, the context in which you find the circle... In other words, circles are circles independent of their size, color, context, material composition... If you think of the size, the color, the context, material composition of the circle as its content, then the algebraic definition of the circle we offered is its form. Thus circles are invariant with respect to size, color... These three examples are very clear instantiations of the form/content distinction.

In a context such as the practice of NLP where the process/content distinction is the touchstone for ethical practice, the fact that a procedure is effective has no impact on whether it is a legitimate or ethical pattern, to be included in the technology of the field.

Let's return to the Satir example offered above in chapter 1 of Part III, *Logical Types and Logic Levels*: had Virginia simply substituted a relatively content free linguistic expression (technically, a variable) for the phrase *hurt feelings* that she imposed by presupposition, we would find the work much closer to the ideal. She could well have said,

> *...now that you have adequately expressed the anger you genuinely felt* (note the past tense of the verb)*, are you willing to talk about the deep feelings that lie behind that anger?*

simply deleting the remnant of the relative clause (*of hurt*) and

> *...the deep feelings of hurt that lie behind that anger?*

convert the phrase to:

> *...the deep feelings that lie behind that anger?*

Perhaps a similar maneuver would convert the hierarchy proposed by Dilts into a process model. For example, in place of some standard content hierarchy such as the one presented by Dilts, perhaps he could argue effectively for using some formal concept - for example, that there is a hierarchy in which changing something at a higher node in the hierarchy would effect change in the lower level. This seems to be the purpose at the heart of his hierarchy,

> *The effect of each level is to organize and control the information on the level below it. Changing something on an upper level would necessarily change things on the lower levels...*

> Dilts, 1991, page 26 [13]

Further instead of making the (presently unmotivated) assumption that the particular string of nominalizations proposed (but not defined) is a standard organizational pattern for humans, he could propose a set of elicitation steps that would allow each client or user of the proposed hierarchy to determine for himself or herself the ordering of these levels, thereby converting the content nominalizations into processes that allow each user to develop his or her own tailored hierarchy, thereby respecting the integrity of the individual users of the model.

Dilts' hierarchy does overlap partially with what we call leverage points – the points in a system where a minimal difference will set in motion significant change within the entire system. For example, in chapter 3, Part II, New Code, the chain of excellence is presented as an explicit example of a set of hierarchically ordered leverage points with respect to performance in which each of the higher nodes in the hierarchy represents a leverage point to change the functioning of the entities below in the chain. Perhaps something along these lines can be made out of the Neuro-Logical levels model.

To be frank, we have our doubts that hierarchies for living systems with the properties enumerated in the quote above exist (*Changing something on an upper level would <u>necessarily</u> change things on the lower levels*). Note the use of the modal operator *necessarily* in Dilts formulation. This would imply in the present listing of nominalizations that changing any one of the levels above behavior would necessarily change behavior.

But this flies in the face of decades of work in the field of therapeutic applications of NLP let alone in associated fields such as psychiatry... As mentioned in the historical section previously in the book, Bandler and Grinder were astonished by the rich and explicit representations that many of the schizophrenics with whom they worked were able to articulate. These representations indicated an exquisite ability to form conscious mind representations that more than adequately described the origins and present functioning of their schizophrenic patterning. None of this precise explicit knowledge had any impact on changing their behavior. In terms of Dilts' hierarchy, this capability and the expressed values of the schizophrenics failed to shift their behavior as demanded by the properties that Dilts requires his hierarchy to have.

In fact, we need not consider the extreme cases represented by schizophrenics as each and every client that walks into the office of an agent of change with the declared value of changing their behavior represents a glaring counterexample to what Dilts is proposing. Clearly, these clients have a declared *value* to change, but still the *behavior* persists. If you urge that such clients are not changing their *behavior* as they have not yet developed the *capability*, you are simply offering an additional counterexample. This is so as the property required by the hierarchy is that changes in the level higher in the hierarchy (quoting Dilts) *necessarily changes things on the levels below*. Since *value* is at a higher level than *capability* (better – ability) and *capability* is at a higher level than *behavior*, such changes should have already occurred. But, in fact, they have not.

Even closer to home, pause a moment and ask yourself:

> *Is there some change in behavior – say your weight, or your physical competence or your ability to pattern or write more lucidly – that you already have as one of your values to upgrade but your behavior has yet to shift?*

Each such *value* without the corresponding shifts in *capability* and actual *behavior* constitutes a compelling counterexample to the claim made in Dilts hierarchy.

The formulation of the properties of the Dilts hierarchy also involves the nominalization *control*,

> *...effect of each level is to organize and <u>control</u> the information on the level below it...*

The art of NLP [application] revolves around choice, not control. Control is one of the illusions entertained by the conscious mind - indeed, one that rests on the Cartesian split – the very same illusion you encounter in absurd expressions of *mind over matter*.

We urge Dilts to reconsider such claims. Something as simple as the answer to meta model challenges to the nominalizations that constitute the levels of the hierarchy plus *control* would serve. Further we would invite Dilts to apply the modal operator challenge to the term *necessarily*. Finally, as mentioned above, we would appreciate his making explicit the ordering principle that generates the hierarchy. All this would be welcome in the extreme. Further, until adequate clarification is forthcoming, we ask that he specifically clarify that the hierarchy does NOT represent logical levels. His response to the issues raised here will subsequently determine whether the model is to be considered a part of the field of NLP at all.

While the determination as to whether Neuro-Logical levels is a part of NLP must await a further explication by Dilts, we are, in any case, left in a quite unsatisfactory position with respect to the key issue involved. For many years, as the co-creator of NLP, I (JG) have argued passionately that the process/content distinction is the difference that makes the difference in two critical areas of practice within NLP:

> 1. the awesome power and effectiveness of the application of the patterning of NLP rests squarely on the process/content distinction and that this is precisely what distinguishes it from other change technologies
>
> 2. the ethical issue – as we stated earlier, *the current practice standards of NLP demand that the practitioner make the content/process distinction and leave the content entirely to the client while manipulating the process shamelessly and effectively.*

In our analysis of the ordering principles by which various hierarchies in NLP are generated, we have been to date unsuccessful in characterizing *formally* the process/content distinction. Either the proposed distinction does not exist or has the status of tacit knowledge yet to be explicated.

Here is the problem we have been exploring in a nutshell. Take any hierarchy generated (e.g. logical inclusion or the part/whole relationship). Select any level, l^i, in the hierarchy and ask yourself whether in fact, the members of this level arbitrarily selected are the contents of the set named at the level, l^{i-1}, immediately above them. Further, does it match your intuitions that the set named at the level, l^{i-1}, immediately above can be usefully understood to be the form for those members? Now consider the set named at the level above level, l^{i-1}, the set at the level of l^{i-2}. With respect to this set, the set that was previously the form for the elements at l^i, namely, l^{i-1}, now becomes the one of the content elements of the set at level, l^{i-2}.

Let's take a concrete example relevant to the ethical issue: in practice, there seems to be good intuitive agreement about where the lines of process and content are to be drawn. For example, a well-trained NLP agent of change is working, guiding a client to access the material to be changed. Consider the difference between the sets of instructions A and B:

Set A

Make an image of what occurred back then

Feel the feelings that you experienced then

Listen to what is being said in the situation

Set B

See who it was who abused you

Feel how violated you felt

Listen to the terrible things said

We suspect that every NLP trained practitioner would classify set A as a set of process instructions and equally so would categorize set B as ethical violations of the client's integrity – an indulgence in content. As a matter of fact, we are sympathetic with this judgment. But intuitive agreement is hardly an adequate base for principles designed to safeguard the integrity of clients. So what then is the specific difference between sets A and B. Consider the presuppositions of the set A

Statements in Set A

Make an image of what occurred back then —→

Feel the feelings that you experienced then then —→

Listen to what is being said in the situation —→

Presuppositions of Set A

something visual occurred then

you experienced feelings

something was being said then and you heard it

Statement of Set B

See who it was who abused you ———→

Feel how violated you felt ———→

Listen to the terrible things said ———→

Presuppositions of Set B

someone abused you then

you were violated and felt it

terrible things were said then

Examine the graphic representation of the hierarchy involved,

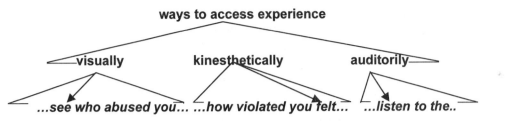

In the hierarchy displayed, the top level is simply the name of a set of possible ways to access the reference experience. The middle level is an enumeration of the principal non-verbal representations through which the reference experience could be accessed. The bottom level is a listing of some specific accesses within each of the representational systems. Critically, the terms in the middle level represent forms with respect to the bottom level and content with respect to the top.

In other words, the set B, taken without controversy to be content violations of the client's integrity, are representations of possible content inside of the reference experiences accessed through the three major representational systems. In that sense, the three major representational systems are formal; they are processes – different strategies for accessing the content of the reference experience. However, with respect to the higher level set - accessing the reference experience, they are content.

Think about it in this way: you bridle at an agent of change imposing by presupposition any of the statements in set B. But what is the difference between that imposition and the imposition represented by the agent specifying which of the representational systems is to be used as the accessing strategy (namely in set A)? Are we to absurdly attempt to quantify the degree of intrusion into content by the agent of change and draw some distinction to the effect that content manipulations at or above some defined level in the hierarchy are acceptable and those below are not? To do so, we would be slipping into a quantitative mode precisely in one of the areas we require a categorical distinction.

You may want to argue that with the exception of people who have lost one of their input sensory channels, any experience from the past will by definition contain images, feelings and sounds – the representations that correspond to the three major representational systems. But we respond by asking how it is that the agent of change is authorized to make the decision as to which of the representational systems is to be used by the client in accessing the reference experience, but that same agent is not authorized to make any of the statements in set B. What in principle makes the difference between the impositions of set A and set B?

If you respond that the agent detected a non-verbal cue (e.g. an eye movement or a physiological shift) that indicated that system X was already activated, we are well satisfied that you have respected the client's integrity; if no such non-verbal indicator can be identified as an appropriate source of the decision to select a particular representational system access, the decision made by the agent of change must be justified by some other criteria. If no other criterion can be proposed and verified, then we are left with a most unsatisfactory situation. In other words, there is no *formal* distinction presently available to us as practitioners in the application of NLP patterning which allows us in principle to distinguish between process and content.

What does emerge from this brief discussion is that *in practice the source of the content is critical.* In this sense, the meta model is an impeccably ethical tool in that the agent of change is restricted to using and challenging only verbal productions that originate with the client and is specifically barred from introducing material – content. Likewise with the application of anchoring, the client has whatever experience – the anchor simply stabilizes access to that experience without adding or modifying the experience in any way, certainly if done with precision and with code words (secret therapy). Equally with sub modalities manipulations, the client presents the differences in sub modalities between a representation that works for him and one that does not. The agent of change simply compares and transfers the differences from one to the other – a formal manipulation. Note that in these cases, the source of the content is uniquely the client, never the agent of change.

Thus we have specific suggestions for the actual practice of ethically applying the NLP patterns in change work:

> 1. the agent of change's task is to behave in such a way that the message is constantly transmitted congruently to the client that the client is responsible for the changes and that the content of the changes need not be disclosed.

> 2. If the client chooses to reveal the content of the experiences and contexts that form the basis of the change work to be accomplished, the agent of change will eschew any attempt to understand the content. He will operate at any level above that content through a manipulation of process however such an agent stylistically chooses to present herself to the client. If the client does not insist upon a disclosure of the content, code words (essentially arbitrary variables) and secret change work are the most highly valued strategy as they ensure the protection of the integrity of the client.

3. We have thus far been unable to develop a formal distinction between content and process. The agent of change is therefore charged with the task of constantly refining his sensory acuity to be competent to detect the ongoing states and strategies being employed naturally by the client at the unconscious level and utilize those unconscious choices and decisions of the client to make the process (content with respect to the level in the hierarchy above) decisions that will guide both to a successful fulfillment of the client's requirements. Calibration is the most fundamental requirement for a well-trained NLP practitioner.

4. Respect the sorting principles developed earlier in the presentation: especially important in this context are the experiences that represent obstacles to the client's continued advancement toward his goals that are represented at FA - the pre-linguistic level. These representations are to be managed at that level without imposing linguistic categories on them.

5. An essential skill of an agent of change employing NLP patterning is to cultivate the use of linguistic variables in their verbal communications so as to offer effective and congruent instructions to the client while imposing a minimum of content (a minimum of partitions) whose source is the agent of change as opposed to the client – or equivalently, making a minimum of decisions for the client. The specific linguistic variables we are referring to fall nicely into the category of intensive definitions.

Using the previous work as an example:

Constants	Variables (intensive definitions)
...see who abused you...	*...an image of what occurred back then*
...how violated you felt...	*...the feelings that you experienced then*
...listen to the terrible...	*...what is being said in the situation*

The notions of constants and variables (intensive definitions) serve nicely here. In retrospect the original source in NLP of the explicit distinctions form/substance or through time, process/content comes from Grinder's work as a professional syntactician doing natural language patterning. In transformational linguistics, the distinction between syntax and semantics is a clear operational division of labor in which syntacticians focus on the discovery and description of syntactic forms that represent well-formed sequences in the language under scrutiny. Linguists with a specialty in semantics work out the meaning relationship among the various lexical items that constitute the vocabulary of the language in question. Chomsky's famous sentence:

Colorless green ideas sleep furiously.

is an icon of this distinction. This sequence of English words is said classically to be well-formed syntactically and decidedly strange semantically. The point of the sequence was to demonstrate that it is possible to have sentences that are perfectly well-formed with respect to their form – their syntactic structure – but which are meaningless – that is, they fail to meet the semantic requirements of the language. If, as was argued historically, the syntax can be studied independently of the semantics, the task for the syntactician is greatly simplified (but hardly simple). Thus the syntactic structure of the sequence is the form and the meaning/semantics is the content – two distinguishable classes of events.

This is the key distinction behind the meta model. In this model, the distinction between form/process and substance/content is cleanly presented and represents a breakthrough model for verbal communication – its effectiveness resting solidly on the distinction we are discussing. The fundamental strategy pursued by Bandler and Grinder in developing the classic code was to push this distinction into non-linguistic areas of human functioning. Phenomena such as anchoring, sub modalities, framing, reframing… are patterns that are products of this research strategy – the form is the leverage point - push the form, leave the content to the client.

With respect to the larger issue, we hope that the NLP community finds the specific suggestions, formalisms and formats (e.g. for reporting patterning) we have proposed here useful, If so, we may anticipate an ongoing public dialogue with the expectation that we will succeed in developing more satisfactory criteria for distinguishing between what traditionally we have pointed to as the process/content distinction. This is a distinction that applies both to the determination of whether a particular putative pattern is formal and therefore to be included as a pattern in the NLP technology as well as the refining of the use of the desired distinction as the basis for the ethical practice in the application of NLP patterning to change work. We hope that it will prove possible to develop a more satisfactory representation – that is, a formal representation - of this critical distinction. Whether and how far this distinction can be extended from the clear cases already mentioned is, as we say, an empirical issue. We invite serious researchers to address this challenge in reporting their work.

Footnotes for Chapter 2, Part III

1. Satir had little skill in making explicit the basis of her superbly effective intuitive work in family therapy. She was often asked questions like

> Virginia, how did you know to do that particular pattern at that specific point in the session?

She predictably responded with the advice,

> Trust your guts!

This, of course, turns out to be excellent advice *if* you happen to have Virginia Satir's guts.

2. Tacit knowledge is, of course, food for the soul of a modeler – someone who is correctly said to have tacit knowledge (or equivalently, excellent intuitions) is someone who is behaving effectively, but who as yet has not explicated her effective behavior. This offers a modeler an excellent challenge.

3. All representations of experiences coded at the level of secondary experience, f^2, are presumed to be already coded at the level of primary experience, f^1. We make good use of this asymmetry in the selection of appropriate interventions.

4. This is an example of one kind of limiting case of rapport – at the conclusion of this maneuver, Grinder may correctly be said to have achieved rapport with the unconscious of the client. We make this comment to correct a common misperception about rapport and the strategies (mirroring or cross over mirroring) made explicit by Grinder and Bandler in the early days of NLP. Rapport, we propose, is established precisely at the point that the agent of change has captured the unconscious attention of the person with whom he wants to achieve rapport. One particular form that rapport can take, then, is trust. The common misperception, mistaking trust for rapport, seems to be the logical level error of identifying a member of a set with the set itself.

5. It should be made clear that the client never (at least up to last contact with her) had any conscious appreciation of the source of her phobia – she simply achieved the choices she came seeking. This ethical principle comes directly from Dr. Erickson. He (and Grinder and Bandler, in turn – certainly in those days) categorized those private communications between practitioner/hypnotist and the client's unconscious mind as privileged communications. As privileged communications, Erickson never revealed to the client's conscious mind material that came through this privileged

medium. His position was that if the unconscious wants the conscious mind to become aware of such information, the unconscious itself will release such information to the conscious mind at a time and in a manner it chooses. Without the express permission of the unconscious, then, a practitioner/hypnotist would be betraying the privileged communications should he present such information directly to the client's conscious mind.

6. Note that this slogan includes reference to two of the critical variables to be managed in such work.

chunk = decompose into units

and

sequence = arrange in some ordering relationship

7. Our apologies to the nautically informed for ignoring the size based distinction between a *boat* and a *ship*. The attentive reader will note the reoccurrence of the boat example from the epistemology section although the point emphasized here is different.

8. These two methods for specifying a set are equivalent to the analytic distinctions *extensive* and *intensive definitions* respectively.

9. We call the reader's attention to the fact that there is no algorithm for mapping upward or downward from any point in the hierarchy. In other words, there are at present no known rules for mapping from some arbitrary point in a natural language hierarchy to the super ordinate or subordinate sets (those above or below the starting point in the hierarchy). Any number of mappings is possible and there are no evaluation metrics that we are aware of to guide us in selecting the higher level sets we will map onto. The list in the text could be extended indefinitely and still meet the formal requirements we have developed.

10. In a sense, this is simultaneously profound and trivial. If you happen to have the epistemological position we have taken here that the formal languages our species has created – algebra, geometry, calculus, number theory, logic, automata theory… and set theory – are a cleaned-up, formalized, explicit language modeled from natural language, then this result is unsurprising. If you have some other epistemological position, then the result is profound. The reader is referred to the section on *The Intellectual Antecedents of NLP* (chapter 3, Part I) where similar crossovers between formalized portions of natural language (e.g. logic, automata theory…) are mapped onto patterning in natural language and the patterning of NLP.

11. Frank Tall also pointed out to us that this second formal characteristic of hierarchical orderings – constriction holds if and only if the sets in the universe of discourse are finite sets.

12. Proper within the frame of the meta model – there are, of course, many *proper* verbal responses outside of the meta model - *proper* in the sense of being effective in assisting the client in developing their mental maps to include an adequate range of choices. For example, the agent of change might choose instead of pursuing any expansion of the client's map through meta modeling to note that if the client's map contains this generalization, it is extremely likely to contain the more important generalization,

> *I don't trust a lot of people*

This conjecture by the agent of change is based on a well attested phenomenon one finds in mental maps – in clinical psychology (originating, we believe, in psychoanalytic practice), this is called *projection*; fundamentally, the insight that what a human feels/believes is true about other people is often true of that same person. In other words, if I have a consistent perceptual filter that leads me to a belief that I don't trust other people, I will strongly tend to project my belief onto them and arrive at the generalization that they don't trust me. A simpler and more formally adequate representation of the process under discussion here would suggest to the agent of change that it is useful to check the client's mental maps by reversing the referential indices in sentences produced by clients. Schematically, given the sentence S^1, by simply reversing the referential index, we can derive sentence S^2

S^1 *X does not trust Y* $\longrightarrow$ *People do not trust me*

S^2 *Y does not trust X* $\longrightarrow$ *I do not trust people*

13. Or again, quoted by M. Hall in the same paper, Dilts states,

> *"Logical levels: an internal hierarchy in which each level is progressively more psychologically encompassing and impactful."*

> Dilts, 1990, page 217

If there is some serious intention involved here, specification of the terms, *psychologically encompassing* and *impactful* is required to allow the rest of the world of NLP to participate intelligently in the discussion.

Chapter 3: Recommendations

In *Whispering,* we have attempted to make explicit a number of issues of concern for us: ones that we have identified as key for the continued development of the field of Neuro-Linguistic Programming and for significantly improving the quality of work within this field. Our intention is to provoke a professional high quality public dialogue among the practitioners of NLP as an integral part of these developments. This final chapter makes recommendations to practicing members within the field of NLP, focusing first on modeling, then on how we may improve the quality of practice in NLP, terminating with a larger social perspective as to how NLP might serve.

The reader will have noted that while we have arrived at certain conclusions in many of the topics treated herein, we have also unselfconsciously presented our thinking and recommendations about topics where much work is yet to be done. We find this entirely appropriate as the field of NLP while having survived its infancy is just now emerging from its adolescence and has yet to develop a stable terminology and a well defined set of methodologies characteristic of older and more mature disciplines. We have worked hard to make explicit the processes and methods of operation that have proven to be successful in the creation and initial development of NLP as well as to define and clarify key terms in the various activities that NLP is presently composed of. We have also indicated what the intentions behind the presentations we have made in *Whispering.* Identifying the intention behind the various portions of our writing is again appropriate as our descriptions, analysis, commentary and recommendations are simply those of two members of the community – for them to be effective will require careful consideration, interactive dialogue and finally acting congruently with these proposals by a significant number of members of the community.

From our point of view, the deepest appeal we are making to other members of the NLP community is for a recognition of and reorientation to the core activity of NLP – the modeling of excellence. Such a commitment by capable practitioners would ensure that NLP will continue to have the same kind of rapid continuous growth and significant impact on associated fields that it has had in its first quarter of a century. For those readers who by choice or by inclination do not find themselves attracted to this core activity of modeling, there remains much to be done in the field of applications and training as we have indicated and which we partially summarize in the recommendations below. In addition, there are myriads of other issues of serious significance for the development and maturation of the field.

Rather than attempt to enumerate these additional points, we will content ourselves with making a series of specific suggestions. At various points in the foregoing text, we have made different proposals about what in our opinion has to occur for NLP to take its appropriate place alongside other scientifically based approaches to the study of human functioning. In this section we collect some of the principal recommendations therein contained with some indications about how specifically these might occur.

Frame: Neuro-Linguistic Programming is the study of the differences that make a difference between the consistent high performance of a genius (either an individual or a team) in some field of human endeavor and the "average" performer in this same field. Its principal defining activity then is modeling.

Modeling itself may be modeled in a number of ways. We have proposed that the following minimum phases can be usefully dissected out of this complex process:

1. Identification of an appropriate model (source of patterning) and the securing of access

2. Unconscious uptake of the patterning of the model with an explicit refusal to consciously understand or codify the patterning being mastered during the uptake phase. This is a critical distinction between what other disciplines refer to as modeling and the form it takes within NLP as we have described here. The importance of this stage cannot be overemphasized. It is precisely at this point that the ability to suspend the requirement to consciously understand one's own behavior (refusing f^2 filters) while in the early phases of modeling opens the possibility of the modeler's securing a deep tacit knowledge of the patterning relatively untransformed by conscious filters (tacit knowledge at FA). Such a process yields a significantly more robust and complete representation of the patterning offered by the source of that patterning – the original model.

Any activity purporting to be modeling but which lacks this operational distinction (the unconscious uptake) belongs to some other area of activity and is to be sharply distinguished from modeling in NLP. While we have offered descriptions of modeling, such description suffered from the same flaw as any verbal description of a complex set of behaviors – it is talking about it rather than doing it. We invite interested and qualified parties to contact Quantum Leap for specific information about seminars and coaching in the art of modeling.

3. Systematic deployment of the patterning incorporated during the unconscious uptake phrase until the performance criteria are satisfied. More specifically, the performance criteria will be satisfied if and only if the modeler is able to reproduce the effects of the patterning modeled from the source. More specifically, the modeler demonstrates the ability to secure the same class of quality responses from clients that the model typically does in approximately the same time frame.

4. Upon reaching these criteria, the modeler begins the task of codifying the patterning now resident in him or herself as well as in the source of the patterning (the original individual or a team). Note that this implies that there are actually two data sets to guide the modeler: observations of the source of the patterning – the original source - and self-modeling, that is, the mapping of the tacit knowledge, now resident in the modeler, to explicit knowledge – the resultant model itself.

5. Testing of the model to determine whether it successfully transfers the patterning codified to interested learners in an effective manner. Equivalently, does the learner achieve mastery of the patterning of the original model in a successful and efficient (that is, within a reasonable) period of time?

With these above definitions and frames fixed clearly in mind, we offer the following:

Recommendations:

For the modeler/designer:

1. that each would-be NLP modeler/designer accept and acknowledge the key distinction on which NLP was created and is defined – namely, modeling. Further, congruent with that acknowledgement, each such practitioner commit to the modeling of excellence with the objective of creating new patterning and models with some frequency on an ongoing basis.

2. that the models that result from this renewed focus on patterning be presented to and reviewed by some select peer group of trusted NLP practitioners who will offer feedback to the modeler about the patterning presented until consensus is reached that the patterning presented represents a new set of patterns or model in NLP. Given the fact that historically, the field of NLP was created and initially developed by Americans and their unimpressive record of achievement in operating in languages other than English, it may be

prudent to establish national or linguistically homogeneous groups for this peer review process. Such linguistically defined groups could then select the best of the models or patterning presented and offer them to an international peer group for dissemination in other languages. Think of this as a best practices strategy.

3. that once the peer review group has reviewed both the process by which the modeling occurred (the five stages of modeling described above) and the effectiveness and efficiency of the patterning in the model (for example, by learning and testing the patterning themselves to determine whether they meet these criteria), the model or patterning will be registered with a date and an author. The modeler who did the actual work as well as the reviewing agents who have tested and are certifying the model should be identified. The model thus certified would then be offered to the NLP community.

4. that the minimum requirements for the presentation of a model or pattern to peer review be those three criteria developed previously in this book, namely:

Presentation of Patterning

    a. <u>Description of the pattern</u>: a relatively sensory-grounded description of the elements in the pattern and their critical ordering (that is, the sequence in which those elements are to be applied – historically, in NLP, this has taken the form of steps in a format which define what the practitioner is to do first, second...).

    b. <u>Consequences of the use of the pattern</u>: a relatively sensory-grounded description of what consequences the practitioner can anticipate through a congruent application of the pattern.

    c. <u>Selection criteria</u>: a relatively sensory-grounded identification of the conditions or contexts in which the selection and application of this pattern is appropriate - for example, in the field of change work, making the distinction between the pattern's appropriateness for 1st and 2nd order changes. This description should include any contraindications (conditions under which the pattern is expressly NOT to be selected and applied).

5. the careful reader will have already noted that the phrase *a relatively sensory-based description of* occurs as part of each element of the proposed presentation format. This phrase points to the fact that it is doubtful in the extreme whether an adequate vocabulary exists for

describing anything of significance in human patterning in sensory-based terms. [1]

The practical question remains in full force – *how are we to present the results of our modeling and patterning in such a way that others can understand and appreciate what we are, in fact, proposing?* Presumably, one of the principal applications of the patterning already available in NLP is its application to effective communication. There is a quite practical solution to this question that has significant appeal – suppose that in addition to the presentation of the three minimum elements proposed above, we as a community, accept the requirement that the NLP practitioner proposing a new model or patterning submit along with the above delineated elements in a verbal description, a video in which the practitioner demonstrates one or more specific examples of the model or patterning being proposed. This would create a reference experience that would offer (via streaming video feed through a website) any one interested in utilizing or testing the pattern direct access to an example of the model or patterning. Naturally, an example of a model or patterning is not the model or patterning itself. It will, however, come significantly closer than what occurs in the typical multiple interpretations that inevitably result from a verbal description alone.

This strategy for ensuring the effective communication of models and patterning suggests an additional task – there are actually a rather limited number of distinctions at present from which the models and patterning of NLP are presently constructed – hardly surprising, given NLP's commitment to a syntactic approach to patterning. We suggest then that a library of such videos (again available via internet video streaming) be developed. Such a library would greatly facilitate understanding and coordination of research within the NLP community to have specific examples of anchoring, framing, verbal patterning, calibration… as common reference points around which further discussion and refinement of patterning could revolve. Great care should be exercised in establishing this library, as it will literally become the central reference point for the definition of the fundamental terms of the entire endeavor called NLP. It would, then, be prudent to invite a number of extremely competent practitioners to submit videos, say, on the technology of anchoring, and to include these multiple representations in the library. There are two movements to be balanced here:

> a) the requirement of stabilizing the fundamental terms of discussion around which research and application in the field of NLP revolves

b) the recognition – deeply rooted in NLP – that multiple descriptions are to be promoted and honored with the caveat that each must meet the minimum professional standards in NLP such as those that we are here proposing...

We are aware that there is an inherent tension between this proposal – one that is common in research communities - and business models where typically such work is viewed as a differentiator. This tension is not unique to NLP – note the developments in the patenting of native plants and their associated use by traditional peoples or in the patenting of specific chemical compounds current in biological research.

6. that in all subsequent patterning work in NLP, the distinction between content models and process models be observed. Further we propose that only process models be registered by the peer review process, respectfully inviting practitioners proposing content models to place their work elsewhere.

7. that the peer group distinguish between variations on models or patterning already registered and genuinely new patterning and register only the latter. This requirement – demonstrating that the proposed patterning be genuinely novel - is similar to those reasonably well-developed criteria observed by the patenting authorities, for example, here in the USA and other technologically advanced countries.

8. that the classic and new code patterning (see Chapter 3, Part II) be grand fathered as registered patterns by the peer group. Further that excellent examples of classic and new code patterning be videoed and offered in the on-line library of the proposed website.

9. that the members of the peer group serve for overlapping periods as part of that group. For example, half of the first group of peer reviewers would serve two years and the other half serve three years and all subsequent peers would serve the full three years so that the group maintains continuity over time.

10. that the practitioners modeling new patterning are explicit about several aspects of their modeling, including

a) the ordering principle contained in the proposed model (see the section on ordering relationships)

b) whether there is good evidence for a discrete or a continuous analysis and the evidence used to make such a determination

11. that those publishers and directors of magazines and those reviewers of articles by authors purporting to represent models and patterning work in NLP adopt the above described criteria (or some comparable explicit set of criteria) for the evaluation of work in NLP as part of their regular processes so as to upgrade the quality of published work in NLP

12. that each NLP center impose a small surcharge (for example, 1% of fees paid to the center) on their students. This surcharge would be forwarded to the peer review group. It would support their efforts by offering some compensation to the reviewers for their work in refining and registering both models and patterning submitted. It would as well serve to defray expenses involved with the establishing and updating of the on-line library of registered NLP models and patterning. Transparent public accountability for the monies should be offered on the website by an independent accountant engaged for that purpose who would be responsible for periodic reviews to ensure activities congruent with the responsibilities assigned to the peer review group and only such activities are being carried out.

13. that a public dialogue begin with the intention of establishing an International Modeling Center (IMC) – a dream that we have carried for some decades. This center would have as its mission the modeling of the special capabilities of geniuses, wherever in the world they may be found.

The IMC would ultimately be staffed by extremely well trained modelers with multiple linguistic capabilities – perhaps selected initially by the peer review group on the basis of models created and registered by participants and subsequently on some rotating basis by past members of the modeling group. The IMC would both dispatch modelers on special assignments and would simultaneously develop within each ethnic and cultural group, individuals from those groups who would continue the modeling within that sphere of influence. This center would then serve as the clearing house for the publication of new models alongside contributions from other participants – that is, fully associated with the peer review group described above that registers and distributes new patterning. It would be worth considering the possibility that the IMC would have a training function as well – more specifically, that the individual or team creating the new model would as a natural part of their responsibility (testing the model) offer trainings to qualified members of participating NLP centers thereby creating a diffusion of the new models and patterning as well as providing a source of material for application and training for the NLP community.

The funding of such a center could be accomplished by tapping a number of sources:

1. NLP centers which would benefit from having the latest models available for marketing to their clients

2. corporate and institutional sponsors which would receive as compensation exclusive access for a limited period of time (six months, for example) to the latest models and patterning and assistance with their application to the corporate context

3. foundations supporting the creation and dissemination of models of excellence (the Ford Foundation, the Rockefeller Foundation, the Carnegie Foundation...)

4. pay-for-modeling clients – it is likely that once the IMC establishes its credentials as a center for the modeling and dissemination of patterns of excellence there will be individuals and groups who will desire to contract with the IMC for modeling of specific abilities of value to their operation.

For the trainer of NLP

14. that all practitioners of NLP engaged in delivering training approach this formidable learning task with certain principles clearly in mind:

a. the basis of effective training is the creation by the trainer of a series of contexts in which through *experience* the student may arrive at his own direct tacit knowledge of the patterning. In other words, the measure of effective training is whether the student can do it, never whether he can talk about it.

b. that all training materials be carefully scrutinized to ensure that only formal (never content) patterning is being presented as NLP patterning. Would be trainers unable to make this distinction are disqualified until they achieve such competency.

c. that the ideal design of training inherently involves

discovery processes by which the student achieves unconscious (tacit) competency prior to achieving explicit verbal competency. A pattern discovered belongs to the discoverer; a pattern presented belongs to the presenter.

d. that the single most important variable in the training context is the congruity of the trainer. Without an appropriate model (the trainer) offering demonstrations of the patterning, the training is unlikely in the extreme to achieve the desired results.

For NLP practitioner involved in NLP application

15. that the practitioner involved in application of NLP patterning master and operationalize the various suggestions made in the above text (see especially Chapter 2 of Part III) such as the distinction between 1st and 2nd order change and their matching interventions, the Iatrogenic principle...

16. that the NLP practitioner accept the responsibility to continue to refine her mastery of the most fundamental of all NLP processes – calibration - with special emphasis on learning to recognize the physiological signals of altered states of consciousness. Such a skill base is a prerequisite for respecting the integrity of the client – a fundamental ethic issue. Similarly, in the final stages of change work with a client, that the practitioner accept only physiologically verifiable responses as evidence that the client has achieved a new set of adequate choices, never simply verbal ones. All change should be considered vague rumor until it has a kinesthetic realization.

17. that the practitioner explicitly recognize (again, through calibration) that the entry of the client into a significantly altered state constitutes an invitation from the client's unconscious to engage in meaningful communication with or without the client's consciousness being involved. We encourage an ongoing learning program to develop multiple methods (non-verbal communication, metaphor...) for establishing and engaging in such communications respectfully.

18. that the NLP practitioner continue to learn to distinguish between form and content in his work as a safeguard for the clients' integrity in their particularly vulnerable states during the change process.

19. that the NLP practitioner clearly recognize that there is an overarching concern amidst all the complex interactions with clients such that she accept the responsibility to conduct herself in such a way as to maximize the independence of the client.

These, then, constitute the set of recommendations we offer to the NLP community. There are multiple additional issues of importance, from our point of view, that do not lend themselves easily to the form of a recommendation. We select one such issue for our final comment in this book.

In setting the historical context for the creation of the new code and in particular, in describing my dissatisfaction with the activities of well-trained NLP practitioners in the early '80's, I (JG) mentioned;

> *There seemed not to be much, if any, concern with larger-frame issues such as aesthetics, ethics or social and political challenges, nor could I detect any movement toward a pro-active approach to such larger issues on their part.*

It is our experience that the patterning thus far coded through NLP modeling projects serves brilliantly to create and carry through to completion actions that make a significant difference in the quality of life of individuals and in communities. Of equal, if not greater importance, is the way in which such projects are conducted – that is, through direct participation, such projects empower people to take actions that matter greatly in developing a sense of their own ability to make a difference – a transformation of victims to pro-active participants in life.

In Brasil, for example, we participated in a project to install a clean drinking water and sewage system in a community just outside of Sao Paulo. This was accomplished through the mobilization of informal leaders in the rural community who, in turn activated the interest and participation of their community members in doing the actual work. Simultaneous negotiation with government representatives resulted in their providing the material, tools and expert guidance to install a clean drinking water and functioning sewage system - a difference that greatly improved the quality of life in the community. The water and sewage system belongs in a deep way to the people of that community – they built it; they own it. You can be certain that they take excellent care of it.

What we are attempting to do here is to invite – better *urge*, even *implore* - those readers already competent with respect to the patterning of NLP to consider carefully the possibilities of generalizing them to such actions in the world around us. Having carefully considered such possibilities, we ask you to select and act effectively to make such differences. We offer the following comments in hopes of stimulating your interest and ability to appreciate how NLP patterning applies to larger issues.

Let's take as a starting point a utilization of Triple Description. We propose that this pattern extends well beyond its application in the new code change format. We offer the following remarks as our way of stimulating the class of thinking we are interested in promoting within the field of NLP.

As mentioned in multiple places in this book one of the consequences of the application of NLP patterning is that it creates genuinely new choices. [2] These choices, however, have a price. As an example, in occidental cultures such as those we find in the Western Europe and North America, the kinesthetic system is privileged: that is to say, the suggestion that a person change an internal representation is generally considered well-formed in such cultures if and only if the representation is visual or auditory. In fact, in some cases, the inability to change such a visual image or internal dialogue is considered to be evidence of so-called "mental illness". Any practitioner of NLP who has had the experience of working with people classified as schizophrenics can attest to the prominence of symptoms that involve either voices or images, that torment the patient – that is, internal representations (visual and auditory) which are involuntary for the patient.

Note, however, any person who develops full choice about her own kinesthetic representations – essentially, a person who chooses what she feels – is awarded a very different title – namely, sociopath. We take it that this negative labeling – sociopath – by the culture is an unconscious recognition at the level of the social system that much of what holds our cultures together is the involuntary nature of the kinesthetic emotional bonds which tie us together in couples, families and larger social units. This involuntary binding is the glue that keeps much of the social system intact. Imagine the differences that would emerge in your marriage, primary emotional relationships, family, business or local community if suddenly the people involved could choose to experience guilt or not to experience guilt or shame or fear or... Yeah, imagine that!

Seen through the NLP filters, it seems clear enough to us that the involuntary nature of feeling (kinesthetic representations) functions as a social control mechanism. From an NLP point of view, kinesthetic representations are simply one of the three major building blocks of the mental maps (FA) we consistently mistake for reality. From this perspective, it is arbitrary, an accident of social development, that western cultures have seized upon maintaining the involuntariness of feelings as a stabilizing variable. [3]

This thesis can be tested – are there cultures where one of the other two major representational systems is selected as involuntary? If the answer is affirmative, then the thesis is supported. For example, does the Sun Dance of the Native Americans of the plains offer an insight into these cultural differences? Does the Sun Dance represent a recognition culturally (unconsciously) among those tribes that celebrate it that it is necessary to break the constraints of a largely involuntary visual representational system? Further does this represent one way to achieve this is by subjecting oneself to such a compelling ordeal that the individual achieves that special altered state in which his life vision is revealed?

These are deep questions and in our acknowledged ignorance, we will await more informed presentations about these critical issues by the native peoples themselves as well as the professionals - the anthropologists who have studied such practices.

The fact that the vast majority of cultures thus far known to us have selected the kinesthetic system as the involuntary one has only the force of a statistical statement, not the force of a statement about human possibility. The study of other intact cultures is an adventure of discovering what alternative forms of social organization, what other cultural possibilities exist. These are investigations into the forms distinct from those that we were born to and are part of what we refer to as the range of human possible experience. Whatever such studies may reveal, we are still empowered by the patterning of excellence to explore additional possibilities – even entirely new forms.

A portion of what we are pointing to involves the misuse of statistics and its misinterpretation in popular culture. We distinguish between the tool known as statistics with its astonishing utility as a method of analysis when properly applied in appropriate contexts and its abuse both in inappropriate applications and its misuse in popular applications – what we refer to as statistical living and the tyranny of the average.

For example, consider rock climbing, one of our passions. The fact that the vast majority of people on the planet would not even consider climbing the vertical face of El Capitan in Yosemite, let alone would be capable and interested in doing so, places no constraints on us. If statistical living were appropriate, we wouldn't bother to have the Olympic Games, as one of the most important points of the games is to explore the extremes of human athletic possibility. The optimal experience of the games is to perform not only outside the statistical boundaries of previous athletic endeavors but expressly to accomplish something that isn't even on the statistical charts – the breaking of a world record; to go faster, or higher, or more gracefully, or... than anyone before us. If statistical living were appropriate, Grinder and Bandler wouldn't have bothered to create NLP. We are reasonably certain that the vast majority of social systems both at present on the planet and historically insofar as we have records have assigned more than half of their populations to a second class, exploited status – namely, women – but that is hardly justification for us to accept such inequitable practices.

By way of explicating the point about the tension between the genuinely new set of choices made available through the application of NLP patterning and the tyranny of the average in popular culture, consider the issue of deep rapport or identification between two human beings in a face-to-face situation. It is quite clear that as human beings, we have naturally occurring neurologically specified circuits for identifying other members of our species. There are studies indicating the presence of specialized receptors for the recognition of other human faces even in the infants only a few days old. [4]

It is equally clear that we are able to learn to ignore or fail to act on the basis of these recognition circuits – look at Kosovo, Rwanda, Northern Ireland, Sierra Leone, Afghanistan, Israel, Palestine or New York on September 11, 2001 in the present or in the shallow past the near extermination of many native peoples in North and South America with the arrival of the Europeans in the new world.

Or perhaps closer to home for some readers, ask yourself what the basis for racism or sexism is. That is, what has to be true for us to fail to make use of our naturally occurring circuits and respond to representatives of other groups different in some way from ourselves? Surely there are multiple answers to this question. However, we are certain that one condition that must obtain for racism (ranging from the extremes of lynchings, torture… to subtler forms such as discrimination, avoidance…) to occur is for the perpetuator of the *–ism* to look into the eyes of the victim and *fail* to recognize and identify with that other human being. Again the same condition applies with respect to sexism and sexual violence (ranging from the extremes of rape and other heinous forms of sexual violence and abuse to the more subtle but insidious forms of acculturation you find in the selection of the toys and games that are offered differentially to children of different genders).

This is surely a discussion about learned filters. Note that what we are implicitly condemning is the exercise of certain forms of disassociation or alienation that result in a failure of identification in certain specified contexts.

Let's suppose as has happened multiple times to each of your present authors, that we come upon a scene where some serious danger or accident with injuries is present.

360

As an example and more concretely, one of your authors on her way home from high school came upon a scene where there was a fire ablaze, burning a low-income residence on the outskirts of Memphis (Tennessee, USA). She saw the faces of several young Afro-American children at one of the windows at the front of the burning house and heard their screams, pleading for help. It was crystal clear to her *in retrospect* that there was great danger in entering the burning structure yet without such consideration, without any hesitation, she rushed into the flames and succeeded in extracting the children from the burning structure with only minor injuries to herself and the children involved.

Or as in the case of the other author, driving to a meeting in San Francisco along highway 92 that connects the coastal highway 1 (from Half Moon Bay) with main arteries into San Francisco from the south (Highways 280 and 101) witnessed an accident in light traffic in a three-lane section on the opposite side of the highway. A small compact car had somehow gotten caught partially underneath the rear end of a large truck. The smaller car was dragged nearly a quarter of a mile before breaking loose and tumbling and skidding to a halt, sitting across two of the lanes of traffic. He pulled immediately over to his side of the highway and dashed across to render assistance to the occupant of the small vehicle. He reached the seriously crunched vehicle nearly simultaneously with another motorist who had reacted similarly – a man who turned out to be a paramedic by profession. The driver of the vehicle was lying unconscious partially on the front seat and partially on the floor, bleeding from a head wound. No other injuries were immediately apparent. However, both your author and the paramedic became immediately aware of the strong smell of gasoline (the gas line had ruptured). While reluctant to move the young woman until they had determined whether there were additional injuries, both of the men realized that there was an eminent danger of fire and a possible explosion – with few words, they coordinated carefully lifting the unconscious woman out of the car, keeping her to the best of their ability in the extended position in which they had found her. They carefully carried her a safe distance from the smoldering wreck. In the meantime, other passing motorists had responded immediately and intelligently to the accident. The driver of the truck involved had radioed for an ambulance and police support; another passerby had arrived with a fire extinguisher and was applying it usefully to the forward section of the car, while yet another motorist was placing flares to re-direct the traffic around the scene of the accident. At the same time, several others, noting what we were doing with the driver of the car had rushed forward with blankets upon which we gently placed the unconscious woman. The ambulance arrived within three to four minutes of our placing the woman a safe distance from her car.

Now consider either one of these situations from the point of view of the respective author involved. Did Carmen feel the terror and panic of the young children trapped in the burning house? Did John, the paramedic or any of the other motorists who stopped to render aid identify with the bleeding unconscious woman in the smoldering vehicle? Was empathy in the form of entering into a matching state a relevant response in either one of these incidents? We propose that the answer is most assuredly *NOT*! No more than empathy or deep rapport is an appropriate response by any of the firefighters or members of the ambulance crew. To make an identification (equivalently, to enter into a state of deep rapport) in such contexts with the endangered or injured people involved is simply to put oneself in an ineffectual state - one that would guarantee that we would not have been resourceful enough to take the decisions and actions required.

Imagine the effectiveness of an ER team if when faced with an injured, bleeding patient, they failed to make the necessary disassociation or responded positively to the tug of identification initiated by those natural circuits that are a part of our legacy as human beings.

Compare the two sets of examples: on the one hand, racism and sexism and their horrific consequences and on the other, the competency and critical nature of the responses required in the face of danger or in situations where rendering aid to injured parties is necessary. These two are identical in the sense that both sets of contexts involve the refusal to respond to our "natural" inclinations – to shift state in identification with the person, to achieve a deep state of rapport. In one case, the consequences are ethically unacceptable and in the other, the consequences are precisely what we desire and applaud. But the choice being exercised is formally identical – the disassociation from the naturally occurring circuits by which we intuitively recognize and identify ourselves with other members of the species. The fundamental differences occur at the levels of intention and consequence.

The point, of course, is that the choice of identifying or not identifying is exactly that – a choice. As such it is neither ethical nor unethical; it is simply a choice. The issue of ethics enters at the point where we ask how specifically and in what context we do or do not exercise the choice – as the contrast between the behavior of a racist and the behavior of a professional ER physician indicates. There are then two associated questions involved:

> *Do you have the choice in each and every significant context of either identifying or not identifying with the human being in front of you?*

Given the choice, are you capable of appreciating the consequences of the choice you have, and of selecting the one most congruent with the ethics you purport to have?

The disciplined practice of NLP allows a resoundingly affirmative answer to the first question – namely, yes, the congruent application of any number of NLP patterns (phobia cure, manipulation of perceptual positions as in Triple Description, re-anchoring…) permits the development of the choice in each and every one of the contexts you might select. This is the art of the application of the patterns of excellence coded through NLP modeling to personal development – that is, the art of choice, pure and simple.

The second question is very difficult. Bateson has argued brilliantly in a number of places (see for example his article *Conscious Purpose versus Nature* in *Steps to an Ecology of Mind*) that we are very poorly equipped to consciously appreciate the long-term consequences of our decisions and actions. We speak often of the unintended consequences of our public policies or our personal decisions.

The field of psychotherapy contains certain relatively technical terms that refer to this phenomenon such as secondary benefit or secondary gain. Economists refer to certain phenomena in their field as knock-on effects or unintended consequences. Ecologists are alarmed by the unintended results of the deliberate or accidental introduction of vectors or predators into an intact ecosystem.

There are sporadic cases of malaria in the immediate vicinity of Charles de Gaulle airport outside of Paris, apparently the consequence of the surely unintentional transport of mosquitoes in commercial airliners whose flights originate in parts of the world where malaria is endemic such as sub-Sahara Africa. New York's Central Park has been demonstrated to harbor vectors carrying West Nile fever.

There are analyses of the collapse of the former Soviet East block that point to the presentation (through radio, television, music…) of differences between the quality of life inside and outside the former Iron Curtain as a major precipitating cause of this collapse.

Biologists are now discovering that a large portion of the drugs consumed by people taking medication is passed through natural processes in significant quantities from the body of the person involved into the water systems where the bacteria naturally present are treated to a hothouse of evolutionary development. One consequence is that we can now have bacterial strains that are resistant to the antibiotics they have learned as a species to cope with.

The Domino theory of the cold war was an attempt to argue for certain secondary and tertiary consequences of permitting or not permitting a change of political leadership in country X.

We as humans are not very good at this sort of thing. If there is any doubt lingering in the reader's mind about this issue, consider the horrifying incongruities between the positive intentions of certain religious movements, from the Inquisitions and crusades of medieval age through the coordination of church and state in the European conquest of the new world to any number of present excesses (Ireland, Afghanistan…) and their actual historical consequences. We just don't do this very well.

The existence of NLP patterning of excellence has the consequence of making choices available, both personally and professionally, that have been available previously to a very limited degree and sporadically, if at all. This is, as we mentioned, the answer to the first question presented above. The price of having these choices is that suddenly and without any preparation through the application of the technology of NLP, we have become responsible for decisions that we have never had to face before for the simple reason that the choices were not systematically available before.

Thus, we propose as a method for beginning to develop the ability to effectively manage these new classes of choices and to take responsibility for the consequences of these new choices the systematic application of triple description. This application offers us as one way to explore how specifically we can come to act responsibly in the face of the new choices generated by the technology of NLP itself. More specifically, we are proposing that prior to making any new choice generated through a congruent application of these NLP patterns, we would accept the responsibility of systematically using triple description. That is to say, before making an important decision, we would step first into our own perceptual position to discover how that decision or action would look, sound and feel from there (1st position). With a separator state to ensure that there is a minimum of contamination, we would then put ourselves in the perceptual position of the other people (2nd position) whose experience would be impacted by the decision or action under consideration, adopting their postures, attitudes, form of thinking… Finally, and again with a separator state to ensure a clean transition, we would move to the observer position (3rd position) from which we could watch and listen to how the decision under consideration might play itself out. [5]

Note that if we attempted to keep all these complex experiences (all three perceptual positions with representations in all three major representational systems) *in consciousness*, we would simply deeply confuse ourselves. Instead, then, we propose that here we have an opportunity to take advantage of the effectiveness of one of the three principal differences between the classic and new codes of NLP. As we stated earlier,

> One of the differences between the classic code and the new code is the aggressive exploitation of the power and wisdom of the unconscious processing – when properly organized and framed

We are proposing that the exercise to be done prior to making a decision is Triple Description – one specific form of proper organization and framing of the unconscious mind. And further, subsequent to the exercise of Triple Description, we leave at least one sleep period for purposes of unconscious integration prior to making the decision or implementing it.

This suggestion to always leave a period for the unconscious to integrate the material developed in the triple description exercise is entirely congruent in our experience with the practice of NLP, especially in its new code format. As an analogy, consider the set of breakthrough discoveries in the history of western mathematics. The prototypic sequence is the following: a gifted mathematician accepts the challenge of some monumental unsolved puzzle in mathematics. He commits himself in a disciplined way to applying every known relevant strategy for solving it. After great labor, he comes to the conclusion (the successful ones, at any rate) that he has exhausted his conscious resources in his attempt to solve the puzzle. So what does he do now?

Surprisingly, the answer is that he does anything else, as long as that anything else is not connected in any significant way [6] with the challenge he is addressing – he takes a nap, chops wood, goes for a walk in the forest, cooks up a superb meal... anything, anything that does not exercise the same circuits he was applying to the challenge.

He, in effect, gives up consciously – an act that releases to the unconscious the possibility of shifting perceptual position, changing the strategy, introducing through metaphor, analogy, or whatever unconscious process a new way of approaching the challenge. And what is the result? Nearly uniformly, the mathematician (again, the successful ones) suddenly, in a blinding flash of insight, with a clarity rarely otherwise achieved, sees the solution. Now, he may spend the next n months developing a proof acceptable by the rigorous standards of mathematics, but the point is nevertheless clear.

This loading up of large amounts of information, much of it inconsistent, in a well-organized and well-framed unconscious confers tremendous benefits. Such benefits extend well beyond the fascinating activities of excellent mathematicians – we propose that you explore and discover the wider and more profound consequences of the application of patterns such as Triple Description concretely through acting.

We have attempted to point to large social and political issues to which NLP has much to contribute. We have also offered a number of specific proposals for the consideration of the NLP community. Our intention has been to make explicit the shifts in focus and practice that will allow NLP to achieve the very excellence it purports to study.

CAVEAT: *Messengers incongruent with the message they purport to bear are not listened to, nor should they be!*

None of the above recommendations or suggestions are relevant nor will they have the desired effect without a congruent personal commitment by practitioners of NLP to a positive, affable attitude to the work of other practitioners. Such an attitude would display tolerance for difference, multiple descriptions and the acceptance of the responsibility to work out such differences in a public and positive spirited manner or at least with a rich vein of humor. This seems to us to be a form of minimum congruency with the practice of NLP. If we are not capable of such self-discipline and self-monitoring, then we have failed to apply the principles of excellence embodied in the multiple models and patterning of excellence in NLP to ourselves.

All of above assumes that there is enough interest and intelligence among the practitioners of NLP to open a public dialogue that surely must take place if the intentions behind these recommendations are to be achieved. These are recommendations worked out by two individuals, Carmen Bostic St. Clair and John Grinder; for them to be effective and to achieve the intention behind them requires a fully participatory response by members of the NLP community – the community must own these recommendations and operationalize them if they are to succeed. Thus, as mentioned in the opening of this book, one of our explicit purposes is to provoke an open, intelligent public multilogue that we hope will result in the explicit adoption of some set of distinctions and quality standards for the future work in Neuro-Linguistic Programming.

On vera!   *Vamos a ver!*   *Wir werden es sehen!*   *We shall see!*   ...

Footnotes for Chapter 3, Part III

1. This is the point explored in Part III, chapter 1 under *The Coding of Pattern* where the readers are invited to educate themselves about the long and interesting series of exchanges in the discussion in the philosophy of science (in particular, we recommend the work of Carl Hempel) about the possibility of sensory based or neutral descriptions. The issue is not unique to work focusing on patterning in humans, although it seems most obvious in such a field of endeavor.

2. The authors are well aware that even within the group of relatively homogeneous cultures of Western Europe and North America, there are significant differences in attitude concerning the possibility and desirability of any profound change. Stereotypically, Americans are perceived by Europeans to have a position that is shockingly ignorant, hopelessly optimistic and quite naïve with respect to this issue while a common American stereotype of the European is that of the somewhat jaded and overly intellectual skeptic unwilling to act.

3. The observation that all cultures seem to regard at least one of the three major representational systems as involuntary may be associated with the limits of conscious processing – that is, with the limitations of consciousness (the 7 ± 2 chunks of processing available), we simply cannot entertain enough of an appreciation of our own processes at one time to manipulate all three of the systems to the point we may experience them as voluntary. If this analysis has any value, it still does not touch on the issue of which of the three major representational systems is chosen (unconsciously) to be involuntary – a fascinating challenge for our anthropologist colleagues.

4. See, for example, *The Scientist in the Crib* by Gopnik, Meltzoff and Kuhl (1999),

5. The description in this portion of the text is a reduced representation of a very precise pattern of application of triple description. The development as well as the application of precise and clean positions is complex to describe and is beyond the scope of this book.

6. Frank Tall, a mathematician at the University of Toronto who is well trained in NLP reports a refined and fascinating confirmation of this do-anything-else strategy as used by one of the current leading problem solvers in mathematics, Professor Saharon Shelah of Hebrew University in Jerusalem. Frank and a colleague, Ann Jane Grieve, approached Shelah with the proposal of modeling his problem solving ability. Shelah agreed to participate in the project if Frank would take the responsibility of writing up the results. For the actual session, Shelah demanded that Frank offer at

least five distinct mathematical problems for him to solve – it turns out that Shelah's strategy involves attacking multiple problems in the same session. Typically, Shelah works on one problem until he feels blocked. At which point, he sets that problem aside and works on a second problem... Faced with this demand, Frank dutifully generated a number of distinct problems. When Frank presented the problem set to him, Shelah objected, stating that the problem set generated by Frank did not contain his minimum of five *distinct* problems. Frank therefore developed a problem set that met Shelah's requirement. Frank later analyzed the sets that Shelah had rejected. The fascinating point was that to a mathematician the first set of five problems proffered by Frank indeed contained five distinct problems. However, what Frank realized was that Shelah's criteria for distinctness of the problems was not based on any external or formal definition of distinctness, but rather on whether the problems in the set required of Shelah himself the application of distinct sets of strategies for solving them. This seems to be an advanced application of the do-anything-else strategy. Frank also noted that Professor Shelah had a practice of tossing a set of keys from one hand to the other while working on significant portions of the problems presented. It occurred to him that this was quite congruent with some of the design features of the new code games developed to induce and sustain high performance states – more specifically in this particular case, the activation of both hemispheres. Frank Tall, personal communication, 2001.

AFTERWORD

Sounds created as air rushes through spaces not occupied by leaves and branches. A white noise familiar in rhythm, tempo, and intensity when at waters edge during a spring thaw – chaotic not unlike water boiling in a teapot.

Movement of ground foliage provides directional data to sheltered observers; pine needles drift in patterns of falling snow. Long stationary dust and other sedimentary matter ride the currents to new locations. Some leaves, replete with natural hitchhikers, ride the lofting current, rolling and dancing; others float to the earth renewed to skip and cartwheel along the surface to provide safe dens for future generations. The wind - breathing new life into that which may have settled.

The wind whispers as an elegant orator – sometimes gentle, sometimes robust – broadcasting the life-giving seeds from its unbounded podium.

And then there are words. What is the legacy of words whispered in the wind?

Bibliography

Articles

A Designer Universe by Steven Weinberg in The New York Review of Books, Vol. XLVI, No. 16, page 46

Endpoints, Why doesn't stainless steel rust? In Scientific American, August, 2001, page 96

Eric Robbie in an article published in NLP World, volume 7, No. 3 November, 2000

Judith Delozier's account of the New Code, NLP World, March, 1995, volume 2, number 1

Letter to the Editor by Charlie Masi, Golden Valley, Arizona in Science News, Vol. 156, No. 6, August 7, 1999

Sign Language in the Brain by Hickok, Ursula Bellugi and Edward Klima in Scientific American, June 2001

Books

A Framework for Excellence: A Resource Manual for NLP by Charlotte Bretto Milliner, preface by John T. Grinder / Paperback / Grinder Delozier and Associates / December 1990

A Guide to Transformational Grammar by John Grinder and Suzette Haden Elgin, Holt, Rhinehart and Winston, Inc., 1973

A History of Experimental Psychology by Edwin G. Boring, Appleton-Century-Crofts, New York, 1950

Abenteuer Kommunikation:Bateson, Perls, Satir, Erickson und die Anfänge des Neurolinguistischen Programmierens by Wolfgang Walker, Klett-Cotta, Stuttgart, 1996

Advanced Techniques of Hypnosis and Therapy edited by Jay Haley, Grune and Stratton, New York, 1967

Aspects of Scientific Explanation by Carl G. G. Hempel, The Free Press, November 1970

At Home in the Universe by Stuart A. Kauffman, Oxford University Press, August 1996

Autobiographical Notes by Albert Einstein, Paul Arthur Schilpp (Editor), Open Court Publishing Company, September 1991

Automata and Computability, Dexter C. Kozen, Springer-Verlag, New York, 1997

Dynamic Patterns: The Self Organization of Brain and Behavior by J. A. Scott Kelso, J. A. Scott Kelso, MIT Press, March1997

Foundation of Cognitive Grammar, Vol.1 by Ronald W. Langacker, Stanford University Press, April 1987

Foundations of Cognitive Grammar, vol. 2 by Ronald W. Langacker / Hardcover, Stanford University Press, July 1999

Frogs into Princes, by Richard Bandler and John Grinder Real People Press, 1979

Generative Grammar by Geoffrey C. C. Horrocks, Longman Publishing Group, January 1987

Introducing Neuro-Linguistic Programming by Joseph O'Connor and John Seymour, Thorson's, November 1993

Introduction to Cybernetics by W. Ross Ashby, Routledge, January 1964

Language and Human Behavior by Derek Bickerton, University of Washington Press, July 1996

Language and Species by Derek Bickerton, University of Chicago Press, March 1992

Leaves before the Wind: Leading Edge Applications of NLP by Charlotte Bretto Milliner, John Grinder and Sylvia Topel (editors), Grinder, Delozier and Associates, November 1994

Mental Spaces: Aspects of Meaning Construction in Natural Language
Gilles Fauconnier, Cambridge University Press, January 1994

Mind and Nature: A Necessary Unity by Gregory Bateson, E. P. Dutton, New York, 1979

NLP in Personal Strategies for Life by Jules and Chris Collingwood, draft version, 2000

Neuro-Linguistic Programming, volume I, by Robert Dilts, John Grinder, Richard Bandler, Leslie Cameron Bandler and Judith Delozier, Meta Publications, Inc. 1979

Noam Chomsky: New Horizons in the Study of Language and Mind by Noam Chomsky, Cambridge University Press, 2000

On Deletion Phenomena in English, by John Grinder, Mouton, The Hague, 1972

Patterns of the Hypnotic Techniques of Milton H. Erickson, M.D., volume I, by Richard Bandler and John Grinder, Meta Publications Press, Inc, 1977

Patterns of the Hypnotic Techniques of Milton H. Erickson, M.D., volume II, by John Grinder, Judith Delozier and Richard Bandler, 1978

Plans and the Structure of Behavior by George A. Miller, Karl H. Pribram and Eugene Galanter, Adams, Bannister, Cox Publishers, January 1986

Precision by John Grinder and Michael McMaster, Precision Models, Bonny Doon, 1980

Principles of Mathematics by Bertrand Russell, 1902

Provocative Therapy by Frank Farrelly, Jeff Brandsma / Hardcover / Meta Publications / July 1974

RedTail Math: the epistemology of everyday life (working title) by John Grinder and Carmen Bostic St. Clair, 2002.

Science and Sanity: An Introduction to Non-Aristotelian Systems and General Semantics by Alfred Korzybski, Institute of General Semantics, January 1994

Selected Philosophical Essays by Carl Gustav Hempel, Richard Jeffrey (Editor), Cambridge University Press / February 2000

Steps to an Ecology of Mind. by Gregory Bateson, Ballantine Books, 1972

Stranger in a Strange Land by Robert A. Heinlein, Ace Books, May 1976

Strategies of Psychotherapy by Jay Haley, Grune and Stratton, Inc., 1963

The Ascent of Science by Brian L. Silver, Oxford University Press, Inc., February 2000

The Doors of Perception, by Aldous Huxley, New York, Harper and Row, 1954

The End of Certainty: Time's Flow and the Laws of Nature by Ilya Prigogine, I. Prigogine. Simon & Schuster Trade, August 1997

The Essential Tension: Selected Studies in Scientific Tradition and Change by Thomas S. Kuhn / Hardcover / University of Chicago Press / March 1979

The Japanese Brain: Uniqueness and Universality by Tadanobu Tsunoda (translation by Yoshinari Oiwa), Taishukan Publishing Company, Tokyo. 1985

The Origins of Order: Self-Organization and Selection in Evolution by Stuart A. Kauffman, Oxford University Press, July 1992

The Philosophy of Carl G. Hempel: Studies in Science, Explanation, and Rationality by Carl Gustav Hempel, James H. Fetzer (Editor) Oxford University Press, November 2000

The Road since Structure: Philosophical Essays, 1970-1993, with an Autobiographical Interview by Thomas S. Kuhn, John C. Haugeland (Editor),James Conant (Editor), University of Chicago Press, November 2000

The Scientific Revolution by Steven Shapin, University of Chicago Press, February, 1998

The Scientist in the Crib by Alison Gopnik, Andrew M. Meltzoff and Patricia K. Kuhl (1999), William Morrow and Company, New York

The Structure of Magic, volume I, by Richard Bandler and John Grinder Science and Behavior Press, 1975

The Structure of Magic, volume II, by John Grinder and Richard Bandler, Science and Behavior Press, 1976

The Structure of Scientific Revolution by Thomas Kuhn, University of Chicago Press, 1970

Therapeutic Metaphors: Helping Others through the Looking Glass. by David Cole Gordon, Meta Publications, January 1978

Turtles All the Way Down, by Judith Delozier and John Grinder, Grinder, Delozier and Associates, 1987

Visual Intelligence: How We Create What We See by Donald D. Hoffman, Norton, W. W. & Company, Inc., January 2000

Tapes

Butterflies and Metaphors by Gregory Bateson (in lectures taped at Esalen Institute)

Contact Page

To inquire about business consulting services (modeling, coaching...) and about seminars in topics such as modeling, new code, metaphor, strategies for developing access to the unconscious and other specialties of Quantum Leap, contact Carmen and John at,

Quantum Leap
245 M Mt. Hermon Rd, #277
Scotts Valley, CA 95044
Fax 831 457 2834

Quantum Leap
3000F Danville Blvd, #368
Alamo, CA. 94507
Fax 925 552 0972

We also invite interested readers to leave comments, proposals... on the following website:

nlpwhisperinginthewind.com

Appendix A

RELEASE

This release and covenant not to sue (hereinafter referred to as "Release") is entered into this 3rd day of February, 2000, between RICHARD BANDLER, individually and as a member of the Society of Neurolinguistic Programming and The Bandler Group, BRAHM VON HUENE, and DOMINIC LUZI (hereinafter referred to as "Plaintiffs"), and DR. JOHN GRINDER, CARMEN BOSTIC-ST. CLAIR, QUANTUM LEAP, INCORPORATED, and UNLIMITED, LTD., a California Corporation (hereinafter referred to as "Defendants"). The Plaintiffs and Defendants are collectively referred to as the "Parties."

In consideration of the covenants contained herein, and in consideration of the statement which is attached to this Release as Exhibit A, the Parties hereto agree as follows:

1. Plaintiffs and their agents, representatives, successors and assigns, and each of them, hereby release Defendants from any and all claims, liens, demands, causes of action (including but not limited to all and any claims for personal injury, general or special damages, or for wrongful death), obligations, damages and liabilities, known or unknown, that the Plaintiffs have had in the past, or now have or may have in the future, against Defendants, or any other persons or entities acting or purporting to act on their behalf, arising directly or indirectly out of or related in any way to the Plaintiffs' claims included in Cases Nos. 78482 and 132495 currently filed in the Santa Cruz County Superior Court, entitled

1

COPY

376

NOT LTD., et al. vs. UNLIMITED, LTD. and Richard W. Bandler, et al. vs. Quantum Leap, Inc., et al..

The Plaintiffs expressly understand and acknowledge that it is possible that unknown losses or claims exist, or that present losses may have been underestimated in amount or severity, and Plaintiffs explicitly took that in account in determining the amount of consideration to be provided for in the giving of this Release, and a portion of said consideration, having been bargained for between the Parties with the knowledge of the possibility of such unknown claims, was given in exchange for a full accord, satisfaction and discharge of all claims, ~~excepting any claims arising out of or related to copyrights~~. Consequently, Plaintiffs hereto expressly waive all rights under California Civil Code §1542, which provides that:

> "A general release does not extend to claims which the creditor does not know or expect to exist in his favor at the time of executing the release, which if known by him must have materially affected his settlement with the debtor."

Nothing Contained Herein Shall Release Any Claims Arising out of, or related to Copyrights.
3   Plaintiffs hereto understand and agree that this Release includes all claims for costs, expenses and attorneys' fees, taxable or otherwise, incurred by Plaintiffs in or arising out of the above-referenced matters. In the event Plaintiffs or Defendants commence litigation to enforce any term or condition of this settlement agreement and release, the prevailing party in such litigation shall be entitled to recover, in addition to any damages suffered, their reasonable attorneys' fees and costs of litigation.

2

377

4.   Plaintiffs hereto acknowledge that the consideration to
this agreement does not constitute an admission or concession of
liability by the Defendants, and that liability for any such
claims or matters is expressly denied by all Defendants.

5.   Plaintiffs hereby warrant that no other person or
entity has claimed or now claims any interest of such party in
the subject of this Release, and that Plaintiffs have the sole
right and exclusive authority to execute this Release, to receive
the aforesaid consideration, and that they have not sold,
assigned, nor otherwise set over to any other person or entity
any claim, lien, demand, cause of action, obligations, damage or
liability covered hereby. Should some or all of the consideration paid under this Release fall into the hands of any third
party lien claimant, Plaintiffs will nonetheless take, and do
take, the position that the action is settled as to the
Defendants.

6.   That this Release shall be binding upon and for the
benefit of the Parties hereto and their respective heirs,
executors, administrators, successors, devisees, and assigns, and
that, in accordance with the attached settlement statement
described as **EXHIBIT A**, all released Defendants have and shall
continue to have the right to teach, train, certify, and produce,
publish and sell materials of any fashion in the field of
Neurolinguistic Programming, including having the right to use
the term "Neurolinguistic Programming."

7.   That each of the Parties warrants, with the exception

3

COPY

378

of the document attached as EXHIBIT A to this Release, no promise, inducement or agreement not expressed herein has been made in connection with this Release, and that this Release constitutes the entire agreement between the Parties herein named. It is expressly understood and agreed that this Release may not be altered, amended, modified or otherwise changed in any respect whatsoever. Each party hereto expressly agrees and acknowledges that it will make no claim at any time or place that this Release has been orally altered or modified or otherwise changed by oral communication of any kind or character.

8. The Plaintiffs and their respective agents, employees, insurers, successors, and predecessors in interest, and each of them, agree that upon the execution of this Release, they will indemnify the Defendants against any claims, demands, actions, or causes of action arising out of or resulting from the above-identified litigation, and further covenant and agree that as against the Defendants, they will never institute any action or proceeding, or cause to be instituted, or participate in any action or proceeding against the Defendants, their servants, employees, insurers, successors or predecessors in interest, or any of them, based upon any claims, demands, causes of action, obligations, damages or liabilities claimed or which could have been claimed in the above-referenced actions.

9. This Release is entered into by the Plaintiffs freely and voluntarily and with and upon the advice of counsel.

10. Should any provision of this Release be held invalid or

4

illegal, such illegality shall not invalidate the whole of this Release, but rather the Release shall be construed as if it did not contain the illegal part, and the rights and obligations of the Parties shall be construed and enforced accordingly.

11. This Release shall be construed and enforced pursuant to the laws of the State of California.

12. Plaintiffs agree to indemnify and hold harmless the Defendants from any lien claim, existing or potential, and will satisfy all valid liens or other such claims as required by law.

DATED: 2/3/2000 _____
RICHARD BANDLER

DATED: _____ _____
BRAHM VON HUENE

DATED: 2/3/00 _____
DOMINIC LUZI

5

In settlement of our legal disputes, DR. JOHN GRINDER AND DR. RICHARD BANDLER confirm that they are the co-creators and co-founders of the technology of Neurolinguistic Programming. Drs. Grinder and Bandler recognize the efforts and contributions of each other in the creation and initial development of NLP. Drs. Grinder and Bandler invite and encourage all interested parties to experience the significant contribution of each of them in the creation of this technology through such public presentations, written materials, programs, and certifications in NLP of such interested parties, as each may choose to offer.

Dr. John Grinder and Dr. Richard Bandler also recognize that each has continued, independently of the other, to create new patterns in the field of NLP, since 1983.

Dr. John Grinder and Dr. Richard Bandler mutually agree to refrain from disparaging each other's efforts, in any fashion, concerning their respective involvement in the field of Neurolinguistic Programming.

If either Dr. John Grinder or Dr. Richard Bandler distributes the terms of this agreement, it will be distributed only in its entirety.

DATED: February 3, 2000   JOHN GRINDER

DATED: February 3, 2000   RICHARD BANDLER

Exhibit A

381